EAT · TASTE · HEAL

EAT · TASTE · HEAL

An Ayurvedic Guidebook and Cookbook for Modern Living

Thomas Yarema md, Daniel Rhoda, Chef Johnny Brannigan | Photographs by Ed Ouellette

Five Elements Press
HAWAII

Published by Five Elements Press, 4504 Kukui St. Suite 13, Kapaa, Hawaii 96746.
Five Elements books may be purchased for educational and promotional use. For more information please write to the above address.

Yarema, Thomas.

    Eat-taste-heal : an Ayurvedic guidebook and cookbook for modern living
/Thomas Yarema, Daniel Rhoda, Johnny Brannigan ; photographs by Ed
Ouellette. -- 1st ed. -- Kapaa, Hawaii : Five Elements Press, 2006.

      p. ; cm.

      Includes bibliographical references and index.
      ISBN: 0-9769170-0-9
      ISBN-13: 978-0-9769170-0-7

      1. Cookery, Indic. 2. Medicine, Ayurvedic. 3. Nutrition. I. Rhoda,
Daniel. II. Brannigan, Johnny. III. Title.

TX724.5.I4 Y37 2005
641.5/63--dc22 0601

Printed in Canada on recycled paper.
      10 9 8 7 6 5 4

Design and typesetting by Adam Prall of thinkingman.com; Recipe design by Paul Murray; Layout design by Daniel Rhoda
Photography by Ed Oullette; Food styling by Denise Vivaldo of Foodfanatics.net; Illustrations by Chef Johnny Brannigan

This book was typset in Berkeley LT and Myriad Pro as body fonts with Trajan Pro as a display font.

First Edition

ACKNOWLEDGEMENTS

WE WOULD LIKE TO THANK THE PATIENTS OF THE Kauai Center for Holistic Medicine and Research for inspiring us to create this book. We would also like to thank the following individuals for their editing eyes, discerning taste buds and ongoing words of encouragement:

Jim Matthews; Sumer Joy, Avalon, and Doris Yarema, along with brother Geoff, sister Stefanie and Valerie; Cecilia, Richard, and Les Rhoda; Helen Evans, Lauran Brannigan, and Robert Brannigan; Dr. Suhas Kshirsagar MD (Ayurveda) and Dr. Manisha Kshirsagar BAMS; Kim Miller, Debbie Ka'auwai, Tsega Abera, Tim Baird, Joe Ulmschneider, Hayes MacArthur, Sarah Lassnig, Nigel Broome, David Walne, Peter Dease, Barbara Curl, Bobbi Spur, Tom Ryan, Elaine Willis, Eric Wall, Dr. Gerald Felcher, Dr. Avinash Lele MD (Ayurveda), Steve Marcus MD and Kay Loomis, Dr. Jay Apte BAMS, Claudette Greene, the monastics of Kauai Aadheenam, and the entire staff of the Kauai Center for Holistic Medicine and Research.

We would also like to thank the following individuals for their unwavering attention to beauty and detail: Ed Ouellette, Adam Prall, Paul Murray, Denise Vivaldo, Norman Kolpas, Andy Sheen-Turner, Jana Rade, Cindie Flannigan, and Katy Randolph.

And lastly, our gratitude goes out to all of the past and present sages who have illuminated this timeless wisdom throughout the ages. Namasté.

CONTENTS

PART II: THE COOKBOOK

EVERY WISDOM TRADITION OF THE WORLD EMBRACES a simple truth: *food is life*. The ritual of eating transcends all boundaries of time, culture, and religion. Food is sacred, and the act of eating is a direct communion with Mother Nature's divine energy. According to ancient Ayurvedic sages, food nourishes our mind, body, senses and spirit on all levels of being. It provides a foundation for personal exploration and evolution. From taking our first sip of mother's milk to sharing meals with loved ones throughout our lifetime, the ritual of eating is deeply ingrained within the human experience.

Eat·Taste·Heal is a celebration of food's ability to heal our bodies and our minds and to nourish our senses. We offer this book as a blessing on your own life's journey. We hope it tantalizes your taste buds and inspires a deeper exploration into your true inner nature.

Dr. Tom, Dan, and Chef Johnny

About the Authors

Dr. Tom

Throughout my medical career, I have always been drawn to common-sense medicine. Amidst prescription pads and sterile hospital quarters, I have frequently asked: What is the most effective way for a patient to truly heal? After 14 years in emergency medicine, I found myself increasingly disillusioned with the infrastructure of the American medical system. I regularly listened to patients express confusion about their illnesses, while witnessing a deeper disconnect to their inner sources of healing. Patients literally seemed to be "dying to get healthy" in a time of unparalleled advancements in modern medicine.

I could fully appreciate how the roadmap to health was missing in my Western medical training. To begin with, there was no definition for what "health" actually meant. The entire model was focused on eradicating illness, rather than improving the quality of life. I knew that my own fulfillment as a physician would be greatly limited in this system. Having studied various forms of alternative medicine, I also suspected there must be a way to effectively bridge together these ancient healing methods with modern science. I knew of a few individuals in the medical field who were trying to forge such cross-cultural paradigms, however, I really had no idea where to begin myself. Ultimately, it took an earthquake to point me in the right direction.

During the Northridge earthquake of 1994 in Southern California, I realized I was the only physician in my neighborhood. Access to hospitals, pharmacies and other healthcare was completely cut off. I found myself questioning: could I be a community health guide using the available supplies and common-sense medicine? I felt that the answer to this question was yes, but I knew I would be leaning much more heavily on my alternative medical training. While my services were only needed for minor injuries that day, this process of self-inquiry provided the spark for making a career change I knew was inevitable.

I left my job in the ER and, for the next three years, placed primary emphasis on furthering my alternative medical training. I worked at a number of alternative cancer clinics in California and conducted research within the emerging field of bio-energetic medicine. During this time, I found myself repeatedly drawn back to the vast wisdom of Ayurveda. I was inspired by Ayurveda's fundamental aim to teach people to take care of themselves naturally, using simple means such as food, herbs, and exercise. This prompted me to deepen my studies of Ayurvedic medicine.

In 1997, I headed to the beautiful Hawaiian island of Kauai and founded the Kauai Center for Holistic Medicine and Research. Located smack dab in the middle of East and West, it felt like a fitting place to marry the medical traditions of these two parts of the globe.

I soon found myself in an economically-challenged community, where affordable, common-sense medicine was the only option for a significant portion of the community. While many people were unable to purchase medical supplies and herbs, I felt it was realistic that people could spend time in their kitchens, utilizing nourishing local foods to promote healing.

I quickly recognized both the practicality and spiritual value of integrating food and cooking into the clinic. In addition to learning how to treat themselves naturally, our patients were developing a deeper appreciation for both food and the ritual of eating. As individuals prepared meals for medicinal use, they were placed back into their kitchens and gardens to discover (or often rediscover) the importance of proper eating in all areas of health. Many also found joy in sharing their healing foods with loved ones. A seemingly simple therapeutic recommendation, the benefits of these practices also began to filter into other aspects of these individuals' lives.

Over time, our patients began to ask for more and more ways to use food as medicine on their healing journeys. So we began to collect recipes and hand them out on loose-leaf sheets of paper. As the stack of papers grew over time, patients began requesting us to write a cookbook. Having always cooked intuitively and never by recipe, I wasn't even sure where to begin. As a primary care physician running a private practice, I also didn't foresee time in my busy schedule to pen a book at night after work. After sitting on the idea for a number of months, we were blessed by the appearance of the two co-authors-to-be: a young patient whose healing path had led him to Ayurveda, and an international Ayurvedic chef looking for a broader arena to share his talents.

The three of us quickly coalesced around certain principles for the book. First, we wanted to demystify the fundamental principles of Ayurveda's ancient vocabulary. Daniel Rhoda's research and writing have been meticulous in this area. I have been awed by his dedication, open-mindedness, and attention to honoring the traditions from which this information originates. Second, we wanted the recipes to be cross-cultural, reflecting the universality of Ayurvedic principles. We also wanted to offer a wide array of recipes to inspire both the kitchen neophyte and experienced cook. Chef Johnny's creative artistry and twenty plus years of cooking around the globe have provided the foundation for this sumptuous endeavor. Lastly, we wanted the book to be sensually engaging. For this, we chose award-winning photographers, food stylists, and designers to help bring the book to life.

This book is our blessing to you. May it inspire your imagination as well as your taste buds. May its recipe pages proudly wear the stains of food over time and its text lead you to quietly remark, "Aha, I knew that all along." May your mealtimes be filled with laughter, levity, and gratitude. And may you and yours be deeply nourished, in a way that provides you with great joy and confidence in expressing your unique manifestation of Inner Light.

DAN

During my junior year of college in 1997, I started developing joint problems which, over the next several years, spread to most of the major joints in my body. After undergoing multiple surgeries, I was left with numerous bottles of prescription pain relievers and a group of eminent physicians scratching their heads. While degenerative arthritis was the closest match symptomatically, it just didn't add up. Why would an active person in his early twenties suddenly develop arthritis in multiple areas of his body?

I knew that working seventy hours a week at a Wall Street investment bank couldn't have helped the situation any. My

meditation, visualization, a firm belief in the ability to heal, and a commitment to the process of healing could, together, dissolve even the most "terminal" tumors.

My personal discovery of Ayurveda provided the spark for my own healing process to begin. In addition to incorporating all of these healing modalities, Ayurveda offered a complete system of individualized medicine. Seemingly unrelated physical and mental problems I had encountered over the years began to fall into place within a much bigger picture. The term "holistic" began popping up with greater frequency around this time. I began to realize, however, that just because a therapy was deemed "natural," did not mean it was actually holistic in origin. Ayurveda, on the other hand, truly felt holistic to me. In addition to treating the physical body, it addressed the mental, emotional, and spiritual components of healing.

It was an appealing yet surprisingly novel concept—to actively engage in my own healing process through a medical system that called for a complete lifestyle change. I was no longer a passive patient relying on the orders of a physician. By learning how to properly feed my body and mind on all levels, I began to rediscover the wisdom that already resided deep inside of me.

I realized that in order to truly heal, I needed to be in a healing environment. So, much to the dismay of family and friends, I packed up and moved to the island of Kauai. It was on this incredible island that my healing truly began. It was also where I met Dr. Tom and this book came into being. After working together as patient and doctor over several months, Dr. Tom asked if I'd like to co-author and produce a book on Ayurvedic nutrition. In a synchronistic turn of events, Chef Johnny arrived at our door step, excited to start cooking.

heart was simply not in the world of bonds and bankers, and I suspected that a more fulfilling path must exist somewhere. What I didn't realize at the time, however, is that some of us require a much bigger kick in the butt to help us find our way.

By the end of my second year in New York, friends were pushing me in a wheelchair at times, and there seemed to be little hope on the horizon. Due to longstanding mental turmoil that greatly intensified during this time, I was also hardly speaking.

While I was recovering from a dual-ankle surgery one day at my family's home in Maine, a dear friend arrived to say goodbye. The doctors had given him three months to live, and he had completely accepted this grim sentence. Sitting there on the couch, observing what a pitiful duo we were, I resolved to start making some serious changes in my life.

Already interested in health and healing, I immersed myself in the study of numerous traditions of alternative medicine. I realized that the typical Western medical path that I had always relied upon would probably leave me in a wheelchair for good this time around. I also felt there had to be something to help my friend Jim recover from cancer. Drawing upon a variety of traditions and methods, we discovered that a healthy diet, exercise, herbs, internal cleansing, laughter,

Soon thereafter, Dr. Tom hired a leading Ayurvedic physician from India, Dr. Suhas Kshirsagar, to join the clinic. I've since had the opportunity to study closely with both doctors and complete a practitioner's training course in Ayurveda. Finding myself drawn to the indigenous healing traditions of North and South America, I've also had the opportunity to study and train within a lineage of Q'uero Incan healers from Peru.

I believe that any effective healing system should focus on nurturing and sustaining life—not solely on treating disease and preventing death. Ayurveda is a Sanskrit word that translates as the "Science of Life." Hence, it is the essence of life itself, and the objective of achieving radiant health, that forms the basis of this timeless science. As you read this book, may these words and recipes inspire you to grow and glow on your own healing journey!

CHEF JOHNNY

By the time I was 13 years old, I was already interested in health and being healthy. There were two reasons for this early need. First, my own mother seemed to be afflicted with just about every ailment known to modern medicine. Consequently, our breakfast table was packed with a colorful assortment of pills and potions. Second, my own health was delicate and unpredictable. I was sure to catch every flu, fever, cold, and chill going around, not to mention agonizing headaches and hours spent on the sofa, clutching my stomach and praying for relief. I also suffered from almost constant worry and anxiety.

It was not until I was 16 that relief came to me, when I was introduced to a branch of Ayurvedic medicine known as Transcendental Meditation. I had already been following a vegetarian diet for one year, due to the influence of a somewhat overzealous friend. After a month without

hamburgers and bacon, I was hooked on rice, curries, salads, and everything (well, almost everything) Italian. Then, two brothers who lived on the street where I grew up in Winchester, England introduced me to the gentle art of meditation.

After about a month of practicing meditation, I began to realize what a great change was occurring in my life. The technique itself was deceptively simple and very pleasant to do. Almost out of the blue, I decided to train as a meditation teacher. If it could help me, I reasoned, it could heal my mother and others who were suffering needlessly.

So, at the age of 18, I traveled to Switzerland to study with Maharishi Mahesh Yogi. To my surprise, I also began to train as an Ayurvedic chef in the wonderful mountaintop and lakeside kitchens of Switzerland. I cooked for people from countless nationalities and began to build up a repertoire of dishes that were truly global. I was completely enthralled and knew that I had a natural feel for the culinary arts. I also began to travel extensively, and everywhere I went, I learned to cook the local fare. During these years, I cooked in Iran,

Thailand, Malaysia, the Philippines, France, Italy, Germany, Spain, Portugal, Croatia, Greece, Denmark, and Austria.

After I was back in England teaching courses in Transcendental Meditation, Maharishi began opening Ayurvedic colleges and clinics all over the world. This awakened me to the further possibilities of healing within this ancient and fascinating wisdom.

Later, I became part of an innovative snack company selling sandwiches and other foods that incorporated Ayurvedic principles of nutrition. The Organic Snack Company was born and I called myself, "The Organic Chef." It was all very exciting and expansive. I wrote countless product recipes and tested them on an eager public jaded with the standard British fare of cheese-and-tomato sandwiches. They were tired of pesticide- and chemical-laden foods and were excited to find healthy alternatives.

Around this same time, cooking shows began overtaking the television programming of England. You couldn't turn on the TV without seeing an excited chef whipping up a new creation. I loved it! The nation's taste buds were coming alive!

In the late 1990's, interest in Ayurveda greatly flourished. I began holding cooking classes in Ayurvedic cuisine. My students begged me for a cookbook. So, for the first time, I began to write it all down.

I then had the opportunity to travel to Hawaii. Immediately, I felt that this was a land closer to the heavens, where one's very thoughts could manifest magically! During everyday conversations in shops and restaurants, it was commonplace to hear, "Yes, I think I'm a Pitta," or "Bananas, they're good for Vata, aren't they?" In Kauai, I met Dr. Tom and Dan and an idea was born to create this sumptuous guide for a life of balance, energy and well-being.

I invite you to learn about the healing effects of home-cooked food, to enjoy the process of creating simple dishes, and to use your intuition to create health and harmony from within. I encourage you to put joy into your food, make it a loving and sacred part of your life, always offer your creations to the highest, to the Divine, and watch your mind, body and spirit soar!

PART I

THE GUIDEBOOK

Ayurvedic Concepts in a Nutshell

Buying, Preparing, & Storing Vibrant Food

The ABC's: Ambiance, Blessing, & Consumption

The Rhythms of Nature

Food as Medicine

1

Ayurvedic Concepts in a Nutshell

Ayurveda: The Recipe for Healthy Living

Ayurveda emerged from the spiritual texts of ancient India, known as the Vedas, or "Books of Wisdom." These date back at least five thousand years and are widely regarded as humanity's oldest literature.

The term *Ayurveda* derives from the Sanskrit words *ayus* and *veda*. Ayus translates as "life" and veda as "knowledge" or "science." Ayurveda thus means the "Knowledge or Science of Life." Ayus extends beyond mere chronological age or physical health. According to Ayurveda: "Ayus is union of the mind, body, senses and soul. It is energy and vitality and is eternal."

Ayurveda peers into the nature of life through the wisdom of Mother Nature herself. As a philosophy of life, Ayurveda teaches us to live in harmony with the basic laws of nature. As a complete medical science, Ayurveda offers us a holistic guidemap for awakening our healing potential. The underlying prescription of Ayurvedic medicine is quite simple: recognize the power of self-healing within, and you will become your own greatest doctor!

According to Ayurveda, health is not a state defined by lab tests or yearly check ups. Health is a continuous and participatory process that embraces all aspects of life: physical, mental, emotional, behavioral, spiritual, familial, social, and universal. Achieving balance on all levels of being is the true measure of vibrant health. The "average person" or "standardized treatment" simply does not exist in Ayurvedic medicine. Every individual is a one-of-a-kind with an equally unique blueprint for health. By providing a universal framework for understanding these blueprints, Ayurveda teaches us to honor and support our true individual natures.

ANCIENT WISDOM

Ancient Ayurvedic scholars combined the wisdom of the Vedas with direct scientific observation and experimentation. *Charaka Samhita*, written sometime during the 5th to 3rd centuries BC, represents the first codification of Ayurvedic medicine and remains an authoritative text on Ayurveda today. In this compilation (*samhita*, in Sanskrit), the great physician and sage Charaka offers the earliest known descriptions of diabetes, multiple sclerosis, Alzheimer's disease, Parkinson's disease, and numerous other conditions. *Sushruta Samhita*, written by the surgeon Sushruta shortly thereafter, includes sophisticated surgical procedures, ranging from the removal of cataracts to skin grafts. Sushruta's instructions for reconstructive operations to the nose influenced the development of plastic surgery by Western physicians. Together, these two works stand among the oldest and lengthiest medical texts in the world.

By the 3rd century AD, Ayurveda included eight branches of medicine: Internal Medicine, Surgery, Eye-Ear-Nose, Toxicology, Gynecology-Obstetrics-Pediatrics, Psychiatry, Aphrodisiacs, and Rejuvenation. Due to its widespread success in India, Ayurveda also became highly respected in many other parts of the world. Students from China, Tibet, Egypt, Greece, Rome, Afghanistan, and Persia traveled to Ayurvedic schools by way of the great silk trading routes. Today, distinct signs of Ayurvedic influence are found in the ancient medical traditions of many of these countries.

After nearly a thousand years of growth and dissemination, Ayurveda's golden age abruptly ended with the foreign conquest of India in the 8th century AD. During this period, Ayurvedic schools perished and classical Indian culture rapidly declined. Foreign rule lasted for the next eleven hundred years, pushing Ayurveda into the villages and homes of India. The practicality and popularity of the science, however, ensured its survival. Physicians also helped maintain

Modern Ayurveda

Upon gaining Independence in 1947, India enjoyed a national re-awakening, leading to a resurgence of traditional Vedic culture. During this period, Ayurveda emerged from the recesses of society to flourish again on a national level. Today, there are more than one hundred Ayurvedic colleges and fifty universities offering Ayurvedic degrees. Although Western medicine has taken its seat at the forefront of India's medical system, Ayurveda remains a widely utilized alternative. The Ayurvedic "kitchen pharmacy" and lifestyle also remain important components within traditional Indian homes.

In traveling beyond the borders of India over the last two decades, Ayurveda has experienced an explosion of interest in many parts of the world. The West, in particular, has eagerly embraced this timeless system of healing. The holistic nature of Ayurveda, combined with its ancient track record, has placed it among the most popular alternative medical systems today. A few of the major pioneers of Ayurveda in the West include Maharishi Mahesh Yogi, Vasant Lad, Deepak Chopra, David Frawley, Bri Maya Tiwari, and Robert Svoboda.

Just as the West embraces this ancient system, Ayurveda embraces the modern medical advancements of the West. At its core, Ayurveda is a non-exclusionary medical system: If something helps heal the human body, mind, and spirit, Ayurveda says all the better. Ayurvedic medicine is currently practiced both on its own and in conjunction with a number of other healing systems. These include allopathy (Western medicine), homeopathy, naturopathy, acupuncture, chiropractic, and massage therapy. Together, these disciplines

Mind-Body Medicine

are helping to pave the way for a new, integrated medical model in the West.

Over the past century, modern science has traveled beyond the static world of Newtonian physics to land in the orderly chaos of the quantum realm. In discovering his monumental theorem $E=mc^2$, Einstein began to unravel the true fabric of the universe. After three hundred years of mechanical science, Einstein shattered the notion that only matter matters. Instead, he proved that matter and energy are simply different sides of the same coin.

Today, quantum physicists have become torchbearers in the realm of the "tinier than tiny." Ten million to one hundred million times smaller than the sub-atom lies the level of the quanta, the new frontier of mind-body research. The source of this quantum level is a field of pure energy, which serves as the underlying intelligence and glue of the entire universe. Sixty-five years ago, quantum physicists labeled this the Unified Field. Nearly six millennia ago, Ayurvedic sages called it the Cosmic Life Force or Field of Pure Consciousness. While modern science is only beginning to understand the implications of this discovery, Ayurveda has been steeped in quantum theory for millennia.

According to Ayurveda, the Unified Field is an underlying field of consciousness, which connects every thought, wave pattern, and particle of our being. At this quantum level, the boundary between the mind and body completely disappears. The mind helps create and renew the body continuously, because the two are unified within this field of intelligence. When unhealthy mental and emotional patterns serve as the backdrop to this dynamic process, the likelihood of physical illness greatly increases. On a cellular level, we begin to grow a body that reflects our inner disharmony. By embracing this essential connection at its core, Ayurveda offers a fully integrated system of mind-body medicine for the future.

A famous saying in Ayurveda acknowledges our fundamental connection with the greater universe:

As is the cosmic body, so is the human body

As is the cosmic mind, so is the human mind

As is the macrocosm, so is the microcosm

The unbounded intelligence that runs throughout Nature on a quantum level dances at the very core of our beings. As is the whole (the macrocosm), so is the individual (the microcosm). Through recognizing this essential connection, we ultimately rediscover the power of healing that lies within.

GETTING TO KNOW YOUR INDIVIDUAL NATURE: VATA, PITTA, AND KAPHA

THE FIVE ELEMENTS: THE OUTSIDE IS INSIDE ALL OF US

When we look to the beauty of Nature, we find that five elements provide the foundation for the entire physical world. Ayurveda recognizes these elements–space, air, fire, water, and earth—as the building blocks of all material existence.

Whether walking headfirst into a strong wind or digging our hands into the soil, we possess an inherent familiarity with the elements. All organic and inorganic substances are combinations of these elements, be it a time-polished rock or a shiny piece of plastic. Every object is unique because it contains a varying ratio of the Five Elements.

Since humankind is a mini-replica of Nature, Ayurveda also observes the Five Elements within the human body. We nourish ourselves with foods from the Earth, and eventually, our body returns to the earthly matter from which it came. Water is our life-sustaining nectar, making up more than 70 percent of our total body mass. Fire provides the body with heat and radiant energy and exists within all metabolic and chemical actions. Air flows freely throughout the body, giving movement to biological functions and feeding every cell with oxygen. Space is ever-present, humbly residing in the background, providing the other elements with an opportunity to interact in this way.

On a quantum level, the Five Elements represent a dynamic continuum of energy, which emerges directly from the Unified Field. This continuum unfolds sequentially, beginning with the subtlest vibration of Space and ending with the densest vibration of Earth. All gross matter derives from the combinations of these basic energies.

From an Ayurvedic perspective, the Water element encompasses more than the substance we call water. It also embodies the physical qualities, biological functions, and energetic properties of this element. For example, Water is liquid, heavy, soft, and cohesive. It governs all bodily fluids and is necessary for chemical reactions to take place in Nature. On the subtler levels of the mind and emotions, Water relates to a calm personality and promotes love, compassion, and contentment.

The Five Elements also explain why substances of the natural world are harmonious with the human body. We easily utilize plants, herbs, minerals, and water, because these substances are the same in composition and character to our own underlying make-up.

THE THREE DOSHAS:
THE KEYS TO YOUR INDIVIDUAL NATURE

Have you ever wondered what actually accounts for differences in people? Why are some people hyperactive and fast moving, while others exude grace and stillness? Why can some people eat a five-course meal with ease, while others can barely finish a salad? Why are some people inherently joyous, while others carry the weight of the world on their shoulders? Modern genetics offers some insight, but what about the characteristics and idiosyncrasies that make every

proportion of these doshas, however, that contributes to an individual's unique mind-body composition.

Just as you are born with a unique genetic makeup, you are also born with a unique proportion of doshas. This doshic make-up derives from the union of your parents' doshas at the moment of conception. According to Ayurveda, you are meant to live into the fulfillment of this underlying nature, called your individual birth constitution, or *prakruti*. Within your prakruti lies the key to harmony. It is your own unique blueprint that brings glowing health to life.

person unique? Ayurveda answers all of these questions with the *Three Doshas: Vata, Pitta, and Kapha.*

The *doshas* are biological energies found throughout the human body and mind. They govern all physical and mental processes and provide every living being with an individual blueprint for health and fulfillment.

The doshas derive from the Five Elements and their related properties. Vata is composed of Space and Air, Pitta of Fire and Water, and Kapha of Earth and Water.

Due to their subtle, energetic quality, the doshas cannot be perceived directly in the body. Their presence, however, is visible through distinct qualities and actions, ranging from complex biological functions to personality traits. Every cell of the body contains Vata, Pitta, and Kapha. It is the varying

A person with a predominantly Vata constitution will have physical and mental qualities that reflect the elemental qualities of Space and Air. That is why Vata types are commonly quick thinking, thin, and fast moving. A Pitta type, on the other hand, will have qualities reflective of Fire and Water, such as a fiery personality and a reddish complexion. A Kapha type will typically have a solid body frame and calm temperament, reflecting the underlying elements of Earth and Water. While one dosha predominates in most individuals, a second dosha typically has a strong influence. This is referred to as a *dual-doshic constitution.* Classically, Ayurveda describes seven major constitutional types: Vata, Pitta, Kapha, Vata-Pitta, Pitta-Kapha, Kapha-Vata, Vata-Pitta-Kapha.

In practice, these seven basic mind-body types are further differentiated to account for various dual-types. For example, a Vata-Pitta type will have Vata as a primary constitution but also embody strong Pitta characteristics. A Pitta-Vata type, by contrast, will identify more with Pitta characteristics, but also have strong Vata traits. The least common constitutional type, known as "tri-doshic" or Vata-Pitta-Kapha, refers to an individual who has an equal proportion of all three doshas.

The doshas are dynamic energies that constantly change in response to our actions, thoughts, emotions, the foods we eat, the seasons, and any other sensory inputs that feed our mind and body. When we live into the fulfillment of our individual natures, we naturally make lifestyle and dietary decisions that foster balance within our doshas. When we live against our intrinsic natures, we support unhealthy patterns that lead to physical and mental imbalances.

If the proportion of doshas in your current state is close to your birth constitution, then your health will be vibrant. A divergence between these states, however, indicates a state of imbalance. *Vikruti* is the term used to describe this imbalanced deviation from prakruti.

An *increased* or *aggravated* doshic state leads to the greatest number of imbalances. Such imbalances can arise from any number of influences, including following a dosha-aggravating diet or, more generally, carrying too much stress in life. You can initiate a restoration of balance, however, when you begin to understand both your unique constitutional make-up and how to harmonize your internal environment and its needs with the external world.

We are most susceptible to imbalances related to our predominant dosha. If you're a Pitta type, for example, you may experience heartburn (a common Pitta disorder) after eating spicy foods. The key to remember is that *like increases like*, while *opposites create balance*. By simply choosing cooling or more alkalizing foods, you can avoid heartburn, while also supporting your underlying make-up.

Ayurveda offers specifically tailored recommendations for every individual, ranging from general lifestyle changes to the treatment of disease (literally, *dis-ease*, or an imbalance from the natural state of ease). For this reason, Ayurveda can truly be called a system of individualized health care, something remarkably different from the Western model's "one-pill-for-all" approach. Since the doshas are used to detect imbalances

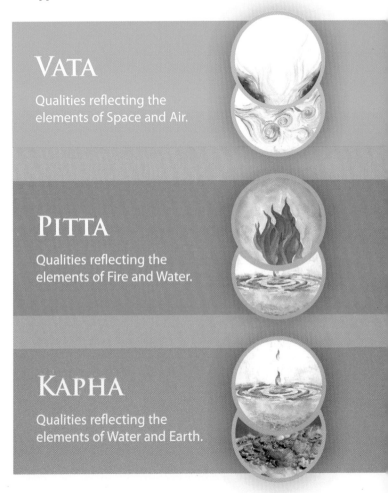

VATA
Qualities reflecting the elements of Space and Air.

PITTA
Qualities reflecting the elements of Fire and Water.

KAPHA
Qualities reflecting the elements of Water and Earth.

before the manifestation of disease, Ayurveda is also a complete system of preventative medicine.

As a general rule to attain balance, you should always pay the greatest attention to your primary dosha. When we refer to a specific doshic type in this book (such as a "Vata type"), we mean any individual with a leading Vata dosha. This may include a pure Vata type or a dual doshic-type such as a Vata-Pitta.

THREE DOSHIC STATES

BALANCED   All three doshas are present in their natural proportions; also referred to as "equilibrium."

INCREASED   A particular dosha is present in a greater-than-normal proportion; also referred to as an "aggravated" or "excess state."

DECREASED   A particular dosha is present in a less-than-normal proportion; also referred to as a "reduced" or "depleted state."

If you're a dual-type, you should also remain aware of your secondary dosha; but do not become overwhelmed by trying to follow two sets of recommendations. As you become familiar with Ayurvedic principles, you will discover that balancing your doshas is largely an intuitive process. If you're a Vata-Pitta type for example, you will naturally desire more Pitta-pacifying foods and activities during the hotter Summer months.

Nurturing your individual nature is a direct pathway to fulfillment in life. As you honor your unique makeup, you live into the fullness of your true potential. One of the greatest ways to create doshic imbalance is to suppress or ignore your natural gifts. Consider, for example, a child who has a passion for painting but is never given an artistic outlet. The suppression of this underlying creative impulse may create a deep-seated imbalance over time. If the child is allowed to embrace this passion, however, greater fulfillment and health will follow.

In the following section, we will delve deeper into the individual qualities and attributes of each dosha. At the end of the section, you will find an extensive dosha self-test to help you determine your own constitutional make-up. With an understanding of your individual nature, you will hold the keys to an incredible wealth of knowledge. We encourage you to use this knowledge as a guidemap for immediately promoting better health and healing!

GETTING TO KNOW YOUR DOSHAS

When you examine the three doshas, always remember one important rule: An individual will never match up exactly with the characteristics of one particular dosha.

We are all unique mixtures of these biological energies. So no single set of characteristics can fully define or encompass an individual being. Under the broader umbrella of the three doshas, an infinite number of physiological and psychological variations exist. These variations may all be categorized in relation to one of the doshas. But two Pitta types, for example, will never have identical physical and mental characteristics, even though their underlying constitutions will ensure some similarity in body and mind.

In reading the defining characteristics of the doshas, do not interpret these too rigidly. A predominantly Vata individual, for example, will identify with most of the traits listed. An individual with a Pitta-Kapha constitution, on the other hand, will identify with characteristics of both doshas. Regardless of constitution, every individual will find recognizable characteristics in tune with his or her unique make-up.

The universal principles of Ayurveda transcend surface measures of differentiation, such as race and culture. Since this book is geared towards a largely Western audience, certain characteristics listed on the following pages reflect this geographic focus. That does not preclude the creation of lists better suited to other audiences around the globe.

When examining the doshas, it's important to make a distinction between a *balanced* versus an *imbalanced state*. As mentioned above, the doshas ensure optimum health in a state of balance and promote disease during a state of imbalance. If your body is in balance, you are not inclined to stop and think to yourself: "Wow, my joints are gliding effortlessly, and my digestion is really humming along smoothly today." Instead, the aches and pains of imbalance grab our attention.

For this reason, we will focus primarily on states of imbalance relating to the physical characteristics of the doshas. Please note, however, that some physical characteristics are broader, defining qualities of a dosha. A small frame, for example, may be found in both a balanced and an imbalanced Vata individual. Since we are more inclined to take note of both positive and negative mental states, we will discuss the psychological characteristics of the doshas in relation to both balanced and imbalanced states.

THE THREE DOSHAS: AN OVERVIEW

Vata: an Overview

Vata derives from the elements of Space and Air and translates as "wind" or "that which moves things." It is the energy of movement and the force governing all biological activity. Vata is often called the "King of the Doshas," since it governs the body's greater life force and gives motion to Pitta and Kapha.

The qualities of Vata are dry, rough, light, cold, subtle, and mobile. A Vata individual will display physical and mental characteristics that reflect these qualities in both a balanced and an imbalanced state.

The main locations of Vata in the body are the colon, thighs, bones, joints, ears, skin, brain, and nerve tissues. Physiologically, Vata governs anything related to movement, such as breathing, talking, nerve impulses, movements in the muscles and tissues, circulation, assimilation of food, elimination, urination, and menstruation. Psychologically, Vata governs communication, creativity, flexibility, and quickness of thought.

In Nature, we observe the Five Elements in both harmony and disarray. A warm breeze on an early Spring day provides a stark contrast to the raging hurricane. These extremes are testament to both the subtlety and sublimity of Mother Nature and her elements.

That same dynamism is found within Vata. Just as the wind in balance provides movement and expression to the natural world, the balanced Vata individual is active, creative, and gifted with a natural ability to express and communicate. When the wind in a Vata type rages like a hurricane, negative qualities quickly overshadow these positive attributes. Common signs of Vata imbalance include anxiety and bodily disorders related to dryness, such as dry skin and constipation.

Physical Characteristics of Vata

Bodily make-up for Vata individuals with a tendency towards imbalance:

BUILD	Thin and bony, little muscle development, protruding joints
WEIGHT	Light; often have difficulty gaining weight
HEIGHT	Usually either tall or short
SKIN	Dry and rough; wrinkles with age
HAIR	Dry and brittle
NECK	Thin, long
HANDS	Thin, dry, cold
NAILS	Rough and weak; lines are common
EYES	Small, dull, and often dark
NOSE	Thin and bony
MOUTH	Small mouths; teeth are often large and crooked, prone to decay
LIPS	Thin, often dark red
TONGUE	Dry or pale, with a grayish coating (especially on the back third of tongue)

Bodily functions/qualities of Vata individuals with a tendency towards imbalance:

APPETITE	Variable, with little consistency from one day to the next
DIGESTION	Poor, with a weak digestive fire
STOOL	Dry, hard, and dark; prone to constipation
URINE	Light in color, frequent elimination
MENSTRUATION	Irregular cycles with severe cramping and scanty blood flow
MOVEMENT	Quick moving
PHYSICAL ACTIVITY	Attracted to physically vigorous exercise
SEXUAL ACTIVITY	Variable sexual desire
SLEEP	Light; prone to insomnia
PULSE	Wiry and fast-moving; said to "slither like a cobra"
VOICE	Weak, tires easily, prone to hoarseness
SPEECH	Fast and often erratic
PREFERRED CLIMATE	Warm and tropical; dislikes cold, windy, or dry environments

COMMON VATA DISORDERS OF THE BODY

- Arthritis
- High or low blood pressure
- Cracking or popping joints
- Bladder/urinary disorders
- Muscle stiffness
- Headaches
- Dry, scaly skin
- Insomnia
- Constipation
- Dizziness, ringing in ears
- Gas and bloating
- Premature aging
- Improper nutrient assimilation
- Chronic fatigue
- Heart disease
- Low energy, depleted life force
- Lower back pain
- Intolerance of coldness and dryness
- Food allergies (especially to wheat and dairy)

Due to the mobile and volatile nature of Vata, nearly 60 percent of all listed disorders in classical Ayurvedic texts are associated with this dosha. While most chronic disorders are linked to Vata, common Vata disorders, such as constipation and low energy, respond quickly to dietary, medicinal, and lifestyle changes. After adjusting to a new regimen, Vata individuals often follow their course of treatment with great dedication and enthusiasm.

Psychological Characteristics of Vata

Qualities of balanced Vata individuals

- Creative
- Strong communicators
- Artistic
- Adaptable
- Alert
- Emotionally sensitive
- Enthusiastic
- Imaginative
- Perceptive
- Spiritually inclined
- Spontaneous
- Heightened intuitive abilities
- Compassionate
- Sensitive to subtle energies
- Charismatic
- Multifaceted in interests and abilities

In balance, Vata individuals are dynamic, just like the wind at their foundation. These individuals experience life "below the surface" and have the natural ability to inspire others.

While Vata types may be inclined to switch careers throughout their lifetimes, they naturally make good teachers, artists, musicians, consultants, counselors, healing arts practitioners, philosophers, foreign ministers, religious ministers, and are also suited to numerous other professions requiring creativity and communication skills.

Qualities of imbalanced Vata individuals

- Overly active thinkers
- Restless; cannot sit still
- Inclined towards fear, anxiety, depression
- Earn easily and spend impulsively
- "Spacey" and ungrounded
- Addictive personality
- Emotionally delicate and thin skinned
- Quick to judge or make decisions
- Shy and introverted
- Disorganized; poor planners
- Lack confidence and boldness
- Tend to procrastinate
- Moody and emotionally volatile
- Talk fast and breathlessly
- Grasp things quickly, but soon forget
- Interrupt or zone-out in conversation
- Impatient

Just as they are prone to physical disease of the body, the delicate nature of Vata types also make them subject to the greatest number of mental disorders. Overly active thinking is a defining characteristic of many of these disorders. Some of the more commonly known include: depression, anxiety, insomnia, bipolar disorder, attention deficit disorder (ADD), obsessive compulsive disorder (OCD), and schizophrenia. Calming the mind through a Vata-pacifying diet and lifestyle can have remarkable results, even for serious mental disorders that are considered chronic in nature.

Ways Vata Becomes Imbalanced

- Eating Vata-aggravating foods
- Eating while anxious or depressed
- Eating on the run
- Drinking alcohol, coffee, or black tea
- Smoking cigarettes
- Following an irregular daily routine
- Going to bed late at night
- Traveling frequently
- Engaging in excessive physical and sexual activity
- Failing to change in accordance with the seasons (especially Fall)
- Surrounding oneself with excessive sensory stimulation (TV, loud noises, etc.)
- Suppressing inner creativity and emotional sensitivity
- Attempting to meld into the routines or societal norms of Pitta and Kapha

Ways to Balance Vata

Key Words to remember: nourishing, warming, routine

Note: Many of the following suggestions will be explained in greater detail throughout this book.

- Eat a Vata-balancing diet.
- Eat in a peaceful environment.
- Engage in wholesome and contemplative activities (like spending time in nature).
- Follow a regular daily routine.
- Go to bed early.
- Meditate daily.
- Do gentle physical exercise like Yoga, swimming, Tai Chi, or walking.
- Incorporate bright, warming colors like orange and green into your surroundings.
- Listen to calming music.
- Laugh and smile more.
- Massage body daily with warm oil (such as sesame).
- Take time to rest during the day (naps are good!).
- Cleanse internally; enemas with added oils (called *basti*) are highly recommended.
- Observe the seasons (especially Fall) and adjust diet and lifestyle accordingly.
- When cold, take warm showers and steam baths when available.
- Sunbathe if prone to coldness.
- Use sweet and warm essential oils, such as lavender and cinnamon for aromatherapy.
- Wear warming gems and stones, such as ruby, lapis and amethyst.
- Follow creative and artistic passions.
- Spend time with engaging and grounded people (like balanced Pittas and Kaphas).

Pitta: an Overview

Pitta derives from the elements of Fire and Water and translates as "that which cooks." It is the energy of digestion and metabolism in the body that functions through carrier substances such as organic acids, hormones, enzymes, and bile. While Pitta is most closely related to the element of Fire, it is the liquid nature of these substances that accounts for the element of Water in Pitta's make-up.

The qualities of Pitta are **oily, sharp, hot, light, moving, liquid,** and **acidic.** A Pitta individual will display physical and mental characteristics that reflect these qualities in both a balanced and imbalanced state.

The main locations of Pitta in the body are the small intestine, stomach, liver, spleen, pancreas, blood, eyes, and sweat. Physiologically, Pitta provides the body with heat and energy through the breakdown of complex food molecules. It governs all processes related to conversion and transformation throughout the mind and body. Psychologically, Pitta governs joy, courage, willpower, anger, jealousy, and mental perception. It also provides the radiant light of the intellect.

When a person has a tendency to "overheat," excess Pitta is usually the culprit. Just as a campfire may turn into a forest fire without proper care, the internal fire of the mind and body must be kept in check.

The balanced Pitta individual is blessed with a joyful disposition, a sharp intellect, and tremendous courage and drive. As the fire of the mind and body becomes unruly, however, the laughing Pitta quickly becomes the yelling Pitta. Anger, rage, and ego replace Pitta's positive attributes, leaving an individual who is bitter with life and overbearing towards others. There is a saying that imbalanced Pitta individuals don't go to hell; they simply create it wherever they go! Pitta imbalances commonly manifest in the body as infection, inflammation, rashes, ulcers, heartburn, and fever.

Physical Characteristics of Pitta

Bodily make-up of Pitta individuals with a tendency towards imbalance:

BUILD	Medium build, developed and proportional musculature
WEIGHT	Average; little problem in gaining or losing weight
HEIGHT	Medium
SKIN	Delicate, oily skin; prone to acne and rashes; moles and freckles common
HAIR	Fine and often lighter in color; premature graying and hair loss common
NECK	Medium thickness
HANDS	Medium size, often hot and sweaty
NAILS	Soft and well-formed; often pink due to heated blood under the nails
EYES	Medium size, bright and penetrating, white of the eyes easily bloodshot
NOSE	Thin and pointed
MOUTH	Teeth are yellow and prone to decay; bleeding gums and canker sores common
TONGUE	Moist, red or pink, with a yellow coating (especially on the front third of the tongue)

Bodily functions/ qualities of Pitta individuals with a tendency towards imbalance:

APPETITE	Strong; become irritable when skipping a meal
DIGESTION	Strong metabolism and digestion; easily aggravated by spicy foods
STOOL	Soft, loose, burning, and lighter in color; regular bowel movements
URINE	Bright yellow, often in excess
MENSTRUATION	Regular cycles, may bleed more heavily and longer due to internal heat
MOVEMENT	Determined stride
PHYSICAL ACTIVITY	Attracted to vigorous exercise and competitive sports
SEXUAL ACTIVITY	Strong sexual appetite, easily aroused
SLEEP	Light, but not easily disturbed
PULSE	Strong and stable; said to "jump like a frog"
VOICE	Loud, often piercing
SPEECH	Sharp and direct
PREFERRED CLIMATE	Low tolerance for sunlight and hot weather; perspire easily

COMMON PITTA DISORDERS OF THE BODY

- Disorders of the stomach and small intestine
- Hot flashes
- Hyperacidity
- Skin rashes and psoriasis
- Ulcers
- Inflammation
- Heartburn
- Diarrhea
- Liver disorders
- Canker sores
- Sore throats and tonsillitis
- Excess hunger and thirst
- Appendicitis
- Bad breath
- Hemorrhoids
- Bloodshot eyes
- Hepatitis
- Other eye disorders
- Infection
- Intolerance to heat (especially hot, humid weather)
- Food allergies (especially to nuts)

The hot, sharp quality of Pitta disorders commonly manifest as infection, inflammation, and hemorrhage and are often acute in nature. In classical Ayurvedic texts, Pitta accounts for roughly 30 percent of all listed disorders. These texts identify more than 70 Pitta disorders related to the eyes alone. Due to their inherent motivation, Pitta individuals usually approach self-healing with great will and enthusiasm. A bigger challenge may relate to their tendency to become overzealous and actually overdo things a bit.

Psychological Characteristics of Pitta

Qualities of balanced Pitta individuals

- Highly intelligent, with penetrating ideas
- Confident
- Able to understand new concepts quickly
- Courageous
- Willful, determined, and ambitious
- Funny
- High achievers; geared for success
- Joyful
- Natural leaders
- Emotionally observant
- Articulate, with clear, direct speech
- Sharp memory
- Perform well under pressure
- Organized, great planners
- Able to focus on single objective at hand
- Strong sense of discernment

In balance, Pitta individuals are smart, enthusiastic, and fun to be around. They find joy in life and radiate this joy to others. Pitta types succeed in most jobs they put their minds to and naturally make good business people, lawyers, professors, doctors, engineers, architects, scientists, politicians, and designers.

Qualities of imbalanced Pitta individuals

- Overly intense
- Manipulative
- Stubborn
- Arrogant
- Jealous
- Materialistic
- Hot-headed; tendency to erupt with anger
- Loud and aggressive
- Controlling of others
- Overly competitive
- Egotistical; enjoy power trips
- Critical and judgmental
- Overly extroverted; like to be center of attention
- Suppressive of emotion
- Demeaning (especially to Vatas and Kaphas)

While not as prone to mental disorders as Vata individuals, the fiery temperament of Pitta types may often burn out of control. Similar to Vata, an overly active mind often defines Pitta psychological imbalances. These thoughts are usually rooted in anger, fear, hatred, and jealousy. Mental disorders include uncontrollable anger, anxiety, obsessive-type behavior, and deep-seated emotional problems.

While fun to be around in balance, the imbalanced Pitta individual can be totally overbearing to others. Cooling the mind through a Pitta-pacifying diet and lifestyle will help re-establish joy and harmony in even the hottest Pitta types.

Ways Pitta Becomes Imbalanced

- Eating Pitta-aggravating food
- Eating while angry
- Drinking coffee, black tea, or alcohol
- Smoking cigarettes
- Over-working
- Being overly competitive
- Allowing oneself to overheat in physical and mental activity
- Failing to make changes in accordance with the seasons (especially Summer)
- Surrounding one's self with loud, aggressive sensory input (like violence on TV)

Ways to Balance Pitta

Key Words to Remember: cooling, calming, moderation

- Eat a Pitta-balancing diet.
- Eat in a peaceful environment.
- Avoid artificial stimulants.
- Engage in calming activities, like spending time in nature.
- Meditate daily.
- Do calming physical exercise, such as Yoga, swimming, Tai Chi, or walking.
- Surround self with cooling colors, like blue, green and white.
- Listen to calming music.
- Take time to rest every day.
- Laugh and smile more.
- Learn to appreciate Vata and Kapha types.
- Observe the seasons (especially Summer) and adjust diet and lifestyle accordingly.
- Do volunteer work.
- Take cool showers.
- Use sweet and cooling essential oils, like sandalwood and rose for aromatherapy.
- Wear cooling gems and stones, such as moonstone, pearl, and blue sapphire.
- Massage body daily with cooling oils (such as coconut).
- Get in touch with emotions, through introspective activities like journaling.

Kapha Overview

Kapha derives from the elements of Water and Earth and translates as "that which sticks." It is the energy of building and lubrication that provides the body with physical form, structure, and the smooth functioning of all its parts. Kapha can be thought of as the essential cement, glue, and lubrication of the body in one.

The qualities of Kapha are moist, cold, heavy, dull, soft, sticky, and static. A Kapha individual will display physical and mental characteristics that reflect these qualities in both a balanced and imbalanced state.

The main locations of Kapha in the body are the chest, throat, lungs, head, lymph, fatty tissue, connective tissue, ligaments, and tendons. Physiologically, Kapha moistens food, gives bulk to our tissues, lubricates joints, stores energy, and relates to cool bodily fluids such as water, mucous, and lymph. Psychologically, Kapha governs love, patience, forgiveness, greed, attachment, and mental inertia. With its earthly makeup, Kapha grounds Vata and Pitta and helps offset imbalances related to these doshas.

Kapha individuals are blessed with naturally good health, rugged bodies, and mental peace. When in a state of imbalance, terms like "couch potato" and "lazy bones" may ring close to home for these types.

Just as a nourishing rainstorm may turn into a rampant flood, the fluids of the body may flood the bodily tissues, contributing to a heavy dampness that weighs down the body and clouds the mind. This dense, cold, and swampy environment becomes the breeding ground for a number of bodily disorders such as obesity, sinus congestion, and anything related to mucous. Mentally, the loving and calm disposition of the Kapha individual may transform into lethargy, attachment, and depression.

Physical Characteristics of Kapha

Bodily make-up of Kapha individuals with a tendency towards imbalance:

BUILD	Heavy bones, broad frames; strong and well-proportioned
WEIGHT	Heavy, often obese; have trouble losing weight
HEIGHT	Shorter or taller than average
SKIN	Oily, smooth, and cool; few moles or wrinkles
HAIR	Thick, oily; often curly and dark
NECK	Thick and often stout
HANDS	Thick, cool, and often clammy
NAILS	Strong, white, and symmetrical
EYES	Large, white, and round; calming
NOSE	Large and thick
MOUTH	Large, strong, white teeth; large mouths
TONGUE	Pink; white coating (especially front third); often swollen

Bodily functions/ qualities of Kapha individuals with a tendency towards imbalance:

APPETITE	Moderate appetite; can easily miss a meal; not hungry upon waking
DIGESTION	Slow metabolism; digestive fire often weak
STOOL	Well-formed, often with an oily coat; regular bowel movements
URINE	White and foamy; infrequent elimination
MENSTRUATION	Regular cycles, mild cramps; average bleeding; prone to water retention
MOVEMENT	Slow and graceful
PHYSICAL ACTIVITY	Capable of vigorous activity, but avoid physical exertion
SEXUAL ACTIVITY	Steady desire for sex
SLEEP	Deep sleep, feel rested upon waking; often snore
PULSE	Smooth; said to move "like a swan"
VOICE	Thick, melodious, often low
SPEECH	Slow and deliberate
PREFERRED CLIMATE	Dry climate; sweat moderately in all climates

COMMON KAPHA DISORDERS OF THE BODY

- Obesity
- Diabetes
- Colds and flu
- Yeast conditions
- Sinus congestion
- Anorexia and bulimia
- Lymphatic system disorders
- Excessive sleeping
- Water retention/bloating
- Allergies
- Excess phlegm and mucous conditions
- Intolerance of cold and damp
- Asthma
- Low thyroid function
- Heart disease

The body of a Kapha individual resembles a stone house: it's solid, rugged, and prepared to weather most of what heads its way. While modern culture has a fascination with being thin, it was undoubtedly the Kapha types that were equipped to brave the elements in ancient times. In classical Ayurvedic texts, only 10 percent of disorders relate to Kapha, with most of these concerning excess fluid conditions. Despite this smaller number, Kapha is closely related to the epidemic rise of illnesses today, such as obesity and heart disease.

Kapha types respond well to dietary and lifestyle changes. They also benefit from cleansing therapies, such as Ayurveda's traditional five-step detoxification program, known as *Panchakarma* (see page 148). Getting a Kapha to adhere to any program of treatment, however, may be the bigger challenge. Once commitment is in place, Kaphas will pursue a healing regimen with determination.

Psychological Characteristics of Kapha

Qualities of balanced Kapha individuals

- Compassionate
- Patient
- Sweet
- Forgiving
- Gentle
- Emotionally stable
- Loving
- Inherent desire to help others
- Calm, mild mannered
- Loyal
- Nurturing
- Accepting of others
- Strong stamina and endurance
- Romantic
- Homebodies; love to feed and entertain
- Sensual
- Community oriented
- Strong long-term memory
- Good listeners
- Deeply satisfied with life

In balance, Kapha individuals are warm, loving, gentle, and a good place to go for a big hug. Kaphas are mentally and emotionally healthy and have a deep satisfaction for life.

Due to their foundation of Water and Earth, Kapha types are well-suited for jobs and activities involving stamina and nurturing. They naturally make good parents, teachers, chefs, healing arts practitioners, construction workers, task force organizers, and community leaders.

Qualities of imbalanced Kapha individuals

- Greedy
- Unchanging; set in ways
- Hoard material things
- Unable to say no
- Easily attached to people and things
- Easily taken advantage of
- Possessive
- Take on other people's problems
- Fearful of letting go
- Overly passive
- Lethargic
- Unable to express thoughts and emotion
- Envious
- Give up easily
- Slow to understand/grasp things
- Depressed for long periods of time
- Introverted
- Complacent; living life on the surface

While the most mentally and emotionally stable of the three doshas, imbalanced Kapha types have a tendency to store emotions, just like extra fatty tissue in their bodies. Kaphas are the least likely to realize they have any psychological problems at all, and are, therefore, unlikely to make self-motivated steps in this direction.

Similar to a bear hibernating in the winter, the inherently good-natured Kapha individual becomes easily introverted, seeking insulation from the cruel outside world. Deep-seated emotions often result in depression and mental lethargy for these types. Their instinctual desire to store may also take on a hoarding quality, manifesting in attachment and greed.

Stimulating the mind through a Kapha-pacifying diet and lifestyle will help Kapha types find peace in the deeper realms of their psyche.

Ways Kapha Becomes Imbalanced

- Eating Kapha-aggravating food
- Overeating
- Eating to offset emotions (like indulging in sweets when depressed)
- Spending too much time in cool, damp climates
- Not engaging in physical activity
- Spending most of one's time indoors (especially on the couch watching TV!)
- Avoiding intellectual challenges
- Storing emotion; not staying emotionally current
- Focusing too much on money and material goods
- Failing to make changes in accordance with the seasons (especially Winter and Spring)

Ways to Balance Kapha

Key words to remember: drying, stimulating, expression

- Eat a Kapha-balancing diet.
- Eat in a loving environment.
- Avoid a luxurious, leisurely lifestyle.
- Focus on non-attachment in daily life.
- Do emotional housekeeping regularly.
- Make time for introspective activities, like meditation and writing.
- Make a distinction between being nice and being taken advantage of.
- Go to bed early and rise early, with no daytime naps.
- Engage in stimulating activities like running, hiking, and more vigorous forms of Yoga.
- Surround self with bright, vivid colors like red, orange, gold and purple.
- Listen to enlivening music.
- Observe the seasons (especially Spring and Winter) and adjust diet and lifestyle accordingly.
- Vary one's daily routine.
- Use warming flower essences like myrrh, eucalyptus, and cedar for aromatherapy.
- Wear warming gems and stones such as ruby and yellow sapphire.
- Take dry saunas when available (and alternate these with cold showers).
- Spend time with interesting and motivated people (like balanced Vata and Pitta types).

Determining Your Doshas

To help determine your constitution, we've provided a brief questionnaire below.

For each statement listed beneath Vata, Pitta and Kapha, write down a score for how much it applies to you. Then, add up the numbers to get a total score for each dosha.

We recommend first answering the questions in accordance with general trends throughout your life. This will give you a better understanding of your underlying birth constitution, or prakruti. Then, use a different color pen to answer the questions in accordance with how you look, feel, and behave today. For example, if you've slept well throughout your life, but just started having sleeping problems, the second set of answers will reflect this current imbalance, or vikruti.

If you're having trouble figuring out your constitution, also have a loved one fill out the questionnaire and then compare answers. Adding this degree of objectivity will often bring greater clarity to your findings. It's important to remember that most individuals have one primary dosha, followed by a prominent secondary dosha.

A simple questionnaire will not always capture the full dynamism of the doshas. For this reason, we also recommend consulting a qualified Ayurvedic practitioner (See Resouce section for more information). In addition to identifying your primary constitution, an Ayurvedic practitioner will identify any current signs of imbalance, while offering recommendations for creating balance in all areas of health.

Legend

For each question, rate your matching characteristics on a scale from zero to five. 0 to 1 doesn't apply, 2-3 somewhat applies, 4-5 strongly applies. Write your answers next to the questions or on a separate piece of paper. Add up your scores for each dosha.

Vata

Physical Characteristics

1 I am slender and don't gain weight easily.

2 I am taller or shorter than average.

3 "Thin" describes many of my bodily features (such as my hair, neck, fingers, and lips).

4 My energy fluctuates and often comes in bursts.

5 My appetite is variable (i.e., high one day and low the next).

6 I have a tendency to become bloated, gassy, or constipated.

7 My skin frequently becomes dry.

8 I tend to have cold hands and feet.

9 I am a light sleeper and often have difficulty falling asleep.

10 I prefer warm, moist weather to cold or dry weather.

Psychological Characteristics

1 I am creative and imaginative.

2 I enjoy artistic forms of expression.

3 My mind is active and often restless.

4 I learn quickly but also forget quickly.

5 I become "spaced out" quite easily.

6 I have a tendency to feel anxious, nervous, and insecure.

7 I speak quickly and use hand gestures.

8 I am always on the go.

9 My lifestyle and daily routine are irregular.

10 My dreams are active and colorful.

PITTA

PHYSICAL CHARACTERISTICS

1 I have a medium build and gain or lose weight easily.

2 My height is average.

3 My physical features are sharp or pointed (such as my nose, chin, and teeth).

4 My energy and activity levels are high.

5 My appetite is strong; I can eat large quantities of food.

6 My bowel movements are regular; I occasionally have diarrhea.

7 I perspire quite easily.

8 My skin is oily and has a reddish tone.

9 My eyes are penetrating and light in color.

10 I prefer cooler weather and become irritable in hot weather.

PSYCHOLOGICAL CHARACTERISTICS

1 I am goal oriented and achieve anything to which I put my mind.

2 I have a good sense of humor.

3 I have a strong intellect and enjoy learning new things.

4 I have a natural ability to lead others.

5 I am a perfectionist.

6 I tend to become irritable, impatient, and angry.

7 I am critical of myself and others.

8 Many people think I'm stubborn.

9 I become irritable if I skip a meal.

10 I enjoy competition.

KAPHA

PHYSICAL CHARACTERISTICS

1 I gain weight easily and lose weight with great difficulty.

2 I am short and stocky or tall and sturdy.

3 "Thick" describes many of my bodily features (such as my hair, neck, fingers, and lips).

4 I have abundant strength and stamina.

5 My digestion is weak and I often feel heavy after eating.

6 My bowel movements are highly regular.

7 My skin is smooth and oily and tends to be pale.

8 I sleep deeply and soundly.

9 I catch colds quite frequently.

10 I prefer hot weather over cold or damp weather.

PSYCHOLOGICAL CHARACTERISTICS

1 I have a big heart and prefer to focus on the good in the world.

2 I am calm in nature and not easily angered.

3 I prefer a slow, relaxed lifestyle.

4 I don't learn as quickly as others, but my long-term memory is excellent.

5 I become sentimental quite easily; I often think about the past.

6 I am methodical in my actions.

7 I am highly protective of myself and family.

8 I let negative emotions build up rather than addressing them.

9 I usually let others take the lead.

10 I am a natural listener and frequently help others with their problems.

THE SIX TASTES OF FOOD

AN INTRODUCTION TO AYURVEDIC NUTRITION

According to Ayurveda, a balanced diet directly nurtures the body, mind, senses and spirit. Food gives strength, sustenance, energy, and radiance. Ayurvedic nutrition is therefore intimately tied to the three doshas and takes into account the unique dietary requirements of every individual.

PULSE DIAGNOSIS

In ancient times, Ayurvedic physicians didn't have high-tech machines to look inside the human body. So they developed an equally sophisticated diagnostic tool, which relies solely on feeling the pulse of the patient. Both a science and art form, pulse diagnosis is a highly prized component of Ayurvedic medicine.

It's common for Westerners to feel a sense of awe after having their pulse read by an Ayurvedic physician (or *vaidya*) for the first time. A vaidya will often start by asking questions based entirely on their pulse reading, such as: "How long have you been constipated?" or "When exactly did you have your tonsils removed?" The ability to discern such information is based upon years of experience and tremendous inner clarity.

In exploring your own constitution, you can use the basic principles of pulse diagnosis to better understand your current state. Simply place the index, middle, and ring fingers of your right hand on the radial artery of your left wrist, as shown in the illustration.

Applying equal pressure, press down all three fingers simultaneously, until you feel a pulse. If you feel a thin, fast moving pulse primarily under your index finger, this suggests that Vata is prominent in your current state. Traditionally, a Vata pulse is said to "slither like a cobra." A strong pulse under your middle finger relates to Pitta. A Pitta pulse is said to "jump like a frog." If you feel a soft and slow pulse under your ring finger, this relates to Kapha. A Kapha pulse is said to "move like a swan."

Eating in accordance with your constitutional makeup promotes balance, while eating dosha-aggravating foods ensures imbalance. Food is the primary preventive tool in Ayurveda, as well as the first step in bringing the mind and body back into balance. That old precept "You are what you eat" extends in Ayurveda to "You are what, how, when and why you eat." Well-being results not just from the type of foods you put into your body, but also from the state of mind, environment, time of day, and season in which you consume them.

In the West, we have separated ourselves from the food we eat. Food plays a role comparable to that of gasoline for a car—something apart from the body, used for fuel and energy. But the same energy dancing at our core is also present in every plant and morsel of food on this planet. Since the energetic foundation of the body and food are the same, we cannot truly separate ourselves from the food we eat. The energy, or *prana*, of food not only nourishes every cell on a gross physical level but also replenishes our underlying life-force.

When feeling run-down, we instinctively eat food to help get us back on our feet. We naturally think of food as providing energy. Ayurveda simply takes it a step further by recognizing that food itself is energy.

Ayurveda classifies different foods in relation to their energetic qualities and specific doshic effects. Modern nutrition, by contrast, classifies foods according to their independent physical components—for example, how many calories, carbohydrates, or grams of protein they contain. This approach echoes the West's greater mechanistic view of the body and fails to capture the true dynamism of food. Ayurveda values these nutrients as a component of a greater synergistic whole—namely, how they intermix along with prana to create vibrant and nutritious food.

Ayurvedic nutrition focuses on the way food affects three major areas: the doshas, the digestion, and the mind. According to Ayurveda, imbalances within the doshas lead to improper digestion. Poor digestion, in turn, plants the seeds for future illness. Ayurvedic nutrition extends to the mind by observing that food directly affects the qualities of the mind (think, for example, of spicy food's ability to fire-up one's temper or passions). Ayurveda also recognizes that we constantly process "mental food" in the form of sensory impressions, thoughts, and emotions. Just as heartburn or bloating can occur after a big meal, failure to digest mental food properly will result in disharmony of the mind, or mental indigestion.

All foods can be examined within an Ayurvedic framework. Questions regarding whether or not certain foods are "Ayurvedic" are irrelevant. Ayurveda offers a universal system of nutrition that teaches us to eat in accordance with our individual constitutions. It goes far beyond a rigid set of one-plan-fits-all dietary guidelines by allowing individuals to tailor diets specifically for themselves. In this sense, Ayurveda inherently offers billions of diet plans!

Ayurvedic nutrition could not be further from the fad diets of today. It's common for patients to arrive at our clinic in a state of utter confusion: "This article says that X diet is good for me, but that TV show said it's bad"; or "This medical study says that such-and-such a food is beneficial, but that study says I shouldn't eat it." Ayurveda, on the other hand, does not demand adherence to a specific set of dietary guidelines. Instead, it shuns dogma and places the greatest emphasis on your own instinctive ability to feed yourself healthfully.

A cornerstone of Ayurvedic nutrition is that food should taste delicious. Mouth-watering food satiates the senses and stimulates the entire digestive system to carry out its job effectively. Ayurveda also supports meeting people where they're at and beginning from there, rather than demanding abrupt dietary and lifestyle changes. Like any sudden change in life, rapid dietary shifts can often lead to physical and mental mayhem. Making gentle, non-invasive changes, on the other hand, ensures that the body will not undergo a state of greater imbalance before getting healthier. After all, why take a step backward if you can take a step forward right from the start?

THE 6 TASTES

OUR GUIDE MAP TO OPTIMAL NUTRITION

Much of the wisdom of Ayurvedic nutrition rests on the tip of your tongue, literally! According to Ayurveda, the sense of taste is a natural guide map towards proper nutrition. For ages, humans relied largely upon taste to discover healthy foods in nature and avoid toxicity. Our tastebuds do much more than simply identify tastes; they unlock the nutritive value of foods and provide the initial spark to the entire digestive process.

Food speaks to us directly through taste. A juicy pear may call out to us with a gentle message of delight, while the flaming chili pepper cries out in warning. As we tune into the tastes naturally desired by the body, we tap into the body's innate wisdom regarding food and nutrition.

Ayurveda identifies 6 Tastes by which all foods can be categorized: *Sweet, Sour, Salty, Bitter, Pungent,* and *Astringent.* Similar to the body's physical and energetic makeup, the 6 Tastes are combinations of the 5 Elements. The inherent wisdom of taste lies within this elemental connection.

Sweet taste, for example, is composed of Earth and Water, just like the bones of the body and Kapha dosha. Nutritional balance is found within the 6 Tastes, because these tastes encompass all 5 Elements of Nature. While the first four tastes are probably recognizable, the last two may not seem familiar. Pungent taste is hot and spicy as found in a chili pepper, while Astringent taste is dry and light as found in popcorn.

Ayurveda recommends two simple principles for achieving a balanced diet through the 6 Tastes:

1 INCLUDE ALL 6 TASTES IN EACH MEAL

The 6 Tastes offer us a user-friendly guide map for how to nourish each of the 5 Elements at our core. Rather than looking at nutritional labels for x amount of protein or y amount of carbohydrates, the 6 Tastes naturally guide us towards our body's nutritional needs. Each taste feeds our mind, body, senses, and spirit in its own unique way. From a modern nutritional perspective, the 6 Tastes satisfy each of the major dietary building blocks. Sweet foods, for example, are rich in fats and carbohydrates, whereas Pungent foods help increase enzymatic activity.

The brain sends the body signals when it requires energy in the form of food. By incorporating all 6 Tastes into each meal, we ensure that these signals are adequately met, thus avoiding food cravings or the over-consumption of certain foods. The 6 Tastes also stimulate the proper sequence of digestion, making it beneficial to include each taste in every meal. The 6 Tastes can be thought of as essential links in a complex digestive chain. When each taste is included in a meal, the digestive process functions smoothly and efficiently. The Sweet taste (the heaviest) is metabolized first, followed by Sour, Salty, Bitter, Pungent, and Astringent (the lightest).

Note that the above sequence does not parallel the order in which foods are typically eaten in the West. We consume rich, heavy desserts at the end of the meal, creating strain on the digestive system. Many European countries, on the other hand, consume salad at the end of the meal. According to Ayurveda, this makes better sense, since the Bitter and Astringent tastes of green leafy vegetables are lighter and easier to digest.

Since foods are often combinations of many tastes, it is not realistic to always eat them in a specific order according to taste. It is more important to be able to differentiate between easy-to-digest tastes and those requiring more energy. With this knowledge, we can make intelligent eating choices that support optimal digestion. And who knows—maybe there is more to a child asking for desert before dinner after all!

6 Tastes	Make-up	Doshas	Make-up	Balancing Tastes	Imbalancing Tastes
Sweet	Earth and Water				
Sour	Earth and Fire	Vata	Ether and Air	Sweet, Sour, Salty	Bitter, Pungent, Astringent
Salty	Water and Fire	Pitta	Fire and Water	Sweet, Bitter, Astringent	Sour, Salty, Pungent
Bitter	Ether and Air	Kapha	Water and Earth	Pungent, Bitter, Astringent	Sweet, Sour, Salty
Pungent	Air and Fire				
Astringent	Air and Earth				

2 ALLOW YOUR UNIQUE CONSTITUTION TO DETERMINE THE PROPORTION OF TASTES YOU EAT

The body naturally desires tastes that balance its doshic make-up and shuns tastes of an aggravating nature. In this sense, things are made pretty easy for us: if we simply follow our natural inclinations, we are led to the proper foods. Vata individuals, for example, are naturally drawn to moist, grounding foods, while Kapha individuals favor light, drying foods.

Two primary elements are found in each of the 6 Tastes (like Water and Earth in Sweet Taste, for example). Since the doshas find balance in opposites, the cool, moist quality of Sweet taste balances the hot nature of Pitta and the dry nature of Vata. If either element making up a dosha (like Ether or Air for Vata) is found in the make-up of a taste, imbalance may result from eating it.

Nutritional imbalance is greatly linked to our cultural bias towards the first two tastes. Excess consumption of Sweet and Salty tastes, without the balancing effect of the other four tastes, is a primary cause for the epidemic of obesity, high blood pressure, diabetes, and heart disease in North America and other countries of the West. Not surprisingly, fast food restaurants incorporate Sweet and Salty tastes in excess. Consider the standard meal of a burger, fries, and soda: the meat has a sweet taste, the fries are salty, and the soda sweet.

After taking the test below, notice whether the ingredients that produced the tastes in your answers are naturally occurring or are man-made additives. Prime examples

THE TASTE TEST

Now, take this simple test to gauge your current relationship with the 6 Tastes. Answer the questions as quickly as possible, writing down the first answers that come to mind:

1 Name 3 foods that are Sweet.
2 Name 3 foods that are Sour.
3 Name 3 foods that are Salty.
4 Name 3 foods that are Bitter.
5 Name 3 foods that are Pungent.
6 Name 3 foods that are Astringent.

Perhaps you noticed that foods for certain tastes came easily to mind, while others were more difficult. If the first three tastes were the easiest, then you're not alone. Western diets are highest in Sweet, Sour, and Salty tastes. These tastes differ from the latter three in that they cause food to be stored as matter. Bitter, Pungent, and Astringent tastes, on the other hand, help liberate bodily stores into energy.

of man-made additives are refined sugar, as found in ice cream and chocolate, and refined salt, as found in potato chips and nuts. Artificial flavoring and colors are also widely used to enhance the taste and appearance of food. You may find that the tastes in the foods you have chosen derive from these types of man-made sources. Once again, you are not alone if this is this case. The majority of foods found in supermarkets today are full of such ingredients.

Now for the good news: the tastebuds regenerate every 10 to 14 days, allowing you to take charge of your diet by developing a palate for all 6 Tastes. In breaking the cycle of habituation and learning to incorporate the 6 Tastes into your daily eating, you can take hold of important keys to unlocking health and balance.

TASTING THE 6 TASTES

Rasa is the traditional word for "taste" in Ayurveda. More specifically, it refers to the sensation that the tongue experiences when consuming a taste. While individual foods are composed of multiple tastes, one rasa predominates. The primary taste of a fresh garlic clove, for example, is Pungent. This means that garlic will balance Vata and Kapha but aggravate Pitta when consumed in excess. In actuality, garlic contains every taste except Salty, a rare occurrence for any plant or herb.

We detect the 6 Tastes on different areas of our tongues. The tastebuds on the tips of our tongues, for example, are receptive to Sweet. That is why we lick ice cream cones and other sweets. We also perceive Salty on this part of the tongue. Sour taste, on the other hand, is most detectable on the sides of the tongue, while Bitter taste is detectable towards the back of the tongue. Pungent taste has a more generalized effect of firing up the mucous membranes of the tongue. Astringent taste

causes these membranes to constrict, creating a puckering sensation in the mouth, such as when eating cranberries.

In the overview of the 6 Tastes below, **–** after a doshic initial refers to a balancing (or decreasing) effect on that particular dosha, while **+** refers to an aggravating (or increasing) effect.

SWEET V **–** P **–** K **+**

Sweet taste results from the combination of Water and Earth and is heavy, moist, and cooling by nature. In the West, sugary foods are most commonly associated with this taste. Sweet taste is also found in milk and milk products (like butter, ghee, and cream), most grains (especially wheat, rice, and barley), many legumes (like beans and lentils), sweet fruits (such as bananas and mangos), and certain cooked vegetables (such as carrots, potatoes, and beets).

Sweet taste naturally increases bulk, moisture, and weight in the body. For this reason, it is excellent for building the body's seven vital tissues (called *dhatus*) of plasma, blood, fat, muscles, bones, marrow, and reproductive fluids. Sweet taste also increases saliva, soothes mucous membranes and burning sensations, relieves thirst, and has beneficial effects on the skin, hair, and voice.

While the nourishing and soothing effects of Sweet taste pacify Vata and Pitta, they naturally increase Kapha. Think of the effect as being similar to giving a large glass of water to someone who already has to urinate urgently. The cool, moist nature of Kapha (Water and Earth) is overloaded by the similar qualities of Sweet taste. An excess of this taste in Kaphic individuals results in disorders such as congestion, phlegm accumulation, cough, lethargy, indigestion, obesity, edema, and diabetes. It also creates imbalances in Vata and Pitta individuals when taken in excess. The satisfying and addictive nature of Sweet taste makes it the most abused of all tastes in the West today.

SOUR V.– P.+ K.+

Sour Taste is composed of Earth and Fire and is hot, light, and moist by nature. It is commonly found in citrus fruits (such as lemon and limes), sour milk products (like yogurt, cheese, and sour cream), and fermented substances (including wine, vinegar, sauerkraut, and soy sauce). Used in moderation, Sour taste stimulates digestion, stimulates circulation and elimination, energizes the body, strengthens the heart, relieves thirst, maintains acidity, sharpens the senses, and helps extract minerals such as iron from food. It also nourishes all the vital tissues (*dhatus*) except the reproductive tissues (the exception being yogurt, which nourishes all the tissues).

Vata benefits from the moist, warming effects of Sour taste. Since Vata imbalance often entails poor digestion, Sour taste is also helpful in stimulating the digestive fire. The heat of Sour taste, on the other hand, increases Pitta and can easily lead to aggravation. An excess of this taste in Pitta individuals may cause acidic pH balance, heartburn, ulcers, rashes, and burning in the throat, chest, heart, and bladder. The heavy and moist quality also increases Kapha, although aggravation occurs less easily than for Pitta. In small amounts, the stimulatory nature of Sour taste can actually benefit Kapha by

BALANCING THE DOSHAS THROUGH TASTE

	MOST BALANCING	MOST AGGRAVATING
Vata	Salty	Bitter
Pitta	Bitter	Pungent
Kapha	Pungent	Sweet

improving digestion and energizing the body. An excess of this taste in Kapha individuals, however, may lead to lethargy, obesity, and indigestion.

SALTY V.– P.+ K.+

Salty taste is composed of Fire and Water and is hot, heavy, and moist by nature. It is found in any salt (such as sea salt and rock salt), sea vegetables (like seaweed and kelp), and foods to which large amounts of salt are added (like nuts, chips, and pickles). Due to its drying quality in the mouth, it may seem counterintuitive to think of Salty taste as moistening. The element of Water in its composition, however, relates to its water retaining quality. Salty taste falls somewhere between Sweet and Sour tastes with regard to its moist quality. While Sweet taste stimulates the greatest water retention and weight gain in the body, Salty taste will have similar effects when used in excess by any of the doshas.

In moderation, Salty taste lubricates tissues, improves digestion, liquefies mucous, improves the flavor of food,

		SWEET	SOUR	SALTY	BITTER	PUNGENT	ASTRINGENT
ELEMENTS		Earth	Earth	Water	Air	Fire	Air
		Water	Fire	Fire	Space	Air	Earth
QUALITIES		Cold	Hot	Hot	Cold	Hot	Cold
		Heavy	Light	Heavy	Light	Light	Heavy
		Moist/oily	Moist/oily	Moist/oily	Dry	Dry	Dry

maintains mineral balance, aids in the elimination of wastes, and calms the nerves. Due to its tendency to attract water, it also improves the radiance of the skin and promotes overall growth in the body. The warming and grounding effects of Salty taste are beneficial for balancing Vata, but increase both Pitta and Kapha. In Pitta individuals, the heat associated with this taste can lead to hyperacidity, high blood pressure, skin rashes, grayness and loss of hair, wrinkles, and eye problems. When used in excess by Kapha individuals, the dense, water-retaining qualities of Salty taste can lead to obesity, swelling, high blood pressure, and edema.

Bitter taste is a powerful detoxifying agent, and has antibiotic, anti-parasitic, and antiseptic qualities. It is also helpful in reducing weight, water retention, skin rashes, fever, burning sensations and nausea. The cool, dry nature of this taste is extremely balancing to the hot, oily make-up of Pitta. It also balances the dense, moist qualities of Kapha, with its lightening and drying effects on the body. Vata is easily aggravated by Bitter taste, since they both derive from the elements of Air and Ether. A Vata individual who eats this taste in excess risks depleting the seven vital tissues (*dhatus*) and developing Vata disorders such as constipation and insomnia.

BITTER V + P − K −

Bitter taste is composed of Air and Ether and is light, cooling, and dry by nature. It is found in green leafy vegetables (such as spinach, kale, and green cabbage), other vegetables (including zucchini and eggplant), herbs and spices (like turmeric, fenugreek, and dandelion root), coffee, and certain fruits (such as olives and bitter melon). While Bitter taste is often not appealing alone, it stimulates the appetite and helps bring out the flavor of the other tastes.

PUNGENT V + P + K −

Pungent taste derives from the elements of Fire and Air and is hot, dry, and light. It is the hottest of all the 6 Tastes and is found in certain vegetables (such as chili peppers, garlic, and onions), and in spices (like black pepper, ginger, and cumin). In small amounts, Pungent taste stimulates digestion, clears the sinuses, promotes sweating and detoxification, dispels gas, aids circulation, improves metabolism, and relieves muscle pain. The stimulating and drying effects of Pungent taste are particularly beneficial for balancing the stagnant and damp qualities of Kapha.

TASTES BY QUALITIES

Hottest to Coldest	Heaviest to Lightest	Moistest to Driest
Pungent	Sweet	Sweet
Sour	Sour	Salty
Salty	Salty	Sour
Sweet	Astringent	Astringent
Astringent	Pungent	Pungent
Bitter	Bitter	Bitter

The hot nature of Pungent taste is aggravating to Pitta, even in small amounts. For an individual with an excess Pitta condition, eating Pungent foods is like throwing gasoline on a fire. It may lead to ulcers, hyperacidity, heartburn, nausea, diarrhea, skin rashes, and a depletion of reproductive fluids. Vata individuals are also easily aggravated by Pungent taste, due to the presence of Air in the taste's elemental makeup. A Vata individual who eats Pungent foods in excess may experience disorders such as insomnia, back and leg pain, tremors, colitis, excessive thirst, and bodily dryness. A small amount of this taste, however, may be helpful for stimulating digestion and circulation in Vata types.

ASTRINGENT V + P − K −

Astringent taste results from the combination of Air and Earth and is dry, cooling, and heavy by nature. It is the least common of all the 6 Tastes and can be found in legumes (such as beans and lentils), fruits (including cranberries, pomegranates, pears, and dried fruits), vegetables (such as broccoli, cauliflower, artichoke, asparagus and turnip), grains (such as rye, buckwheat, and quinoa), spices and herbs (including turmeric and marjoram), coffee, and teas (such as black and green tea). Astringent taste is not as cold as Bitter taste, but has a greater cooling effect on the body than Sweet taste.

Astringent taste is classified more in relation to its effect on the tongue than its actual taste. It creates a puckering sensation in the mouth, as caused by cranberries or pomegranates, or a dry, chalky feeling as found in many beans. Foods such as broccoli or cauliflower have a mildly Astringent taste that is less detectable. Dry foods such as crackers and chips, most raw vegetables, and the peels of fruit, also have Astringent qualities.

Taken in moderation, Astringent taste balances Pitta and Kapha. Its contracting and drying quality stops bleeding, absorbs water, tightens tissues, dries fat, and heals skin wounds, ulcers, and mucous membranes. Beans, for example, are typically soaked in double the amount of water, due to this absorptive or spongelike quality. Astringent taste also has antibiotic and antibacterial effects. Vata is naturally aggravated by the cool, dry nature of this taste. A Vata type who consumes Astringent foods in excess may experience slow digestion, constipation, heart problems, loss of weight, excessive thirst, and blockages in the body's channels (called *shrotas*).

TASTES BY ACTIONS

TASTE	PRIMARY ACTIONS	COMMON SOURCES
Sweet	Builds tissues, calms nerves	Fruit, grains, natural sugars, milk
Sour	Cleanses tissues, increases absorption of minerals	Sour fruits, yogurt, fermented foods
Salty	Improves taste of food, lubricates tissues, stimulates digestion	Natural salts, sea vegetables
Bitter	Detoxifies and lightens tissues	Dark leafy greens, herbs and spices
Pungent	Stimulates digestion and metabolism	Chili peppers, garlic, herbs and spices
Astringent	Absorbs water, tightens tissues, dries fats	Legumes, raw fruits & vegetables, herbs & spices

CRUNCH

Chef Johnny identifies Crunch as the unofficial 7th taste of food. Commonly found in Salty and Astringent foods, Crunch provides that certain gratification to the senses that soft foods simply can't fulfill alone!

THE QUALITIES OF FOOD

In addition to the 6 Tastes, Ayurveda considers the general qualities (or *gunas*) of food. When we described Sweet taste above, we said it was "heavy, moist, and cooling" by nature. These terms refer to the qualities or gunas of Sweet taste. Foods that have a predominantly Sweet taste will share the same qualities. Classically, Ayurveda uses ten pairs of opposite qualities to analyze food. Of these, the top three pairs are the most significant.

- Heavy / Light
- Hot / Cold
- Moist / Dry
- Dull / Sharp
- Smooth / Rough
- Solid / Liquid
- Soft / Hard
- Firm / Flexible
- Subtle / Gross
- Clear / Viscous

The gunas refer to physical qualities of food (such as weight or temperature) and also to the physiological and energetic effects of food. Any food item eaten hot, for example, will create a mild heating effect in the body. Foods that are high in the Fire element (such as Sour, Salty, or Pungent foods) will create an even greater heating effect, by increasing metabolism and acidity. Cooling foods, on the other hand, being high in the Earth, Water, and Air elements (as found in Sweet, Bitter and Astringent foods), decrease metabolism and increase alkalinity.

"Heavy" refers to foods that are dense in nutrients and prominent in tastes containing the Earth and Water elements (such as Sweet and Salty foods). "Light" foods require less energy to digest, due to the elements of Air and Ether in their make-up (as found in Pungent and Bitter foods). "Dry" foods extract moisture from bodily tissues, through the elements of Fire, Air, and Ether (as found in Pungent, Bitter, and Astringent foods). "Moist" foods build and lubricate the tissues through the elements of Water and Earth (as found in Sweet, Sour, and Salty foods).

If this all sounds a bit confusing, there's no need to worry! The food recommendations and recipes in this book take into account all of these factors. We've also included detailed food lists for each dosha in the Appendix. When you see kale in a Pitta-balancing recipe, for example, it takes into account the taste (rasa) and qualities (gunas) of kale (i.e., Bitter, cooling, and dry), which help balance the hot, oily nature of Pitta.

Similarly, there is no need to become overwhelmed by trying to memorize dosha-specific food lists (such as those on page 319). Instead, just refer to the underlying qualities of the doshas and the food itself. For example, if you know you're a Pitta type, but you can't remember whether a specific food is balancing or not, just consider its qualities. Is it oily and spicy (like Pitta itself) or alkalizing and sweet (unlike Pitta itself)? The key lies in choosing foods with opposite characteristics to the dosha you're trying to pacify.

As you tune into your underlying constitution, you'll notice that you naturally desire dosha-balancing foods. For example, if you're a Vata type and feel internally dry or mentally ungrounded, you'll naturally desire warm, heavy, and comforting foods to help you regain balance. Ultimately, this type of intuitive self-guidance is your greatest nutritional guidemap of all.

General dietary tips: Vata, Pitta and Kapha

Vata General Dietary Tips

- Favor foods with Sweet, Sour, and Salty tastes.
- Favor heavy, moist and warming foods.
- Eat fewer Bitter, Pungent, and Astringent foods.
- Enjoy three or four smaller meals at regular times each day.
- Eat a balanced breakfast each morning.
- Avoid eating when nervous or anxious.
- Sit down to eat and always avoid eating on the run.
- Take note of any signs of poor digestion (such as gas, bloating, or constipation).
- Eliminate white sugar and caffeine.
- Use warming spices to improve digestion.
- Avoid cold and carbonated beverages.

Grains

Heavier whole grains such as rice, wheat, quinoa and oats are best for Vata. Corn, millet, rye, and puffed cereals, on the other hand, are too light and drying. Some Vata types may have difficulty digesting wheat, due to their weak digestion or food allergies. Yeasted bread also aggravates Vata, due to its gas-promoting qualities.

Fruits

Vata types do well with most fruit. Heavier fruits with Sweet and Sour tastes are particularly beneficial, such as mangoes, bananas, dates, oranges, grapes, and grapefruit. Dry fruits and astringent fruits (such as cranberries) are less beneficial.

Vegetables

Heavy, moist vegetables such as squash, sweet potatoes, avocado, and cooked carrots are excellent choices for Vata. Broccoli, cabbage, cauliflower, and raw onions create gas in Vata types. Allergies to nightshades (such as tomato and eggplant) are also common in these types.

Cooked or steamed vegetables are best suited for Vata. Raw vegetables are less suitable, due to their rough, hard nature and stronger digestive requirements. Salads should be eaten at room temperature (instead of straight from the refrigerator), along with oil or a creamy dressing. Juicing raw vegetables also makes them easier to digest for Vata types.

LEGUMES

Vata types frequently have difficulty digesting legumes. Mung beans are best suited for Vata, while lentils, chickpeas, and tofu can be eaten in smaller amounts. Soaking legumes before cooking will improve digestibility and decrease gas. Cooking the legumes with Pungent spices (such as cumin, ginger, or asafetida) will offer similar effects.

NUTS AND SEEDS

All nuts and seeds are good for Vata, especially in the form of nut butters and milks, which are easier to digest. Roasting nuts with a little salt, or simply soaking them in water, is also highly beneficial for Vata. Soaked and peeled almonds, in particular, are great for pacifying Vata.

DAIRY

Vata benefits from the grounding and nourishing effect of dairy. Yogurt, ghee, and cow's milk are particularly beneficial for Vata. Since Vata types are the most prone to food allergies, however, cow's milk may pose a problem. To help avoid such problems, always boil milk and allow it to cool to room temperature before drinking. Vata types also do better with soft cheeses rather than hard varieties.

OILS AND FATS

Oils are an important component of the Vata diet. Sesame oil, olive oil, and ghee are the best choices.

SEASONINGS

Most spices are beneficial for Vata, especially sea salt, ginger, and garlic. The overuse of Pungent spices like cayenne, however, may aggravate the dry nature of Vata.

SWEETENERS

Vatas can use any natural sweetener in moderation, but should always avoid white sugar and use honey in moderation due to its drying quality.

DRINKS

Drinking plenty of water each day is particularly important for Vata types. Adding lemon or lime to the water is beneficial. Fruit juices (especially Sour) and herbal teas are also beneficial. Wine is okay in moderation, but beer and hard alcohol quickly create imbalances within these types.

MEATS

Vata types are the most suited for meat consumption, due to its grounding and nutrient-rich quality. Deepwater fish, chicken (both meat and eggs), red meat, and duck, are all Vata-pacifying. Ayurveda, however, does not recommend the regular consumption of meat for any doshic type, due to its difficulty to digest (both physically and mentally).

Pitta General Dietary Tips

- Favor foods with Sweet, Bitter, and Astringent tastes.
- Favor cool, dry, and slightly heavy foods.
- Eat fewer Salty, Sour, and Pungent foods.
- Eat at regular times each day.
- Eat a balanced breakfast and early lunch.
- Avoid refined sugar.
- Limit alcohol and caffeine.
- Avoid conducting business while eating.
- Don't eat poorly, just because your digestion can handle it!

Grains

Most grains are beneficial for Pitta. Basmati rice, barley, couscous, quinoa, pasta, and wheat are particularly balancing. Barley is considered the best Pitta grain, due to its cooling, drying, and alkalizing effects. Corn, millet, rye, and buckwheat, on the other hand, are less recommended, due to their heating effects.

Fruit

Sweet, cooling, and Astringent fruits are most beneficial for Pitta, such as pears, mangoes, apples, coconut, figs, cranberries, and pomegranates. Sour fruits such as grapefruit and pineapple are the least recommended.

Vegetables

Pitta types do well with most vegetables. Bitter and cooling vegetables are especially beneficial, such as kale, broccoli, zucchini, potatoes, squash, cucumber, and peas. Sour or heating vegetables, such as mustard greens, tomatoes, radishes, garlic, and eggplant are not recommended. Pitta types benefit from both cooked and raw vegetables.

Legumes

Pitta types are well-equipped to digest most legumes, due to their strong digestive fires. Pre-soaking legumes before cooking is recommended to improve digestibility. Adding digestive spices during cooking is also recommended. Mung beans, lentils, adzuki beans, chickpeas, soybeans, and split peas are all balancing to Pitta.

NUTS AND SEEDS

The oily and heating nature of nuts and seeds make them less suitable for Pitta. Coconut, sunflower seeds, and soaked and peeled almonds are the best choices. Peanuts, cashews, pistachios, and all salted nuts are Pitta-aggravating.

DAIRY

Pitta benefits from the cooling and nourishing effects of dairy, such as cow's milk, ghee, cottage cheese, panir (fresh cheese made from whey), and unsalted cheese. Sour cream, along with hard or salted cheeses, easily aggravates Pitta. Yogurt is fine in moderation for Pitta types, but it's best taken slightly watered-down.

OILS AND FATS

Pitta types are naturally oily by nature, so they require less dietary oil. Cooling oils and fats such as ghee, sunflower and coconut oils are the best choices. Olive and sesame oils are also fine in moderation. Peanut and mustard oils are not recommended for Pitta types.

SEASONINGS

Pitta benefits from cooling spices and herbs such as dill, fennel, cardamom, cilantro, coriander, and saffron. Heating spices such as garlic, cumin, sea salt, black pepper, and asafetida are best taken in moderation by Pitta types. Highly Pungent herbs such as cayenne and horseradish are best avoided.

SWEETENERS

Pitta benefits from all types of natural sweeteners in moderation, except molasses, due to its heating quality. Honey should also be taken in smaller quantities, due to its mildly heating quality. White sugar is best eliminated altogether.

DRINKS

Drinking plenty of water each day is important for Pitta types. Sweet and Astringent fruit juices such as apple, pear, cranberry, and pomegranate are especially balancing for Pitta. Cooling herbal teas (such as mint) are also beneficial. Beer is fine in moderation, but wine and hard alcohol easily aggravate Pitta.

MEATS

Meat is oily and heating in nature, and should therefore be consumed less by Pitta types. White meats and freshwater fish are the best choices for Pitta. Red meat, saltwater fish, shellfish, and egg yolks are the most aggravating.

Kapha General Dietary Tips

- Favor foods with Bitter, Pungent, and Astringent tastes.
- Favor light, dry, and warming foods.
- Eat fewer Sweet, Sour, and Salty foods.
- Eat less in quantity and frequency.
- Eat at regular times each day.
- Eat a light breakfast (or skip it entirely).
- Eat a light evening meal.
- Avoid frequent snacking and late-night eating.
- Eliminate white sugar and greasy foods.
- Use warming spices to improve digestion.
- Favor warm beverages.

Grains

Kapha types require fewer grains than Vata and Pitta types, due to the moist, heavy nature of most grains. The light, dry, and heating qualities of corn, millet, rye, and buckwheat make them the best choices. Wheat, oats, and rice should be consumed less frequently. Bread is best taken toasted. Popped grains (such as corn and amaranth) make great snacks for Kapha.

Fruit

Kapha benefits from light and Astringent fruits such as apples, pears, cranberries, pomegranates, and dried fruit. Sour, juicy, and heavy fruits are least recommended, such as pineapple, oranges, melon, and banana.

Vegetables

Kapha benefits from most vegetables, including root vegetables, broccoli, mushrooms, celery, kale, green beans, eggplant, and a wide range of other vegetables. Heavy, Sweet, and Sour vegetables are least recommended, such as avocado, sweet potato, and tomato. Vegetables are best taken lightly steamed and spiced, due to the cold nature of Kapha. Lighter, raw vegetables are also beneficial for Kapha, such as salads and sprouts. These should be eaten at room temperature rather than straight from the refrigerator.

Legumes

The Astringent taste and drying quality of most legumes make them a balancing choice for Kapha. These include mung beans, adzuki beans, black beans, lentils, pinto beans, red lentils, and well-cooked tofu.

Nuts and Seeds

The heavy, oily quality of most nuts and seeds make them less suitable for Kapha. As a protein source, however, they're preferable to meat and dairy. Pumpkin seeds and sunflower seeds are the best choices for Kapha. Coconut, almonds, sesame seeds, peanuts, pine nuts, and walnuts are Kapha-aggravating.

Dairy

Kapha types should generally avoid dairy, due to its heavy, moist, and oily properties. Dairy products easily create mucous and congestion in Kapha types. Yogurt, goat's milk, and goat cheese are fine in moderation. Soy milk is also a healthy alternative to cow's milk.

Oils and Fats

Kapha types are oily by nature, so they require less dietary oil. Light oils such as sunflower, canola, and safflower are best suited for these types. Ghee is also fine in moderation. Heavier oils and fats such as sesame, butter, and olive oil are Kapha-aggravating.

Seasonings

All spices benefit Kapha, especially Pungent spices such as garlic, ginger, cumin, black pepper, cloves, turmeric and cayenne. Salt should be consumed sparingly by Kapha types. Sour condiments such as vinegar and relish are Kapha-aggravating, due to the heavy, moist qualities of Sour taste.

Sweeteners

Sweeteners naturally increase Kapha, so they should be used in small quantities. Raw honey is the best choice, due to its drying and heating qualities. According to Ayurveda, cooking with honey transforms it into a toxic substance that clogs the channels of the body. Adding honey to tea or hot water, however, is fine. Rice syrup and stevia are also beneficial options for Kapha. White sugar should be eliminated completely.

Drinks

Kapha types require less water than Vata or Pitta types, due to their natural tendency to store water in the tissues. As a rule, it's best for Kapha types to only drink when they're thirsty. Hot, spicy drinks such as ginger tea or chai are great for Kapha. Coffee and black tea are also fine in moderation. Vegetable juices are better than Sweet fruit juices & wine is better than other types of alcohol.

Meats

Kapha types are naturally abundant in bodily tissues and, therefore, require animal foods the least. The heavy, oily nature of meat aggravates Kapha. White meat, poultry, and freshwater fish are better choices than beef, pork, and saltwater fish. When cooking meat, it's best for Kapha types to roast, broil, or bake it rather than frying or sautéing.

Dual-Dosha Recommendations

Dual-dosha individuals should pay attention to the dietary tips for both doshas in their make-up. However, as we mentioned, it's important to pay the greatest attention to your primary dosha, while remaining aware of your secondary dosha. A Pitta type with a strong secondary Kapha dosha, for example, will be able to handle more heating foods than a purely Pitta type (due to the cooling influence of Kapha).

Seasonal influences are also important to consider. This is because a particular season will naturally increase a dosha with similar qualities to itself. During the hot months of Summer, for example, Pitta becomes more pronounced in

the body. Vata becomes more pronounced during the dry, cold weather of Fall and early Winter. Kapha becomes more pronounced during the late Winter and Spring, when Nature begins to liquefy again. A Vata type with a strong Pitta influence should, therefore, take greater care not to eat overly heating foods in the Summer. A Pitta type with a strong Kapha influence, on the other hand, would incorporate Kapha-balancing foods during the wet Spring season.

We've kept the recipes in this book simple by presenting them in a uni-doshic format (that is, designed to balance one specific dosha). This will help familiarize you with the ingredients that are most balancing for each dosha. At the same time, we've included doshic alternatives at the bottom of each recipe that make them easily tailored for dual-types. Considering that individuals in the same family will often have different doshas, we've also included a section on page 169 on how to cook Ayurvedically for your family.

General guidelines for Dual-Doshic types

Vata-Pitta: Follow a Vata diet in the Fall and Winter and incorporate more Pitta-balancing foods in the Spring and Summer. Sweet taste is particularly beneficial, since it balances both Vata and Pitta. Pungent taste should be consumed less frequently, since it increases both doshas.

Pitta-Kapha: Follow a Pitta diet from Summer through early Winter and incorporate more Kapha-balancing foods from early Winter through Spring. Bitter and Astringent tastes balance both Pitta and Kapha, while Sour and Salty tastes increase both doshas.

Vata-Kapha: Follow a Vata diet in the Summer and Fall and incorporate more Kapha-balancing foods in the Winter and Spring. Salty taste balances both Vata and Kapha, while Bitter taste increases both doshas.

Note: You can analyze any other doshic combinations in this same way.

THE POTENCY & POST-DIGESTIVE EFFECTS OF FOOD

The depths of Ayurvedic nutrition and herbology extend far beyond the reaches of this book. Ayurveda also classifies food according to two other primary characteristics: potency (called *virya*) and post-digestive effect (called *vipak*). These concepts are slightly more complicated than the 6 Tastes, however, there is no need to become overwhelmed with theory. These components are inherent within the recipes and food recommendations throughout this book (including the Dosha Food Lists on page 319).

Virya refers to the immediate heating or cooling effect that a particular food or herb has on our physiology. Foods predominant in cooling tastes such as Sweet, Bitter and Astringent have cooling viryas, while Pungent, Salty, and Sour foods have heating viryas.

Ayurveda also acknowledges that tastes change during the course of digestion. Vipak translates as "the final taste after digestion" and describes how food ends up building our bodily tissues after digestion. There are three types of vipak: Sweet, Sour, and Salty. The effects of these final tastes are consistent with the 6 Tastes. A Sweet vipak, for example, will benefit Vata by adding bulk to the tissues, but will aggravate Kapha for the same reason.

Of the 6 Tastes, Sweet and Salty lead to a Sweet post-digestive effect on the tissues. Pungent, Bitter, and Astringent tastes lead to a Pungent post-digestive effect. And Sour taste leads to a Sour post-digestive effect.

THE 6 TASTES AND THE MIND

A glimpse into the way we speak today offers insight into the impact of the 6 Tastes on our mind and emotions. We're all familiar with common words and phrases such as "sweetheart", "sourpuss", "salty dog", "left a bitter taste in my mouth", "let's spice things up", and "a dry sense of humor." Ayurveda describes mental and emotional effects such as these in relation to the three doshas.

Sweet taste promotes love and satisfaction in all doshas. It helps calm the anxious Vata mind and cool the fiery Pitta mind. So-called comfort foods are typically high in this taste. When consumed in excess, Sweet taste creates lethargy and attachment (especially in Kapha types).

Sour taste sharpens the Vata mind and senses. It easily irritates Pitta types, causing them to become angry, manipulative, or overly critical. Kapha types may become envious or jealous when consuming too many Sour foods.

Salty taste calms the anxious Vata mind but easily excites the Pitta mind, leading to stubbornness and anger. When consumed in excess by Kapha types, it promotes greed.

Bitter taste cools the fiery Pitta mind and clears the foggy Kapha mind. When taken in excess by Vata types, it promotes grief and depression.

Pungent taste enlivens the Kapha mind and causes all doshas to become more extroverted and expressive. In Pitta types, however, it quickly excites anger and resentment.

Astringent taste draws in (or constricts) the over-confidence of Pitta types and the over-complacency of Kapha types. When consumed in excess by Vata types, it promotes fear and insecurity.

DIGESTING FOOD, THOUGHTS, AND EMOTIONS

AN INTRODUCTION TO THE DIGESTIVE SYSTEM

According to Ayurveda, health begins with proper digestion. To reap the benefits of eating healthfully, we must properly digest and assimilate the foods we eat. The digestive process is one of the many wonders of the body, highlighting its innate intelligence and underlying unity. The digestive system operates with great precision, coordination, and teamwork, ultimately ensuring that every cell of the body is fully nourished.

The primary function of the digestive system is to bring essential nutrients into the body's internal environment. It accomplishes this by breaking down complex food molecules into simpler ones, thereby facilitating the absorption of nutrients into the body. This process takes place along the digestive tract, also called the gastrointestinal (GI) tract.

The main organs of the digestive tract are the mouth, esophagus, stomach, small intestine, colon (also called the large intestine), and rectum. Important accessory organs to the digestive process include the five sensory organs, salivary glands, tongue, teeth, liver, gallbladder, and pancreas.

The digestive system offers a glimpse into the underlying unity of the body. Proper digestion provides fuel and energy to all bodily organs and systems. The ability to digest food itself, however, hinges upon the proper functioning of these organs and systems. The nutritive fuel of digestion, for example, nourishes the nervous, endocrine, and immune systems. These, in turn, play essential roles in the chemical breakdown of food.

Important signs of proper digestion include regular bowel movements, feeling hungry at regular times, and having a light, energetic feeling in the mind and body after digestion.

According to Ayurveda, digestion begins with the five sensory organs. The taste, sight, smell, touch, and sound of food stimulate the salivary glands to excrete moist, enzyme-rich saliva. The process of chewing continues to generate saliva, in order to help break down and pre-digest food particles. This process also begins to unlock the underlying intelligence of the 6 Tastes. Food then travels to the stomach, where it mixes with digestive juices to create a dough-like substance. Kapha governs this first stage of digestion (called the "Sweet phase"), in which the Earth and Water elements are prominent in the solid food particles and liquid secretions.

Pitta governs the second stage of digestion, in which enzymatic and acidic secretions further transform the food. This occurs in conjunction with the liver, gall bladder, pancreas, and small intestine. The Fire and Water elements create the "liquid fire" of this second stage (the "Sour phase").

Vata governs the third and final stage of digestion. During this stage, the usable nutrients of food travel to the tissues of the body, while the unusable parts (or waste materials) travel to the colon and bladder. The Air and Fire elements govern this process of separation and transportation (the "Pungent phase").

Today, the importance of proper digestion is widely neglected by modern medicine. Symptoms such as indigestion, heartburn, bloating, and constipation are treated as normal occurrences. Ayurveda, on the other hand, reminds us that digestive problems are not simply unavoidable misfortunes; they are directly related to how well we nourish ourselves. Even a slight complaint regarding the digestive system can offer important clues to specific imbalances in the body. A heavy or tired feeling immediately after eating, for example, indicates a Kapha digestive disturbance. This may point to a greater Kaphic imbalance in the body. Gurgling noises or burning sensations within an hour or two after eating relate to excess Pitta. Feelings of bloating and gas after two or more hours relate to excess Vata.

AGNI: THE DIGESTIVE FIRE

Deep inside all of us, there is a burning fire—not a fire of flames in the typical sense, but a biological fire that stimulates the metabolic breakdown of the foods we eat. Central to the Ayurvedic understanding of digestion is the strength of this digestive fire, called *agni*. Composed of various acids and enzymes, agni is seated within the lower stomach and small intestine and relates to Pitta dosha.

Ayurveda refers to an individual's overall digestive capabilities in relation to agni ("Her agni is balanced," for example). While it's common to use the terms agni and "digestive fire" interchangeably, there are in fact a total of 13 different agnis governing all metabolic functions of the body. Any process involving heat, light, transformation, and conversion relates to agni. On a universal scale, agni is the creative flame of intelligence that is present in all life.

The digestive fire (*jathara agni*) presides over all other agnis and ultimately ensures that the body absorbs necessary nutrients. For this reason, we will use the term agni in relation to the digestive fire. According to Ayurveda, we are not simply what we eat but, instead, what we are able to digest!

After an individual's current doshic state, agni is the most important factor in determining dietary needs. It's a readily observable fact that we all digest food differently. One individual may gleam with satisfaction after a meal, while another person may clutch his stomach in agony after eating the exact same thing. For this reason, terms like "iron stomach" and "eating like a bird" have become everyday terms.

Ayurveda identifies four main states of agni: balanced (*sama*), irregular (*vishama*), sharp (*teekshna*), and weak (*manda*). A person with constitutional harmony will have balanced agni. When in balance, agni ensures proper nourishment, balanced energy levels, regular elimination, strong immunity, a clear complexion, excellent circulation, and overall strength and vitality.

Balanced Pitta individuals are the least likely to experience digestive problems. The fiery nature of Pitta naturally helps break down and assimilate food into the body. A Pitta-imbalanced individual, however, runs the risk of actually stoking the digestive fire too high. Sharp or excessive agni can lead to hyperacidity, heartburn, acid reflux, diarrhea, excessive hunger, and bodily dryness.

The cool, damp nature of Kapha runs the risk of causing the digestive fire to burn too low. Kapha-imbalanced

CAUSES OF WEAK AGNI

Common ways agni becomes weak or aggravated include: eating out of accordance with one's constitution; habitually eating the same foods, overeating, eating tasteless foods, drinking too much water with meals, staying up late, eating at irregular times, and resisting the urge to eat.

individuals, therefore, commonly have weak agni. Symptoms of weak agni include slow digestion, obesity, hypertension, diabetes, excess mucous, coughing, clammy skin, loss of appetite, and lethargy.

Ayurveda identifies numerous ways to improve agni. Adding Pungent spices to food (such as cumin or cayenne) or drinking spicy teas (such as ginger tea) are two of the easiest ways to spark the digestive fire. Physical activity also strengthens agni by stimulating the overall metabolic activity of the body. For variable agni conditions, eating meals at regular times each day is highly beneficial, while eating Pitta-pacifying foods will help balance sharp agni conditions.

AMA: THE TOXIC BYPRODUCT OF POOR DIGESTION

If water and blood are the sweet nectars of the body, *ama* is the rotten sludge. Ama is undigested food residue that lodges itself within the organs and channels of the body. With the consistency of a sticky paste, ama is whitish-yellow in color and has a putrid smell.

AMA

To get a better sense of ama, stick out your tongue in front of a mirror. If you see a white coat on your tongue, then you are directly observing ama accumulation. To get an even better sense, scrape your tongue with a metal tongue scraper or edge of a spoon. The slimy substance you perceive is pure ama. To directly observe how toxic foods create ama, put a sugar cube on a toothpick and light it with a match. The melting tar and soot that you'll find becomes the sticky "tissue tar" ama when digested by the body.

When our ability to digest food becomes impaired, the body can no longer absorb essential nutrients. Undigested and partially digested food lingers in the body, leading to the formation of ama. Ayurveda views ama as one of the most threatening opponents to good health, linking the majority of health disorders in some way to the presence of this substance. Simply stated, ama is undigested food that begins to eat you!

Although there is no equivalent in Western medicine to ama, it is widely accepted that toxins typically originate in the GI tract. The closest known substance is cholesterol, but the scope of ama far exceeds the properties of cholesterol. Ama initially accumulates in the colon and small intestine. It then travels through the blood to become lodged in various channels, tissues, and organs of the body. In creating toxic breeding grounds throughout the body, ama acts as the physiological precursor to disease. Ama, however, does not result from poor digestion alone. Toxic food substances, even when digested properly, will also result in ama accumulation.

The presence of ama pushes the body's underlying constitution into a state of imbalance. Kaphic individuals are most easily plagued by excess ama conditions, due to the cool, damp nature of Kapha and their weak digestive fires. Most symptoms of poor digestion for these types are linked to excess ama. Vata individuals are also highly prone to ama accumulation, due to their irregular digestion and tendency towards constipation. The underlying heat of Pitta individuals usually burns away ama, making these types the least hampered by this toxic substance.

In a state of balance, the body removes ama with its own self-cleansing mechanisms, through the bladder, bowels, and skin. We will examine dosha-specific ways to reduce ama and encourage these natural cleansing mechanisms in Chapter 5, entitled "Food as Medicine."

According to Ayurveda, nutrition extends beyond the domain of the tongue and digestive system. The experiences we take in within any field of perception are also forms of "food." For this reason, ama extends beyond the physical body alone. Undigested thoughts, emotions, and sensory impressions will also lead to the formation of mental ama. Deep-seated anger or the tendency to store emotions, for example, will cloud the true nature of the mind. Regular or excessive use of drugs and alcohol will have similar effects. Surrounding oneself with constant noise or activity also leads to mental ama, exhausting the nervous system over time.

From an Ayurvedic perspective, many forms of mental illness relate to the presence of mental ama. Depression and anxiety, for example, are often associated with the improper digestion of thoughts and emotions. Mental ama is subtler than its physiological counterpart, although the two are completely interrelated. Poor mental digestion leads directly to physical illness, while poor physical digestion eventually creates imbalances within the mind.

Ayurveda identifies numerous ways to prevent the accumulation of ama. A balanced diet, lifestyle, and exercise routine are important places to begin. Inward practices such as meditation are also important for staying in touch with the true essence of your inner nature.

Ayurveda also identifies numerous ways to rid the body of excess ama. Sweating through physical exercise, for example, is a highly effective way to release ama from the tissues and channels of the body. After breathing, sweating is the second largest method of detoxification for the body. Special dietary practices, such as drinking cleansing teas or fasting, are also effective. We will discuss these in detail in Chapter Five.

One of the most effective methods is Ayurveda's traditional five-step method of detoxification, known as *Panchakarma*. These highly effective cleansing programs are specifically tailored to an individual's constitution by an Ayurvedic doctor. Treatments include detoxifying diets, therapeutic sweating, medicated oil massage, herbal and oil enemas, and a wide variety of other therapies. Please see page 326 for more information on Panchakarma therapy.

If you would like to get a general idea of your current ama levels, fill out the questionnaire below. For each question, rate your matching characteristics on a scale from zero to five: 0-1 doesn't apply, 2-3 sometimes applies, 4-5 strongly applies. Add up your total. A score between 0-19 indicates a low level of ama, 20-34 indicates a moderate amount of ama, 35-50 indicates a high amount of ama.

Ama Questionnaire

1 I often feel a sense of blockage in my body (such as constipation or congestion).
2 I often have difficulty digesting food.
3 I feel foggy when I wake up in the morning.
4 I tend to feel weak for no apparent reason.
5 I often feel lethargic and unmotivated.
6 I feel the need to cough regularly.
7 I become easily exhausted, both mentally and physically.
8 I frequently feel depressed.
9 I often have no taste for food.
10 I catch a cold several times a year.

OJAS: THE END-PRODUCT OF PERFECT DIGESTION

Since there's a physical by-product of poor digestion (ama), there must also be an end-product of perfect digestion. Ayurveda refers to this substance as *ojas* and cherishes it as one of the most health-promoting agents of the body. If ama is the great enemy, ojas is the beloved partner in maintaining and improving health.

The proper digestion and assimilation of food governs the production of ojas. According to Ayurveda, ojas directly influences physical, mental, emotional, and spiritual life. One can, therefore, view ojas as the reward for eating healthfully. It's common to use terms such as "high" and "low" to describe ojas levels. An individual with high ojas enjoys energetic vitality, an impenetrable immune system, and a feeling of overall contentment and joy in life. A low-ojas individual, on the other hand, frequently feels tired and weak and is prone to physical and mental disorders.

Ayurvedic texts identify ojas as a whitish-gold liquid that is transparent and oily in nature. Unlike ama, ojas is not readily observable to the human eye. The presence of ojas, however, is easily detectable through the vibrancy of an individual's eyes or the radiance of the skin. While there is no equivalent in Western medicine, modern researchers have drawn parallels between ojas and the basic living substance of all cells, known as protoplasm. Parallels have also been drawn to biochemical substances of the brain relating to emotions, such as neurotransmitters and neuropeptides.

Along with eating a balancing diet, one can increase ojas in a variety of ways. General guidelines are to love yourself and others, live a healthy lifestyle, and always take time to appreciate the joys in life. Other ways to increase ojas include:

- Laugh and smile a lot.
- Take time to relax.
- Meditate regularly.
- Spend time in nature.
- Exercise your creativity.
- Offer your gifts to others.
- Follow your heart's passion.
- Engage in physical activity.

One can also diminish ojas through living a reckless, anti-health lifestyle. Along with improper diet, ojas-decreasing mental states and activities include:

- High stress levels
- Fear and anxiety
- Feelings of hate and anger
- Not respecting yourself

- Overworking
- Overindulgence in sex
- Abusing drugs and alcohol
- Sleeping too little or too much
- Excessive hunger or fasting

It's especially important to monitor ojas levels during periods of imbalance. This can be determined by overall energy levels, mental and emotional stability, and the vibrancy of your eyes and skin. If your ojas is low, you should adjust your diet and lifestyle accordingly. As ojas becomes strong again, your body will rebound (often with great speed).

HOW FOOD BECOMES YOUR BODY

THE DHATUS: THE BODY'S SEVEN MAJOR TISSUES

We all know that food is required for life. The way in which food actually feeds the body, however, is often not understood. Ayurveda identifies seven vital tissues that provide nourishment, growth, and structure to the entire body. These tissue layers, called *dhatus*, are strikingly similar to the major tissues identified by modern science. Ayurveda expands upon modern interpretation, however, by also including tissues in liquid form.

The 7 Dhatus are:

1 Plasma (*Rasa*)

2 Blood (*Rakta*)

3 Muscle (*Mamsa*)

4 Fat (*Meda*)

5 Bone (*Asthi*)

6 Bone marrow and nerve (*Majja*)

7 Reproductive fluid (*Shukra/Artava*)

Once food is fully digested, the building of tissues commences. Beginning with plasma, the tissues form sequentially, with each layer building upon the layers that come before it. Muscle, for example, derives from both Plasma and Blood. The complexity of tissues increases with each new layer, culminating with the reproductive fluids. An imbalance within any tissue will, therefore, affect all subsequent tissues. Unhealthy plasma, for example, will affect all layers. Agni is at the heart of this tissue-building process, through its role in helping transform one dhatu into another. A weak agni condition will, therefore, result in the improper formation of tissues.

Proper diet and digestion ensure excellent tissue renewal. Plasma is rich in digestive nutrients and actively transfers these nutrients to subsequent tissue layers. In this way, even the deepest and most complex tissues are nourished by the foods we eat. Ojas is the ultimate "essence" of each dhatu. The most effective way to improve the health of the dhatus is to increase ojas. Improper diet and digestion, on the other hand, will lead to ama formation in each tissue layer.

The dhatus are integrally linked to an individual's doshic state. Balance within the doshas creates harmony in the tissues, while imbalance creates disarray. A dosha in excess quantity disperses throughout the body and relocates in the weakest tissues and organs. Most illnesses, therefore, have a pathological component in the tissues. As an individual creates doshic balance through dietary and lifestyle changes, the development of healthy tissues will follow.

Malas: The Unusable Byproducts of Digestion

Good old #1 (urine) and #2 (stool) may be dubbed "waste" products. However, their critical role in maintaining and improving health is befitting of a much grander title. At the end of the digestive process, unusable food is converted into waste materials that exit the body through excretory channels. Along with urine and stool, Ayurveda identifies sweat as a primary *malas*, or waste product. Secondary waste products include mucus, tears, ear wax, and oily secretions of the skin.

While stool and urine are the waste products of food, the other malas are more closely related to the tissue layers. Sweat, for example, is considered a waste product of fat, whereas mucous is a waste product of plasma. The malas are of central importance to Ayurveda for their cleansing, toning, and purifying functions. It's not so much what the malas do for you, however; it's what doesn't happen to you due to their efficient removal.

The inability to properly eliminate waste materials commonly results from imbalances within the doshas. A poor diet alone can lead to these imbalances. Symptoms of improper elimination can range from a slight bloated feeling to life-threatening situations in which impurities are reabsorbed and circulated throughout the body.

Malas should always be eliminated when the natural urge arises. In total, Ayurveda identifies thirteen natural urges that should not be resisted. They include urination, defecation, hunger, thirst, sex, passing gases, burping, vomiting, yawning, sneezing, coughing, crying, and sleeping. The resistance of natural urges can lead to a variety of disorders. The majority of these relate to the obstruction of Vata dosha.

Ayurveda also identifies urges that should be resisted. They include:

- Working beyond our capacity
- Unhealthy thinking, speech, and actions
- Negative emotional tendencies, such as desire, anger, greed, pride, addiction, fear, worry, and jealousy

The Srotas: The Channels of the Body

The human body is home to a vast network of transportation channels, called *srotas*. These consist of gross channels like the GI tract, lymphatic system, and urinary tract, as well as subtle channels such as the blood vessels and energetic pathways. The srotas are the channels through which the doshas, dhatus, and malas move throughout the body.

The entire digestive process depends upon clear, smoothly functioning channels in order to distribute nutrients and eliminate wastes efficiently. Blockages in the srotas prohibit these functions, eventually leading to illness. The srotas are the primary target areas for ama accumulation. As ama builds up in these channels, transportation both into and out of the body is greatly hindered. Maintaining good digestion is an important key to avoiding such blockages.

Food and the Mind

The Mind

When we hear the word "mind," we may instinctively think of the brain, since the brain is considered the thinking center of the body. But what exactly is the mind and where is it located? We know the mind exists, because we all possess a distinct sense of self-awareness and individuality. Our ability to think, perceive, reason, and feel is also rooted within the underlying consciousness of the mind. If we open up the brain, however, will we find a little blob of matter that we can label "mind"?

According to Ayurveda, the mind is found throughout the entire body. Although the brain is the primary organ through which the mind functions, the mind is in no way confined to the brain alone. A stream of consciousness and intelligence flows through every cell of the body. This is the non-localized mind at work. The source of this stream is the same universal life-force, dancing at the core of the body. Ayurveda recognizes the inseparable connection between mind and body.

It follows that our thoughts and emotions directly affect our physiology. If we are joyful, our body experiences joy on a foundational level. If we are fearful, our body experiences fear on this same core level. For this reason, physical disease always has a mental/emotional component, and mental disease, when left untreated, eventually manifests in the physical body.

Modern medicine has started to recognize this connection through making clinical links between chronic stress and conditions like ulcers. Unfortunately, the widely used term "psychosomatic illness" often takes on a negative connotation: namely, "it's all in the patient's head." Used in this way, it becomes a fall-back term for conditions eluding typical diagnosis, rather than a positive step toward bridging the mind-body gap.

Despite the slow integration into allopathic medicine, modern science has made fascinating discoveries regarding the mind-body connection over the last two decades. In the late 1980's, Dr. Candace Pert, a psychoneuroimmunologist who remains on the cutting edge of mind-body research today, made a landmark discovery. She identified biochemical molecules called neuropeptides that respond instantaneously to all of our thoughts, moods, and emotions. Through the discovery of a single molecule, Dr. Pert helped validate what ancient cultures had known for thousands of years: that the mind and body are unified on the level of consciousness.

In her research, Dr. Pert shows how neuropeptides continuously wash through the bloodstream, attaching themselves to specific cell receptors throughout the body. As a result of this biochemical process, every thought and feeling creates an immediate response on the cellular level. A feeling of joy, for example, causes a cell to vibrate in a positive way. The vibratory quality and frequency of this "happy" cell is shown to have health-promoting effects on the body. Anger, on the other hand, creates an entirely different vibratory quality, leading to "angry" cells throughout the body and ill effects on overall health. In this way, the entire body is viewed as a dynamic, pulsating mind, a concept celebrated within the ancient wisdom of Ayurveda.

SATTVA, RAJAS, AND TAMAS: THE THREE QUALITIES OF THE MIND

Ayurveda recognizes three primal qualities of Nature that manifest in every mind. These subtle essences and energies govern the mind, as well as the three doshas. They are known as *Sattva*, *Rajas*, and *Tamas*.

Sattva is the quality of purity, knowledge, truth, and light. Rajas is the quality of change, activity, and movement. Tamas is the quality of dullness, darkness, and inertia. Each of these qualities, or *gunas*, is naturally present in the mind at all times. We have the ability to increase or decrease each of the gunas through the course of our thoughts, choices, and actions.

Sattva promotes love, peace, fulfillment, clarity, health, and stability. In nurturing both a sattvic mind and lifestyle, one becomes less attached to the binding constraints of ego and begins to recognize the underlying connection of all life. A sattvic lifestyle is a life of simplicity and honesty in which excess materialism is discarded and concentration is focused on spiritual development. If you're thinking that this sounds great for a monk but is impractical in your own world, don't worry!

Bringing sattva into our lives is as simple as opening our eyes a little wider and walking our paths with love and awareness. Engaging in calming and peaceful activities increases sattva, along with all of the ojas-increasing activities on page 64. One of the greatest ways to increase sattva is through the foods we eat.

In today's world, basic necessities like working to eat and pay bills also demand the energy of rajas. Rajas promotes outward action, change, and motivation. In excess, rajas leads to mental turbulence, self-motivated action, and the desire to seek happiness outside of ourselves. A rajasic lifestyle is fueled by short-lived pleasure and inevitably results in pain and suffering. The key is, therefore, to keep rajas in check through nurturing sattva, something done through simple dietary and lifestyle changes.

Tamas gives us the desire to stop and rest, thereby allowing things to come naturally to an end. Of all the gunas, tamas is required in the smallest proportion. In excess, tamas creates ignorance and delusion, leading to attachment and depression. A tamasic lifestyle is marked by lethargy, oversleep, and dullness. Physical and mental ama promote a tamasic quality of mind. Increasing sattva is the way to break out of this dull mentality.

Think of sattva as taking a refreshing walk through the woods or along the ocean on a beautiful, clear day. There is joy, purity and lightness in this experience. Rajas, on the other hand, is like taking a walk through a crowded city, with sensory impressions bombarding you from every direction. While there are elements of stimulation, intrigue, and excitement in this experience, they may become overwhelming or unsettling in excess. For tamas, the walk is skipped entirely in lieu of the couch and remote control!

FOOD AND THE 3 QUALITIES OF THE MIND

Since the mind and body are completely interrelated, it follows that we feed our mind as we feed our body. Ayurveda, therefore, also categorizes food in relation to how it evokes the three gunas. Eating fresh fruit, for example, will create a light, energetic feeling that leads to clarity of the mind. A decadent ice cream sundae, on the other hand, will initially lead to a sugar high and then transform into a heavy fogginess. Sattvic foods help the mind remain light, clear, and focused. Rajasic foods have a stimulatory effect that enlivens and provokes the mind. Tamasic foods weigh down the mind, dulling the senses and creating heavy emotions.

In relation to food, it's helpful to take a step back and view the gunas from a broader perspective. One should regard these qualities as general guidelines to eating rather than detailed roadmaps, like the 6 Tastes. While it's beneficial to incorporate sattvic foods into one's diet, the 6 Tastes are still emphasized.

A Kaphic-imbalanced individual, for example, will not benefit from a purely sattvic diet, due to the Sweet taste of most sattvic foods. Since Ayurveda recommends incorporating all 6 Tastes into one's daily diet, however, a

Kaphic individual can make an effort to incorporate Sweet tastes that are sattvic in nature.

The gunas offer incredible insight into the subtle effects of food on the mind. When used within the greater context of our individual constitutions, the knowledge of these qualities enhances our ability to choose healing foods. These qualities also extend to the methods in which foods are farmed, prepared, and consumed.

Sattvic Foods

Sattvic foods are fresh, pure, and vibrant. These include natural, organic ingredients that are free from chemicals, pesticides, fertilizers, and preservatives. The body easily digests sattvic foods, leading to high ojas production and harmony of the mind. The regular consumption of these foods prevents disease and promotes physical, mental, and spiritual health. Many sattvic foods are sweet by nature and thus have a rejuvenating effect on the body and a calming effect on the mind. Sattvic foods typically grow above the ground in the presence of sunlight, making them lighter in nature than foods grown below the ground.

Examples of Sattvic foods

- Most fresh fruits, vegetables, and freshly-prepared grains
- Many types of beans, including black, mung, soy, & fava
- Lentils
- Cow's milk
- Fresh yogurt
- Ghee
- Honey
- Sesame and sunflower seeds
- Cashews, almonds, walnuts, and macadamia nuts

Rajasic Foods

Rajasic foods are stimulating by nature and are naturally comprised by Salty, Sour, Bitter, and Pungent tastes. Many rajasic foods are only palatable after developing a taste for them. Used in moderation, these foods provide the body with vital energy and help kindle agni. In excess, however, these foods create imbalances within all three doshas, leading to anger, jealousy, and egotism. It's important to maintain a balance between sattvic and rajasic foods in one's diet.

Examples of Rajasic Foods

- Peppers
- Tomatoes
- Lemon and lime
- Kidney beans
- Red lentils
- Garlic
- Peanuts
- Pickles
- Avocado
- Eggs
- Onions
- Sour cream
- Vinegar
- Hot spices
- Salt
- White sugar (short-term effect)
- Coffee
- Alcohol (in small amounts)

Tamasic Foods

Tamasic foods are dull and lifeless. Artificial processes such as canning, freezing, and microwaving render food tamasic, even if it is sattvic by nature. Tamasic foods suppress agni and require large amounts of energy to digest. The consumption of these foods leads to the formation of ama. While it's important to balance between sattvic and rajasic foods, one should try to avoid tamasic as much as possible. Since this may be challenging at first, it's important to remember there are degrees of tamas—a fried piece of meat that is frozen for a week, reheated, and then consumed will lead to greater mental lethargy than frozen and microwaved vegetables.

Examples of Tamasic Foods

- Leftovers
- Stale food
- Deep-fried foods
- Meat and fish
- Margarine
- Ice cream
- Frozen foods
- Garlic
- Microwaved foods
- Overcooked foods
- Onions
- Mushrooms
- White sugar (long-term effect)
- White flour
- Alcohol (in large amounts)
- Cheese

2

Buying, Preparing & Storing Vibrant Food

BUYING, PREPARING AND STORING VIBRANT FOOD
WHY BUY ORGANIC?

Consider two apples sitting side by side: The first is picture-perfect, almost plastic looking, while the other has a few minor blemishes and looks like it was just picked from a tree. Biting into the first apple, you experience a bland flavor and chalky texture. Biting into the second apple, sweet juice literally trickles from the corners of your mouth.

The first apple is a creation of modern industrial farming. Sprayed with pesticides from infancy and then polished and waxed with more chemicals after picking, it harbors a toxic secret. It looks flawless, but contains residues from these harmful chemicals.

The second apple is organic. It didn't require any chemicals, pesticides, or artificial beauty treatments—just sunlight, rain, and the nurturing forces of Mother Nature.

Rather than settling for the first apple, consumers are beginning to demand the organic variety in record numbers. Organic foods are now the fastest growing sector of the food industry in the United States, Canada, and Europe.

Despite being a now-familiar term, many still wonder what "organic" actually means. Organic foods are those produced in rich, fertile soils without the use of synthetic pesticides, herbicides, or fertilizers. Organic farming also shuns genetic modification, irradiation, and the use of sewer sludge as fertilizer. In addition to organic fruits and vegetables, you can now also buy organically grown grains, legumes, nuts, oils, sugars, teas, wines, and a variety of other foods and beverages.

3 Reasons to Buy Organically

While we could spend many pages discussing why organic foods are good for you, three main reasons provide ample support for switching to organic.

Organic Foods are Better for You

Organic foods are grown in bio-diverse soil that is rich in vitamins, minerals and other micronutrients. Recent studies suggest that the nutrient levels in conventionally grown foods, by contrast, have declined over the past twenty-five years as fertile topsoil has eroded.

Currently, little long-term research has been conducted comparing the nutritional contents of organic versus conventionally grown foods. A study in the *Journal of Applied Nutrition*, however, suggests that organic foods are higher in several essential nutrients. In comparing conventionally grown apples, potatoes, pears, wheat, and sweet corn over a two-year period, the study found that organically grown foods averaged 63 percent higher in calcium, 73 percent higher in iron, 118 percent higher in magnesium, 60 percent higher in zinc and 29 percent lower in mercury than the conventionally raised foods.

According to Ayurveda, organic foods also contain a higher concentration of energy or *prana*, thus nourishing both mind and body on deeper levels. In eating organic food, you can also feel safe knowing you're eating clean, vibrant food.

You Support a Healthier Environment

Organic farming is a reciprocal process: we take care of the land and the land takes care of us. This arrangement is in harmony with an understanding of the interconnectedness of all life.

Conventional farming treats land as a commodity. Vegetables are likened to money springing up from the soil. Thousands of consecutive acres are typically planted with the same crop, without giving the soil a chance to regenerate between harvests. This type of mono-crop farming has resulted in depleted topsoil and a consequential deficiency of vital nutrients in our food supply.

When we choose to eat organic foods, on the other hand, we celebrate a natural cycle of life that has taken place for millennia. We also support a sustainable farming method that will allow this cycle to continue for millennia to come.

You Support the Small Farmer

Farming has traditionally been a great art form—women and men living in accordance with nature, getting to know the ins and outs of every plant and season. Over the last three decades, however, multinational corporations have

virtually wiped out this ancient tradition. Today, for example, five companies account for 90 percent of the food consumed in the United States.

Organic farming has given rise to a new era of small farmers. A common misconception about these farmers is that the higher retail prices of organic foods bring them greater wealth. In reality, most organic farmers work on much smaller, less cost-effective scales and therefore don't enjoy the same profit margins as larger companies.

Another common misconception holds that organic foods cost significantly more than conventionally grown foods. Some people claim they'd love to buy organic foods, but they can't afford to double their grocery bills. In reality, prices for organics are closer to 15 to 25 percent higher on average than their conventionally produced counterparts. Fresh produce and dairy products, however, may be higher depending on the store and season.

One way you can verify this for yourself is to price five regular items in your supermarket against comparable items in the health food aisle (or your local health food store). You may find that you can only afford select organic items. This is fine. Even buying one organic staple each week represents a conscious decision to improve the quality of the food you eat. One way to cut prices dramatically is to buy directly from your local farmers. Often, you will end up paying less than you would for conventionally grown items. As organic farming becomes more widespread, the prices of these foods should also drop, making them available to a broader spectrum of society.

Through buying organic foods, you directly support the small farmer. Even if you buy items from a larger organic food company, you still support organic farming as a

movement. This, in turn, helps small organic farmers, since larger companies frequently will also buy their raw materials from a number of smaller producers.

As organic foods have grown in popularity, however, huge conglomerates have begun to create subsidiaries dedicated to tapping into this profitable market. If you prefer not to support such conglomerates, do a little research to determine what companies are behind the products you're buying.

ORGANIC LABELING

Until recently, a number of private and state agencies have regulated organic standards in the United States. In October 2002, the United States Department of Agriculture (USDA) implemented a set of organic labeling guidelines. These are currently the most extensive organic labeling standards in the world.

Some may say they're also the most confusing guidelines. To help you untangle them, see the sidebar on page 77.

AYURVEDA AND VEGETARIANISM

People frequently ask whether Ayurveda is a vegetarian science? The answer to this question is slightly more complicated than a simple "yes" or "no". Ayurveda promotes eating fresh, vital food that is easy to digest and promotes mental clarity. Meats (including beef, poultry, fish, and other animal proteins) are heavy, difficult to digest, and lead over time to the formation of physical and mental toxins or ama. Within this framework, the daily consumption of meat is not advised for any constitutional type.

In classical Ayurvedic texts, however, meat is recommended for treating a number of conditions. Most of these relate to debilitated Vata conditions, in which tissues require quick rebuilding. Meat was also used for its rajasic or stimulating effects on the mind. Soldiers, for example, were instructed to eat meat before battle to stimulate the mind and emotions. An animal was only considered safe for human consumption if found in its natural environment and freshly slaughtered using non-poisonous means. Even then, it was acknowledged that over-utilizing meat would lead to greater physical and mental imbalance.

From an Ayurvedic perspective, modern meat farming practices compromise the healing properties naturally present in meat. Animals are raised in artificial (and often brutal) conditions and injected with hormones and other chemicals. Their meat is often packaged in plastic and may be frozen for days before consumption. This transforms the meat into devitalized or tamasic food, which leads to ama formation and illness.

Over-consuming even the cleanest organic meat will have the same result, due to the inherent chemical structure of meat. It's no coincidence that modern medicine draws a direct correlation between diets high in animal fat and illnesses such as obesity, heart disease and colon cancer. The body is unable to digest large amounts of saturated fat, so it converts this fat into bad cholesterol (LDL) and fatty tissue. In Ayurvedic terms, these relate directly to excess ama.

Ayurveda favors a vegetarian diet rich in whole grains, beans, fresh vegetables, fruits, nuts, and seeds. Dairy foods, including cow's milk, goat's milk, ghee, yogurt, and soft cheeses, are also recommended in moderation. According to Ayurveda, a vegetarian diet promotes optimal digestion, metabolism, and tissue nourishment. It also supports the production of vital energy or ojas, leading to increased immunity and vitality. From a spiritual perspective, the higher vibratory frequency, or sattvic nature, of an organic

USDA GUIDELINES FOR THE ORGANIC LABEL

"100 PERCENT ORGANIC"

- Must contain only organically produced ingredients, excluding water and salt.
- The USDA seal may be used on these products.

"ORGANIC"

- Must contain at least 95 percent organic ingredients, excluding water and salt.
- The USDA seal may be used on these products.

"MADE WITH ORGANIC INGREDIENTS"

- Must contain at least 70 percent organic ingredients, excluding water and salt.
- May list up to three of the organic ingredients or food groups on the main display panel.
- The USDA seal may not be used on these products; however, the certifier's seal or mark may be used along with the percentage of organic ingredients.
- Non-organic ingredients (30 percent or less) may not be genetically modified, bio-engineered, irradiated, or fertilized with sewage sludge.
- Must not contain added sulfites or nitrates, except wine, which may contain added sulfur dioxide.

PRODUCTS MADE "WITH SOME ORGANIC INGREDIENTS"

- May contain less than 70 percent organic ingredients, excluding water and salt.
- May only identify organic ingredients in the ingredient statement and may not use the USDA organic seal or a certifier's seal or mark. When organic ingredients are identified, the total percentage of organic ingredients must also be given.

plant-based diet raises our own vibration by purifying the mind and body. This provides an excellent platform from which to experience higher states of consciousness.

VATA

Of the three doshas, Vata types are best suited to meat consumption because the heavy nutrient-rich quality of meat grounds the light, airy nature of Vata. According to Ayurveda, a Vata-pacifying vegetarian diet can offer the same effect, while also balancing the delicate Vata mind.

PITTA

Pitta types digest meat more efficiently than Vata and Kapha types, due to their strong digestive fires. However, the heating quality of meat, particularly red meat and saltwater fish, is highly aggravating to Pitta. It's common for imbalanced Pitta types to have a voracious appetite for meat because it adds fuel to their underlying fire.

KAPHA

Kapha types often enjoy the taste of meat. It leads quite easily, however, to imbalances such as obesity and high cholesterol. This is because the heavy, oily nature of meat closely resembles the underlying makeup of Kapha.

Vedic philosophy acknowledges the interconnection of all life. It embraces the principle of non-violence, or *ahimsa*, towards all living beings. This includes non-violence in our thoughts, words, and actions (even towards ourselves). As Ayurveda developed alongside vegetarian religions in India, this principle became more deeply rooted in practice. Although meat is recommended in classical Ayurvedic texts, it is traditionally eaten with discernment. A line is drawn between consuming animal foods out of medical or geographic necessity and consuming them merely to please the senses. While plants are also part of the greater web of life, Ayurveda considers a vegetarian diet the most compassionate choice in nourishing ourselves.

AYURVEDA FOR NON-VEGETARIANS

If you're thinking: "Ayurveda isn't for me, since I'm not a vegetarian," don't go away just yet. As mentioned many times throughout this book, Ayurveda favors personal experience over dogmatic adherence to rules. If you feel like you need meat to function in a balanced state, this is a decision only you can make. Ayurveda will offer you recommendations, but you ultimately have to determine what works best for you. Whatever dietary path you choose, it's important to feel good about it. Becoming a doubtful vegetarian is no better than feeling like a guilty meat-eater.

While Ayurveda favors a vegetarian diet, it also offers specific guidelines for improving a meat-based diet. Choosing meat in accordance with your individual constitution is an important place to begin. Lighter meats are recommended for all the doshas, unless you're using meat for specific medicinal purposes like building the tissues. Beef and pork are least recommended for daily consumption, due to their heavy, ama-promoting qualities.

Vata types benefit most from oily meats that are rich in high-quality fats and protein, such as salmon and other cold-water fish. Beef is also beneficial for helping rebuild tissues in these types. Pitta types benefit from white meats, such as the breast meat of chicken and turkey; but they should limit their consumption of red meats, which are highly Pitta-provoking. Freshwater fish is also preferable over saltwater fish, due to its lower salt content. Kapha types also do better with white meats and freshwater fish, due to their lighter nature and lower salt content.

The proper seasoning of meat is another valuable tool for improving a meat-based diet. Pungent spices such as cumin and fennel greatly improve the digestibility of meat.

Proper cooking methods are also beneficial. For example, Pitta and Kapha types benefit from broiling or roasting meat rather than pan-frying it in oil. Vata-types, on the other hand, may benefit from this added oil. Food-combining principles are also beneficial to consider, due to the incompatibility of certain foods. For example, consuming meats with dairy products or fruits creates greater strain on the digestive system.

If you eat meat daily, try cutting back your serving sizes while experimenting with a larger variety of legumes and vegetables. Also try decreasing the frequency with which you eat meat. If you currently eat it two or three times a day, try including it in just one meal a day (preferably lunch, since agni is strongest during this time). You may also consider setting aside a meat-free day each week to give your digestive system a break.

What if you just really like the taste of meat? By no means does Ayurveda deny the fact that meat can be pleasing to the senses. Like anything, however, moderation is essential. It's also important to remember that during states of imbalance, you may crave dosha-imbalancing foods. That is why it's beneficial to consider your constitutional make-up in relation to your meat-consuming tendencies. For example, if you're a Kapha individual who eats beef every day, this may point to an underlying imbalance.

In the recipe section of this book, we've included a number of chicken and fish recipes for each dosha. We encourage you

to explore this section in order to better understand how to include meat in your Ayurvedic diet. Of course, we encourage you to explore the other recipes as well, since a balanced diet also requires a healthy variety of plant foods!

AYURVEDA FOR NEW VEGETARIANS

If you aren't a vegetarian now but think you'd like to become one, Ayurveda can also help. Adopting a constitution-balancing diet and lifestyle is the first step in making the transition to a meat-free diet. There's no magic formula for going vegetarian, although a gradual transition is always recommended to allow your mind and body to adjust gently to your new regimen.

Eliminate the heaviest animal foods first (such as beef) and gradually work your way to eliminating the lightest foods (such as fish). At each stage, give yourself ample time to adjust. For example, if you just cut beef out of your diet, it may take you a few weeks (or longer) to feel comfortable giving up the next-heaviest meat (such as pork or chicken). That is totally fine. Trust your instincts and don't push yourself too quickly.

In order to make a successful transition, it's essential that you add foods into your diet to make up for those you're taking away. This will require exploring a greater variety of foods. (Use the Stocking Your Ayurvedic Pantry section on page 106 to familiarize yourself with basic vegetarian staples.) Begin incorporating more protein-rich plant foods into your diet, such as beans, tofu, tempeh, nuts, and seeds. If you eat dairy foods, increase your intake of soft cheeses, yogurt, and milk. We've given you over 150 recipes to get started!

You can also use the fish and poultry recipes in this book to help you transition away from heavier meats. Eggs may also provide a useful tool for satisfying meat cravings. Once you feel like you're ready to stop eating meat altogether, make the step confidently.

As you start feeling vibrant from your new diet, it's important to remember this little piece of vegetarian etiquette: *Never yuck someone else's yum!* Choosing a vegetarian diet doesn't place you on a dietary pedestal. Making people feel bad about the foods they eat doesn't contribute positively to anything. If someone wants to learn about the benefits of a vegetarian diet, then by all means share with them your experiences. But also learn to exercise restraint for those times when your dining partner orders a 12-ounce ribeye steak.

AN OVERVIEW OF MODERN VEGETARIANISM

Today, the number of vegetarians in the West continues to grow in record numbers. No longer viewed as a passing fad of the "flower power" 1960's, vegetarianism is now recognized as an important dietary option in Western society.

According to a June 2003 position statement jointly issued by the American Dietetic Association and Dietitians of Canada:

Well-planned, vegan [pure vegetarian] diets and other types of vegetarian diets are appropriate for all stages of the life cycle, including during pregnancy, lactation,

VATA	PITTA	KAPHA
Buffalo	Buffalo	Chicken (white meat)
Chicken (dark meat is best)	Chicken (white meat)	Eggs
Chicken (white meat)	Egg whites	Fish (freshwater)
Duck	Fish (freshwater)	Rabbit
Eggs	Turkey (white meat)	Shrimp
Fish (fresh and saltwater)	Shrimp	Turkey (white meat)
Beef (for medicinal purposes)	Venison	Venison
Seafood		

For more detailed information on making the switch to a vegetarian diet, we recommend *Transition to Vegetarianism* by Rudolph Ballentine, M.D. The book offers practical guidelines for becoming vegetarian. It also combines modern nutritional theory with the wisdom of Ayurveda.

infancy, childhood, and adolescence. Vegetarian diets offer a number of nutritional benefits including lower levels of saturated fat, cholesterol, and animal protein as well as higher level of carbohydrates, fiber, magnesium, potassium, folate, and antioxidants such as vitamin C and E and phytochemicals. Vegetarians have been reported to have lower body mass indices than non vegetarians, as well as lower rates of death from ischemic heart disease; vegetarians also show lower blood cholesterol levels; lower blood pressure; and lower rates of hypertension, type 2 diabetes, and prostate and colon cancer.

There are three primary types of vegetarian diets:

- Lacto-ovo vegetarian

  A diet that includes eggs and dairy products

- Lacto-vegetarian

  A diet that includes dairy products but not eggs

- Vegan

  A diet that excludes all animal products, including honey

In addition to the health benefits of a vegetarian diet, millions of people are becoming vegetarian for the following reasons:

ENVIRONMENTAL SUSTAINABILITY

It's no longer a secret that our personal health is inseparably linked to the health of our planet. In response to the rampant misuse of our natural resources, environmental awareness has grown exponentially in recent years. World hunger, pollution, topsoil erosion, deforestation, global warming, and a dwindling water supply are just a few of the many stark environmental issues facing our planet today. A vegetarian diet is one way to promote an environmentally conscious lifestyle.

MORAL & ETHICAL RESPONSIBILITY

A striking paradox exists today between the pet-loving people of the United States and the brutality present in the nation's modern meat-farming industry. Cats and dogs are treated as part of the family, while cows, chickens, and other animals are treated as profit-making machines. If loving pet owners had a chance to visit the modern slaughterhouse or chicken factory, the number of people eating factory-farmed meat may rapidly decline.

The modern consumer is not forced to think about how animals are raised or treated. Packaging and advertising portray happy animals living on idyllic farms, so there's no reason to think otherwise. Unless you're buying organic meat, however, the source of your protein was most likely raised in artificial and oppressive conditions. The following information derives largely from John Robbin's pioneering research into modern farming practices. For more information, we recommend his book *The Food Revolution*.

FOOD SAFETY

As the factory farm has replaced the family farm in modern times, food safety has become a bigger issue. Raising animals using artificial methods is not a foolproof way to increase profits. Crowded factory farms provide fertile breeding grounds for food-borne diseases such as *salmonella, e.coli, listeria*, and *campylobacter*. Recalls of contaminated meat have increased significantly over the past decade. The presence of hormones, vaccines, pesticide residues, and other chemicals in meat also pose a threat to human health today. This includes toxins in fish (such as PCB's and mercury), resulting from factory farming practices and environmental pollution.

Mad cow disease is an example of unnatural farming practices gone awry. Bovine Spongiform Encephalopathy (BSE), commonly known as mad cow, was first reported in 1986 in the United Kingdom. The disease is believed to have originated from feeding cattle the ground up meat and bones of contaminated sheep. The disease causes a slow death by eating small holes through the brain tissue of cattle. Today, nearly 40 countries around the world have found traces of BSE in their cattle supply.

Creutzfeld-Jacob Disease (CJD) is the human variation of BSE. Until recently, it was thought that humans could only

FOOD FOR THOUGHT

- Half the agricultural land in the United States is devoted to cattle grazing.

- American livestock consumes 10 times more grain than the American human population each year.

- Nearly 80 percent of U.S. corn and 95 percent of U.S. oats are fed to cattle.

- It takes 2,500 gallons of water to produce 1 pound of beef.

- An acre of land devoted to legumes will yield 10 times more protein than an acre devoted to livestock.

- More than half of the world's species are found in rainforests. Millions of acres of rainforests are being clear cut each year to support cattle grazing. Most of this meat is sold to Western fast-food chains.

contract the disease by eating contaminated meat. Blood transfusions, however, have also been shown to transmit the disease. Over 150 people have reportedly died from CJD, and many more could be infected. It's difficult to estimate this number, because the disease typically lies dormant in the body for 10 to 30 years before symptoms appear.

In 1997, the U.S. passed a law prohibiting the use of animal tissues in cattle feed. It remained legal, however, to use cattle blood, chicken excrement, and chicken feathers in cattle feed, all of which remain common practices today. Consumer groups have argued that rendered beef pellets are routinely fed to chickens, thus allowing for cross-contamination. The first U.S. case of BSE was found in December 2003, leading to the implementation of new governmental testing measures for beef. Consumer groups

are calling for a more thorough approach to combating BSE. This would entail also addressing the underlying farming practices that contribute to the disease in the first place.

VICES AND VIRTUES

According to Ayurveda, one person's medicine will always be another person's poison. Broad generalizations about food fail to recognize the inherent differences in human nature. A Kapha type, for example, may feel great after eating a bucket of popcorn, while a Vata type may feel gassy and bloated. Generalizations about food also ignore the qualitative differences in food itself. A health crusader may call for a ban on all sugar. However, this lumps sugar into a single, harmful category. Ayurveda, on the other hand, differentiates between refined sugar and natural sweeteners that can actually help balance certain individuals.

The closest Ayurveda comes to making a blanket statement about food involves the consumption of unnatural foods. Quite simply put, it's always best to choose natural foods over artificially farmed, processed, and packaged foods. Many of the health problems in the West today have their roots in the consumption of inferior, often toxic foods.

Even the dietary vices so commonly vilified today are difficult to label definitively as bad. Often, a virtuous counterpart exists when such foods are consumed in the right forms and by the appropriate doshic types. Eating the proper quantity of food is another important factor. We've included an overview of the most common vices in the modern food chain. While the damaging effects of these substances are severe, many of them also provide important nutritional benefits.

FOOD ADDICTION

A particular food only becomes a vice through addiction. A cup of coffee or a glass of wine is not inherently harmful. Rather, it's our misuse, abuse, and lack of discretion in choosing these substances that create imbalance. Food addiction is largely fueled by the highly concentrated nature of artificial foods. Refined sugar and caffeine are two of the most widely abused substances in the West today. While these addictions are easily ignored, in the long run, they lead to highly damaging effects.

Addiction includes anything we crave in excess. This may include food, drugs, thought patterns, emotions, sex, attention, and even exercise. All addictions begin with improperly nurturing our individual natures. In an effort to find balance, gratification, or pleasure in life, we may choose foods, substances, and activities that lead to greater imbalances over the long run. Food addictions, for example, may stem from a simple desire to satisfy the senses, or they may extend to deeper issues such as unresolved emotions.

Recognition is the first step in addressing any form of addiction. Even though a food addiction may not present itself as a major problem, it's beneficial to examine any unhealthy dietary habits in your life. For example, if you need sugary foods to help get you through the day, then you should consider whether you have a mild addiction to this potent substance. You should also ask yourself why you have this daily craving. Does it stem from mere habit, or is it a chemical dependency resulting from years of over-consumption? Or is it possibly a substitute for a lack of emotional sweetness in other areas of your life?

The answer to this question is less important than the actual process of reflection. As you develop greater awareness about your dietary habits, you will begin to form a healthier

FOOD FOR THOUGHT

- Up to 100,000 broiler chickens (the ones that end up on the dinner plate) are frequently crammed into a single building. The toes and beaks of the chickens are clipped off to avoid profit-reducing casualties. It's estimated that 8 billion broiler chickens are slaughtered in the United States each year.

- Dairy cows are forced to remain pregnant for most of their lives. They are injected with hormones that artificially increase milk production from 10 to 15%.

- A cow must legally be knocked unconscious with a stun gun before being slaughtered. In practice, many are still conscious when they are killed.

- Over one third of the world's fish supply is now factory farmed. This entails keeping hundreds of fish in a single holding pool with little room to swim.

- The veal calf lives in a 2x3 foot stall for its entire four month life. In order to ensure tender meat, the calf is never allowed to take a step or lie down.

relationship to food. If these habits are linked to deeper psychological issues or longstanding patterns of addiction, we encourage you to seek professional guidance. Often, the vicious cycle of addiction is too much for a person to conquer alone. That is why a strong support network of family and friends is also important. Overcoming any addiction ultimately requires self-love and a commitment to healing. When these components are in place, our natural impulse to evolve replaces the impulse toward addiction and suffering.

SUGAR

Two centuries ago, sugar was still a luxury in the West. Today, the average American eats nearly 140 pounds of sugar each year. White, refined sugar is one of the most addictive ingredients in the modern food chain. It's also one of the most common ingredients, finding its way into the majority of packaged and processed foods. Sugar addiction begins in childhood and lasts until we make a conscious effort to break the habit. If you find yourself needing that frequent sugar fix, then it's time to drop white sugar for good.

Unlike most foods, refined sugar absorbs directly into the blood stream. This forces the liver, stomach, and pancreas to work harder in an effort to regulate blood sugar levels. The body eventually loses its ability to process sugar efficiently and waste products (or ama) collect in the intestinal tract. Medical research has linked the over-consumption of refined sugar to a wide variety of physical and mental illnesses. A partial list includes hyperactivity, anxiety, diabetes, arthritis, multiple sclerosis, learning deficiencies, adrenal dysfunction, depression, and certain types of cancers.

In modern nutritional terms, a *carbohydrate* is a compound made up of carbon, hydrogen, and oxygen molecules. Carbohydrates are an essential source of fuel and energy. The most basic carbohydrates are known as simple sugars. These are found in white sugar, fruits, vegetables, and other sweeteners. A *calorie* is a unit of measurement for the amount of energy that food provides. Simple sugars have the most calories of all foods. When the body takes in more energy (or calories) than it needs, it ends up storing these calories as excess fat and other harmful substances.

Refined sugar contains "empty calories," since it provides the body with energy but offers no nutritional value. Natural forms of simple sugars (such as those found in fruits, sweet vegetables, and honey), on the other hand, provide the body with both energy and nutrients. All simple sugars cause blood sugar levels to spike temporarily, so even natural sugars can create an excess sugar burden for the body.

When several simple sugar molecules link together, they form a *complex carbohydrate*. These are found in quality whole foods such as grains, legumes, vegetables, and nuts. Complex carbohydrates provide the body not only with energy but also with important vitamins, minerals, fats, and proteins. They also release sugar (in the form of glucose) into the blood at a much slower rate, creating balanced energy levels.

Both Ayurveda and modern nutrition favor a diet rich in complex carbohydrates and natural forms of simple sugars (or simple carbohydrates). From a doshic perspective, Kapha types are the most sensitive to carbohydrates. Eating processed, simple sugars results in weight gain for these types. While they do need complex carbohydrates for fuel and nutrients, these will also lead to weight gain when consumed in excess. Vata and Pitta types do well with most carbohydrates, due to the predominantly Sweet taste of these sugars.

Honey is the best sweetener for Kapha. Used in moderation, its warming and Astringent properties can actually decrease ama in Kapha types. Ayurveda also values honey for numerous other healing properties. Stevia, which is gaining popularity in the West today, is another good option for Kapha. The plant is 30 times sweeter than sugar and doesn't raise blood sugar levels. It's now available in both powdered and liquid form. Vata and Pitta types do well with most natural sweeteners, but should consume honey in small amounts, due to its drying and heating properties.

FAT

In the United States, the ages-old expression "fat of the land" has been downgraded to the "land of the fat." Revered throughout human history as an essential building block for life, fat has become vilified in modern times. The flaw, however, lies within our over-consumption and adulteration of this mighty nutrient. Fats and oils serve a multitude of biological functions. They also provide taste, aroma, and texture to the food we eat.

From a dietary perspective, fat is the most concentrated source of energy available to the human body. We utilize it constantly for maintaining energy levels and supporting growth. Fat enables the body to store and circulate fat-soluble vitamins (such as vitamins A, D, and E), while providing an important layer of insulation just beneath the skin. It also governs hormone production, lubricates bodily tissues, and protects and supports our vital organs. Fat also composes over 60 percent of the brain, making it one of the most important nutrients for brain function.

Fats are composed of molecular building blocks known as *fatty acids*. There are three major categories of fatty acids: *saturated*, *polyunsaturated*, and *monounsaturated*. Saturated fats are commonly found in meat, dairy products, tropical oils (such as coconut and palm), margarine, lard, and vegetable shortening. Polyunsaturated fats are found in legumes, vegetables, nuts, and seeds such as soybeans, corn, and sunflower seeds. The oils of certain fish are also high in polyunsaturates, including salmon, mackerel, and albacore tuna. Monounsaturated fats are found in a variety of foods, including olives, avocado, flax seeds, and peanuts.

The most important key to understanding fat is to remember that *not all fats are created equally*. The fat phobia present in today's dieting culture stems primarily from the harmful effects of saturated fats. The liver uses saturated fats to manufacture LDLs (*low-density lipoproteins*) or bad cholesterol. Saturated fats are also extremely high in calories and cause blockages within arteries. Heart disease, high cholesterol, arteriosclerosis, and obesity are at the top of a long list of illnesses related to the over-consumption of saturated fats.

From an Ayurvedic perspective, saturated fats (particularly those deriving from animal flesh) are the most difficult foods to digest and, therefore, promote ama formation. Ghee, or clarified butter, is an exception to this rule, because it stimulates agni and balances all three doshas. While Ayurveda also recommends other dairy products for balancing the doshas (particularly for Vata and Pitta), saturated fats should never comprise a large portion of any individual's diet.

Fat-free diet fads fail to recognize the essential role that fat plays in maintaining health. Unlike saturated fats, polyunsaturated and monounsaturated fats have actually been shown to reduce the risks of high cholesterol and heart disease when they are processed correctly and consumed in moderate quantities. Sesame oil, which is widely used in Ayurveda, is composed of roughly half polyunsaturated and half monounsaturated fats, making it another healthy option.

The benefits of Omega-3 and Omega-6 fatty acids have also received a great deal of attention in recent years. These polyunsaturated fats are referred to as "essential fatty acids," since they are needed for health but cannot be produced by the body. Both Omega-3 and Omega-6 are widely recognized for their anti-inflammatory and immune-enhancing properties. Omega-3 is most abundant in cold water fish such as salmon, mackerel, and herring. It is also found in flax seeds, hemp seeds, and to a lesser degree in soy, canola, walnuts, and pumpkin seeds (and the oils of these plants). Omega-6 is found in a large variety of foods and oils including sesame, corn, soybean, olive, pumpkin, borage, and primrose.

The second most important key to understanding fats is to remember that *not all oils are processed equally*. When oil comes into contact with air, it rapidly begins to oxidize or spoil. This process changes the molecular structure of the oil, creating a rancid substance that is toxic to the human body. When exposed to heat, oil begins to oxidize at an even faster rate. The majority of commercial oils today are processed at temperatures of 500 degrees or more. This maximizes the amount of oil expelled from each plant and creates a clear, odorless substance. Numerous chemicals are also used during this process. Polyunsaturated oils such as soy, corn, canola, and vegetable oils are the most likely candidates for becoming rancid.

Trans-fatty acids are synthetic or man-made fats that the body cannot efficiently utilize or eliminate. Hydrogenation is a process in which unsaturated or liquid fats are artificially saturated in order to create solid fats. *Hydrogenated* oils

contain the largest concentration of these fats. These are commonly found in margarine, vegetable shortening, peanut butter, sweets, and many other processed and packaged foods. Over-consuming trans-fats, rancid fats, and chemically treated fats can lead to a wide variety of illnesses including heart disease, high cholesterol, arthritis, and cancer.

In choosing your cooking oils, it's always best to favor organic, cold-pressed oils. These oils are free from harmful chemicals and are processed at temperatures below 110 degrees. According to Ayurveda, ghee has the highest heat tolerance of any oil, making it a valuable cooking tool. Olive oil (preferably extra-virgin) and sesame oil also withstand higher temperatures without becoming rancid. These oils can be stored safely at room temperature. When using sunflower, safflower, soy, canola, and other oils, greater care should be taken in order to avoid overheating the oil. These oils should always be kept refrigerated in order to prevent them from turning rancid.

It's also beneficial to choose oils in accordance with your constitution. Vata types do well with heavier oils such as sesame oil, olive oil, and ghee. Pitta types benefit from cooler oils such as sunflower oil, ghee, and coconut oil. Kapha types do best with light or heating oils such as sunflower, safflower, and mustard oils.

SALT

Salt is essential to human life. It performs numerous functions in the body and acts as the great magnifier for other foods and tastes. Historically, salt was prized for its ability to preserve food, granting it a regal position within many ancient cultures. Roman soldiers were given "salt money" or *salarium argentums* as partial payment for their services. The English word "salary" derives from this Latin term.

From a biological standpoint, salt regulates fluid levels in the body while maintaining the acid/alkaline levels of the blood. It also absorbs nutrients across cell membranes, transmits electrical nerve impulses, and aids in muscle contraction. As one of the primary Six Tastes of food, Salty taste adds its own defining quality while bringing out the splendor of the other five tastes.

Similar to sugar and fat, however, not all salt is created equally. The average salt shaker contains one of the most heavily refined foods available today. After being mined from deep within the ground, refined salt is chemically cleaned, bleached, and treated with anti-caking agents. This leaves a tainted sodium chloride molecule that the body cannot efficiently utilize or eliminate. In total, salt is stripped of nearly 60 important trace minerals. "Iodized" salt has been further processed chemically to bond the essential nutrient iodine with table salt.

Most processed and packaged foods today contain large amounts of salt in an effort to increase shelf life and make up for their inherent lack of flavor. Numerous diseases are now linked to excess salt intake, including high blood pressure, stomach ulcers, heart attack, fluid retention, and osteoporosis.

When choosing salt, it's always best to pick a minimally refined or non-refined variety. Sea salt is one of the healthiest choices available today. Made from evaporated sea water, sea salt retains important trace minerals while offering a high level of culinary quality. Classically, Ayurveda mentions eight primary types of salt. Of these, rock salt is considered the most beneficial for daily consumption. You can find it at many health food stores, Indian grocery stores, or Ayurvedic supply companies (see Resources, page 333). Even when consuming the best quality salts, it's important to always keep things in moderation. Excess salt consumption, especially for Pitta and Kapha types, will quickly lead to imbalance.

COFFEE

If you find yourself needing that third cup of coffee to carry you through the day, then you may be riding the caffeine rollercoaster. The rapid ups and downs of caffeine use make it one of the most widely abused substances in the West today.

Coffee provides convenient compensation for an unbalanced lifestyle. It allows a person to work when tired, to have a bowel movement when constipated, and to keep up with the hectic pace of modern culture. The over-consumption of coffee will always fuel a greater cycle of imbalance. Modern medicine has linked coffee to illnesses such as heartburn, high cholesterol, anxiety, adrenal dysfunction, liver dysfunction, nervousness, acid reflux, and fatigue.

According to Ayurveda, our misuse of coffee gives the bean a bad name. Coffee is rich in Bitter and Astringent tastes, which are lacking in today's diet. This may explain why people are initially drawn to coffee in the first place.

For a Kapha individual, a cup of coffee after a meal will help kick-start the digestive system. Taken before a meal, however, coffee will neutralize important digestive enzymes. A Pitta type can tolerate coffee in small quantities, although its acidic and rajasic qualities will aggravate Pitta with regular use. Coffee is least suited for Vata types. Its Bitter and Astringent tastes, combined with the stimulatory effect of caffeine, are a recipe for Vata disaster. Coffee excites the temperamental Vata mind, while creating extreme dryness in the body.

If you drink coffee, it's always best to buy organic beans. Numerous chemicals are used in the manufacturing process of coffee, especially decaffeinated varieties. When buying decaf, favor brands that have been water decaffeinated, sometimes referred to as "Swiss process." It's also best to grind your coffee beans freshly before use, since they oxidize rapidly.

If you take sugar in your coffee, choose natural sweeteners over refined sugar and non-sugar substitutes. Adding a pinch of cardamom and a tablespoon of cow's milk to coffee will also help decrease harmful effects to your liver (especially if you're a Pitta type). If you enjoy the taste of coffee but don't like the side effects, natural coffee substitutes offer a healthy choice. These are made from a wide variety of ingredients, including chicory, barley, rye, carob, and dandelion (See page 183 for Chicory "Coffee").

CHOCOLATE

The Aztec, Maya, and Inca prized the cacao bean for its energizing properties. Our own use of the bean dates back to these ancient Mesoamerican cultures. Modern chocolate, however, bears little resemblance to its noble predecessor. Composed of white sugar, hydrogenated oils, and other harmful substances, chocolate is now a poster-child for junk food.

White sugar and theobromine (an element similar to caffeine) are a formidable duo. Offering instant pleasure and energy, these substances quickly lead to cycles of abuse. In ancient times, cacao beans were heated, crushed, and beaten with water into a bitter, frothy drink. The refinement of chocolate today uses a much higher concentration of beans, creating a powerful substance that can easily overwhelm the digestive system.

If you enjoy the occasional chocolate treat, favor organic, semi-sweet chocolate. We've included a few recipes in the Expanded Recipe section as a guide. If you start developing

a craving, however, then you know it's time to re-evaluate your relationship to this highly addictive food. It's also helpful to consider your doshic make-up. A Vata type may benefit from the grounding quality of chocolate, but the caffeine is bound to create unrest. A Pitta type may enjoy the Bitter taste of chocolate, but its acidic and rajasic qualities can easily lead to imbalance (much like coffee). The sweet-natured Kapha may find joy or comfort in chocolate, but its heaviness will eventually disrupt the Kapha mind and body.

If you're lacking Bitter taste in your diet, you may find yourself drawn to dark chocolate. Use this as a cue to start eating more Bitter foods, such as dark leafy greens. If you're a full-fledged chocoholic, then it's time to do a chocolate fast in order to break the cycle of addiction (that means staying away from chocolate, not choosing it as your sole dietary staple!). Carob provides a useful alternative to chocolate. The powdered form of the plant has a similar taste and texture to cocoa powder. It's also caffeine-free and requires less sweetening. Large amounts of sugar are used in many processed carob products, however, so it's best to eat these in moderation.

ALCOHOL

Alcohol abuse taxes the mind and body and creates chemical dependency over time. Whether wine or whisky, the liver and kidneys have to work harder to process any form of alcohol. After repeated abuse, the body loses its ability to eliminate alcohol toxins efficiently, leading to a slow, vile poisoning of life.

As with any addictive substance, it's important to consume alcohol with awareness. If the occasional drink becomes a daily necessity, ask yourself why you're drinking more. Most of the time, people simply self-medicate in a highly inefficient way. Drinking provides an easy outlet for stress. It also serves as a short-term bandage for our deepest fears and frustrations. Rather than working towards inner harmony, we choose a path of instant relaxation and happiness. This is a fleeting solution that only leads to greater suffering in the long run.

If you drink, choose your alcohol wisely. Vata individuals are highly sensitive to alcohol, so moderation is essential. The yeast, carbonation, and cold temperature of beer will easily aggravate these types. Hard alcohol will do the same, due to its highly concentrated nature. Small amounts of red wine, on the other hand, may actually stimulate agni and improve circulation in some Vata and Kapha types.

With a nickname like "fire water," it's no surprise that alcohol can severely aggravate Pitta. Beer is less heating than wine or hard alcohol, so it's a better choice for fiery types. Kapha individuals have the greatest tolerance for alcohol, although its dulling or tamasic effect heavily weighs down the Kapha mind and body. Alcohol initially stimulates the senses and motor organs, creating a temporary rajasic effect. It proceeds to dull these faculties, leading to a greater tamasic effect. The drunken stupor and morning hangover are examples of extreme tamas in the mind and body.

Ayurveda uses naturally fermented herbal wines (called *arishtas*) for treating a large number of imbalances. These may contain a dozen or more herbs, thus making them highly medicinal in nature. Their heating qualities make them particularly beneficial for kindling the digestive fire and improving circulation.

MODERN FOOD CONCERNS

GENETICALLY MODIFIED FOODS

Now consider two potatoes side by side. The first potato is a large, fresh, organic variety. The second is also large and fresh, but a little different. Lab technicians inserted artificial genes into this potato, in order to create bacterial pesticides in each of its cells. After nibbling from this variety, beetles and other insects will die. The first potato is an ancient staple of agrarian life. The second is a technological creation.

ABOUT FIBER

Unlike most nutrients, the benefits of fiber stem from its indigestible nature, rather than its assimilation into the body. There are two primary types of dietary fiber: *soluable* and *insoluable* fiber. Choosing a diet that's rich in whole foods is the best way to ensure adequate intake of both fibers.

Soluable fiber is found in fruits, vegetables, legumes, oat bran, brown rice, barley, rye, sesame seeds, and psyllium husks. It nourishes the friendly bacteria in the intestines, decreases the rate at which sugar enters the blood stream, and helps expel heavy metals from the body. Diets high in soluble fiber have been shown to reduce the risk of heart disease and colon cancer, while significantly lowering "bad" cholesterol levels.

Insoluable fiber keeps waste materials moving through the body with ease. You'll find it in wheat bran, whole grain breads and cereals, brown rice, fruits, vegetables, nuts, and beans. The widespread occurrence of constipation in the West today relates to the over-consumption of fiberless foods.

Genetically modified foods (or "GM" foods for short) go by a variety of different names. Some of these include "genetically modified organism" (GMO), "genetically engineered" (GE), and "transgenic." The corporations behind these foods have pumped millions of dollars into marketing and advertising to improve public opinion about biotechnology, and what they call "genetic enhancements" or "genetic improvements."

The most common GM foods include varieties of soy, corn, cotton, and canola designed to withstand large sprayings of chemical herbicides. When using herbicides produced by the same company as the crops themselves, farmers have the ability to kill weeds without damaging their crops. Biotech companies state that these herbicide-resistant crops require less chemical usage than conventional varieties. Research suggests that farmers are actually spraying these crops with more herbicides. It may come as no surprise that the five leading biotech firms are also the world's leading producers of herbicides and agricultural chemicals.

While the newer potato may sound less appetizing and even a bit frightening, this type of genetically modified food is entering our food chain at a staggering rate.

The genetic modification of food is a process in which genes from one organism are inserted into another, usually unrelated organism, in an attempt to transfer a desired trait. Foreign genes may derive from non-related plants, bacteria, fungi, insects, viruses, or animals. In 1996, genetically modified crops accounted for 4 million acres of farmland world-wide. By the year 2001, these crops accounted for over 100 million acres.

Today, five multi-national biotech corporations control more than 95 percent of the market for genetically modified foods. Despite claims by these companies that they are making foods healthier and more abundant, research has done little to support their claims. What we do know, however, is that these companies are profiting financially in a big way.

Other GM foods currently on the market include tomatoes, papayas, daikon, sugar beets, potatoes, yellow crookneck squash, zucchini, radicchio, and flax. The genetically-modified growth hormone, rBGH, is also widely used to increase milk production in cows. Dozens of other foods are currently in advanced stages of testing. These include salmon that grow four times faster than normal breeds, cantaloupes that ripen at slower rates (for longer shelf-life), and corn that produces pharmaceutical proteins for blood clotting medications and other drugs. These last "biopharmaceuticals" are among the most controversial uses of genetic engineering in agriculture, because of the ethical issues surrounding the insertion of human genes into food crops.

No long-term studies have been conducted on the physiological effects of GM foods on humans. In reality, the technology is too young even to begin to understand the health impacts of these foods. Scientists, however, have raised concerns regarding the creation of GM-related food allergens in the human body. In short-term studies, for example, GM corn has been shown to trigger mild allergic responses. Soybeans containing the genes of Brazil nuts have also triggered responses in people with pre-existing allergies to this nut.

On a fundamental level, we know that manipulating the genetic structure of food immediately alters billions of years of evolution. The question arises whether humans contain adequate blueprints from nature to digest and utilize these foods properly? Only time and further testing can truly determine the subtle effects of these foods on the mind and body.

The long-term environmental effects of GM foods are also unknown. In short-term studies, these crops are shown to cross-pollinate at rates nearly 20 times greater than conventionally grown crops. That means GM crops are more likely to spread their genes to non-GM varieties via wind, insects, or birds. Through cross-pollination, the genetic structure of a non-GM crop is permanently altered, thereby posing a threat to an entire species of food. Scientists have similar concerns regarding the threat GM fish may pose to natural breeds should one be mistakenly released into the wild.

Lack of soil biodiversity is another area of environmental concern surrounding GM foods. Similar to conventional farming methods, thousands of consecutive acres are being planted with the same GM crop. Couple these mono-crop practices with increased chemical spraying, and the threat to important soil bacteria and related organisms is greatly magnified. GM crops have also proven to kill non-targeted

insects such as the monarch butterfly, indicating a threat to overall ecological diversity.

The United States is the most vocal supporter of GM foods in the world. It is estimated that over two thirds of the U.S. soybean crop and one third of the U.S. corn crop is genetically modified. Further, nearly two thirds of all foods in U.S. supermarkets may now be genetically modified, largely due to the fact that soy oil and corn syrup are two staple ingredients of processed foods. There are currently no labeling or safety requirements for GM foods in the U.S. One may, therefore, conclude that most Americans are unknowing participants in a massive experiment.

While the U.S. continues to support GM foods, over 30 countries around the world have turned their backs upon these foods. These include Japan, Australia, New Zealand, China, North Korea, countries in Africa, most of the European Union, and additional countries in Asia. Citing insufficient research, many have banned all imports on GM foods. Others have implemented strict labeling standards for products containing GM ingredients. Developing countries such as Zimbabwe have declined foreign food aid due to the unknown affects GM crops may have on their own farming systems, public health, and ecosystem. Even in the U.S., many non-organic companies are now committing to 100 percent GM-free ingredients in their products.

At this point, you may be wondering how to avoid GM foods in your own diet. Under the new USDA organic labeling guidelines, organic foods may not contain any GM ingredients. Buying organically is therefore one way to avoid these foods. If you are not able to buy organically, then you can familiarize yourself with common GM ingredients and avoid these when possible. The biggest culprits include non-organic soy, corn, and canola products. With regards to soy and corn, watch out for these following foods and ingredients:

- Soybeans: margarine, unspecified vegetable oils, soy oil, soy flour, soy protein isolates, soy lecithin, and textured vegetable protein
- Corn: fresh corn, canned and frozen corn, corn sweeteners (including corn syrup and high-fructose corn syrup), corn oil, corn flour, and corn starch

Today, the genetic modification of food is one of the most important issues threatening our world food supply. As biotechnology continues to advance, attempts to improve upon nature will also continue. Only by demanding safe, clean food can we ensure that long-term collective health wins out over short-term corporate profits.

FOOD ADDITIVES

Food additives have fallen in stature since their days as the crowning achievements of modern nutritional technology. With the invention of chemical additives in the 1930's, the storage and shipment of food suddenly became much easier. Many foods also became cheaper, as spoilage-caused waste dropped. Consumers could suddenly enjoy the agricultural bounty of distant lands that had vastly different growing climates. As the profits of chemical companies increased, the additive industry expanded with relentless force. Hundreds and eventually thousands of additives made their way into the U.S. food chain. Today, over 3,000 additives are used in the U.S. food industry.

These additives have become the defining characteristics of most processed and packaged foods. Common additives include coloring and flavoring agents, sweeteners, preservatives, bleaches, emulsifiers, binders, and anti-caking agents.

Similar to the case with GM foods, the testing and research to justify the widespread use of food additives does not exist. What we do know, however, is that all chemical additives are artificial. That means our bodies have to work harder to process and remove these additives. While some additives serve useful purposes and appear to be safe for human consumption, we also know that many others substances are proven toxins, carcinogens, and allergens.

Consumers are told that small amounts of substances such as Red Dye #3 are completely safe for human consumption. This fails to take into account, however, the damaging effects of these chemicals on the body over time. After becoming lodged in the tissues of the body, they can lead to free-radical damage, weakened immune function, and a host of other medical problems.

Over the last fifty years, our senses have been conditioned to artificial additives. The taste, look, feel, and smell of foods are widely governed by these agents. In the commercial food industry, every measure is taken to make the nutritionally void appear and taste appetizing. Crops grown on nutrient-deficient lands are augmented by artificial tastes and coloring agents. Even the smells in the typical fast-food meal today are concocted in chemical labs.

If it seems like the infiltration of additives into our food is irreversible, consider this fact: while the United States allows thousands of food chemicals, some European countries allow fewer than 20. Once again, we have a case of corporate profits winning out over collective health. Buying unrefined, fresh, organic whole foods is a direct way to curb the market for artificial food products.

REFINED FOODS

The term "refined" may evoke notions of knowledge, wealth, and sophistication. When it comes to food, however, this term is a euphemism at best. Once upon a time, "white foods" or refined carbohydrates were considered a delicacy in the West. Brown bread and other whole grains were looked down upon as the food of the poor. In actuality, people were paying more money for less nutrition.

Refinement is a process by which the two outer layers of a grain, know as the bran and germ, are stripped away. Most of the nutrients in grains, such as fiber, iron, calcium, vitamin E, and the B vitamins, are stored in these outer layers. In order to make up for this nutrient loss, many refined foods are "enriched," by the addition of small amounts of nutrients back into the food. An increased shelf life is the primary economic motive for such refinement. The stripped away nutrients also receive a premium in today's booming supplement market.

According to Ayurveda, refined foods disrupt the normal course of metabolism. A diet high in refined foods creates ama in the body. Foods such as white flour, white rice, and white sugar are also often bleached, increasing their toxicity. The lack of fiber and roughage in such foods also makes it more difficult to pass them through the digestive tract, as evidenced by the widespread problem of constipation in the West.

MICROWAVE OVENS

Microwave ovens are one of the most common appliances in modern kitchens. The way they actually cook food, however, remains a mystery to many. Accidentally discovered in the 1940's as an offshoot of military radar technology, microwave ovens use radio waves to heat food from the inside out. These waves increase the vibrational rate of water and food molecules, which in turn generates heat that cooks the food.

Research has shown that microwave cooking alters the molecular structure of food. Studies have also shown that eating microwaved food may promote harmful changes in blood composition. It's a well-known precaution that you should avoid standing in front of microwave ovens while in use, due to the possible effects of the emitting waves. Little regard, however, is given to the effects these waves may have on the foods placed inside of them.

And you may be thinking…yes, but microwaves are so easy and convenient! There's no question about it; they're about as easy and convenient as it gets. This degree of convenience, however, often breeds unhealthy dietary choices. Leftovers, along with instant and precooked foods, are the tamasic staples of microwave cuisine. Instead of relying on your microwave, we encourage you to engage in the cooking process. The preparation of vibrant food is an act of loving creation. Regarding microwaves and any other enticing technology that comes along, just remember that it's best to keep things as natural as possible.

IRRADIATION

Irradiation is a process of passing food through nuclear-derived gamma rays before packaging. This process has become increasingly popular with the food industry in recent years as a way to increase shelf-life and combat food-borne diseases such as *E. coli* 0157:H7 and *salmonella*. In the 1960's, the U.S. military first began serving irradiated foods to its personnel. The FDA halted the use of these foods, however, after irradiated sugar was shown to damage human chromosomes and affect cell growth.

causing properties, the European Union limited food irradiation to spices and dried herbs.

Proponents of food irradiation emphasize its important role in making foods safe. Similar in function to taking a pill to mask the symptoms of an illness, however, irradiating food does not address the underlying problem. It merely allows unhealthy and inhumane cycles of growing and production to continue. Only by breaking this cycle will change occur—a change we can all support by refusing to purchase irradiated foods.

WATER

Water is the universal elixir of life. It makes up more than 70 percent of our total body mass and covers the same proportion of the Earth's surface. We can live without food for a month or more, but we will perish in a matter of days without water. It's widely known that drinking enough water each day is an essential key to health. The quality of the water we drink, however, often gets overlooked.

Today, we are blessed with remarkable convenience in obtaining the water we drink. While some people still hike for miles to find fresh water, we simply turn on a faucet or run to the nearest store. Such convenience, however, also breeds less care regarding the quality of water we drink.

Basic chemistry tells us that water is composed of two hydrogen atoms and a single oxygen atom. Unfortunately, this doesn't mean that all water is created equally.

Most of the global water supply is no longer the pure substance that cultures have cherished for millennia. Water is now widely tainted with harmful chemicals and inorganic materials. Pollutants from farming, industrial dumping, and decaying pipes are among the biggest threats. These include

International food scares such as mad cow disease brought irradiation back with a vengeance in 2000, when the USDA legalized the irradiation of beef and other animal products. Most foods are now approved for irradiation in the U.S., including grains, nuts, seeds, fruits, and vegetables. While labeling is required for any irradiated product sold in a store, restaurants and cafeterias are not required to label these foods.

Currently, no long-term studies have been conducted on food irradiation. Short-term studies have shown irradiation to produce free radicals and other potentially carcinogenic by-products in the body. It has also been shown to destroy important vitamins and enzymes in food. After European studies demonstrated that irradiated fats contain cancer-

mercury, iron, lead, copper, arsenic, various fertilizers and pesticides, asbestos, cyanide, radium, and other industrial chemicals. Despite extensive water treatment methods, trace amounts of these substances often remain in drinking water. Repeated exposure to these toxins has been linked to cancer, Alzheimer's disease, and a wide range of other illnesses.

The chemicals added to sanitize water have also raised concerns in recent years. These include chlorine, phosphate, lime, soda ash, and aluminum phosphate. Chlorine, in particular, has attracted considerable attention. Studies have shown that chlorine forms carcinogenic chemicals when interacting with organic matter commonly found in water. Ingesting small amounts of chlorine over time has also been shown to drop vitamin E levels in the body and destroy beneficial intestinal flora.

In the U.S. and Europe, the fluoridation of water has been another controversial topic. Fluoride is added to water as a type of medicine for the masses, with the stated objective of creating stronger teeth and bones. Opponents of fluoridation, however, make the following distinction: chemically derived *sodium fluoride*, a by-product of the aluminum industry, is added to drinking water, not the naturally occurring *calcium fluoride*. Studies have shown that small amounts of calcium fluoride strengthen teeth and bones. No study has ever proven the same for sodium fluoride. Certain illnesses, on the other hand, have been linked to this substance, including, ironically, tooth decay as well as skeletal fluorosis, a bone and joint condition. Yet, today, more than half the cities in the United States fluoridate their water supplies.

So what is pure water and how can you get it? Water should be clear and have a refreshing taste and aftertaste. If you turn on your tap and find cloudy, discolored, or sediment-laden water, it's a sign to take caution. Similarly, if the water tastes metallic or otherwise "off" in any way, it's probably impure. If you'd like to test your water for harmful substances, a number of private labs now offer this service. (See Resources on page 333 for more information.) Your local water company should also provide free information on chlorine, fluoride, and mineral levels.

Water filtration is one of the safest and most affordable options for purifying water today. There are three primary types of filtration: activated carbon, reverse-osmosis, and steam distillation. Carbon filters are highly effective, moderately priced, and available in a variety of styles, from pitchers to whole-house units. Just note that filters require frequent changing. Reverse-osmosis technology is also highly effective. Such countertop units get rid of more contaminants than carbon filters, although they also cost more and waste large quantities of water. Steam distillers are the most thorough purifiers, but they're expensive, difficult to maintain, and strip water of all essential minerals, thus creating lifeless water.

This raises an important consideration regarding the mineral content of our drinking water today. Truly vitalized water spends time deep within the earth or mountains, collecting minerals and other nutrients. It then naturally filters through rocks and other sediments, which aerate, purify, and mineralize the water. From an Ayurvedic standpoint, such minerals relate to the greater Earth element at our core.

Most of our drinking water today derives from surface sources devoid of this natural process. Filtering water through any of the methods above will further remove important minerals. If you suspect you have mineral-depleted water, we recommend adding trace minerals to your water. These derive from natural sources, such as saltwater lakes, and are available at most health food stores. Ayurveda also recommends placing water in a natural, unglazed clay pot overnight to help add back minerals. For this to be effective, it's important that both sides of the pot are unglazed.

As awareness of water quality has increased in recent years, bottled water sales have boomed. Relying solely on bottled water, however, is more costly and less environmentally friendly than investing in a quality filtration system. Chemicals from plastic bottles can also leach into the water, particularly if bottles become hot. When you do buy bottled water, always check the source listed on the bottle. If no source is listed, the water can legally be tap water. "Natural Spring Water" and "Artesian Water" are healthy choices, since they derive from underground sources and flow naturally to the Earth's surface.

According to Ayurveda, drinking pure water nourishes the Water element at our core. Modern nutritional theory recommends drinking at least six to eight glasses of water a day. While this quantity is in line with Ayurveda's general recommendation, other factors must also be taken into account. These include an individual's doshic make-up, age, and activity level. Seasonal and geographic factors should also be considered. For example, an active Pitta type living in a hot climate will require more water during the Summer months. A busy Vata individual living in a dry climate will require more water during the Fall. An inactive Kapha type living in a wet climate will require less water during Spring. Since the body naturally becomes drier with age, all doshic types benefit from greater hydration during these years.

Water is the body's most potent purifier. It naturally flushes out ama and other harmful toxins, while enhancing immunity. Drinking water is also one of the greatest ways to enliven and re-invigorate the energy or *prana* of the body. When we don't drink enough water, our bodies become a breeding ground for disease. Many of the major illnesses in the West today are linked to chronic dehydration. Coffee, tea, alcohol, soda, and other man-made drinks have widely contributed to this phenomenon. Along with replacing water as the drink of choice, these substances force the body to eliminate water at a faster rate due to their diuretic properties. According to Ayurveda, our ability to taste the 6 Tastes of food is also integrally linked to adequate water consumption, making it an essential component of balanced nutrition.

In determining how much water you should drink, listen to your thirst above all else. Remembering to do this during a hectic schedule is one of the most important keys to proper hydration. Keep water nearby and take small sips throughout the day. If necessary, even develop a more structured approach such as designating certain hours during the day as "watering" times. It's also important to remember that too much water can be detrimental. Flooding the body with gallons of water each day will dampen the digestive fire and lead to other imbalances. Always let common sense and your body's own innate wisdom be your guides.

Cow's Milk

Cow's milk is heralded by the modern dairy industry as one of nature's most wholesome foods. Classical Ayurvedic texts agree with this notion, although a major point of difference exists: the highly prized milk of ancient times is barely comparable to the substance we call milk today.

Similar to GM crops, U.S. milk production may be likened to a large-scale science experiment. Cows grow up on factory farms where they receive regular injections of growth hormones and antibiotics. Instead of grazing on grass, they eat legumes, grains, and other foods that may contain dangerous herbicides and pesticides. Residues from these drugs and chemicals leech directly into the cows' milk.

This prompted the European Economic Community in 1990 to ban the importation of hormone-treated U.S. milk (an embargo that still holds today). The widespread use of the genetically engineered hormone rBGH has rekindled this international debate in recent years. This hormone artificially increases a cow's milk production from 10 to 15 percent.

From an Ayurvedic perspective, the pasteurization and homogenization of cow's milk renders the food dull or tamasic. While these processes increase the safety, shelf life, and aesthetic appeal of commercial milk, they deplete its vitality. Important enzymes and beneficial bacteria are destroyed in the pasteurization process, making milk difficult to digest. Homogenization is the process of breaking up the fat globules in milk so they remain evenly suspended rather than separating into a layer of cream. From an Ayurvedic standpoint, this artificial process changes the qualities and molecular structure of the milk, making it more difficult to digest. The methods used to create low-fat and non-fat milk have similar effects on digestion. Low-agni conditions (common in Vata types) and excess-ama conditions (common in Kapha types) also inhibit the body's ability to digest milk properly.

Lactose intolerance occurs when an individual is unable to produce the enzyme lactase, which is responsible for digesting the milk sugar lactose. Characterized by gas, bloating, cramping, and diarrhea, this increasingly common condition may be partly explained by the digestive factors discussed above. A broader geographic focus must also be taken into consideration. In areas where dairy farming has been conducted for thousands of years such as northern Europe, India, and certain African countries, lactose intolerance is less common. In cultures not based on dairy farming, by contrast, there is a greater susceptibility to this intolerance.

Ayurveda favors fresh, raw, organic milk. Unless you have your own cow or personally know a dairy farmer, it's difficult to find raw milk in the West today. Organic milk is the next best option. Regardless of the source, Ayurveda always recommends boiling milk before consumption to break down complex protein molecules, making the milk lighter and easier to digest (while retaining the important enzymes and beneficial bacteria). Simply bring the milk to a boil and let it cool down to room temperature before consuming. Adding a pinch of ginger or cardamom will also increase the digestibility of milk.

Ayurveda never recommends drinking milk straight out of the refrigerator. Cold milk extinguishes the digestive fire, which neutralizes important digestive enzymes and promotes the formation of mucous (or ama). Combining milk with incompatible foods will have similar effects. As a rule, it's best to drink milk either on its own or with other Sweet foods, such as grains. Consuming milk with fish is a particularly ill-suited combination that leads to digestive disturbances and skin problems. It's also best to avoid drinking milk with meats, yeasted breads, sour fruits, bananas, and melons.

Vata types benefit from the grounding and strengthening properties of milk. Milk nourishes the deeper tissues of the body and supports the production of the vital fluid ojas. Some Vata types, however, may not tolerate milk due to their greater susceptibility to food allergies. Pitta types benefit from the cooling and calming effects of milk. Kapha types are the least suited to milk consumption, due to its high fat content and mucous-forming effects.

If cow's milk doesn't agree with you, there are a number of healthy substitutes available today. Soy milk is one of the most popular options, due to its pleasant taste and high protein content. Other plant-based milks derive from rice, barley, almonds, cashews, oats, and potatoes. It's best to choose these substitutes in accordance with those foods best suited to your primary dosha. We also recommend buying organic brands when possible, especially for soy milk. Organic goat's milk is another available option. Kapha types do well with goat's milk due to its mildly heating property and non-mucous forming effect. Vata and Pitta types, however, do better with plant-based milk alternatives (See Almond Milk on page 232).

DECREASING THE DEEP FREEZE

It's hard to imagine modern life without refrigeration. The ease with which foods can be stored has played a major role in the developing world. Over-reliance upon the freezer, however, often leads to suboptimal nutrition. We've probably all noticed that defrosted food never tastes quite as good as fresh. Could you ever imagine a description on the menu of a fine restaurant boasting, "defrosted vegetables cooked just two days ago"? We place a premium on fresh food because it looks and tastes better. The vibrancy of food is directly related to the prana or energy contained in it. The process of freezing, or even just leaving leftovers in the refrigerator for a few days, depletes its life-force.

You can observe this fact by placing a defrosted food item next to a similar fresh one out on your kitchen counter. You'll notice that the defrosted food begins to decompose much faster, often becoming dry, colorless, and odorous in a short period of time. This is because the life-force of the food is already compromised. Ayurveda, therefore, characterizes frozen food by its dull, tamasic quality.

As a rule of thumb, always to try to eat fresh foods. Storing something in the refrigerator, however, does not render it useless. The food will still provide the body with important nutrients. Just remember that the longer something stays in the refrigerator or freezer, the more lifeless it will become.

EVERYDAY TOOLS OF THE TRADE

In beginning to explore the world of Ayurvedic cooking, it's beneficial to stock your kitchen with a few key items. If you already cook, you probably already have most of these tools. Rather than filling every inch of counter space with the latest high-tech gadgets, Ayurveda recommends going back to the basics. Concentrate on equipping your kitchen with high-quality, practical tools that never become outdated.

As a rule, Ayurveda holds that *natural is best*. Preparing and cooking foods using natural methods helps protect their energetic integrity. Overuse of some electrical appliances, such as microwave ovens, may actually disrupt the vibrational quality of foods, making them less nourishing on subtle levels.

At the same time, this book aims to bring Ayurveda into the modern kitchen. In today's busy world, most people (ourselves included) do not have time to prepare everything from scratch. So there's no need to toss out your trusty blender or food processor. If these tools make cooking a reality for you, then do what works best. The most important thing is that you're in the kitchen cooking, an increasingly rare occurrence in the West today. Just take note of what appliances you have, and get rid of those you don't really need. You'll find that decreasing kitchen clutter will promote a clearer energy with which to exercise your culinary creativity. You'll also notice that returning to basic cooking methods will refine your sensitivity to this creative process.

The Kitchen Basics

In the list below, we've included basic kitchen tools. By no means do you need each of these things to get started; they are simply the tools Chef Johnny uses most frequently. The list even includes a few electric appliances that you may find useful for saving time and expanding creative possibilities.

Knives   Chefs often herald a good knife as the most important kitchen tool. Sharp, stainless-steel knives are a valuable component of most any cooking. Using dull knives, or knives that are ill-suited to particular jobs, can make cooking a tedious and even dangerous process. Despite the wide range of cutlery choices out there today, you only need four or five good-quality knives:

- A paring knife, for peeling
- A 6-inch knife, for both peeling and slicing
- A 10-inch chef's knife, for general slicing and chopping
- A heavy cleaver, for cutting denser foods like root vegetables
- A large serrated knife, for cutting breads

Sharpen your knives at the first sign of dullness. Alternatively, sharpen them every few weeks, whether or not they feel dull. Using a traditional whetstone with a little oil or running water is one of the easiest ways to sharpen knives. You can purchase a whetstone wherever quality knives are sold.

Cutting Boards   A spacious cutting board helps you cook without feeling cramped. Wood is the best option, since it's a natural material and the most forgiving on sharp knives. It's beneficial to have one primary cutting board for fruits and vegetables and a separate cutting board for garlic, onions, and anything else with a strong flavor that may linger on other foods. Non-vegetarians should also have a separate cutting board reserved exclusively for meats, to avoid the risk of cross-contamination from bacteria.

Keep your cutting boards clean, washing them thoroughly with hot, soapy water, and dry them thoroughly after each washing. This is doubly important if you are cutting meat, since bacterial residue may cling to the board. Rubbing a few drops of grape seed extract on the board after washing helps cure and clean the wood. If you prefer plastic cutting boards, use those made with a composite surface.

Pans   Favor durable, stainless-steel pans with bases of copper-and-silver alloy. These distribute heat evenly and withstand the test of time. Also look for pans with handles that don't conduct heat, and reinforced rims that ensure smooth pouring. Basic pan sizes include: 6 ¼ inches, 8 ½ inches, and 9 inches. A shallow 4-inch pan is also useful for heating herbs and spices. High-quality pans will cost more, but they also last much longer and produce far better results, making them a worthwhile investment for any kitchen.

Note that the word "pot" is often used synonymously with "pan" in the West. A pan is a cooking vessel with a single, long handle. A pot, on the other hand, has two small handles on either side.

Sauté Pans and Frying Pans   Sauté pans are practical and versatile. Since you can cook just about anything in them, it's always good to have a 10-to-12-inch sauté pan on hand. Most sauté pans have sloping sides and are fairly lightweight. Traditional frying pans are slightly heavier, a bit deeper, and have straight sides. The functions of these pans are similar, so you can choose whichever works best for you. Having a pan with a lid is helpful when you want to retain moisture and heat while slow-cooking foods.

Always choose stainless-steel or cast-iron pans. Nonstick, aluminum, and other varieties may leech harmful substances into food as they deteriorate.

Pots   A large, stainless-steel stockpot is useful for cooking larger quantities of soups or stews.

Mortar and Pestle   Hand-grinding foods with a mortar and pestle has a wonderfully ancient quality to it. While the task is a little more work, manually grinding herbs and spices unlocks their hidden flavors with surprising precision. Often, when you use an electric grinder, it's easy to overdo such tasks.

Stone mortars and grinding slabs are widely employed in traditional Ayurvedic cooking. Wooden, metal, and ceramic mortars are also commonly used around the world. If you use a wooden mortar, note that the wood will retain the odor of whatever you grind. So you may want to reserve it only for select items such as garlic or pungent spices.

Spoons   Wooden spoons are inexpensive and stay cool in your hand during cooking. Buy a set of wooden spoons with a variety of sizes. A metal soup ladle and slotted spoon (the one with holes in it) are also useful.

Whisks   Whisks are used to beat, whip, or lightly mix ingredients. There's a wide variety of whisks tailored to different culinary tasks. Metal balloon whisks are great for smoothing out lumps in sauces. Wooden or straw whisks are helpful for more delicate mixing needs.

Steaming Baskets   Collapsible steaming baskets are commonly made from stainless steel. These baskets fold and unfold like the petals of a flower to fit the cooking vessel in which you place them, while remaining elevated a few inches above water. To use a steaming basket, put a few inches of water in the bottom of a pan, place food in the basket, and cover the top with a lid. Within minutes, the steam will begin cooking the food. Chinese stackable bamboo steamers, which sit on top of a cooking vessel and come with their own lids, work in a similar way and add a beautiful element to food presentation.

Grater/Shredders   An upright box grater/shredder is typically used for grating fine particles or cutting thin or thick shreds of vegetables and hard cheeses. Smaller handheld versions are useful for adding bits of these foods to individual plates.

Measuring Cups and Spoons   If you're just learning to cook, you'll find these to be essential tools. As you become more familiar with measurements, you'll find that you can often simply eyeball amounts and know they're correct. Many cooks attribute their creative flair to this style of improvisational cooking.

There are two basic kinds of measuring cups: one for dry ingredients and one for wet. Dry measuring cups have a straight rim that allows for evenly leveling off ingredients, while wet measuring cups have an indented rim to make pouring easy. Sets of measuring spoons are also useful for smaller ingredients such as herbs and spices.

Baking Sheets　Baking sheets are useful for baking a wide variety of foods. They usually have a ½-inch raised side and vary greatly in length and width. Be sure to choose a tray that will fit easily in your oven.

Strainers　Fine-meshed metal strainers are useful for straining pasta and vegetables. They're also handy for sifting flour and for rinsing vegetables, grains, and dried legumes.

Timer　Your senses will provide you with the most information about whether or not food is ready. A timer, however, may come in handy as a reminder if you're doing many things at once.

Pressure Cooker　Many people shy away from cooking beans because the soaking and cooking process is too lengthy. A pressure cooker greatly reduces the cooking time for beans and requires no presoaking. It's also great for speeding up the cooking time of dense, hearty vegetables such as beets and potatoes.

Tea Kettle and Bulk Tea Strainer　Did we mention that Chef Johnny is English? A high-quality, stainless-steel or copper tea kettle is a useful part of any Ayurvedic kitchen. While you can always simply heat up water in a pan, a whistling kettle is a convenient tool.

It's also helpful to have a small tea strainer for bulk or loose-leaf teas. They come in a variety of sizes and styles and can be used for either a single cup or larger pots.

ELECTRICAL APPLIANCES

Blender　Whether puréeing a soup or making a smoothie, a blender is one of the most useful appliances around. Handheld blenders let you blend directly in a glass, bowl, or pot.

Food Processor　Food processors are time-saving, do-it-all-for-you appliances. They chop, grate, mix, shred, slice, and grind. Although food processors take you away from the intimate process of cooking, they may prove invaluable when you're short on time or cooking for a large number of people.

Spice Grinder　If a mortal and pestle is too time-consuming for you, try using an electric coffee bean grinder for grinding spices and herbs. It requires little effort and is useful for powdering roasted spices. Designate a separate grinder for coffee to avoid mixing flavors.

Crock Pot or Slow Cooker　Crock pots are popular because you don't really have to do much to cook. Simply put in the ingredients and let them sit for hours. If you have limited cooking time, this may be a valuable option. Highly regarded dishes in Ayurveda, such as Kitchari (see page 212) and one-pot meals, can be made easily in a slow cooker.

Basic Techniques and Practical Routines

Kitchen Sattva

"Your kitchen is a sanctuary and your cooking is an expression of love…"

According to Ayurveda, the consciousness of the cook directly affects the food itself. Sattva is the essence of purity, creativity, and light. A sattvic chef naturally infuses loving energy into every dish. An angry or resentful chef, on the other hand, infuses food with negativity. Cooking is an opportunity to create, share and discover. As you participate in this celebration of life, nourish yourself and others with vibrant, healing foods.

Sattva extends to the kitchen environment itself. A clean kitchen, with adequate air flow and light, sets the stage for creation. Indoor plants, fresh flowers, fruit, and music will transform even the dullest kitchen into a space of inspiration and beauty. Personal cleanliness is also essential. Always wash your hands before cooking and tie

your hair back if necessary. When cooking for others, keep a separate utensil nearby for testing the food. Be sure to rinse this after each testing. Traditional Ayurvedic cooks prefer never to test food while it's cooking, taking cues, instead, from the other four senses.

Developing Practical Routines

It's probably no surprise to you by now that different constitutional types will approach cooking differently. The creative Vata type may scoff at ever following a recipe, while a Pitta type may follow every recipe down to the last fraction of a teaspoon. A Kapha type may favor recipes passed down through generations and shy away from anything new or different.

No matter what your cooking style, establishing simple routines will make the act of cooking a graceful process. Routines are meant to facilitate a smooth, enjoyable flow within the kitchen, rather than restrict creative flair. If you're new to cooking, creating practical routines will allow you to experiment without becoming overwhelmed by the details of cooking.

Create Shopping Lists

If you're a Pitta type, you probably have this one covered already. While it's permissible to substitute ingredients, a good cook knows that one ingredient can make or break a dish. By creating shopping lists, you're more likely to have your bases covered when it's showtime in the kitchen. Taking time to create lists will also help familiarize you with dosha-specific ingredients. In beginning to shop Ayurvedically, we recommend referring to the section entitled, Stocking Your Ayurevdic Pantry on page 106 and the Dosha Food Lists on page 319.

PRE-PLAN MEALS AND MENUS

Take some time over the weekend to write down a quick outline of the week's meals. While this outline can change at any time, the very act will reduce stress over the thought of "What's for dinner tonight?" You may find that you have an Italian dish planned one night, but you're really in the mood for Mexican. So make the Mexican dish and reserve the other dish for another night. Pre-planning meals is particularly helpful if you're cooking for a family.

RECRUIT HELP FROM YOUR FAMILY

If you typically carry most of the responsibility in the kitchen, try recruiting your family to help. Designate jobs and make these a regular fixture. All of the peripheral tasks associated with cooking, such as setting and clearing the table, washing the dishes, and even chopping the salad ingredients can be divided up among your tribe.

The five senses are highly valued tools in the Ayurvedic kitchen. By engaging your senses in the cooking process, you will develop a deeper understanding of the qualities of food. Feeling unique textures in your hands, smelling distinct aromas, and learning to prepare foods from their fresh, natural states all impart valuable information about food's effect on the body. And by participating more directly in the process of cooking, you impart more of your own loving spirit (the most essential ingredient!) into the food you prepare.

You may also find that trading off cooking days will provide you with greater creative inspiration in the kitchen. If you're not responsible for cooking every single meal, it's easier to put more time and effort into the meals you do cook.

PREPARE A FEW CARRY-OVER ITEMS EACH WEEK

Ayurveda always recommends eating fresh foods rather than leftovers. But if it's a matter of eating a pre-packaged, microwave dinner over a freshly cooked meal from yesterday, we say go for the leftovers. If you don't have time to cook every day, prepare a few dishes each week that will last more than one meal. Grains and beans are two of the best foods to carry over in this way. They stay relatively fresh and lend themselves to a variety of dishes. That said, however, try to avoid eating leftovers that are more than a day old.

MISE EN PLACE

Pronounced *meez ahn plahs*, this French term from professional kitchens means "put in place." Before starting to cook, have all of your ingredients prepared and measured as directed in the recipes and lined up in the order you'll be using them. Also have all the kitchen tools and serving pieces you'll need ready to go. This is a great way for novice cooks to become more prepared and organized in the kitchen.

SOAK AND SPROUT IN ADVANCE

By pre-planning meals, you're less likely to fall into the dilemma of wanting to cook a specific recipe but not having, say, any soaked legumes on hand. Since many legumes must be soaked overnight, it's wise to have plenty of foresight in this area. The same goes for sprouts, since many take a number of days to germinate. If you know

BASIC COOKING TECHNIQUES

All great cooks have a few basic cooking techniques at their disposal. These serve as the underlying foundation for all culinary exploration.

For readers who are new to cooking, we've defined the most important techniques to help familiarize you with the language of cooking. In reading these, you'll be able to navigate the recipes in this book with greater ease.

Bake   To cook uncovered, within the hot, dry air of an oven.

Blanch   To boil in water for a short time and then plunge into cold water. Or to pour boiling water over food and then drain it immediately. Blanching is used to pre-cook some foods before combining them with others, for more evenly cooked final results.

Boil   To cook in boiling water or other liquids. Liquid is at a full boil when large bubbles continuously rise to its surface.

Braise   To brown in oil, then slowly cook in a covered pan with added liquid over low heat. Braising can be done on top of the stove or in the oven.

Broil   To cook under the direct heat of a broiler element, usually found in the tops of most home ovens.

Grill   To cook food on a metal rack or grid suspended over an open flame or glowing coals.

Pan-Fry   To cook in a frying pan, sauté pan, or skillet in a small amount of oil.

Poach   To cook gently in water, broth, wine, or other liquid that is barely simmering. Spices, herbs, and other flavorings are typically added to the liquid.

Purée   To liquefy solid foods.

Roast   To cook uncovered in a hot oven. Roasting is similar to baking but usually done at higher temperatures.

Sauté   To cook smaller or thinner pieces of food quickly over high heat until brown on all sides. Usually done in a sauté pan using a small amount of oil.

Sear   To quickly brown all surfaces over high heat, using a small amount of oil in a pan or skillet. Similar to sautéing but usually done for a shorter period of time and as the preliminary step in a longer cooking process, rather than as an end in itself.

Simmer   To cook in liquid at a low temperature.

Steam   To cook over boiling water or another liquid.

Stir-Fry   To cook in a wok or pan in a small amount of oil, while rapidly stirring. A wok is a deep bowl made of thin metal, popular in Asian kitchens.

SOAKING & SPROUTING

Soaking is an effective way to increase the digestibility of nuts, seeds, dried fruit, dried sea vegetables, and other ingredients. It's particularly beneficial for making dry foods more Vata-friendly. See the chart below for sample soaking times.

Sprouting, the process by which certain grains, nuts, seeds, and legumes germinate and send out tender shoots, is a method used to maximize the energetic vitality of these nutrient-rich ingredients. Sprouts abound in vitamins, minerals, enzymes, phytonutrients, and protein. There are several common methods of sprouting. Using a glass jar is one of the easiest and safest methods.

GLASS JAR SPROUTING

You will need a wide-mouth glass jar (1 quart) and a fine mesh screen (available at health food or hardware stores). Some health food stores also sell sprouting kits specifically designed for this purpose.

1 Place the seeds, grains, nuts, or legumes in the jar and secure the mesh screen over mouth of jar with a rubber band.

2 Fill the jar with filtered water and soak according to the chart on page 328.

3 Drain the water and rinse the seeds at least two times, draining all water.

4 Keep the jar at room temperature, away from direct sunlight, and positioned at an inverted angle to ensure further drainage (a raised dish rack works well).

5 Rinse the seeds 2 or 3 times per day until ready; see the chart for approximate sprouting times and the lengths of sprouts when ready to eat.

Sprouts begin to spoil quite rapidly, so it's best to use them as soon as they're ready. Storing sprouts in the refrigerator will retard spoilage, but it will also lessen their vitality. Lightly stir-frying sprouts in a small quantity of oil will make them easier to digest (especially for Vata types). The versatility of sprouts makes them a valuable cooking ingredient. You can use them as simple salad toppers or as the primary ingredients for main dishes. See page 174 for Johnny's Sprouted Wheat Bread. Also, see the Sprouting Chart on page 328 for approximate sprouting times.

SOAKING CHART

Sprout	Time	Water Temperature
Almonds*	10 hours	Warm
Walnuts	10 hours	Warm
Flax seeds	6 hours	Cool
Sunflower seeds	6 hours	Cool
Raisins	30 minutes	Warm
Prunes	30 minutes	Warm
Nori	30 minutes	Warm

* Almond skins can irritate the intestinal lining. It's best to remove them before consuming.

you're going to require chickpeas on Tuesday night, for example, include a note next to your Monday night menu plan to begin soaking them.

STOCKING YOUR AYURVEDIC PANTRY

To help you begin to cook Ayurvedically, we also recommend stocking up on a few basic food items. These are items that you'll either use repeatedly in cooking or want to keep stocked in your "kitchen pharmacy" for medicinal uses. Some of the items (especially the spices) may be new to you, but you should be able to find them at your local health food store. In many cases, you can also find these spices at larger supermarkets. Buying in bulk is the cheapest way to stock your pantry. Store bulk items in airtight glass containers (such as mason jars). And, as always, favor organic ingredients whenever possible.

STORING FOOD

Always use glass containers for storing ingredients over longer periods. These create an airtight seal that keeps food fresh. Many plastic containers are oxygen permeable. They can also leech harmful chemicals into food, making them unhealthy options. If you use plastic containers for short-term storage (such as for leftovers), avoid placing hot food directly into them. Heat causes the chemicals in plastic to release more quickly. Metal tins and thermoses are also convenient for short-term storage, such as for work lunches and snacks. Also choose waxed paper or freezer paper over plastic wrap and aluminum foil.

It's best to store cooking oils in cool, dark places. Favor brands that come in opaque glass containers, and avoid oils packaged in clear plastic. Most oils should be kept

refrigerated after first use in order to avoid rapid oxidation. Stable oils such as ghee and olive oil are exceptions to this rule.

SEASONAL FOODS & SUSTAINABLE SOLUTIONS

Eating fresh, local, seasonal foods is a great way to connect to the land around you. Through eating seasonally, you attune yourself with the cycles of Mother Nature. There's a reason juicy peaches ripen in the Summertime and root vegetables prosper in colder seasons: the qualities of the foods naturally balance the elements at play in nature.

We require more hydrating and Pitta-pacifying foods in the Summer, so Mother Nature offers us sweet, delectable fruits literally bursting with juices. In colder seasons, we require more warming, Vata-pacifying foods, so heavier grains and vegetables are offered in abundance. If you've ever eaten fresh foods from a garden or local farm, you know the experience is nothing short of divine. The food tastes particularly vibrant, and you may even sense a greater degree of harmony in the way your body utilizes the food.

Getting to Know Grains

Despite the multitude of whole grains available today, it's common to be able to identify less than five. If you're only familiar with a few grains, try taking a "grain quiz" the next time you stock your pantry. Buy small amounts of as many grains as you can find and place them in labeled mason jars. Turn the labels away from you and see how many you can identify. This is an easy way to learn about new grains. Better yet, use the cooking chart on page 327 to taste each grain over a period of time.

Buying Spices

Start by buying an ounce of the spices you desire, along with a case of glass spice bottles, individual labels and a spice rack. You can also buy pre-bottled spices, however this will be more costly.

Fresh Foods
- A variety of fresh fruits & vegetables
- Chilis
- Herbs (cilantro, mint, rosemary, etc.)
- Garlic bulbs
- Ginger root
- Lemons & limes
- Milk
- Onions
- Yogurt

Nuts & Seeds
- Almonds
- Flax seeds
- Peanuts
- Pine nuts
- Pumpkin seeds
- Sesame seeds
- Walnuts

Grains
- Amaranth
- Basmati rice, white & brown
- Brown rice, short-grain
- Barley
- Buckwheat
- Couscous
- Millet
- Oats
- Quinoa

Sweeteners
- Brown rice syrup
- Maple syrup
- Raw honey
- Stevia
- Sucanat
  (*brand name for organic dehydrated cane sugar juice*)

Legumes
- Black beans
- Black-eyed peas
- Brown lentils
- Chickpeas
- Mung dhal, whole
- Pinto beans
- Red lentils
- Split mung dhal

- Tempeh
- Tofu

Oils
- Ghee
- Olive oil
- Sesame oil
- Sunflower or safflower oil

Dried Fruit
- Dates
- Raisins

Basic Spices & Herbs
- Asafetida (*a.k.a.* Hing)
- Bay leaves
- Black pepper
- Cumin seed, whole, ground
- Cardamom, whole, ground
- Cayenne
- Cinnamon sticks, powder
- Cloves, whole
- Coriander seed
- Curry powder

- Dill seed
- Fennel seed
- Fenugreek seed
- Garam masala powder
- Garlic powder
- Ginger powder
- Mint
- Mustard seeds, black & yellow
- Nutmeg, ground or whole
- Oregano
- Paprika
- Parsley
- Sage
- Rosemary
- Saffron
- Sea Salt
- Tarragon
- Thyme
- Turmeric
- Vanilla

As food consciousness has increased in recent years, it has become much easier to buy local and seasonal foods. Farmers' markets, self-pick farms, and roadside stands are now staples once again in many communities. Food Co-ops and CSA (Community-Supported Agriculture) have also risen in popularity in recent years. If you're unfamiliar with these terms, we've provided a quick overview below. Supporting sustainable agricultural practices is a better choice for your health, your tastebuds, and the planet.

Food Co-ops

Food co-ops adhere to the motto: "Food for people, not for profit." Co-ops are worker- and customer-owned businesses that offer high-quality foods without the middle-man costs. Co-ops may take the form of traditional retail stores or community buying clubs. Every member is part owner and enjoys significant cost reductions and decision-making rights. Most co-ops also support their local communities by selling organic, seasonal produce grown on local family farms. (See Resources on page 333 to find a co-op in your area).

Community-Supported Agriculture (CSA)

CSA is a strategy for connecting local farmers with local consumers. A community of supporters buys shares in a particular farm, in return for a commitment by the farmers to supply seasonal, fresh produce (usually organic) throughout the growing season. Member shares cover the yearly operating budget of the farm, with one share typically providing the weekly vegetable needs for a family of four. Fruit, honey, eggs, meat, dairy products, and flowers are also often provided.

In addition to its cost-saving advantages, CSA provides an opportunity to connect with the people who till the soil to produce your food. By bringing the act of food purchasing closer to home, you know exactly what's on your plate and also form a deeper relationship to the seasonal growing patterns in your area. The roots of CSA trace back thirty years to a model started by a group of Japanese women concerned about the impacts of food imports on local farming. This model, called *teikei*, translates as "putting the farmer's face on food." Today there are thousands of CSA farms across the United States, Canada, and Europe. (See Resources on page 333 to find CSA opportunities in your area.)

Composting

Composting is the process of transforming food, plant remains, and other organic matter into nutrient-rich fertilizer. It's cheap, easy, and is an ancient practice that benefits both you and the environment. All you have to do is make or buy a compost bin for your yard and commit to throwing natural items such as fruits, vegetables, and leaves into this bin. As compost breaks down, it feeds millions of tiny microorganisms, which release nitrogen, potassium, and phosphorous into the compost matter. Adding these nutrients to soil improves fertility and supports healthy root development. Compost is ready to use when it turns into a dark brown, earthy-smelling matter. After letting the matter break down for usually 6 to 8 weeks, depending on what materials you're composting, you're left with rich, healthy fertilizer to use in your garden or flower beds. You can compost a wide variety of organic matter.

Do Compost	Don't Compost
Fruit and vegetable scraps	Dairy products
Cardboard (small quantities)	Fats and oils
Cardboard tubes	Meat
Paper towels	Fish
Egg boxes	Salad dressings
Eggshells	Nut butters
Tea bags	Newspaper
Coffee grounds	Glossy paper
Flowers	
Grass cuttings	
Weeds	
Hedge clippings	
Straw and hay	
Autumn leaves	
Animal manure (chicken, cow, horse)	
Wood ash	

Grass cuttings, and young weeds are great activators to speed up the composting process. It's recommended always to include both "greens" (such as kitchen scraps and grass clippings) and "browns" (such as dried leaves and paper products) to create a balanced ratio of nitrogen- and carbon-rich ingredients. It's also best to break down paper products and other tough materials by tearing or chopping them before adding them to your bin.

An outdoor bin is used to contain the compost during the maturation process. You can build your own bin or purchase one at any lawn and garden center. These are made from wood, wire, or plastic and are available in a variety of shapes and sizes. They require little yard space and can be chosen to blend in with their surroundings. You should also keep a small, airtight bin in your kitchen to collect wastes. Empty this into the outdoor bin whenever it gets full, being sure to cover the additions with a few inches of brown matter each time.

Today, it's estimated that one-third of all landfill space is used for dumping organic matter. Most of this could be better used for creating rich, fertile soil. Whether used for home gardening or larger-scale farming, the benefits of composting are mutual: We take care of the planet and are rewarded with one of nature's greatest fertilizers.

If you live in an apartment or don't have a garden, there are still ways to compost your kitchen wastes. For example, many urban centers now have compost drop-off locations, usually located at farmers' markets. Or if you have a friend or neighbor who composts, they will almost certainly welcome more matter into their own bins. (See Resources on page 333 for further information on composting).

Herb Gardening

Planting your own herb garden is the best way to keep stocked up on fresh herbs. Home-grown herbs also taste better, cost less, and are a great way to enjoy the beauty and bounty of your land, even if that land is confined to a window box. It also feels wonderful to eat something you planted yourself.

Sustainable Solutions

1 Recycle whenever possible; especially glass, plastic, aluminum, paper products, and organic waste (through composting).
2 Purchase reusable canvas bags for grocery shopping.
3 Use nontoxic, biodegradable products in your household.
4 Drive a fuel efficient car; carpool, bicycle, walk, and use public transportation more often.
5 Plant an organic garden.

3

THE ABCS: AMBIANCE, BLESSING & CONSUMPTION

Ambiance: Setting the Stage
Blessing: Giving Thanks
Consumption: How We Eat to Heal

AMBIANCE: SETTING THE STAGE

When you think of an important family dinner or a romantic dinner for two, what kind of ambiance comes to mind? Most likely, it doesn't include a messy table or the buzz of a television set in the background. Instead, you take extra measures to create a beautiful and peaceful dining environment. You put greater care into the food, ensuring it's freshly prepared and appetizing to both the eyes and the tastebuds.

Rather than making such habits a once- or twice-a-year rarity, we encourage you to make it the norm. That doesn't mean you have to break out the fancy dishware and spend hours preparing for every meal. Instead, just try to give greater attention to the entire process of eating, from how the dining environment feels to how good the food looks on your plate.

A pleasing ambiance complements the entire digestive process. When the senses are satiated and the body is relaxed, the digestive process is able to carry out its job more effectively. Loud background noises, heated conversations, and rushed meals create underlying tensions in the body. These force the body to work harder, thus inhibiting optimal digestion and assimilation. Mealtime should be a time to relax while enjoying the company of family, friends, and great food.

When you dine out, also choose restaurants with a pleasing ambiance. If budgetary constraints limit your options, always try to pick tables that are a healthy distance from foot traffic and kitchens. And never feel embarrassed to ask to switch tables. Even in places with no ambiance, you can usually find a way to make things a little more comfortable.

Simple recommendations for improving dining ambiance at home:

- Thoroughly clean the dining space.
- Simplify the space, making it less cluttered.
- Place fresh flowers and plants on or near the table.
- Play gentle, soothing music in the background.
- Dim the lights a bit or eat by candlelight.
- Coordinate tableware and dishware with the meal.
- Turn off any TVs, radios, or telephones.
- Leave reading materials outside the dining area.
- Fill the room with a subtle, soothing fragrance before the meal, such as candles, incense, or essential oils.
- Bring beauty into the space through decorations and art.
- Dress a little nicer than usual.
- Bring a calm disposition to the table, leaving all battles behind.

BLESSING: GIVING THANKS

The gift of food nurtures and sustains all life. Giving thanks for food is one of humanity's most ancient forms of expression and prayer. While typically an acknowledgement of some higher power or divine order in life, this act is not bound to any one faith or correct method. It is an integral part of all religious and spiritual traditions and may be expressed in an infinite number of ways.

Offering a blessing, prayer, or simple thought of gratitude before a meal, either out loud or in silence, is a way to honor the gift of food and the greater blessings of life. It's also a wonderful opportunity to downshift a few gears and harmonize with your fellow diners and environment. During this time, the mind becomes quiet as attention is turned towards the food and the blessing.

By welcoming food into the body in this way, you also bring greater awareness to the act of eating itself. With this heightened awareness, you'll find that poor eating habits will naturally transform into healthier ones. For example, instead of gulping down a lunch with hardly a thought, you'll be more inclined to chew and savor your food thoroughly. You'll also be more likely to consider whether the food is balancing to your overall constitution.

Offering food to a higher power through prayer, ritual, chanting, or any other mindful, spiritual practice is another important form of blessing. Cultures around the globe have offered their food in these ways for millennia. According to Vedic wisdom, *prasadam*, or offered food, becomes charged with Divine energy.

CONSUMPTION: HOW WE EAT TO HEAL

10 TIPS FOR **HOW** TO EAT HEALTHFULLY

1 **Eat in a Quiet, Settled Atmosphere**

A quiet, settled atmosphere promotes ideal digestion. Dividing your eating time by watching TV, reading, or engaging in heated discussions, on the other hand, compromises the entire digestive process. If eating is just another obligation on your daily to-do list, try approaching it as a time both to relax and to recharge. Also try focusing on the food itself while savoring its flavors and textures.

2 **Offer a Blessing or a Simple Thought of Gratitude Before Eating**

See *Blessing: Giving Thanks.*

Blessings

A few blessings from around the globe:

Sahanavavatu-Let's be together. *Sahanau bhunaktu*-Let's share a meal together. *Sah veeryan karvavahai*-Let's be vital together. *Tejas vina vadhi tamastu ma vidvishavahai*-Let's be radiant together and dispel darkness and negativity in the world around us. *Om Shanti Shanti Shanti!* May peace prevail!

- Traditional Vedic Blessings

Spirit, Changing Mother, We are grateful for the two legged, four legged, wingged, plant and mineral kingdoms, finned and creepy crawlies, all those that have sacrificed so that we might be sustained. For our lives we are grateful. And bless the cook! Daaiina (and so it is).

- Quero Apache blessing

Bread is a lovely thing to eat; God bless the barley and the wheat. A lovely thing to breathe is air; God bless the sunshine everywhere. Alive is a lovely thing to be; Giver of life, we say, bless thee.

- Anonymous

The silver rain, the shining sun, The fields where scarlet poppies run, And all the ripples of the wheat, Are in the bread that I do eat, So when I sit for every meal, And say a grace, I always feel, That I am eating rain and sun, And fields where scarlet poppies run.

- Anonymous

As this food and its life energy enters our bodies and becomes our bodies, may our minds be opened, our hearts be inspired, and our bodies be nourished, so that our words and actions be living manifestations of our unique expressions of the Divine Love within.

- Dr. Tom

3 Only Eat When You are Hungry

As simple as it sounds, eating when you are hungry is one of the most important components of healthy eating. When you are hungry, agni is burning hotter. That is why your stomach may growl when you haven't eaten for a while. These messages are an indication that your body craves nourishment. When agni is burning strong, the entire digestive process is primed to carry out its job effectively. Eating when you are not hungry, however, is like putting too much wood on a fire—the digestive fire will eventually be snuffed out. This in turn leads to sub-optimal digestion and assimilation, thus creating ama, the toxic by-product of poor digestion. So, eat when you are hungry, and resist eating when you are not. It certainly sounds simple enough!

4 Wait Until the Previous Meal is Digested Before Eating Again

It usually takes three to six hours to digest a meal, depending on an individual's constitution. A Pitta person, for example, will digest faster than a Kapha person, due to a faster metabolism. In order to avoid dousing the fire as mentioned above, you must allow the digestive system ample time to do its work. That is why Ayurveda recommends waiting until a meal is digested before eating again. You'll know it's time to eat again when you feel hungry and have a sense of lightness in your belly. For snacking, it's always important to take into account your unique constitution. Through choosing lighter snacks that balance your constitution, you can satisfy those between-meal cravings without overwhelming your digestive fire.

5 Chew Your Food Thoroughly and Eat at a Moderate Pace

If hunger seems to trigger an unconscious "inhale" mechanism when you eat, remember to chew, chew,

chew. Proper digestion and assimilation require that food be sufficiently broken down and pre-digested before reaching the stomach. That is why we are equipped with sharp teeth and enzyme-loaded saliva. It's estimated that we digest over 40 percent of complex carbohydrates during the process of chewing alone. Ayurveda, therefore, considers proper chewing an integral component of any weight-loss program. Chewing your food thoroughly will also automatically regulate your eating pace, while unlocking the true flavor and essence of the food itself.

6 Eat to a Point of Comfort

How many times have you ended a meal and thought or said, "I just knew I shouldn't have eaten that last piece of (fill in the blank)"? To avoid this, try eating up until the point you feel satisfied but not yet full. If you fill your stomach with too much food, there's simply not enough room for the digestive process to take place. Since it's often dessert that puts us over the edge, take this into consideration ahead of time by leaving room for dessert. The stomach expands when we eat, so also make sure you're not experiencing false hunger. Take time to pause during a meal and observe whether your body truly desires that last helping.

7 Postpone Eating If You are Upset

If you've ever eaten after an argument (or worse, during an argument), you've probably noticed that your stomach doesn't respond well. The tightening muscles and tension directly counter the mechanisms required to digest food properly. Or maybe you have experienced reaching for the ice cream when you're upset, only to feel worse later. It's always best to postpone eating when you're in an emotionally heightened state—particularly a negative state, though excess excitement can also hinder the proper course of digestion. That is not to say eating should be devoid of the laughs and sharing that make dining such an integral component of the human experience. Instead, just learn to check in with yourself to assess whether you need some time to calm down before eating.

8 Always Sit Down to Eat

In an age where eating on the run is a common occurrence, remembering to sit when you eat is even more important. Sitting down to eat helps the body to relax, thus allowing the digestive process to begin effortlessly. Food eaten while standing or walking, on the other hand, requires greater energy and effort to digest. Therefore, always try to sit down when you eat, even if it's just for a snack.

9 Eat Around the Same Time Each Day

The body is a truly awesome yet delicate timepiece. Attuning this timepiece with the natural rhythms of nature is one of the fundamental aims of Ayurveda. It's not a coincidence that lunchtime coincides with noontime each day: at this point of the day, the sun is highest and agni is strongest. By eating in accordance with the rhythms of nature, you directly support your body's underlying makeup. Eating meals at regular times also ensures you're properly nourished and energized throughout the day. It's also a great way to keep food cravings in check and to avoid overeating.

10 Rest for a Few Minutes After Each Meal

Similar to sitting down when you eat, resting for a few minutes after a meal allows digestion to begin effortlessly. So rather than jumping up after your last bite of food, take a few minutes to relax and enjoy the feeling of being satiated.

5 Tips for **What** to Eat Healthfully

1 Include All 6 Tastes in Each Meal

The 6 Tastes of food (Sweet, Sour, Salty, Bitter, Pungent, and Astringent) offer a complete guidemap to balanced nutrition. By including the 6 Tastes in each meal, we nourish the three doshas at our core. Each taste feeds the mind, body, senses, and spirit in its own unique way. From a modern nutritional perspective, the 6 Tastes satisfy each of the major dietary building blocks. By incorporating the 6 Tastes into each meal, we encompass the complete nutritional spectrum.

2 Eat According to Your Individual Constitution

As you begin to tune into your underlying nature, you'll instinctively seek out foods with balancing tastes, while avoiding those of an aggravating nature. You may find that Pungent salsa fires up your underlying Pitta constitution, while Bitter leafy greens are cooling. Or perhaps a Sweet dessert feels like a weighty brick to your Kaphic constitution, while an Astringent snack like popcorn is both light and energizing.

Ayurveda favors experiential learning over dogmatic adherence to a set of rules, so experiment to establish what works best for you. Seemingly random attractions, reactions, or distastes for certain foods will suddenly become much clearer. As you develop awareness for your true dietary needs, you'll discover the ability to fine-tune your health through food. If you're currently in a state of imbalance, you'll also learn to self-treat with every bite of food you eat.

3 Favor Fresh, High-Quality, Organic Foods

In order to eat healthfully you must first make a conscious decision to buy or grow healthy foods. Always favor fresh, natural foods over processed and packaged foods.

Also avoid food additives such as artificial sweeteners and colors. As a general rule, the fewer wrappers you have to open, the more natural your diet will be!

Buying organically is the best way to ensure you're eating high-quality, natural foods. It's also the only way to avoid residues from pesticides and herbicides, as well as genetically modified ingredients. In addition to essential nutrients, fresh, clean foods are packed full of prana, the greater life force that gives us energy and vitality.

4 Avoid Cold and Carbonated Drinks with Meals

Drinking cold fluids with meals directly inhibits the digestive fire. Cold drinks serve as a mild shock to the entire digestive system and are particularly ill-suited to Vata and Kapha types. Carbonated drinks hamper digestion by creating excess gas in the stomach. If you're prone to reach for soda at mealtimes, try replacing it with warm water or tea. Pitta types have the greatest tolerance for cold drinks, but are still advised to avoid them with meals.

In general, it's also best to avoid drinking too many liquids at mealtime. Small sips of warm water or tea, however, will aid the digestive process without diminishing agni. Ayurveda also recommends drinking a glass of room temperature water an hour after eating, while food is in the Pitta stage of digestion.

5 Practice Proper Food Combining Techniques

You've probably noticed that certain foods simply don't go together. Beyond just taste and culinary sense, however, certain combinations of food actually create unwanted by-products in the gut. Drinking orange juice and milk at breakfast, for example, may create a curdling in the stomach that makes digestion difficult. Ayurveda identifies a number of food combinations to avoid,

Quick Tips by Food Group

Fruit and Vegetables

Favor organic, in-season fruits and vegetables. Gently wash all fruits and vegetables with filtered water before eating.

Grains

Steamed whole grains are easiest to digest. Mixing grains together is also a beneficial way to broaden the nutritional spectrum of a meal. Equal proportions of brown basmati rice, quinoa, and wild rice make an especially protein-rich combination.

Legumes

Mung beans are the easiest legume to digest for all three doshas. Pre-soaking legumes and adding proper spices while cooking greatly increases their digestibility. Onions, cumin, asafetida, cayenne, and salt are particularly beneficial.

Dairy

Always favor organic cow's milk over conventional milk. Bringing milk to a boil and allowing it to cool greatly increases its digestibility. Spicing milk with digestive herbs such as ginger, cardamom and cumin also makes it more digestible. Black pepper, cumin, cayenne, and salt improve the digestibility of yogurt.

Meats

Cooking meat with digestive herbs and spices, such as cumin, fennel, garlic or salt greatly increase its digestibility. Avoid buying meat packaged in foam and sealed with plastic wrap, due to potential toxicity.

Oils

Choose organic, cold-pressed oils to avoid rancidity.

Nuts and Seeds

Favor organic nuts and seeds to avoid rancidity and pesticide toxicity. If buying non-organic nut butters, favor non partially-hydrogenated varieties.

Sweeteners

Favor natural sweeteners such as raw sugar, honey, and maple syrup, while avoiding white sugar altogether.

Condiments

Favor freshly prepared condiments, such as chutneys and churnas (spice mixtures).

Herbs and Spices

Favor garden-fresh herbs and non-irradiated herbs and spices.

many of which relate to combinations with dairy foods.

It's important to note that longstanding habits may not produce recognizable symptoms of imbalance. For example, your body may have adapted to eating a morning omelet with cheese. That, however, does not mean you are any better served by this combination than someone who experiences symptoms of indigestion.

FOOD COMBINATIONS TO AVOID

- Milk with meat, fish, eggs, bananas, yogurt and sour fruits
- Yogurt with milk, eggs, hot drinks, cheese, fish, nightshades (tomatoes, potatoes, and eggplant) and lemons
- Eggs with milk, meat, fish, yogurt, cheese, fruit and beans
- An equal proportion of ghee and honey (i.e. 1 teaspoon ghee and 1 teaspoon honey) creates a subtle toxin in the tissues
- Fresh fruits with any other foods, since many create sour juices or "wines" in the stomach. Cooked fruits are easier to digest with other foods.

4

THE RHYTHMS OF NATURE

THE RHYTHMS OF NATURE: STYLING YOUR LIFESTYLE

If asked to describe your lifestyle, how would you answer? Would you begin by talking about your work, or by offering a general adjective such as "comfortable" to describe your financial means? Or would you talk about your true style of life—how you love, eat, sleep, exercise, play, think, and thrive?

In the West, we often use the term "lifestyle" to denote external or material elements of our lives. In reality, lifestyle—our attitudes and approach towards life—is one of the most significant internal relationships we have to the external world. The importance we place on our health is directly reflected in how we carry out our daily lives. For this reason, lifestyle is an equally powerful component in creating balance or disease.

For millennia, humans rose with the sun, ate fresh locally grown food, celebrated the passing of the moons and seasons, and gave thanks for the abundance of Mother Nature. Human life was intimately interwoven with all forces of nature. As modern technology advances, however, it becomes easier to forget these essential connections. Why should we spend an hour cooking a fresh meal when we can zap a package in the microwave? The answer: because deep down, we truly we want to!

Even when we lose connection with Nature, we retain her vast intelligence in every cell. This is because the same life force and elemental structure permeate the very fabric of our being. A century of electricity or the ability to ship food around the world will not suddenly erase these natural impulses. Instead, they will breed artificial ways of living that end up, over time, creating cycles of imbalance.

That is not to say you need to turn your back upon the modern world. After all, there's much to be said about the way modern life allows us to experience being human in new and exciting ways. Rather, it's about fostering balance in your life in a way that brings you back to your inner wisdom. This wisdom is inseparable from nature's intelligence, so try taking cues from the natural world more often.

Daily, Nightly, Monthly, and Seasonal Rhythms

The Daily Rhythm

I move with the infinite in Nature's power.
I hold the fire of the soul.
I hold life and healing. —Rig Veda

Every day, nature conducts a vast symphony in accordance with certain master cycles. These cycles run parallel to the twenty-four hours in a day, but they long predate our invention of time. The Sun and Seasons are the composers of these underlying cycles, from which the rooster knows when to crow and the flower knows when to bloom.

In studying the daily cycles of the human body, modern science has made some puzzling observations. For example, why are our hands hottest around two o'clock in the morning, and why do people with inflammatory conditions often wake up around that time? Or, why are breathing problems more pronounced in the morning, and why do we typically weigh the most at around seven o'clock in the evening?

Ayurveda answers these questions by identifying inner cycles of the body that correspond to the outer cycles of

nature. These cycles are governed by the rising and setting sun and are characterized by an integral relationship to the three doshas.

Every day, two primary cycles of change occur in the body, each containing a Kapha, Pitta, and Vata phase. The first cycle takes place between sunrise and sunset, and the second takes place between sunset and sunrise. This progression always begins with Kapha characteristics, and is followed by Pitta and Vata characteristics.

The approximate times for these cycles are listed on the following page. Please note that these are general windows of time rather than exact timetables, since the Sun rises and sets at different times throughout the year. Different geographic regions will also experience slight variations within the times associated with these cycles.

Daily Cycle

- 10:00 AM PITTA
- 2:00 PM VATA
- 6:00 AM KAPHA
- 6:00 PM

First Cycle (Daily Rhythm)

KAPHA	6:00am-10:00am
PITTA	10:00am- 2:00pm
VATA	2:00pm- 6:00pm

Second Cycle (Nightly Rhythm)

KAPHA	6:00pm-10:00pm
PITTA	10:00pm- 2:00am
VATA	2:00am- 6:00am

During the daytime cycle, the Sun heats both the Earth and our bodies. We absorb energy from the Sun, as well as information from our surrounding environment. We also absorb nutrients into our bodies through the foods we eat. For these reasons, the daytime cycle is also known as the *accumulation phase*.

The nighttime cycle is a time when both the Earth and our bodies cool down and rest. It's also called the *release phase*.

During this time, our attention turns inward to digest the information, food, and energies of the day. During sleep, nutrients are transformed into bodily tissues, and our daily thoughts, emotions and experiences become our dreams.

Any period of the day or night that corresponds to your predominant dosha will create a greater sensitivity for you during that period. For this reason, it's important to take extra balancing measures during these times.

Sunrise to mid-morning: Sunrise to mid-morning is Kapha in quality. That is why your body may feel a bit slow or heavy during these hours. It's also why you may experience a certain calmness and serenity upon waking. Kapha individuals, in particular, should take extra measures to jump-start their systems during this period.

The digestive fire (agni) is generally low in the morning, especially if you ate a late dinner the night before. Breakfast should, therefore, be easily digestible. Poor digestion at the start of the day quickly leads to ama accumulation. Since this is the Kaphic time of day, Kaphic individuals must be particularly attentive to eating a balanced breakfast. Light, energizing foods are the best choices. Adding heating spices to these foods is also a great way to enliven the digestive fire and quicken metabolism.

Vata individuals frequently have weak agni upon waking, due to their cold, light natures. While they may instinctively want to skip breakfast due to this fact, a nourishing breakfast is especially important for these types. Slightly heavier foods that are highly nutritious yet easily digestible, are the best choices for keeping Vata balanced. A healthy breakfast will also prevent mid-morning low-blood sugar crashes that are common in these types.

Pitta individuals, due to their naturally high digestive fires and strong constitutions, can eat heartily or lightly. Their doshic power will carry them through easily until lunch. Since Pitta types typically hit the ground running in the morning, it's important for them to spend breakfast time sensitizing themselves to the tastes of the food, the environmental ambiance, and the quality of the day about to unfold.

Please see the *Breakfast Archetypes* on page 171 for simple recipes for all three doshas.

Late-morning to mid-afternoon: Late-morning through mid-afternoon is Pitta in quality. The sun and digestive fires hit their peak around noontime. Ayurveda therefore recommends eating the largest meal of the day around this time. There is also a great capacity for both physical and mental tasks leading up to lunch. That is why it's especially important for Pitta types to take time away from work to eat lunch. They should avoid eating in front of computers or conducting business over lunch. Taking a short walk outdoors following lunch will also aid digestion and give the mind a break before heading back to work. Kapha and Vata individuals also benefit from eating lunch in a pleasant atmosphere and taking a walk after lunch.

A need to nap after eating demonstrates that more digestive power is required before energy is available for external expenditure. Many cultures honor this tradition through taking a "siesta," a short nap after lunch. Vata types in particular may benefit from a quick nap to recharge their systems. Kapha types are better served by taking a brisk walk to aid digestion and to counterbalance their natural tendency towards sleepiness.

Please see the *Lunch Archetypes* on page 185.

Mid-afternoon until sunset: Mid-afternoon until sunset is Vata in quality. During this time, the body becomes light and the mind becomes clear, as the digestion of the lunch nears completion. Physical and mental activities also increase in preparation for the day's end. This is a great time for Vata individuals to express themselves and create. It's important, however, for these types to remember to stay grounded during this period, which may require eating a nutritious snack during mid-afternoon. If Pitta and Kapha types are hungry during these hours, they should favor light, energizing snacks.

Please see the *Snack Archetypes* on page 219.

The Nightly Rhythm

Sunset until late evening: Sunset until late-evening is Kapha in quality. During this period, we unwind from the day and enjoy relaxing time with family or friends. By late evening, Kapha becomes heavier as the body and mind prepare for sleep. It's beneficial for Kapha types to perform light activities before dinner, in order to avoid falling asleep too early.

The cooling of both the Earth and our bodies after sunset makes it important not to overwhelm the digestive fire during these hours. Ayurveda recommends eating a light evening meal and allowing food to digest for a few hours before going to bed. It also recommends taking short walks after dinner to stimulate digestion. Food should be freshly prepared, so the vital energy (prana) in the food will properly nourish the body and mind. Eating lifeless or overly heavy foods in the evening will result in ama accumulation. This is particularly the case for Kaphic individuals.

Well-utilized food ensures a sound night's sleep and proper growth of the tissues. Feeding children in accordance with these natural rhythms will also assist in helping them to fall asleep more easily and will also improve their quality of sleep.

Pitta individuals who eat late at night—especially spicy, sour, and salty foods—commonly suffer insomnia or heartburn, due to creating excessive heat in the body. Similar to breakfast time, Vata individuals need to be attentive to their *agni* at dinner time. They will sleep soundly after warming, nourishing, and highly digestible meals. Inappropriate dinners will lead to gas, bloating, and the failure to achieve refreshing sleep. Colic in babies is an example of overtaxing the digestive fire, which in turn aggravates Vata and creates gas and discomfort for the child.

Please see the *Dinner Archetypes* on page 201.

Late evening through early morning: Late-evening through early morning (i.e., a few hours after midnight) is Pitta time. This is a dynamic and paradoxical time. It is the most energetically active time of night, similar to its noontime counterpart, but the energies and consciousness are diverted inwards. The evening meal digests during these hours, along with all of the day's activities, thoughts, feelings, and experiences. The body is also busy both detoxifying and synthesizing new tissues. Individuals whose daily routine, diet, or behavior exceeds their energy capacity during the day will not perform these nightly duties effectively. The quality of sleep will also be diminished, leading to insomnia or intermittent sleep.

It's important for all doshic types to be asleep during these hours for optimal rest and regeneration. This is particularly important for Pitta types who have the natural ability to stay up late. As mentioned above, late dinners and Pitta-aggravating foods will lead to discomfort in Pitta types during these hours.

Early morning through dawn: Early morning through dawn is Vata time. During this period, our bodies' energies and consciousness begin to emerge gently back into our waking environment. Active dream sleep ('rapid eye movement' or REM sleep) increases during this time. Involuntary nervous system activity, such as the peristalsis of the intestines and the circulation of energy into the muscles, also increases. Imbalances within the body will manifest during this time in the form of waking up to use the bathroom, excessive tossing and turning, or awakening due to arthritic or neurological pains. Vata individuals need to pay particular attention to their daily routine to ensure a graceful entry into the new day.

Ayurveda recommends waking up before sunrise and beginning one's daily routine during this phase. The ability to arise refreshed at this hour, after a productive day and a good night's sleep, is a standard of health. Most of us have noticed that when oversleeping in the morning, we feel heavy, groggy, and often more tired than if we had awakened earlier. This is due to waking up within the inertia of the Kapha phase.

Conversely, if you already wake up early in the morning, you know there is a magical quality about this time of day. In giving ourselves ample time in the morning, we're able to establish a healthy morning routine that carries over into the day. To help assist in eliminating wastes, Ayurveda recommends drinking a glass of warm water with a squeeze of lemon upon waking. After clearing the bowels, it then recommends taking time to do gentle yoga postures, breathing exercises, and meditation. This allows the mind and body to transition gracefully from the sleep state into waking consciousness. (See page 136 for more on these practices.) Not having to rush in the morning also gives us time to enjoy a healthy breakfast, rather than merely grabbing food on the run. A balanced morning routine also allows us to arrive at work feeling calm, grounded, and prepared for whatever comes our way.

THE MONTHLY LUNAR CYCLE

If a group of women live and work closely together, they will soon notice that they will begin to menstruate at the same time. They will also notice that their cycles follow the phases of the Moon. Ayurveda provides great insight on how to care for this deep relationship with the monthly lunar cycle.

During the childbearing years, the monthly cycle prepares a woman's body for conception and giving birth. If no conception occurs, it cleanses and rejuvenates the body for the next monthly cycle. Illnesses such as hypertension and heart disease typically appear after the cessation of menstruation in women. This is largely due to the internal cleansing mechanisms of the menstrual cycle.

A few days after the completion of the menstrual flow, the Kapha or building phase of the female cycle begins. The slow, steady build-up of bodily fluids and tissue continues until after ovulation. During this time, Ayurveda recommends limiting foods that naturally aggravate Kapha (i.e., Sweet, Sour, and Salty foods) such as refined sugar, excess salt, excessive citrus, fermented foods, and deep-fried or oily foods, like rich meats and aged cheeses. This will help prevent excessive fluid retention, painful breast swelling, and general heaviness and dullness in the body and mind.

With a receptive uterine lining formed by Day 17, the Pitta phase of the female lunar cycle begins. Pitta's accelerated warming ensures that if a fertilized egg arrives, it has the best possible home to be nurtured in its rapid phase of growth. If no fertilized egg arrives, then Pitta's transformative power dynamically causes the lining to slough.

To help prevent symptoms of PMS, such as irritability, intense cramping, constipation, and headaches, Ayurveda recommends avoiding acidic and un-grounding foods. These include refined sugar, fried foods, alcohol, salt, salty cheeses, highly processed foods, seafood, hot peppers, garlic, nightshades (potatoes, tomatoes, peppers, and eggplant), and large amounts of citrus. Consuming a lighter diet with extra dark-green leafy vegetables (or vegetable juices) and cooling foods like cucumber or melons will also assist in keeping the fires of the body in check (especially for Pitta types).

The Vata phase of the menstrual cycle is marked by the flow of menses out of the body. The loss of blood during this period welcomes iron- and mineral-rich foods such as broths, soups, and stews; and nutrient-dense foods such as high-quality oils and proteins. Warmed milk with added ghee and gently heating spices, taken during the early morning or before bed, is also highly nourishing. These rejuvenating techniques should be continued until the woman feels restored again before ovulation. For information on how to nourish pregnancy appropriately, please see page 155.

SEASONAL RHYTHMS

When we observe animals in nature, we witness an intrinsic harmony with the seasons. A squirrel knows what foods to store for the Winter, just as a dog knows how to keep cool in the Summer. Since we're also linked to the greater cycles of Nature, it serves us to change in accordance with the seasons.

A dosha naturally increases during seasons with similar qualities to itself. For example, the dry, cool nature of Fall is aggravating to Vata, while the warm, moist nature of Spring is soothing. A Vata type must, therefore, take extra balancing measures during Fall.

It's important for everyone to make changes in diet and lifestyle during each new season. While a Pitta type needs to take extra measures to stay cool during late Spring and Summer, all constitutions should observe the greater changes in climate and condition. Since a season naturally balances a dosha with opposite qualities to itself, seasonal changes may often be quite small. This may particularly be the case when following a regimen for a specific doshic imbalance.

Whether you've stopped to think about it or not, you already do many things to keep yourself balanced during the seasons. Wearing shorts in the Summer or eating warm

Oil Self-Massage

Abhyanga or "head-to-toe oil massage" is a highly prized component of the Ayurvedic lifestyle. Regular self-massage nourishes the skin, relaxes the nervous system, removes impurities from the plasma and blood, and feeds the inner tissues of the body. Vata and Pitta types benefit from daily abhyanga, while Kapha types should perform it less frequently. They should favor dry brush massage instead, using silk or cotton gloves. As simple as it may sound, a few minutes of massage each morning is one of the most effective forms of preventative medicine.

If you're a Vata type, favor rich, warming oils such as sesame or almond oil. Vata types benefit the most from oil massage, due to its calming and grounding qualities. If you're a Pitta type, favor lighter, cooling oils such as coconut or olive oil. And if you're a Kapha type, favor light oils such as sunflower or grapeseed oil. Since we absorb oil directly through the skin, it's important to always use high quality oils (preferably organic and cold-pressed). Adding a few drops of essential oil to this base is a great way to further pamper your senses (see page 160 for more on essentials oils).

Ayurvedic massage is performed with the balls and palms of the hands, as well as with the fingers. In general, use circular strokes over the joints and abdomen, and up-and-down strokes over the limbs.

Gently heat the oil before starting, by putting it in a clear plastic squeeze bottle and then setting it in a cup of very hot water. When finished the massage, leave the oil on for 15 to 30 minutes and follow with a hot shower or bath. This allows the pours of the skin to open, thus bringing the oil into the deeper tissues of the body. In performing self-massage, it's important to always keep a nurturing attitude towards your body. Abhyanga is an opportunity to love yourself and to deepen your commitment to healing.

foods in the Winter are instinctive balancing measures. Ayurveda simply brings greater awareness to other ways you can create seasonal balance. Doing a cleanse at the start of each season, for example, is an important tool for offsetting imbalances associated with seasonal transitions, such as the flu in the early Winter and allergies in early Spring. (See page 146 for general cleansing tips.)

GENERAL GUIDELINES FOR SEASONAL ROUTINES

SUMMER

Summer is hot and bright, just like Pitta  dosha. The Sun is at its strongest and physical activity is high. Everyone should take measures to avoid overheating during this time. Pitta individuals must take extra care in following a Pitta-reducing diet and lifestyle from late Spring through Summer.

General Recommendations (suitable for all doshas):

- Eat more cooling foods.
- Wear light, breathable clothing.
- Take cool baths and showers.
- Avoid overly spicy foods.
- Drink more water.
- Avoid exposure to the sun between noon and 3PM.
- Take a short nap during the day.
- Favor cooling exercises such as swimming.
- Take walks under the moonlight.

FALL

Fall is cool, light, dry, and windy,  just like Vata dosha. Vata types must, therefore, take extra care in keeping balanced during this time of year. As the weather becomes colder in late Fall, it's beneficial for all types to favor warmer food and drinks. Plenty of rest and relaxation are also advisable, since Fall is an active time in which all of nature prepares for the upcoming Winter.

General Guidelines for Fall:

- Favor warm food and drinks.
- Include more heavy and oily foods in your diet.
- Include warm oil massage in your morning routine.
- Cover your head on windy days.
- Avoid sleeping in cold drafts.
- Avoid fasting.
- Keep well-hydrated.

WINTER

Winter is cold, damp, and heavy, just  like Kapha dosha. Kapha types should stay active during this time of year, rather than hibernating inside. It's also important for Vata types to stay warm in Winter, while taking measures to offset the dryness associated with indoor heating. The digestive fire is strong in Winter, so everyone can enjoy slightly heavier foods.

General Guidelines for Winter:

- Favor warm food and drinks.
- Always wear a hat in cold weather (over 60 percent of body heat is lost through the head).
- Keep your neck warm with a scarf or clothing.
- Use humidifiers in your home.
- Include warm oil massage in your morning routine.

- Avoid taking naps during the day.
- Exercise more.
- Do things that make you feel good (to avoid the Winter blues).
- Wear bright colors.

SPRING

Spring is warm, liquid, and soft, like Kapha dosha. During this season, the heat from the Sun awakens the vibrancy and beauty of nature. Accumulated Kapha begins to liquefy in the early part of the season, leading to the common occurrence of colds, sinus congestion, and allergies. Ayurveda emphasizes internal "Spring cleaning" for all doshic types.

General Guidelines for Spring:

- Favor a lighter diet.
- Follow some type of cleansing program or fast (see Panchakarma on page 148).
- Wake up earlier.
- Participate in outdoor activities.
- Avoid taking naps during the day.
- Keep cool as the weather heats up in late Spring.
- Enjoy the beauty of nature.

THE SEASONS OF YOUR LIFE

In addition to the changing seasons of nature, Ayurveda observes three greater seasons of our lifetimes. Each season is governed by one of the three doshas. Making small changes in accordance with these seasons is considered an important key to graceful aging.

INFANCY THROUGH ADOLESCENCE IS GOVERNED BY KAPHA

During childhood, the bones and tissues of the body become strong with the help of Kapha dosha. Soft, smooth skin and baby fat reflect the high proportion of Kapha in the body during this time. If you've ever pinched the cheeks of a baby, you've directly experienced the qualities of Kapha. A greater need for sleep, along with common childhood ailments such as colds and asthma, also relate to Kapha.

Because of rapid growth, this is an important time to support the Kapha dosha, rather than decreasing it through Kapha-pacifying foods and activities. This is done through eating a balanced diet that incorporates all 6 Tastes, maintaining healthy agni, and properly eliminating wastes.

The epidemic of childhood obesity and diabetes in the U.S. today reflects daily routines that deplete agni, such as snacking throughout the day and not getting enough physical exercise. It also relates to the consumption of ama-producing foods (such as refined sugar and fast foods), and inadequate psycho-emotional support during the developmental years.

EARLY ADULTHOOD THROUGH MIDDLE AGE IS GOVERNED BY PITTA

Pitta dosha helps fuel the transformative process of puberty. That is why Pitta conditions such as acne and tonsillitis are common around this time. After the teenage years, we enter a more focused and driven period of life, relating to education, career, and raising a family. If our underlying flame of ambition burns too high during this time, inflammatory problems and anger will appear with greater frequency.

Eating dosha-balancing foods is important during these years, particularly for Pitta types. It's also important to favor foods that are high in vital energy, while avoiding refined sugar and greasy foods.

LATE MIDDLE AGE THROUGH OLD AGE IS GOVERNED BY VATA

As we get older, the proportion of Vata in the body becomes higher. This increases bodily dryness and decreases mobility, thus making wrinkles, arthritis, and nervous system disorders more common. An increase in leisure time during these years allows us to devote more energy to doing the things we enjoy. It's also a time to communicate the wisdom of life with those in the Kapha and Pitta phases.

Consuming highly digestible foods will protect against the depletion of agni during the later years of life. Mineral-rich homemade vegetable broths are a great addition to meals. Incorporating high-quality oils into the diet is also necessary for nourishing bodily tissues. In general, caloric needs will generally fall during this time, along with appetite levels. A pleasant social ambiance will also greatly enhance the digestion and assimilation of nutrients.

	SEASON	STAGE OF LIFE
Vata	Fall	Old Age
Pitta	Summer	Middle Age
Kapha	Spring	Childhood

By this point, you may be wondering how you can possibly keep all of these recommendations straight? Between the qualities of the doshas themselves, the time of day, the season, and your age, you may feel like you'll never have the understanding or dedication to balance so many elements. Once again, it's important to emphasize that the understanding is already within you. As you become aware of your underlying nature, you will instinctively start to bring this wisdom into all areas of life. The information above merely provides guidelines to help direct you back to this inner wisdom.

Rather than becoming frantic about trying to balance all of the categories meticulously, begin by making small changes in your lifestyle. Remember that balance is a dynamic, constantly changing state that only you can define. No list of recommendations will ever fully encompass your unique requirements. So take what works, leave what doesn't work behind, and most of all, don't be afraid to explore. Life is the greatest laboratory, and it's only though personal experience that we find balance.

HONORING YOUR TEMPLE

SLEEP

Ayurveda describes sleep as the "diet of the mind." Sleep repairs and rejuvenates both the mind and body. Since you spend almost a third of your life sleeping, it's important to bring awareness to how you sleep.

Vata types are light sleepers by nature. In order to replenish the nervous system, Vata types need plenty of sleep (at least 8 hours a night). It's also beneficial for them to take a nap during the day. Pitta types sleep soundly and require less sleep than Vata types (6 to 8 hours). Sleep is an important time for these types to relax and refuel. Kapha individuals sleep like rocks and often spend too much time in bed. It's best for these types to decrease the amount they sleep (to 6 to 7 hours), while avoiding naps throughout the day. It's also beneficial for them to rise either before or with the Sun.

As modern society falls out of sync with Nature's rhythms, sleeping problems are becoming more widespread. While these problems are often complex disorders, establishing a healthy routine is one of the quickest ways to improve your quality of sleep. The doshas provide valuable insight into the underlying nature of common sleeping problems.

If you suffer from insomnia, restless sleep, or always feel tired upon waking, excess Vata may be the culprit. If you can't fall asleep due to excessive thinking, Pitta may be the culprit. Waking up during the night with hot pains or excessive sweating also points to high Pitta. If you go to sleep like a baby, but have to be dragged out of bed, excess Kapha is probably the culprit. Snoring and congestion are also usually linked to high Kapha.

DREAMS

When we sleep, the mind withdraws the senses from the outside world, and we connect to our unconscious minds. Ancient cultures have valued dream experiences for millennia. By remaining open to our dreams, we have the ability to derive valuable insight into our waking lives.

Dreams often reflect characteristics related to our primary doshas. For example, if you're a Vata type, you may have active, colorful, and fantastical dreams. These may involve flying, jumping, falling, and elements that don't seem to make any sense. Of the three doshas, Vata types are also the most likely to experience disturbing dreams or nightmares. Pitta types often have intense dreams, which may involve figuring out problems, fighting, or dealing with waking life issues. They also commonly have dreams with elaborate story lines that resemble a book or movie in complexity. Kapha types often have gentle, pleasurable dreams that

TIPS FOR MORE RESTFUL SLEEP

- Go to bed at or before 10PM. It's said that the hours of sleep before midnight are the most rejuvenating of the night.

- Go to bed at a regular time each night.

- Create a clean, pleasant bedroom environment.

- Take a few minutes before you sleep to bring attention to your breath. This will help you avoid processing the day's events.

- If you have problems falling asleep, take a warm bath before going to bed. You can also try listening to gentle, soothing music.

- If you typically fall asleep reading, try reading before getting into bed. This will prevent you from waking up in the middle of the night to turn off the light or move the book.

- Wear a cloth cover over your eyes if you have sleeping problems.

- Drink a glass of warm milk with a pinch of cardamom and nutmeg before going to bed.

feature lakes, oceans and mountains. Kaphas are the least likely to experience unpleasant dreams.

A noticeable change in your dreams may provide clues for a particular doshic imbalance. For example, if you suddenly start having intense, fiery dreams, you should consider whether your Pitta is heightened for some reason. It could relate to a passing component of your life or signal a deeper imbalance. Rather than over-analyzing things, it's best to treat these as helpful signs, and not as definitive indicators of imbalance.

SEXUAL INTIMACY

Sexual intimacy is one of the greatest creative forces through which we express and share our love. It's a source of tremendous pleasure and has the ability to positively influence our health, vitality, immunity, and ojas, the vital essence of the body.

A healthy relationship to sex is required for overall health. As with anything pleasurable, it's important to keep things in moderation. Overindulgence in sex leads to the excessive loss of reproductive fluids and to the depletion of ojas. Over time, this reduces vitality and immunity, leading to a wide range of doshic imbalances. A healthy emotional relationship to sex is also extremely important. Lust, addiction, and self-centered desire undermine the sharing and expansive nature of intimacy. Mutual trust and satisfaction are essential requirements for any healthy sexual relationship.

Ayurveda also recommends honoring your personal constitution in relation to sexual activity. Vata types typically have variable sexual appetites and are sensitive lovers by nature. They may, however, be overly mental about sex and become easily imbalanced by excess sexual activity. Pitta types are passionate lovers with strong sexual appetites and, therefore, risk overindulging at times. They may also have the tendency to be inattentive to a partner's needs or to become fixated on personal performance. Kapha types have the greatest sexual stamina and make romantic lovers. They may, however, have the tendency to overindulge or to outpace a partner's own sexual desires.

Ayurveda also recognizes the importance of the time of day and seasons in relation to sexual activity. Nighttime is considered the best time for lovemaking, while the morning and daytime are not as well-suited. Regarding the seasons, sex can be enjoyed more often in the colder months, when there is naturally less physical activity. In the hotter months, sex is recommended less, due to the greater loss of fluids and energy from the body.

To restore strength and ojas after lovemaking, Ayurveda recommends simple rejuvenating techniques. These include taking a cool bath or shower and drinking water or a little wine. Drinking warm milk with honey and ground almonds is also a great remedy for rebuilding ojas. Always remember to bring the milk to a boil first and then allow it to cool. Eating foods with natural sugars is also helpful for restoring the vital fluids of the body.

PHYSICAL EXERCISE

Regular exercise keeps the inner motors of the body running with ease. Through exercising in accordance with your underlying make-up, you have the ability to keep your body young and vibrant. Exercise also helps bring clarity to the mind and improves the flow of energy or prana within the body.

There's a notion in the West today that all exercise is good exercise: if you're taking the time to do physical activities for your health, then you must be doing something correct. Ayurveda agrees that you are doing something important, but also encourages a degree of discernment within the activities you choose. Along with your constitution, aspects such as age, strength, physical condition, diet, time of day, and time of year are important factors to consider in choosing the best forms of exercise.

That is not to say that choosing an exercise needs to be a tedious process. Instead, just ask yourself why you're choosing a particular exercise. Most importantly, do you think it will bring balance to your mind and body? Also use common sense in relation to the factors mentioned above. If you're a Pitta type, you should avoid exercising under the midday sun. If you're just beginning to exercise regularly, you should take a slow, gradual approach to any form of exercise. And if you just ate a meal, you should allow your body time to digest before beginning an activity.

According to Ayurveda, regular exercise should not strain or over-exert the body. Traditionally, it recommends exercising up to one-half of your full capacity. This is typically indicated when sweat begins to form on the brow, under the arms, and along the spine. Another sign is when respiration quickens to the point you are forced to breathe out of your mouth. Vigorous and challenging forms of exercise are most suitable for Kapha types. While it's good for Kaphas to jump-start their systems, it's still recommended for them to avoid over-exerting.

Today, it's common to see people become fanatical about exercising. This often points to an underlying doshic imbalance. High-Pitta individuals, for example, often push themselves in activities until the point of injury. High-Vata types typically become attracted to exercises involving constant movement and changing stimuli. And high-Kapha types may be committed to not wanting to exercise at all.

The desire to over–exercise is often rooted in underlying psychological and emotional issues. Whether attempting to sculpt society's version of the "perfect" body or seeking a daily release for anger, individuals search for external activities to pacify these thoughts and emotions. Ayurveda recommends turning inwards instead, through practices such as meditation.

Vata

Aerobics, low-impact	Swimming
Bicycling, easy	Tai Chi
Dancing	Walking
Gymnastics	Yoga

Pitta

Archery	Mountain climbing
Basketball	Skiing
Bicycling	Soccer
Football	Surfing
Ice Hockey	Tennis
Ice Skating	Yoga
Martial Arts	Weight-lifting

Kapha

Aerobics	Rock climbing
Basketball	Rowing
Bicycling	Running
Football	Tennis
Jogging	Yoga

Many forms of exercise in the West use forceful methods to build muscles and eliminate fat. Ayurveda favors exercises such as yoga postures, which strengthen, tone, and loosen the muscles through non-strenuous means. It also recommends cardiovascular activities such as walking, hiking, and swimming that promote deep, rhythmical breathing.

INNER DISCOVERY: YOGA, BREATHING EXERCISES, & MEDITATION

YOGA

While Ayurveda may have been a new word for you upon opening this book for the first time, you've almost certainly heard of yoga by now. In a relatively short period of time, it has become one of the most popular forms of exercise in the West.

Yoga is primarily known today for its physical postures (or *asanas*) that stretch, strengthen, and purify the body. In its traditional form, yoga is presented as a complete system of spiritual development. Physical postures are practiced along with meditation and other techniques designed to promote self-discovery. The *Sanskrit* word *Yoga* translates as "union" or "to yoke or harness," and refers to the union of mind and body and, more broadly, to an individual's union with the Divine.

Despite the wide array of yoga practices available in the West today, choosing one doesn't need to be a daunting process. Honoring your personal constitution will always lead you to the most suitable practice. It's also beneficial to seek out practices that incorporate other branches of yoga, such as meditation and breathing exercises.

In general, Vata types should favor gentle yoga postures that calm the mind and ground the body. Sitting postures are particularly beneficial for Vata, though most postures are fine if done gently and routinely.

Pitta types benefit from most forms of yoga, although it is best to favor practices that calm the body and mind. These individuals are often drawn to physically demanding postures, due to their highly driven natures. While they have a capacity for such practices, it's important for Pitta types to remember not to overdo things.

Kapha types should favor more vigorous forms of yoga that stimulate the body and clear the mind.

Here are a few general guidelines for any yoga practice:

- Always learn from an experienced teacher before starting an extended home practice. Books and videos can help in the initial stages of practice, but a teacher will offer greater degrees of refinement that are necessary to ensure a safe and rewarding practice.
- Practice yoga on an empty or near-empty stomach. Also remember to keep hydrated during asana practice.
- Don't take yourself too seriously. Yoga should be an enjoyable journey of self-exploration.

(See Resources on page 333 for information on where to learn yoga).

BREATHING EXERCISES

According to Ayurveda, breath is the single most important food. Through the process of breathing, we feed every cell of our body with prana, or life-force. Breath is, therefore, the essential bridge between matter and consciousness, linking body, mind, senses, and spirit.

BREATHING TECHNIQUES

DIAPHRAGMATIC BREATHING

The diaphragm is a dome-shaped muscle located at the base of the rib cage, between the stomach and lungs. During inhalation, the diaphragm naturally contracts, pulling the bottom of the lungs downward, in order to bring in oxygen and prana. During exhalation, the diaphragm releases, allowing carbon dioxide to flow outward.

A baby naturally takes full, deep breaths, allowing the diaphragm to perform its job effectively. As we get older, stress and busy lifestyles often limit the movement of the diaphragm, leading to shallow or upper-chest breathing. This quick exercise is a great way to recharge the cells of the body with energy, while bringing greater awareness to how you breathe.

Begin by sitting on the front edge of a chair with your spine straight and feet flat on the floor. Keep your upper chest, neck and shoulder muscles as relaxed as possible.

1 Placing one hand on your abdomen, take a slow, deep breath through your nostrils. As you inhale, you should naturally feel your stomach and lower rib cage expand outwards.

2 Then, exhale slowly through your mouth, feeling your ribs and stomach pull gently inward.

Repeat this exercise for a round of ten breaths, then slowly build your practice up to five minutes a day.

ALTERNATE-NOSTRIL BREATHING

This is a widely used breathing exercise in Ayurveda and Yoga. It helps balance all three doshas, and is particularly well-suited for balancing excess Vata conditions of the mind. Perform it sitting on the floor in a cross-legged position or on the front edge of a chair, keeping your spine straight and both feet flat on the floor. We recommend doing a few test runs as you read the instructions.

1 Relax, close your eyes, and gently close your right nostril with the thumb of your right hand. Take a short exhalation through your left nostril (this helps create a "clean slate" for the exercise). Next, slowly inhale through the left nostril, feeling your stomach expand outwards.

2 Gently close your left nostril with the ring and middle fingers of your right hand and slowly exhale through your right nostril.

3 Keeping your left nostril closed, inhale through your right nostril. Close your right nostril with your thumb once again and exhale through your left nostril.

This marks the completion of one full cycle. In starting, try completing five full cycles and slowly work your way up to a five-minute daily practice.

Ayurveda recommends specific exercises to develop greater awareness and control of the breath. *Pranayama* translates as "control or regulation of the breath" and is a general term used for these exercises. A regular breathing practice creates clarity of the mind, energizes the vital forces of the body, and helps balance the linear-thinking, left hemisphere of the brain and the more creative right hemisphere.

As with yoga, it's always best to learn breathing practices from an experienced teacher, due to their powerful effect on the mind and body. We offer a few simple exercises here as starting points to developing a daily practice. Regularity is important for getting the most out of any practice. Even just two to five minutes a day can provide immediate health benefits.

Exercise Suggestions

Vata types should favor exercises that are gentle and flowing in nature. Pitta types do well with most forms of exercise, but should avoid overdoing things or becoming overly competitive. Kapha types benefit from stimulating exercises that utilize their natural strength and endurance. (The lists on page 135 contain balancing activities for each dosha. Please note that these are only partial lists.)

Meditation

Day after day, we process an endless stream of thoughts and sensory impressions. Even during much of sleep, the mind actively churns with dreams and images. Perhaps you've felt a need at times simply to quiet down your mind or decrease mental chatter?

Meditation is one of the easiest ways to give your mind a break (or brake, for that matter!) While the word "meditation" may seem foreign to some, it's not a mystical or exclusionary practice: any person of any faith can meditate. The practice of meditation is found in all corners of the globe and is not bound to any one correct method.

Many feel it's impossible to meditate because they simply can't "empty" their minds. This degree of mastery, however, is not required to reap the physical and mental benefits of meditation. Even simple meditation exercises such as those listed on the following page, will result in a clearer mind and more energized body. Modern scientific research has shown regular meditation practices to increase positive emotions and immunity, while having the ability to reduce anxiety, blood pressure, cholesterol, and muscular tension.

Chef Johnny likens meditation to taking a highly concentrated capsule of deep rest, which refreshes and rejuvenates the mind and body, while dissolving fatigue and stress. During this daily taste of deep peace, mental activity is reduced to its simplest state of awareness, to a field of silence that underlies our thoughts, desires, and emotions. Ayurveda states that through experiencing this vast silence within, we directly touch upon our true inner nature, which is inherently blissful.

In choosing a regular meditation practice, we recommend learning from an experienced teacher. Meditation has a powerful effect on the mind and body, so it's best to have a teacher to guide your practice and to answer questions should they arise. (See Resources on page 333 for information on where to learn meditation.)

SIMPLE MEDITATION EXERCISES

In starting these exercises, first choose a quiet area in your home. According to Ayurveda, early morning and early evening are particularly good times to meditate.

We recommend sitting on the front edge of a chair with your spine straight and both feet flat on the floor. If it's comfortable, you can also sit on the floor with your legs crossed. Placing a small cushion on the floor directly under your tail bone will assist in keeping your spine straight. Performing a few minutes of breathing exercises (see page 137) will naturally quiet the mind and lead you gracefully into meditation.

COUNTING YOUR BREATHS

Begin by taking a few deep breaths, while exhaling slowly through your nose. Then begin counting each inhalation and exhalation until you reach ten. That means counting "one" after the first inhalation and "two" after the first exhalation. When you reach ten, begin with "one" again on the next inhalation. After becoming comfortable with this practice, you can begin counting only the exhalations.

FOLLOWING YOUR BREATHS

Begin in the same way as the counting exercise. Rather than counting your breaths, simply allow your attention to focus on the breaths coming in and out of your nasal passages. Alternatively, you can focus on the rising and falling of your stomach as you breathe.

Begin by practicing either of these meditations for two to five minutes per sitting, while slowly working your way up to 15 or 20 minutes. These exercises may sound exceedingly easy at first; but you'll probably find that it takes practice for your

TRANSCENDENTAL MEDITATION

Maharishi Mahesh Yogi first brought Transcendental Meditation (TM) to the West in 1958. Over the past four decades, millions of Westerners have learned TM, and it remains the most scientifically researched form of meditation. A type of Vedic mantra meditation, TM is described as an 'effortless' technique. Its name refers to the process of 'transcending,' or going beyond, the normal activity of the mind to an underlying field of silence, also referred to as pure consciousness. (Please see the Resource section for information on Transcendental Meditation).

mind to become quiet. As thoughts arise, simply turn your attention back to the counting or the sensation of breathing.

MANTRA MEDITATION

Traditional forms of Ayurvedic meditation commonly use *mantras*, or sacred sounds, as vehicles to quiet the mind through directing the thoughts into a single point. These Sanskrit syllables are also highly charged vibrations that exhibit specific effects on the body, mind, and subtle energy reserves of the body (called *chakras*). For this reason, we encourage you to seek out a qualified teacher when learning traditional mantra meditation.

5

FOOD AS MEDICINE

YOUR BODY ONLY WANTS TO HEAL

"Let food be thy medicine and medicine be thy food."
- Hippocrates (460-377 B.C.)

"With proper diet and lifestyle, medicine is of no need.
With improper diet and lifestyle, medicine is of no use."
- Ayurvedic Proverb

"Food is the best medicine. No, actually, laughter is the
best medicine, unless you're really hungry."
- Dr. Tom

While great health is often looked upon with awe in the West, it is an inherent reality that health lives within the core of every being. Health, not illness, is our natural state—it's usually just a matter of finding it tucked beneath the layers of imbalance that have accumulated over time.

In working towards greater constitutional balance, there's an important rule to remember: *Your body only wants to heal.* When you get a cut, your body immediately begins the mending process. When one of your doshas becomes aggravated, your body retaliates with an elaborate series of self-regulating mechanisms.

With repeated imbalances over time, this powerful system becomes overwhelmed, eventually leading to disease—literally, a lack of ease or balance. Even during major illnesses, however, the body retains its natural inclination to heal. The key to activating this healing potential lies in treating health with wholeness.

In the West, we usually don't pay attention to imbalances until painful or undeniable symptoms arise. Consider the following example:

One day you feel a mild burning sensation in your stomach, but dismiss it as a temporary nuisance. The pain becomes more frequent over the next few weeks, so you try taking an over-the-counter antacid. After two months, the pain begins keeping you up at night, so you finally go see a doctor. The doctor finds a large ulcer and says you're fortunate you didn't wait any longer to get examined.

This example would be much different with a basic understanding of the doshas and your unique constitution. The mild burning in your stomach would notify you that Pitta is slightly aggravated. If you were a Pitta type by nature, you would immediately start eating more cooling and alkalizing foods. You would also take a moment to consider your overall lifestyle: are you stressed out and pushing yourself too hard again? If so, you would bring more calming and nurturing activities into your daily routine.

If you were a Vata or Kapha type, you would also take measures to balance Pitta. Since you're not typically prone to overheating, however, these measures may be less intensive. For example, maybe you simply need to soothe your stomach after eating overly spicy foods. A cup of mint tea could quickly do the trick.

If you feel the imbalance is more deeply rooted, you would consider what factors in your life could be increasing Pitta. Is it the middle of summer, perhaps, or did you suddenly start working longer hours? If so, you would incorporate more Pitta-pacifying measures into your lifestyle, while staying aware of any changes in your underlying constitution. As soon as Pitta feels likes it's back in check, you would focus again on keeping your primary dosha in balance. If you have Pitta as a strong secondary dosha (say you're a Vata-

Pitta type), you would take extra care on a continuing basis to keep Pitta balanced.

THE SIX STAGES OF DISEASE

"Any treatment that attends only to the symptoms is not a good therapy. The best treatment is one that balances the whole and does not create any other disorder."
- Charaka Samhita

As discussed throughout this book, Ayurveda views health as a dynamic process, rather than a static state. Disease is an equally dynamic process, with many factors leading to imbalance. It's generally the habitual excesses of certain foods, activities, emotions, or ways of thinking that begin the disease process.

You don't simply wake up one day with a particular illness. Instead, repetitive imbalances over time kindle an underlying disease process that may span weeks, months, or even years. Ayurveda identifies six stages of disease and always aims to treat imbalances at the earliest stage. The foods we eat are an integral component within all six stages.

STAGE 1: ACCUMULATION

According to Ayurveda, doshic imbalance stands behind all disease. During the first stage of disease, an aggravated dosha accumulates in its home seat. Eating dry and cold foods such as chips and iced drinks every day, for example, may cause Vata to increase in the colon (the primary seat of Vata). If Vata increases at a faster rate than the body can naturally expel or pacify, accumulation occurs. At this stage, you may feel slight discomfort or no symptoms at all. It's common for people to ignore minor symptoms altogether.

Luckily, the body strives to restore balance on its own during the Accumulation stage. It does this largely through desiring foods and activities of a balancing nature. Let's say, for example, there's a fresh cake in the house. Over a two-day period, you eat a piece with lunch and dinner. By the third day, you feel sluggish and the cake isn't appetizing anymore. Instead, you crave light, spicy foods. This is your body's way of saying you need to balance Kapha. By listening to this inner intelligence, you have the ability to stop the disease process at its root. In general, incorporating all 6 Tastes into your diet and "circuit-breaking" dietary habits are important steps during the Accumulation phase.

STAGE 2: AGGRAVATION

If the disease process is not stopped during the first stage, the imbalanced dosha remains in its home seat and symptoms intensify. A Pitta imbalance involving an unsettled stomach during the first stage, for example, may lead to acid indigestion during the Aggravation stage, when provoked by Pitta aggravating foods. The imbalanced dosha also prepares to move into other parts of the body.

With a little awareness, you can easily reverse the disease process during the second stage. By paying attention to any feelings of imbalance, and then making appropriate dietary and lifestyle changes, you will quickly return to your natural state of balance.

Breaking improper dietary habits through eating a lighter diet is important during this stage. Drinking dosha-balancing herbal teas or skipping the evening meal is also highly effective.

Common ways the doshas become provoked during this stage include not getting enough rest for Vata types, drinking alcohol or eating spicy foods for Pitta types, and falling out of a regular exercise routine for Kapha types.

STAGE 3: SPREADING

During the third stage of disease, the aggravated dosha spreads from its home seat, overflowing into the general circulation of the body. Symptoms will often begin appearing in other parts of the body during this stage but will be fluctuating or inconsistent in nature. While these symptoms will be more noticeable than the second stage, they still may not seem like major problems.

The first three stages of disease relate to general imbalances within the doshas, rather than particular diseases. If you pacify an imbalanced dosha before the fourth stage, it will be much easier to regain constitutional balance.

During the Spreading phase, Ayurveda recommends specific techniques of cleansing, such as fasting and the traditional system of detoxification known as Panchakarma (see page 148). Intervention and prevention are also major components during this period. It's important to look back over the previous few months (or longer) and identify dietary and lifestyle patterns that may have created the imbalances. Ayurveda then advises changing these through choosing dosha-pacifying foods and activities.

STAGE 4: RELOCATION

If the spread of the imbalanced dosha is not stopped by the third stage, the dosha will deposit itself into weak organs and systems throughout the body. Weakness can result from many factors, including genetic predisposition, trauma, unresolved emotions, energetic blockages, addictions, infections, and external pathogens. After entering a weak area, the dosha mixes with the tissues (dhatus) in that area, thereby creating functional imbalance at a much deeper cellular level.

In the West, we usually start paying attention to symptoms at the fourth stage. If the condition is not treated at this stage, it will typically become a full-blown disease. Since treatment becomes more difficult with the advancement of the disease process, Ayurveda recommends professional assistance at this point (or earlier if possible). A skilled practitioner will identify and treat imbalance at a core level, thus avoiding further complications of the disease. Primary treatment will typically include herbal medicines, dietary guidance, detoxification therapies (such as Panchakarma), and lifestyle changes. These therapies are geared towards pacifying the imbalanced doshas, cleansing impurities from the tissues, eliminating ama, and enlivening agni.

STAGE 5: MANIFESTATION

By the fifth stage, the symptoms of disease become clearly pronounced. If you walk into a medical doctor's waiting room, most people you see will be at this stage or beyond. This is largely because modern medicine relies upon the examination of symptoms to diagnose and treat disease.

The excess dosha becomes further embedded within the tissues during the Manifestation stage. Symptoms are treated at this stage and then purification therapies are used to restore the health of the tissues. Utilizing the same treatment methods as described in the previous stage, the disease process can still be successfully reversed at this stage.

Breaking poor dietary habits through favoring fresh, vibrant foods is essential during the Manifestation stage. One should also place greater emphasis on eating dosha-

EARLY SYMPTOMS OF IMBALANCE BY DOSHA

VATA

Anxiety or confusion, constipation, gas

PITTA

Irritability, alternating dry and loose stools, pressure or heat above the neck

KAPHA

Sluggishness, congestion, bloating

balancing foods and eating smaller quantities to avoid further ama accumulation.

STAGE 6: CHRONIC

At the sixth and final stage, the disease process is fully manifested, with symptoms becoming more severe. This stage is also commonly known as "Differentiation," because specialized features of disease become clear. For example, diabetes may be recognized at Stage 5, but it's not until Stage 6 that it takes on the characteristics of Type 2 diabetes. Structural changes and complications to other organs also take place during this final stage.

While chronic disease falls within the sixth stage, the entire disease process can still be reversed with the proper treatment and willpower. Purification through Panchakarma or other detoxifying measures is the first mode of treatment during this stage. Pacification (or balancing) therapies incorporating herbal medicines and dietary and lifestyle changes are then incorporated after the removal of the excess doshas and ama. Lastly, rejuvenation therapies using foods and herbs are used to rebuild and strengthen the tissues.

According to Ayurveda, disease is never absolute. Even in the most serious illnesses, an underlying current of healing potential remains. Tapping into this current with an open heart and a belief in the ability to heal can help cure even the toughest illnesses.

FOODS FOR CLEANSING AND LIGHTENING-UP

AN AYURVEDIC OVERVIEW OF FASTING

Fasting is an effective way to kindle agni and burn away ama from the body and mind. It also eliminates gas, makes the body light, improves mental clarity, and preserves overall health. Ayurveda favors regular, short-term fasting over infrequent, long-term fasting. This could entail fasting on the same day each week or setting a few days aside each month to fast, depending on your constitution and cleansing requirements. According to Ayurveda, abstaining from food or water for extended periods of time depletes bodily tissues, leading to doshic imbalance.

THE PRIMARY TYPES OF FASTING IN AYURVEDA

- Consuming light foods only (such as Kitchari and Kanjee, recipes follow)
- Consuming fruits, vegetables, or juices only
- Abstaining from solid foods while drinking water or herbal teas
- Abstaining from both food and water

In determining the appropriate type and length of a fast, it's important to take into account your constitution, digestive strength, level of ama, and overall vitality. It's never advised to deplete your energy during a fast. If you're new to fasting or have a chronic illness, we recommend consulting an Ayurvedic practitioner for specifically tailored guidance.

THE SIGNS OF EFFECTIVE FASTING

- Lightness in the body, clarity in the mind, and increased energy
- Regular bowel movements with no gas or bloating
- A clean tongue and fresh breath

It's best to choose a fasting period in which you'll be able to follow a peaceful, non-stressful routine. We recommend following the daily and nightly routine recommendations in Chapter 4. It's also important always to break your fasts properly. The most important rule to remember is to begin eating again gradually, slowly working your way up to solid foods. This gently allows agni to regain its power of digestion. Always avoid overeating directly following a fast, even if you have the urge to devour everything in sight. In general, start with vegetable broths and light soups for breakfast. For lunch, move to semi-solid foods such as soupy dhals (see page 250), soupy kitchari (recipe follows), or kanjee (recipe follows). For dinner, move to easily digestible solid foods, such as steamed vegetables and kitchari (see page 259). If you're ending a longer fast, it's beneficial to maintain this diet for a few days to allow agni to become strong again.

Fasting for the Doshas

Vata Fast

Vata types are the most sensitive to fasting, due to their light, airy natures. Fasting in moderation, however, is a good way for these types to improve low-agni and excess-ama conditions. As a general rule, Vata types should favor lighter food or juice fasts over total fasts.

Kitchari Mono-Diet

Eat only kitchari for 24 to 48 hours. Kitchari is a grain-and-legume dish cooked with mildly heating spices. It's both cleansing and nourishing, thus keeping Vata balanced.

1 CUP	basmati rice
1 CUP	split yellow mung dhal
6 CUPS	filtered water
1 TABLESPOON	ghee
1 TEASPOON	ground cumin
1 TEASPOON	ground coriander
½ TEASPOON	salt
½ TEASPOON	black pepper

1 Soak the mung dhal for 1 to 2 hours.

2 Thoroughly rinse the rice and mung dhal twice.

3 Put the rice, dhal, ghee, and water in a medium saucepan. Bring to a boil and boil for 5 minutes, uncovered, stirring occasionally.

4 Reduce the heat to low and cover, leaving the lid slightly ajar. Add the spices after 15 minutes. Cook until tender, about 25 to 30 minutes.

Note *If you can only find green (or whole) mung beans, soak them overnight before cooking to improve their digestibility.*

Simple Kanjee

10 cups filtered water

1 cup organic brown rice

pinch salt, ginger powder, ground cumin

1 In a large pot, bring the water and rice to a boil. Allow to boil for 1 hour until the rice becomes swollen and broken.

2 Stir and strain, leaving in small pieces of the rice.

3 Add a pinch of salt, ginger powder, and ground cumin. Pour into a thermos and drink 1 to 2 liters (around 4 to 8 cups) throughout the day.

Note *Kanjee is an easily digestible form of carbohydrate, which allows one to maintain energy during a fast.*

Pitta Fast

For Pitta types, regular, light fasting cleanses impurities in the blood and reduces overall heat in the mind and body. Juicy whole fruits and fruit and vegetable juice fasts with added fiber are especially good. These help flush ama and inflammatory toxins out of the body, while cooling down the gastro-intestinal tract. Total fasts (no food or water) are not advised for Pitta types, due to their natural tendencies to become irritable without food.

FRUIT FAST

Consume only fruit for 24 to 48 hours. Mildly Astringent fruits (raw or cooked) such as pears and apples are particularly beneficial. Eat the fruits with the skins on for added fiber. Melon and sweet orange are also recommended for Pitta. Always favor fresh, organic produce and rinse it thoroughly before juicing. Eat small portions of the fruits in the morning and afternoon and other times you may feel hungry throughout the day.

FRUIT OR VEGETABLE JUICE FAST

Fruit and vegetable juices are also cleansing for Pitta types. Leave in the pulp of the fruits or vegetables for extra fiber. You can also add ground psyllium husks, oat bran, wheat bran or ground flaxseeds. For simple juice fasts, use diluted grape, prune, pomegranate, or cucumber juice. Mixing dark leafy green vegetables with celery or carrot is also a highly beneficial juice combination.

KAPHA FAST

Fasting is beneficial for balancing excess Kapha conditions such as obesity, water retention, lethargy, mucous accumulation, and food addiction.

WATER FAST

Consume only water for 24 to 72 hours. Drink eight 12-ounce glasses of filtered water each day. You may drink more if you're thirsty. The water should be warm or hot (avoid cold water) with a squeeze of added lemon. This is a helpful fast for releasing accumulated ama, fat, mucous, drugs, and other toxins. Avoid this fast if you have edema or other problems with water retention.

TOTAL FAST

This is a more vigorous fast. Do not consume any food or water for 24 hours (also called an "Air and Sunshine Fast"). Begin this fast in the evening and spend time in the sun during the day.

PANCHAKARMA: REJUVENATING DETOXIFICATION

Panchakarma is a Sanskrit word meaning "five actions or treatments." As the primary method of detoxification in Ayurveda, Panchakarma rids the body of toxic materials left by disease and poor nutrition. It also expels excess doshas from the body. Therapies are individualized based upon constitutional types, doshic imbalances, age, digestive strength, immune status, season, and a host of other factors. Panchakarma promotes deep purification within the tissues, using safe, gentle methods.

Preparatory treatments to Panchakarma include light fasting, steam therapy, herbalized oil massage, and the intake of herbal decoctions or oils. These procedures help loosen accumulated toxins (ama), which then enter the major channels of the body for elimination. The five primary treatments of elimination include: herb-induced emesis or vomiting (*vamana*), herb-induced purgation (*virechana*), herbal decoction enema (*asthapana basti*), medicated oil enema (*anuvasana basti*), and the nasal administration of medication (*nasya*). Depending on an individual's needs, all five or only select treatments are used. There are also several adjunct treatments, such as the luxurious *shirodhara*, in which a continuous stream of warm oil is gently poured between the eyebrows (on the "third eye") of the patient.

Like any medical procedure, Panchakarma begins with an initial consultation by a qualified health professional, who can determine an individual's *prakruti* (birth constitution), the nature of the health problem, and the appropriate therapies. Ayurveda also recommends Panchakarma for healthy individuals as a preventative measure, particularly at the junction points between the seasons. In the West, treatment programs typically span from 3 to 14 days. During this time, individuals are encouraged to rest, relax, and welcome internal cleansing on all levels of the mind and body. Optional instruction is also provided in daily practices such as yoga, breathing exercises, and meditation. (For information on where to find Panchakarma, please see the Resources on page 333).

Foods for Common Illnesses and Ailments

Ayurvedic wisdom celebrates the "kitchen pharmacy," or the notion that simple food preparations, herbs, and spices can combat imbalances before they turn into full-blown illnesses. Below, we've offered classical Ayurvedic home remedies for a number of common illnesses and ailments. We encourage you to give these a try next time you find yourself reaching for an over-the-counter drug. Unlike synthetic drugs, these remedies improve outer symptoms, while naturally supporting the inner intelligence of the body to reharmonize the underlying imbalances. While deceptively simple, these preparations have been tried and tested for centuries and hold tremendous healing properties.

Using Herbs & Spices as Medicine

A defining characteristic of Ayurvedic cooking is its distinctive use of herbs and spices. In addition to providing mouthwatering appeal to dishes, these ingredients provide medicine in every bite.

The science of herbology constitutes an enormous branch of Ayurvedic medicine, with thousands of plants still in

Simple Detoxifying Teas

Sipping warm teas throughout the day is also a highly effective way to flush out ama and other toxins from the body. Below, we offer basic detoxifying teas for each dosha. Simply place the ingredients in a medium saucepan with 4 cups filtered water, bring the water to a boil for 5 minutes, and then steep for 2 to 5 minutes. Always add the lemon while the tea is steeping. Strain into a tea pot or thermos.

Vata Tea

1 TEASPOON	fennel seeds
1 TEASPOON	cumin seeds
½ TEASPOON	coriander seeds
½ TEASPOON	fresh grated ginger
SQUEEZE	lemon juice
(TO TASTE)	raw organic sugar, such as Sucanat

Pitta Tea

1 TEASPOON	fennel seeds
1 TEASPOON	coriander seeds
½ TEASPOON	cumin seeds
10	fresh mint leaves
SQUEEZE	lemon juice
(TO TASTE)	raw organic sugar, such as Sucanat

Kapha Tea

1 TEASPOON	cumin seeds
½ TEASPOON	coriander seeds
1 STICK	cinnamon or licorice
10	fresh basil leaves
SQUEEZE	lemon juice

FOOD ALLERGIES & INTOLERANCES

A food allergy is an immune reaction produced by the body after eating a certain food. It typically takes place moments after eating (although delayed reactions are also common) and may include sneezing, itching, swelling, breathing difficulties, and other symptoms. Food allergies are essentially misdirected responses by the immune system that can stem from many causes. Modern science has shown that genetic predisposition, environmental factors, and stress may all play a role in creating these allergies. From an Ayurvedic standpoint, food allergies most frequently occur in Pitta types, in response to foods that are acid-forming and high in protein such as nuts, shellfish, and egg yolks. The rancid oils often found in commercial nuts also contribute to these allergies.

Food intolerances occur when the body is unable to digest a certain food properly. Wheat, milk, and eggs are the three most common food intolerances in the West today. Due to their high protein contents and heavy natures, these foods require stronger agni to digest. When the digestive fire becomes weak over time, due to dietary and lifestyle imbalances, the ability to digest these foods becomes less. Food intolerances such as gluten intolerance, lactose intolerance, and candida, commonly occur in Vata and Kapha types, due to a combination of weak agni and ama accumulation. Although many individuals in the West view these as life-long conditions, Ayurveda recommends internally cleansing the body, strengthening agni, and then gradually reintroducing these foods over time.

use today. Similar to foods, herbs are classified according to their predominant taste (rasa), heating or cooling effects on the physiology (virya), and post-digestive effects on the tissues (vipak).

SIMPLE FOOD-BASED HOME REMEDIES

Note *For all remedies containing milk, always bring the milk to a boil first and then set to cool. Serve according to instruction.*

DIGESTIVE DISTURBANCES

HYPERACIDITY

- 1 cup milk, 1 teaspoon rose water, and 1 to 2 pinches cardamom powder. Serve cool.
- 1 cup milk and ¼ teaspoon baking powder. Serve cool.
- 1 cup pomegranate or apple juice

LOW APPETITE/WEAK AGNI

- 1 teaspoon roasted fennel seeds, ½ teaspoon roasted cumin seeds, and 1 pinch salt. Dry roast the seeds together in a cast iron skillet until golden brown, about 3 to 5 minutes, and then add the salt. Chew ½ teaspoon of the mixture 15-30 minutes before each meal. For indigestion, chew the same quantity immediately after each meal.
- ½ teaspoon grated ginger with a pinch of lemon, salt and black pepper. Mix together and eat 15-30 minutes before each meal.
- Tea made from equal portions of cumin seeds, coriander seeds, and fennel seeds. Use 1 teaspoon of the mixture per 1 cup filtered water. Boil for 5 minutes, steep for 2-5 minutes, and strain. Drink 30 minutes before each meal.

CONSTIPATION

- 1 to 2 tablespoons aloe gel. Take on an empty stomach in the morning.
- 3 tablespoons yogurt, ½ teaspoon honey, and 1 tablespoon psyllium husk powder. Mix together and eat in the evening.
- Soak 3 figs and 3 prunes in hot water overnight. In the morning, eat the fruits and drink the water. For children, use 1 to 2 figs and prunes.
- 2 tablespoons castor oil in 1 cup hot water or orange juice. Take in the morning on an empty stomach.

GAS

- 1 teaspoon fennel seeds, ¼ teaspoon black pepper, ½ teaspoon chopped mint leaves. Mix together in a blender and place 2 pinches in a small quantity of warm water. Store the rest in a glass jar.
- Rub castor oil directly onto the skin around the navel area.

DIARRHEA

- ½ teaspoon ginger powder, ¼ teaspoon black pepper, and ½ teaspoon ghee. Mix together to form a paste and take a small quantity (roughly ¼ teaspoon) multiple times throughout the day.
- 1 cup filtered water, ¼ cup yogurt, ¼ teaspoon ginger powder, and 1 pinch salt.
- 1 peeled and chopped apple, ¼ teaspoon nutmeg powder, and 1 teaspoon honey.

OTHER ILLNESSES AND AILMENTS

ARTHRITIS

- ½ teaspoon ginger powder, ½ teaspoon turmeric, ¼ teaspoon black pepper, 1 teaspoon ghee, and ½ teaspoon honey. Mix ingredients together and eat alone or place on a cracker or piece of bread. Eat at least one hour after breakfast and then again as a snack in the late afternoon.
- 1 cup milk, ½ teaspoon ghee, and ½ teaspoon turmeric. Drink warm in the evening.
- 1 cup water, 1 to 2 tablespoons castor oil, and ½ teaspoon ginger powder. Boil the water and then add the other ingredients. Drink before going to bed.
- Perform regular self-oil massage with sesame oil (See Abhyanga, page 129). Leave on for 20-30 minutes and follow with a warm shower or bath.
- For more serious arthritic problems, consider undergoing an internal cleansing program, such as Panchakarma (see page 148).

OBESITY

- 4 cups water, 1 teaspoon grated ginger, and ½ teaspoon lemon juice. Boil all ingredients together for 5 minutes, steep for 2 minutes, and strain into a thermos. Sip warm throughout the day. Alternatively, use the Kapha Tea recipe on page 149. This is a highly effective way to flush fat and ama out of the body.
- 1 teaspoon ginger powder, ½ teaspoon cinnamon, ½ teaspoon licorice powder, ¼ teaspoon black pepper, and ¼ teaspoon ground clove. Mix ingredients together in a spice or coffee grinder and add 1 tablespoon honey. Eat at least one hour after breakfast and then again as a snack in the late afternoon. The

HERBS & THEIR DOSHIC EFFECTS

Below, we've listed some of the most common herbs and spices that you'll see repeatedly throughout the home remedies and in Chef Johnny's recipes. We've listed them according to their doshic effects and primary actions. Please note that every herb has a number of medicinal actions—we've just listed a few. We recommend taking time to experiment with any ones that are unfamiliar to you, while also taking care to consult with a health-care professional on any problems of a more serious nature.

The symbol − after a doshic initial refers to a balancing (or decreasing) effect on that particular dosha, while + refers to an aggravating (or increasing) effect.

*The symbol * indicates this herb is OK to consume in moderation.*

V	P	K	HERB	PRIMARY ACTIONS
−	+	−	Ajwan	Increases appetite, improves digestion, eliminates ama, relieves congestion
−	+	−	Asafetida	Increases appetite, aids digestion, decreases abdominal pain
−	+*	−	Basil	Relieves coughs, colds, headaches and fevers, improves immunity
−	+	−	Bay Leaf	Improves digestion, decreases abdominal pain, increases urination
−	+*	−	Black Pepper	Improves digestion, eliminates ama, liquefies mucous
−	−	−	Cardamom	Calms nerves, aids digestion, freshens mouth
−	+	−	Cayenne	Improves circulation, decreases congestion, burns away ama
−	−	−	Cilantro	Cools the GI tract, improves digestion, promotes urination
−	−	−	Coriander	Improves digestion, offsets spicy foods, relieves gases, promotes urination
−*	−	+	Clove	Improves digestion, reduces ama and congestion, soothes coughs
−	+*	−	Cinnamon	Improves circulation, relieves coughs and colds
−	+*	−	Cumin	Stimulates agni, eliminates ama, relieves congestion
−	−	−	Fennel	Stimulates agni without increasing Pitta, improves digestion, promotes breast milk flow
−	+	−	Fenugreek	Promotes breast milk flow, strengthens bones, regulates sugar metabolism
−	+	−	Garlic	Improves digestion, strengthens immunity, strengthens heart
−	+	−	Ginger	Improves digestion, relieves constipation, reduces ama and inflammation
−	−	−	Mint	Soothes stomach, improves digestion
−	+	−	Mustard Seeds	Improves digestion, clears sinuses
−	−	−	Nutmeg	Promotes sleep, relieves cough and colds, decreases morning sickness
−	+	−	Rosemary	Beneficial for headaches, eases menstruation
−	−	−	Saffron	Purifies blood, improves digestion, calms nerves
−	+	−	Thyme	Soothes coughs, improves digestion, decreases gas
−	−	−	Turmeric	Improves digestion, strengthens immunity, decreases inflammation, adds luster to skin

heating spices in this mixture are great for burning away ama from the tissues.

- 2 tablespoons castor oil in ½ cup orange juice or hot water. Drink in the morning and follow a liquid diet for the rest of the day (once a week). This is a highly effective 1-day cleanse.

- 1 to 2 cups hot water, 1 teaspoon honey, and a squeeze of lemon. Drink immediately upon waking every morning. This gently stimulates the bowels and eliminates toxins through the urine.

OTHER RECOMMENDATIONS

- Follow a Kapha-balancing diet. Make sure to include plenty of fresh fruits, vegetables, and whole grains.

- Adopt Kapha-balancing lifestyle recommendations, such as: eat a light breakfast or skip it entirely, make lunch the largest meal of the day, avoid snacking throughout the day, favor a light evening meal, fast for one day each week, get plenty of exercise, sweat regularly, and undergo an internal cleansing program, such as Panchakarma (see page 148). Ayurveda also recommends dry brushing the skin each day with silk or cotton gloves (available at most health food stores). This stimulates circulation and helps regulate the fat metabolism of the body.

- Keep a daily food journal. Take a few moments in the evening to record what you ate for the day. Note if any foods made you feel particularly light and energetic or heavy and dull. This simple exercise brings greater awareness to the foods you eat and allows you to identify the most effective foods in helping you to lose weight.

INSOMNIA

- 1 cup milk, ¼ teaspoon nutmeg powder, and 5 to 6 strands saffron. Place the ingredients in a pan and bring to a boil. Drink warm before going to bed.

- 1 cup milk, 2 to 3 teaspoons poppy seeds, 2 pinches cardamom powder, 1 teaspoon ghee, and 1 teaspoon maple syrup. Soak the poppy seeds for 30 minutes. Place the ingredients in a pan and bring to a boil. Drink warm before going to bed.

- 1 teaspoon chamomile, ½ teaspoon gotu kola, and ¼ teaspoon valerian root. Boil water and steep ingredients together for 5 minutes. Drink before going to bed.

- Massage soles of feet with coconut oil or ghee before going to bed. This helps relax the nervous system.

COLDS/FLU

- For a cough with mucous, mix ¼ teaspoon black pepper powder and 1 teaspoon honey. Take following meals.

- For a dry cough, mix ½ teaspoon ginger powder and 1 teaspoon ghee.

- For a sore throat, blend together 1 teaspoon whole cloves, ½ teaspoon celery seeds, ½ teaspoon turmeric, ¼ teaspoon ginger powder, 1 teaspoon ghee, and ½ teaspoon honey. Take ½ teaspoon multiple times throughout the day. Alternatively, chew one whole clove followed by the black inner seeds of 1 cardamom pod (spit out the remainder of each when finished).

- For sinus congestion and general symptoms of the cold or flu, mix ¼ teaspoon black pepper powder with ½ teaspoon honey. Take 3 to 4 times throughout the day.

FATIGUE

- 5 fresh dates, 2 figs, 2 dried apricots, and 1 cup milk, soy milk, or any other grain-based milk. Soak the fruits in water overnight, strain, and blend with the milk. Drink in the morning.

- 1 ripe mango, 3 to 4 tablespoons ground almonds or cashews, and 1 cup milk. Blend together and drink in the morning.

- 1 cup fresh orange juice with a pinch of salt. This is good for reducing fatigue and rehydrating the body after exercise.

LOW LIBIDO

- 1 cup whole yogurt with 1 tablespoon honey at breakfast.

- 1 ripe banana, 1 cup milk, and ¼ teaspoon cardamom. Blend and drink for breakfast.

- In general, add more onions and garlic to your diet.

- ¼ teaspoon clove, ¼ teaspoon nutmeg, ¼ teaspoon cardamom powder, and 1 tablespoon honey. Mix together and eat away from meals in the morning and evening. This is particularly beneficial for premature ejaculation in men.

PMS

- ½ teaspoon ginger powder, ½ teaspoon ground comfrey root, ½ teaspoon ground rosemary, 1 teaspoon licorice powder, and 1 teaspoon ground dandelion root, and 2 cups filtered water. Mix ingredients together and drink 3-4 times a day, 5 to 7 days before menstruation.

- ½ teaspoon black pepper, ½ teaspoon licorice powder, ½ teaspoon chamomile, 1 teaspoon mint, 1 teaspoon fennel seeds, 1 teaspoon cumin seeds, 1 cup filtered water. Boil for 5 minutes, steep for 2 minutes,

and strain. Drink in the morning on an empty stomach 5 to 7 days before menstruation.

- Beneficial vegetables and fresh herbs for PMS include squash, broccoli, asparagus, dill, and cilantro.

- Avoid salt, caffeine, chocolate, sugar, tobacco, and greasy foods 5 to 7 days before menstruation.

- For a painful menstrual cycle and scanty blood flow, eat more papayas, apples, and pineapple.

- For heavy bleeding, eat more grapes, raisins, figs, and other sweet fruits. Avoid sour fruits and papaya.

ANXIETY

- Vata Tea (see page 149). Keep in a thermos and sip throughout the day.

- 10 raw almonds, ½ cup filtered water, ½ cup coconut milk, 1 ripened banana, and 1 pinch cardamom powder. Soak almonds in water overnight, peel off the skins, and blend with the other ingredients.

- Favor warming and grounding foods (Vata pacifying), especially at breakfast. See Spiced Oatmeal with Bananas and Almonds on page 172.

- Place a few drops of Vata-pacifying essential oils (such as lavender) on your pillow before going to bed. (See page 160 for more on essential oils.)

HEADACHE

- For dull, aching headaches, often associated with sinus congestion, make a topical paste by mixing 2 teaspoons ginger powder with 2 teaspoons water. Apply over forehead and leave on until paste begins to flake off, about 5-7 minutes. Alternatively, boil 4-6 fresh basil leaves in 1 cup filtered water. Strain and drink.

- For sharp or migraine headaches, blend 1 cup filtered water with ¼ cup yogurt, ½ teaspoon rosewater,

2 teaspoons honey, and a few fresh cilantro leaves. Alternatively, apply 2 drops of ghee (melt over low heat to make liquid and allow to cool) or coconut oil into each nostril.

- For throbbing headaches, often associated with dehydration, mix 1 tablespoon organic sugar (such as Sucanat), ¼ teaspoon salt and 10 drops lime juice in 2 cups water.

Skin Problems

- For hives or skin rashes, blend together 1 cup honeydew melon, 1 cup cantaloupe, 2 cups filtered water, 2 tablespoons aloe gel, and ¼ teaspoon black pepper.
- For general skin health, make a tea using ½ teaspoon triphala powder (see Triphala on page 157) and ¼ teaspoon turmeric powder. Boil water, steep the ingredients for 5 minutes, and strain. Drink before going to bed.
- Drink plenty of good quality, filtered water throughout the day.

Foods for Pregnancy & Breast Feeding

Everyone knows that nutrition starts in the womb. Little emphasis, however, is given to proper nourishment during pregnancy. Rather than focusing on balancing foods that support pregnancy, attention is typically given to foods a mother should avoid (such as alcohol), as well as a few beneficial supplements (such as folic acid).

Including all 6 Tastes in one's diet and favoring dosha-balancing foods are particularly important during pregnancy. Incorporating vital foods, complete proteins, and high-quality oils is also essential for properly building the structural tissues and nervous system of the child. Eating mineral-rich foods such as vegetable broths and leafy green vegetables will protect against dehydration, muscular tension, and pregnancy-related hypertension. Avoiding depleting substances such as alcohol, caffeine, and refined sugar will also decrease pregnancy-related complications and the risk of poor nutrition for the child. Lastly, eating in a calm environment, chewing properly, and following other healthy rituals of eating are also important during pregnancy. See Chapter 3 for additional recommendations.

As any mother knows, each trimester of pregnancy presents its own unique challenges. Simple food-based remedies can greatly assist during these times.

1st Trimester

Morning sickness is the hallmark of the first trimester. Small servings of carbohydrates (such as salty crackers) with a few slices of freshly grated ginger and a squeeze of lemon are highly effective for decreasing nausea. Simply holding a sliced lemon close to the nose and inhaling is also remarkably effective.

2nd Trimester

During this period, the energy reserves of the body typically decrease as greater energy is provided for the developing fetus. Protein-rich foods such as soaked nuts and nut butters are particularly beneficial. Nourishing drinks such as warm milk with ghee, raw sugar, and spices are also helpful in restoring vital energy or ojas. See page 306 for Warm Cardamom Milk with Ground Cashew Nuts.

3RD TRIMESTER

In the final three months of pregnancy, the digestive fire typically weakens as the stomach becomes compressed due to the expanding womb. During this time, small, frequent, and easily digestible snacks with digestive spices are recommended. For example, adding 1/3 teaspoon ginger powder to the Rosewater and Currant Rice Balls (page 189) provides a satisfying snack that also stimulates agni. Cooked fruit, such as Baked Apples with Cranberry and Clove (page 200), is also beneficial. Getting plenty of rest is also extremely important during this final phase.

FOODS FOR BREASTFEEDING

While breastfeeding, it's important for a mother to include additional high-quality fats and proteins in her diet. This allows for the healthy production of milk while maintaining overall energetic vitality or ojas. The warm, nourishing qualities of Vata-pacifying foods are particularly beneficial during this time. Excessively dry foods, by contrast, limit milk production and lead to colic in babies.

Foods such as cow's milk, ghee, olive oil, nut butters, and seeds assist in milk production. Since breastfeeding is associated with Kapha, however, it's important not to overload on excessively Sweet foods. Incorporating Bitter and Astringent foods into the diet will help retain balance with respect to Kapha. Animal proteins such as eggs, fish, and chicken are helpful for quickly rebuilding bodily tissues during breastfeeding. Ayurveda also recommends cooking with "galactogue" (or milk-promoting) herbs and spices such as fennel seed, dill seed, and fenugreek seed. Eating overly heating spices is not advised, due to their stimulating effects on the infant. Adding fresh fenugreek sprouts to the Split Mung Dhal on page 251, while eliminating the asafetida and

mustard seeds, makes a great dish for breastfeeding. (See Sprouting on page 105).

Dehydration commonly occurs during breastfeeding, so it's also important to drink plenty of water and other liquids throughout the day. Soaking dried fruits such as raisins, figs, and dates in water and then eating the fruits and drinking the water is a great way to nourish the plasma of the body (the first dhatu or tissue) and prevent dehydration. Drinking 12 to 16 ounces of warm water with a squeeze of lime and a pinch of raw sugar and sea salt is another simple home remedy for quickly rehydrating the body. Nourishing drinks made with milk, ghee, nuts, and spices are also recommended (see "2nd Trimester," above). Calming herbal teas such as chamomile and Vata Tea (page 149) will also help relax the mother's nervous system while promoting restful sleep for the infant.

FOODS FOR BEAUTY & LUSTER

We've all heard the saying, "Beauty is only skin deep." It implies that a pretty face or sculpted body is not the true measure of a person's beauty. Ayurveda agrees with this notion, but also states: "Beauty is never only skin deep." That is because the essence of beauty always lies within. And only by nurturing beauty from the inside-out do you become outwardly radiant.

Today we are told we can purchase beauty in the form of the newest cosmetic product, weight-loss program, or surgical procedure. If beauty from the outside-in actually worked, however, we'd all be glowing by now. Instead, we're left grasping at external sources of beauty that always fall short of expectations.

As you tune into your underlying nature, you will discover the not-so-hidden secrets of creating and maintaining

Common Ayurvedic Herbs & Supplements

In addition to basic herbs and spices, a number of Ayurvedic herbal supplements are becoming widely available in the West today. A fundamental principle of Ayurvedic herbology is: "Use the herb as a whole, and treat the patient as a whole." Rather than stripping away select chemical compounds of a plant, Ayurveda maintains that the synergistic effects of the plant or herb as a whole bring greater balance to the mind and body. We've listed a few of the most common Ayurvedic herbs and formulas below.

Triphala

Actually a combination of three herbs, triphala balances all three doshas and is highly effective as a gentle, non-habit-forming laxative. Ayurvedic lore describes traditional physicians (or *vaidyas*) who would use triphala as the sole herb of an entire practice, due to its innumerable healing properties and uses.

Guggulu

Guggulu is a type of plant resin that is helpful in ridding the body of unwanted fat and ama, while reducing arthritic pain and inflammation. There are different balancing guggulu formulations tailored for each dosha.

Brahmi

Also known in the West as "gotu kola," brahmi calms the nerves, improves memory, and promotes restful sleep. It helps balance all three doshas.

Chavanaprash

Amla, an immunity-enhancing fruit containing high amounts of Vitamin C, forms the basis of this rejuvenating jam. Chavanaprash benefits all three doshas by strengthening the tissues and enhancing overall vitality or ojas. It's not recommended, however, for individuals with high-ama conditions, such as obesity.

Ashwagandha

Ashwagandha is a widely used herb in Ayurveda for its calming effects on the mind and nerves and its strengthening effects on the bones and muscles of the body. It is particularly beneficial for reducing anxiety in men and women, as well as reversing sexual debility in men.

Shatavari

Shatavari is excellent for treating female disorders relating to menstruation, menopause, infertility, low libido, and hormonal imbalances. It also increases the production of breast milk, and decreases digestive disturbances, such as ulcers and hyperacidity in both men and women.

lasting beauty. Beauty is rooted in vibrant health, and as you nourish health on all levels, you radiate beauty outwardly. Ayurveda views beauty as an expected by-product of balance. No matter what physical features you were born with, living a life of balance will create lustrous skin, sparkling eyes, shining hair, and an indescribable glow.

Ojas is the subtle nectar of beauty that lies within. The key to producing ojas lies in reconnecting to your inner nature. As you nurture balance in all areas of life, you burn away the veils clouding your true self. Through developing outward practices such as conscious eating, and inward practices such as meditation, you will discover this fountain of beauty deep within yourself.

The desire for beauty is a natural human impulse. We like to look beautiful because we like to look at and experience beauty. Whether viewing a vast sunset or a brilliant smile, the senses are satiated by observing beautiful things. There's no reason to diminish this impulse by labeling it vanity. Only when we begin to define ourselves through beauty (or lack thereof) does the unhealthy relationship arise. This often occurs when we adhere to society's latest definition of beauty. It's important to remember, however, that true beauty will always transcend society's latest projection of the "perfect" face or figure. After all, what's considered beautiful in today's fashion world—a Vata imbalanced body—would have been considered unfortunate in past eras.

Ayurveda identifies many foods, beauty-care formulas, and treatments that directly target beauty through balance. The majority of these are made with food ingredients. Ayurveda thus adheres to the motto: "Beauty products so good you can eat them!" We've listed a few of these below. For more on Ayurvedic beauty care, please see the Resource section.

BEAUTIFYING FOODS

- Include all 6 Tastes in your diet.
- Follow a dosha-balancing diet.
- Eat fresh, vibrant, organic foods, including plenty of fruits and vegetables.
- Include high quality oils and fiber-rich foods in your diet.
- Drink good quality, filtered water throughout the day.
- Avoid excessive amounts of coffee, sugar, and alcohol.

SPECIFIC BEAUTY-PROMOTING FRUITS & VEGETABLES

FRUITS

- **Luster:** mango, grapes, watermelon, avocado, fresh coconut
- **Skin tone:** apples, pears, avocado, and papaya
- **Blood circulation:** guava, prunes, grapes, watermelon, pomegranate
- **Moisturizing:** avocado, fresh coconut, lemon

VEGETABLES

- **Luster:** carrots, red beets, pumpkin, kale, spinach
- **Skin tone:** sweet potato, broccoli, squash, turnip
- **Blood circulation:** zucchini, cabbage, cilantro, green onion, bitter gourd
- **Moisturizing:** cucumber, asparagus, okra

OTHER BEAUTY-PROMOTING FOODS

- **Nuts, Seeds, and Dried Fruits:** almonds, raisins, figs, sunflower seeds, walnuts, pine nuts, prunes, flaxseeds, and hemp seeds

- **Grains and Legumes:** amaranth, oats, brown rice, mung beans, buckwheat, barley, soy beans, and black eyed peas
- **Spices:** turmeric, saffron, peppermint, fennel, nutmeg, cinnamon, clove, cardamom, and rose water
- **Herbs:** turmeric (root), neem, aloe, licorice, gotu kola, sandalwood, hibiscus, and triphala
- **Dairy:** ghee and cow's milk

MOISTURIZERS

All doshic types benefit from regularly moisturizing their skin. This keeps the skin soft, while forming a barrier of protection from bacteria and make-up. Many commercial moisturizers contain glycerin or alcohol, which create tissue dryness in the long run. Ayurevda recommends applying moisturizers after every shower or bath.

A NOTE ON COSMETICS

If you buy cosmetics over the counter, favor high-quality, natural products. Avoid those containing synthetic or chemical substances, mineral oils, dyes, preservatives, or artificial fragrances. Also, try making a positive shift in your attitude towards cosmetics, wearing make-up to enhance your natural beauty instead of covering up any flaws you might perceive.

OTHER BEAUTY TIPS
- Practice yoga, breathing exercises, and meditation (see page 136).
- Smile more.
- Be sparing with soap.
- Regularly blow up balloons to strengthen your facial muscles.
- Perform regular self-oil massage (see page 129).

ALL-PURPOSE FACIAL MOISTURIZERS

Place the cocoa butter and carrier oils together in a small pan. Heat until the cocoa butter melts. Add the essential oils and allow to cool. Gently apply a small quantity to your face and neck after bathing. Always use organic ingredients when possible.

V VATA

1 OUNCE	cocoa butter
2 OUNCES	almond oil
3 TO 4 DROPS	rose oil or geranium oil

P PITTA

1 OUNCE	cocoa butter
2 OUNCES	extra virgin olive oil or sunflower oil
5 TO 6 DROPS	sandalwood oil or rose oil

K KAPHA

1 OUNCE	cocoa butter
2 OUNCES	almond oil
3 TO 4 DROPS	lavender oil or rosemary oil

FEEDING YOUR BODY, MIND, SENSES AND SPIRIT

According to Ayurvedic philosophy, we are all created of spirit and light rather than mere flesh and bones. The physical body is a temple that houses the finer domains of the mind and soul. As recognized by ancient cultures and religions around the globe, we are actually spiritual beings having a human experience, rather than the other way around. We are crafted from the same energy that weaves together all of life.

To truly understand how to "feed" ourselves, we must, therefore, extend beyond the physical body alone. According to Ayurveda, anything that affects our consciousness is

Feeding Your Senses

Taste (Foods)	Balances Dosha
Vata	Sweet, Sour & Salty
Pitta	Sweet, Bitter & Astringent
Kapha	Pungent, Bitter & Astringent

Smell (Essential Oils)	Balances Dosha
Vata	Warm, sweet, & sour: lavender, vanilla, grapefruit
Pitta	Cool & sweet: rose, peppermint, sandalwood
Kapha	Stimulating & spicy: cedar, eucalyptus, clove

Sight (Colors)	Balances Dosha
Vata	Warming & calming: green, gold, orange
Pitta	Cooling & soothing: blue, white, pastels
Kapha	Stimulating & energizing: red, yellow, purple

Touch (Massage)	Balances Dosha
Vata	Gentle & nurturing, with sesame or almond oil
Pitta	Slow, moderate pressure, with coconut or olive oil
Kapha	Deep, stimulating, with sesame or mustard oil

Hearing (Music)	Balances Dosha
Vata	Slow paced, calming rhythms & melodies
Pitta	Medium paced, calming rhythms & melodies
Kapha	Quick-paced, invigorating rhythms & melodies

considered food. Yoga, breathing exercises, and meditation are thus highly charged types of food, because they directly nourish our deeper consciousness.

The realm of the senses also provides direct nourishment to the finer domains of the mind and soul. For example, a soothing sonata and a blaring car alarm are merely different types of food on the level of the mind and senses. The subtle effects of these sensory impressions feed the mind, much like the 5 Elements feed the physical body. The mind, in turn, nourishes both the physical body and, ultimately, the spirit or soul.

Ayurveda offers many recommendations for properly feeding our senses. The recipes and cooking methods in this book are designed to provide nourishment on all levels of the senses. We've also listed a number of simple tips for feeding the senses in the text box to the left.

THE SEVEN CHAKRAS

Beyond the realm of the senses, even subtler forms of energy impact the nutrition of the body, mind, and spirit. The *chakras* are the seven primary points within the energetic body where energy and matter meet. Just as we are all born with the same number of bones, we are also born with the same energetic anatomy. Knowledge of these centers of consciousness is found throughout the healing traditions of numerous ancient cultures.

Prana flows through three primary channels in the energetic body (called *sushumna, ida,* and *pingala*). These channels intersect at seven major points along the spine. The Sanskrit word *chakra* translates as "wheel" and refers to the swirling disks of heightened energy that occur at these points. The chakras spin in a clockwise direction about three to four inches outside the physical body. They converge inwards towards the body in the shape of a funnel, and link directly to the spine and central nervous system. The chakras are the main points through which the physical, mental, emotional, and spiritual bodies interact. Each chakra governs certain biological functions, thoughts, emotions, and aspects of spiritual development.

Just as we utilize food through the gastro-intestinal tract, we absorb and metabolize energy through the chakras. Freely flowing prana within the body leads to vibrant health. When we are unable to digest certain energies, prana becomes obstructed, causing the chakras to become storehouses for unresolved emotions, fears, and traumas. A primary focus of Ayurvedic and yogic practices is to remove these obstructions. Following a balancing diet and lifestyle is an important step in beginning purification on this subtle energetic level.

As we direct awareness upwards through the chakras, we refine our energetic and spiritual bodies. Instead of acting out of fear through the lower chakras, we begin acting out of love, compassion, and knowledge through the higher centers. The seventh chakra is depicted by the blooming, thousand-petalled lotus, representing the state of enlightenment.

Chakra	Location	Governing aspects	Signs of blockage
1 Muladhara	between anus, genitals	survival instincts	fear, ungroundedness
2 Svadhisthana	just below navel	passion, sexuality, creativity	sexual problems, aggression
3 Manipura	solar plexus region	fulfillment of dreams, personal power	low self-esteem, egoism, digestive problems
4 Anahata	center of chest	universal love, compassion	heart and lung problems, grief
5 Vishudda	base of throat	communication, learning	fear of expression, lying
6 Ajna	between eyebrows	intuition, spiritual insight	lack of concentration, nightmares
7 Sahasra Padma	crown of head	enlightenment, transcendence, bliss	confusion, ignorance, delusion

10 Essential Ingredients for Health

One whose doshas are balanced, whose tissues and wastes are functioning normally, whose appetite is good, and whose body, mind, and senses remain filled with bliss, is called a healthy person. - Sushruta Samhita

1. Love, Be Loved... & Love Some More

Love is the ultimate elixir. When you have an open heart and allow yourself to love life, every cell of your body is positively charged. Love the people and the world around you. Also remember to fall in love with your own life. So often, it's easier to love others than to truly let yourself be loved (whether by yourself or others). As you bring more love into your life, you will develop greater understanding, compassion, and self-awareness. Experience beauty and connect with the universal love that fills all life. Illness has no chance against this brilliant, unbounded love. By knowing this, you hold the single most important key to health and healing.

2. Live Into the Fullness of Your Unique Constitution

Life purpose is not limited to a job title or a single achievement. We all have dynamic, constantly changing purposes that make life exciting and challenging. Living into the fullness of your unique constitution is a guidemap to nurturing your deepest talents and passions, leading directly to true fulfillment in life.

A hallmark of health is to "grow" your talents and passions throughout your lifetime. Often, our inner gifts get swept under the carpet by other life events. Maybe they were not allowed to flourish during childhood, or perhaps the demands of a job relegated them to the backburner of your mind. It's important to remember that it is never too late to exercise these gifts. Simply set aside more time in your life for activities that the inner you knows you should be doing. This could include pursuing some mode of artistic expression, or maybe you'll find you need to make a career change altogether. It's through growing your talents and passions that dreams ultimately become realities.

3. Feed Yourself Proper Fuel

Feeding yourself proper fuel is one of the fastest ways to influence health positively. Incorporating all 6 Tastes into your diet and eating in accordance with your unique constitution ensures that food becomes nourishing fuel rather than toxic junk. The concept of feeding yourself also extends beyond food and nutrition. What activities and sensory impressions do you feed your body and mind each day? Are you a Pitta individual who thrives under pressure, or perhaps a Vata individual whose life is scored by background noise and bustle? If so, try making a conscious effort to avoid activities and impressions with similar qualities to your underlying constitution. Pitta individuals should favor things that cool their fiery natures, while Vata individuals should favor things that soothe their sensitive natures. By feeding yourself proper fuel on all levels, you approach health with wholeness.

4. Exercise Your Body and Mind

Physical activity keeps the inner motors of the body running with ease. Through exercising in accordance with your underlying make-up, you have the ability to keep your body young and vibrant. As you tune into your unique make-up, you may find that a brisk run better serves your underlying Kapha nature than a gentle walk. If you're a Vata individual, you'll probably find that a gentle walk brings you greater balance than a brisk run. In order to keep your mind clear and bright, also remember to exercise those inner talents and passions as mentioned above. If you regularly exercise your body and mind, you will help exorcise all imbalance and illness.

5. USE YOUR SENSES SENSIBLY

Our 5 senses of taste, sight, sound, smell, and touch unlock the joy and grandeur of life. Because our senses constantly feed our physical, mental, emotional, and spiritual beings, it's important to use them wisely. Common ways we often misuse our senses include eating aggravating foods, watching violence on TV, surrounding ourselves with noise, over-using chemical products, and neglecting the body's inherent need for touch. As you begin to step into greater balance, you will naturally desire sensory impressions of a balancing nature. Since we don't live in isolated bubbles, you will also learn to digest efficiently those impressions you could have easily done without.

6. USE YOUR INTELLECT INTELLIGENTLY

We are all intelligent beings. That, however, does not mean we always make the best decisions regarding health. Many times we get sick or become imbalanced simply because we disregard our inner wisdom. You may find that you have a "gut" instinct to avoid a particular food or perform a certain activity, but you do it anyway. Or maybe you replay the same emotional dramas in your life, despite swearing they would never happen again. As you truly honor your intuition and self-guidance, you will learn to recognize what brings you balance or imbalance in life. And with this knowledge, you will equip yourself with the most powerful form of preventative medicine.

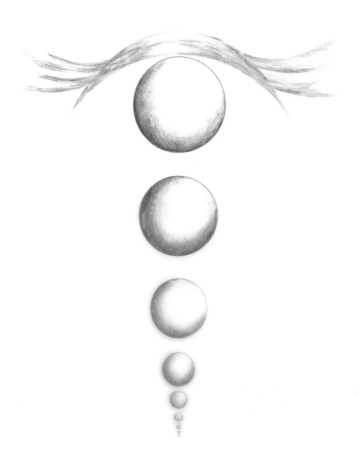

7. MAKE TIME TO STILL YOUR MIND

Taking time to still your mind each day is a way to dissolve stress and nurture creativity. Ayurveda cherishes meditation for its ability to connect us to our true inner natures. It can be thought of as a daily homecoming to your deeper essence, the part of you that lies beyond chattering thoughts, grocery lists, and all fears or desires.

If you look out over an ocean, you will see a seemingly infinite number of waves rippling across the horizon. If you were to visit the ocean floor, however, you would experience vast, uninterrupted stillness. Ayurveda describes the nature of the mind in much the same way. By going beyond our thoughts, we access the underlying field of silence that lies within.

Many people assume they could never completely empty their minds, so they shy away from learning to meditate. The point of meditation, however, is not to do it correctly.

It's to promote inner growth through regularly accessing a deeper part of yourself. All it takes is proper instruction, a little practice, and a regular meditation schedule. In taking time to meditate each day, you will be rewarded by a clearer, calmer, healthier you.

8. Change with the Seasons

Since we are integrally linked to the greater natural environment, it serves us to change as it does. A dosha naturally increases during a season that has similar qualities to itself. For example, the dry, cool nature of Autumn is aggravating to Vata, while the warm, moist nature of Spring is soothing. While an individual with Vata tendencies must take extra measures during Autumn, it serves everyone to makes small changes in diet and lifestyle during each season.

It's also important to observe the greater seasons of one's lifetime. Kapha governs childhood, Pitta governs puberty through middle age, and Vata governs old age. It's no coincidence that babies have baby fat, teenagers have acne, and "the Autumn of one's life" refers to old age, a time when the body becomes dry. Each of these characteristics reflects the underlying qualities and functions of its governing dosha. Through making balancing changes throughout your lifetime, you can ensure that aging is a graceful transition of the seasons.

9. Practice Clarity in Relationships

Relationships are present in all aspects of life. You are constantly relating to everything around you, whether it's the elements of nature, the foods you eat, the people you love, or the money you earn. You're also constantly relating to your own physical and mental well-being. The important question is: How well do you relate?

Practicing clarity in relationships first requires being honest with yourself. By establishing a healthy relationship with your inner self, you will be better prepared to relate to the external world. As you become clear with your own intent, all relationships become healthier. Avoiding a particular food because you listen to your body is an example of practicing clarity. Making a conscious effort to communicate openly with a loved one is another important example. By bringing clarity into your life, you ensure that life is smooth and gratifying rather than bumpy and terrifying.

10. Cultivate Awareness
(Be Aware or Beware!)

Without awareness, things become automated in life: thoughts, words, and actions stem from habit, rather than heart. You may make avoidable mistakes or say things you regret simply because you do not fully participate in life. Cultivating awareness, however, is a way to tap into a more conscious and loving way of life.

As you cultivate awareness, you begin living in the present. You are no longer bound to past actions and future expectations. In this "nowness," the trials of life become easier because answers present themselves with clarity. As you choose to live with greater awareness, positive impulses will begin overriding negative ones. The entire science of Ayurveda can be viewed as a guide-map for helping you to rediscover this unbounded awareness that resides within the very core of your being.

In accessing this awareness, you breed a heightened sensitivity to your own needs and to those of the world around you. Your ego becomes humbled by an appreciation of your interconnectedness to all life. You also begin demanding more from life, since you are no longer content merely to skim across its surface. By choosing to cultivate awareness, you ultimately choose a path of fulfillment and freedom.

PART II

THE COOKBOOK

An Introduction to the Recipes

The Recipe Archetypes

Ayurvedic Basics

The Expanded Recipes

An Introduction to the Recipes

The Recipe Archetypes

THROUGHOUT the writing of this book, Dr. Tom, Dan and I have always referred to this section as the "Archetypes"—and the name stuck! These are quick, easy-to-prepare dishes that are particularly beneficial for each dosha. Throughout, I provide general menu options for Vata, Pitta, and Kapha for each meal of the day. Rather than including one fixed menu for each meal, however, I've included several options. Under the Breakfast recipes for Vata, for example, you'll find several choices, ranging from simple fruit dishes to more hearty options such as Spiced Oatmeal with Bananas and Almonds (page 172). I've purposely kept the recipes short and sweet (and sour, salty, bitter, pungent and astringent, of course!) in order to better familiarize you with the basic principles of Ayurvedic cooking.

In the short introductions at the beginning of each recipe, you'll find helpful shopping tips for those lesser-known or exotic ingredients, useful preparation guidelines, and short explanations of how ingredients and their particular tastes affect the doshas. Occasionally, I also may wax poetically about the wonders of a particular dish to enliven your taste buds and to inspire you to start cooking!

The Expanded Recipes

In the last section, I've included dishes with a touch more flair and complexity for the experienced or adventurous cook. The section is divided into 16 categories, ranging from Main Dishes to Sauces and Desserts. As with all of my recipes, they reflect my cross-cultural cooking style and passion for finding new ways of interpreting the world's awe-inspiring variety of mouthwatering dishes. In this section, I

Ayurvedic Basics

In this section, you'll find simple instructions for preparing basic Ayurvedic ingredients at home. These include vegetable stock, ghee, dosha seasonings, and other ingredients that I use frequently throughout the recipes. While you can find many of these items in health food stores, I recommend making them fresh whenever possible to create vibrant, delicious food. You may find it a surprise that you can make fresh cheese such as panir in ten minutes or a balancing spice mixture in just a few minutes.

Cooking Ayurvedically for Your Family

After reading about the doshas and their balancing tastes in Chapter 1, you may have wondered how you would go about cooking Ayurvedically for an entire family. "If I'm predominantly Vata, my husband's Kapha, and my children are Pitta, how could I possibly cook three meals at once to keep everyone in balance?"

First off, it's important to remember that everyone contains all three doshas at their cores. That's why including all 6 Tastes in a meal is the most important way to nourish each dosha (and thus every person) at a fundamental level. Furthermore, most of us have a strong secondary dosha, which greatly expands the number of foods that help balance our overall constitution. Ayurveda teaches us simply to become more aware of what foods are most effective in keeping our minds and bodies in balance. If you're a Pitta-Kapha type, for example, you will do fine with a little extra spice in your diet. If you know you have a Pitta imbalance, however, you should listen to that inner voice that tells you to avoid heating foods.

If you look at your family as a whole, you'll usually find distinct doshic trends. After becoming acquainted with your own constitutional make-up, take some time to identify these trends. You may determine that Pitta and Vata are the primary doshas at play in your family. In this case, you would put greater focus into preparing meals to help balance these doshas.

Another important way to satisfy different nutritional requirements at a single meal is to offer a variety of dosha-pacifying dishes. This is actually a cornerstone of Ayurvedic cuisine that greatly differs from the single-main-dish dining style of the West. By offering small quantities of a variety of foods, you bring a greater degree of enjoyment to the senses, while also covering a broader nutritional spectrum. Easy-to-prepare starters, side dishes, breads, and condiments are a great way to get started.

Although most Indian restaurants in the West are not Ayurvedic, many of their recipes and practices are still rooted within these same principles. The wide array of complementary side dishes and condiments, for example, incorporate a variety of the 6 Tastes, thus catering to different constitutional types.

Throughout the recipes, I've included suggestions for dishes that work well together. I also encourage you to try different combinations of dishes to see what you enjoy best. A simple dhal or legume soup (like that on page 250), for example, makes a versatile and protein-rich starter that balances each dosha. On days that your cooking time is limited, you can focus on simple ways to incorporate the 6 Tastes into a meal, such as through the dosha seasonings on page 228.

A key to Ayurvedic cooking is to develop a working knowledge of the doshas and their qualities, rather than adopting restrictive rules such as: "I'm a Kapha, so I can only eat Kapha-balancing foods." The recipes in this book are presented as a launch pad for your own exploration of Ayurveda. After a little practice, cooking balancing foods for yourself and family will become second nature. It's also important to remember that cooking Ayurvedically extends beyond choosing dosha-pacifying foods. Eating fresh, clean foods, and taking into account factors such as ambiance, consumption, season, time of day, and proper food combining techniques are all integral components of balanced nutrition. In beginning to pay attention to any one of these areas, you make an important step towards achieving greater health!

USING THE RECIPES

I've kept the recipes simple by presenting them in a uni-doshic format (that is, designed to balance one specific dosha). This will make it easier to familiarize yourself with specific dosha-pacifying ingredients and dishes. It will also allow you to use the recipes therapeutically, if you sense one of your doshas is out of balance. At the same time, I've included doshic alternative boxes at the bottom of most recipes to make them easily changeable for other doshas.

HERE'S HOW TO USE THESE BOXES

- If a P Pitta recipe appeals to you, but you feel like you need to balance Kapha, simply substitute the ingredients by the small box labeled K.

- If you want to make a Pitta dish more suitable for a dual-doshic constitution (say Pitta-Vata), simply substitute some of the ingredients next to the box labeled V.

- In general, rely on your knowledge of the doshas to select the different proportions of ingredients for dual-doshic recipes. For example, if you want a predominantly Pitta-balancing recipe, but also want the dish to be quite grounding, simply choose a hearty Vata-pacifying ingredient that's not overly heating. Most recipes also contain dairy and gluten alternatives for individuals following a Vegan diet or for those who have trouble digesting such foods.

This may all sound a little subjective to you at first, but that's exactly the point. The goal is to enable you to create your own dishes based upon the timeless principles of Ayurveda. The test of whether or not you're effective is in how good they make you feel, not by rigidly following a set of rules or instructions. We recommend using the dosha food lists, cooking charts, and glossary of less common ingredients in the back of the book to help guide you in your acts of culinary creation.

My last word to all you budding Ayurvedic chefs is to remember that this ancient system of healing is an art as much as a science and that cooking uses the heart just as much as the mind. The love, care, and nourishment that go into your food preparations will bring benefits that far surpass any technical details to which you adhere. So with this in mind, remember to keep seeking the source and goal of Ayurveda; namely, the wisdom, peace and inner joy which come from nourishing the body, delighting the senses, expressing emotions, continually purifying the heart and mind, and looking to the highest inspiration that guides us all to greater fulfillment in life.

STEWED APPLES
with Dates & Cinnamon

This comforting homestyle dish is great for balancing Vata. Cooked fruit is easy to digest and helps keep the body clean. Serves 2

Ingredients

2 apples, peeled, cored, and sliced
4 *or* 5 dried apricots, soaked in hot water for 20 minutes
4 dates, preferably Medjool, pitted and cut in half
2 cups filtered water
1 tablespoon maple syrup
1 tablespoon grated fresh ginger
¼ teaspoon ground cardamom
¼ teaspoon ground cinnamon

1   Put all ingredients in a medium saucepan. Bring the mixture to a boil over high heat. Reduce the heat to medium-low, cover, and simmer for 5 minutes.

2   With a ladle, transfer about a third of the contents, including the juice, to a blender or a food processor fitted with the stainless-steel blade. Blend or process until puréed. Stir the purée back into the pan. Serve warm.

P Omit the grated ginger.

K Substitute raisins for the dates.

Dairy- and gluten-free

 # SPICED OATMEAL
with Bananas and Almonds

The key to making oatmeal truly delicious is to use plenty of water so that the resulting dish is creamy and smooth. If you make it too thick and paste-like, nothing you add to it will produce acceptable results! This is an ideal energy breakfast, especially in Winter and Autumn for Vata and Pitta types. Serves 2

Ingredients

3 cups filtered water
1 cup rolled oats
2 tablespoons seedless raisins
¼ teaspoon ground cardamom
¼ teaspoon allspice powder
¼ teaspoon ginger powder
1 banana, peeled and sliced
⅓ cup sliced soaked almonds
⅓ cup organic whole milk *or* cream
2 tablespoons maple syrup

1   Place the almonds in 1 cup filtered water overnight. Peel off the skins and slice.

2   In a medium saucepan over medium heat, bring the water to a boil. Stirring continuously, pour in the oats and then add the raisins and spices.

3   Reduce the heat and simmer, stirring occasionally, until the mixture reaches a smooth, creamy consistency, 7 to 9 minutes. Stir in the banana.

4   Serve in a bowl with cream or milk and maple syrup.

P   Add ¼ teaspoon cinnamon powder; omit the allspice and ginger powder.

K   Substitute tapioca for the oatmeal, use just 2 cups of water, and cook a little longer; also, replace the milk with soy milk. After letting the tapioca cool for a few minutes, sweeten with honey instead of maple syrup and stir in a touch of ground ginger.

For dairy-free, substitute rice milk or soy milk.
Gluten-free

 # VERY ORANGE
Vegetable Juice

Try this lively variation on a classic glass of OJ. To ensure optimal digestion, it is best to drink fruit and vegetable juices on their own or at least 20 minutes before eating. Serves 2

Ingredients

3 carrots, washed and thoroughly scrubbed with a vegetable brush
Juice of 1 large orange
1 teaspoon lime juice
1 tablespoon ginger, fresh grated
6 mint leaves *or* cilantro leaves

1   If using a juicer, cut the carrots into chunks small enough to fit through the feed tube. If you do not have a vegetable juicer, simply grate them very finely and then either press them in a sieve or just squeeze them firmly in your hand. Juice the carrots and pour the juice into a pitcher with a watertight lid.

2   Pour in the orange juice, lime juice and ginger. Add the mint leaves, cover, and shake well before serving.

P   Also recommended

K   Use apple or apricot juice in place of orange juice.

Dairy- and gluten-free

STEAMED ASPARAGUS
& Bok Choy with Tahini and Tarragon Dip

Who said you can't eat vegetables for breakfast? Asparagus and bok choy are loaded with important vitamins and minerals to help kick-start your day. Tahini, a paste made from ground sesame seeds, can be found in health foods stores or in the ethnic section of some grocery stores. Serves 2

Ingredients

For the vegetables:
1 bunch asparagus, trimmed and cut into bite-sized pieces
4 stalks baby bok choy

For the tarragon dip:
1 tablespoon chopped fresh tarragon leaves *or* 2 teaspoons dried tarragon
1 tablespoon tahini
2 teaspoons grated fresh ginger
¼ teaspoon paprika
1 teaspoon lemon juice
1 teaspoon brown rice syrup *or* maple syrup

1 Bring the water to a boil in a steamer or in a saucepan with a steamer insert. Add the asparagus and bok choy leaves, cover, and steam until the vegetables are just tender when pierced with the tip of a small, sharp knife, 10 to 12 minutes.

2 While the vegetables are steaming, prepare the dip. Place all the dip ingredients in a mixing bowl. Whisk until smooth.

3 To serve, arrange the hot vegetables on a serving platter. Pour the tarragon dip over them.

P Substitute mint for the tarragon.

K Add ½ teaspoon mustard powder and a tiny pinch of cayenne pepper.

Dairy- and gluten-free

SPROUTED WHEAT BREAD
with Ghee, Nut Butter or Cream Cheese

The hearty, grounding qualities of this bread and spread make a great breakfast pairing for Vata. Sprouted wheat berries can be found in health food stores, or sprout them yourself following the directions on page 328. Makes 1 small loaf

Ingredients

2 tablespoons caraway seeds
2 cups (about ¼ pound) sprouted wheat berries
1 carrot, grated
1 apple, grated
2 tablespoons freshly ground flax seeds
½ teaspoon salt
Cornmeal, for dusting
Ghee (p. 227), almond butter, cream *or* cottage cheese, *or* sunflower seed butter

1 Preheat the oven to 350°F. Spread the caraway seeds in a single layer on a dry baking sheet. Bake them, stirring occasionally, until lightly browned and aromatic, 5 to 10 minutes. Transfer to a dish to cool, and set aside. Grease a clean baking sheet.

2 Grind the sprouts to a coarse purée in a mortar with a pestle or by processing them in a food processor with the stainless-steel blade. Transfer the wheat berries to a mixing bowl, add the carrot, apple, caraway, flax, and salt, and stir to form a fairly thick dough.

3 With your hands, gather the mixture into a large ball. Wrap it in cheesecloth and squeeze over the sink to remove excess moisture.

4 Dust the baking sheet with cornmeal. Form the dough into a loaf shape and place it on the prepared baking sheet. Alternatively, press the mixture into a small loaf pan and then unmold it onto the baking sheet. Dust the top of the loaf with more cornmeal.

5 Bake the loaf until it forms a nice crust and is firm but still moist inside, 3 to 4 hours. Alternatively, dehydrate it in a kitchen dehydrator set at 115°F for 8 hours.

6 Use a serrated bread knife to cut the loaf into slices ⅓ to ½-inch thick. Serve with ghee, nut or seed butter, tahini, or cream cheese.

P Also recommended

K Substitute sprouted wheat with sprouted barley, millet or buckwheat.
Dairy-free, Contains gluten

V FENNEL & CARDAMOM TEA

For an even more exotic taste, try adding 1 teaspoon licorice powder to the saucepan. Gently crush the cardamom pods with the flat side of a knife for a stronger flavor and delightful aroma. Always favor untreated cardamom pods, which are typically pale green, over bleached white varieties. Serves 2

Ingredients

2 cups filtered water

2 teaspoons whole fennel seeds

5 whole cardamom pods

Organic cream *or* milk

Raw organic sugar, such as Sucanat *or* maple syrup

1 In a small saucepan over high heat, bring the water to a boil. Add the fennel seeds and cardamom pods. Reduce the heat and simmer for 5 minutes.

2 Pour the tea through a strainer into 2 cups. Stir in cream or milk and sugar or maple syrup to taste. (If you are lactose-intolerant, boil the milk first.)

P Also recommended

K Substitite soy milk for the cream and stevia for the sugar.

Dairy-free if made with almond milk, rice milk, or soy milk
Gluten-free

P FRESH FRUIT SALAD

Fresh fruit salads are colorful and easy to prepare. Letting the bowl sit for 30 minutes allows each unique juice to mingle and blend in culinary harmony. Try substituting different fruits, but avoid using sour fruits for Pitta. Serves 4

Ingredients

Juice of 2 ripe oranges
1 tablespoon maple syrup
1 ripe mango, peeled, pitted, and cut into bite-sized pieces
1 pint strawberries, sliced
6 dates, pitted and chopped
1 ripe pear, peeled, cored, and cut into bite-sized pieces
¾ cup red seedless grapes, halved
12 mint leaves, torn
Pinch cardamom

1 In a mixing bowl, stir together the orange juice and maple syrup. Add the remaining ingredients and stir gently until thoroughly combined.

2 Cover the bowl and chill in the refrigerator for 30 minutes.

3 To serve, spoon the salad into chilled bowls or wide-mouthed cocktail glasses.

V Add ½ teaspoon ground ginger.

K Use peach or apricot juice in place of the orange juice and add ½ teaspoon ground ginger.

Dairy- and gluten-free

P MINT TEA

Mint tea is soothing to the digestive system and cooling for Pitta types, especially when served chilled. Serves 2

Ingredients

1 pint filtered water
12 fresh mint leaves, 2 teaspoons dried spearmint *or* peppermint leaves, *or* 1 organic peppermint tea bag

1 In a saucepan over high heat, bring the water to a boil. Reduce the heat to a simmer and stir in the mint leaves.

2 Pour the water and mint into a teapot and let it brew for 10 minutes. (Alternatively, let the mint leaves steep in the saucepan and strain.)

3 Pour the tea through a strainer into teacups. Serve hot or refrigerate and serve cold over crushed ice.

V Also recommended when served hot

K Also recommended when served hot

Dairy- and gluten-free

 STEAMED CAULIFLOWER
& Green Beans with Dill Herb Sauce

With its mild taste and wonderful texture, cauliflower helps keep the fires of Pitta in-check. Dill is also one of the great Pitta pacifying herbs of the Ayurvedic kitchen apothecary. For a sudden burst of wonderful aroma, pour the sauce while the vegetables are still steaming. Serves 4

Ingredients

For the sauce:
2 tablespoons chopped fresh dill
¼ cup organic cream of coconut *or* coconut milk (p. 233)
1 teaspoon maple syrup *or* brown rice syrup
¼ cup filtered water
Pinch turmeric
Salt

For the vegetables:
½ cup bite-sized pieces fresh green beans
1 small head cauliflower, trimmed and broken *or* cut into bite-sized florets

1   First, make the sauce: In a mixing bowl, stir together all the ingredients. Cover and refrigerate for at least 1 hour.

2   Bring the filtered water to a boil in a steamer or in a saucepan with a steamer insert. Add the green beans, cover, and steam for 5 minutes. Add the cauliflower, cover, and continue steaming until the vegetables are tender but still slightly firm, 6 to 7 minutes more.

3   When the vegetables are done, arrange them on a platter, in a serving dish, or on individual plates. Pour the sauce over them and serve immediately.

V Substitute fennel for the cauliflower.

K Substitute honey for the maple syrup and goat cheese mixed with 1 tablespoon water for the cream.

Dairy-free
Gluten-free

P COCONUT, CUCUMBER
& Watercress Smoothie

Coconut milk is highly alkalizing and rich in nutrients. Combined with cucumber and watercress leaves, it provides the foundation for a cooling Pitta smoothie. There's a saying in Ayurveda: "Drink your food and chew your juice." By savoring this smoothie for a few extra seconds in your mouth, you pass along important nutritional information to the stomach, thus improving digestion. Serves 2

Ingredients

1 small cucumber

1 cup organic coconut milk, preferably fresh (p. 233)

1 cup organic rice milk

3 cups coarsely chopped watercress *or* cilantro leaves

1 teaspoon maple syrup

1 Juice the cucumber using an electric juicer.

2 Pour the cucumber juice into a blender and add the remaining ingredients. Blend until smooth.

3 Pour the smoothie into chilled tall glasses and serve immediately.

V Also recommended

K Not recommended due to the sweet, heavy qualities of coconut milk.

Dairy- and gluten-free

P CRISP POTATO PATTIES

These crisp patties make a satisfying side dish for hungry Pitta types. Try them with Scrambled Tofu (recipe follows) or Panir Cheese (p. 231). Serves 3-4

Ingredients

1 pound potatoes, scrubbed thoroughly *or* peeled, cut into 1" pieces

4 ounces organic unsalted butter, at room temperature

2 tablespoons finely chopped fresh parsley

Salt

Freshly ground black pepper

½ cup fine rice flour

½ cup shelled sunflower seeds, partially ground in a spice mill *or* food processor

Ghee (p. 227) *or* extra-virgin olive oil, for frying

1 Put the potatoes in a large saucepan and add filtered water to cover well. Bring to a boil over high heat. Then, reduce the heat. Simmer gently until the potatoes are just tender enough to pierce easily with the tip of a sharp knife, about 30 minutes. Drain the potatoes and leave them in the colander for about 2 minutes to let excess moisture evaporate.

2 Transfer the potatoes to a mixing bowl and, using a handheld masher, mash them thoroughly.

3 Add the butter, parsley, and salt and pepper to taste and mash until thoroughly incorporated. Set the mixture aside.

4 In a small bowl, stir together the rice flour and sunflower seeds. Sprinkle the mixture onto a flat, dry work surface. Scoop up the potato mixture into 6 equal portions of about ⅓ cup each, emptying each portion onto the prepared surface. With a spatula, flatten and shape each portion into a square about ½-inch thick. Then, gently turn each square over to coat its second side with the sunflower seed coating.

5 In a large, nonstick skillet, heat the ghee or oil over medium heat. Add the potato patties and fry until golden brown, 2 to 3 minutes per side.

6 Briefly drain the patties on paper towels, then serve hot.

V Substitute sweet potato, use ghee for frying, and season with black pepper and salt.

K Instead of pan-frying, brush the patties with sunflower oil and sprinkle them with black pepper or paprika. Broil until golden brown, 7 to 8 minutes per side.

Dairy-free if made without the butter or ghee, Gluten-free

SCRAMBLED TOFU
or Panir with Cilantro & Zucchini

Try this tasty, Pitta-balancing alternative to scrambled eggs. Panir (p. 231) is a fresh unripened cheese, traditionally used in Indian cuisine. Serve with Crisp Potato Patties (see previous page) or Chapatis (p. 305). Serves 4

Ingredients

1 tablespoon ghee (p. 227)
1 teaspoon whole cumin seeds
1 small zucchini, thinly sliced
¼ teaspoon ground turmeric (optional)
1 cup soft tofu *or* panir, cut into ½ -inch pieces
3 tablespoons chopped fresh cilantro leaves
2 tablespoons organic cream
Salt

1 In a large sauté pan, heat the ghee over low heat. Add the cumin seeds and cook, stirring frequently, until it becomes aromatic and begins to brown, 1 to 2 minutes.

2 Stir in the zucchini and sauté for 3 to 4 minutes. Add the turmeric and continue to sauté for 1 minute more.

3 Stir in the tofu or panir and cook, stirring continuously, for 1 minute. Stir in the cilantro, cream, and salt to taste and continue cooking until heated through, about 1 minute more. Serve immediately.

V Try asparagus in place of the zucchini. Use sesame or sunflower oil in place of the ghee and season with salt and black pepper.

K Use sunflower oil in place of ghee and omit the cream.

Dairy-free with tofu, olive oil in place of the ghee, and coconut milk or soy cream in place of the cream
Gluten-free

HOT QUINOA CEREAL
with Warm Spiced Soy Milk

Quinoa, pronounced "keen-wah," is a delicious, protein-rich grain that dates back to the time of the Incas. Look for it in health food stores or in the rice and pasta section of grocery stores. Combined here with pungent spices, this warming dish will satisfy hungry Kapha types without weighing them down. Serves 4

Ingredients

1 cup quinoa
2 cups filtered water
2 cups organic soy milk
½ teaspoon ground ginger
¼ teaspoon ground cinnamon
¼ cup honey *or* brown rice syrup

1 Put the water and quinoa in a small saucepan and bring to a boil over high heat. Reduce the heat and simmer, stirring occasionally, until the quinoa is tender and the mixture thickens, about 20 minutes, adding more water if necessary.

2 When the quinoa is almost done, put the soy milk, ginger, and cinnamon in another small saucepan. Warm the mixture over low heat.

3 Divide the quinoa among 4 serving bowls. Pour the warm soy milk over each serving and drizzle with honey or brown rice syrup.

V Use cow's milk in place of soy milk.

P Substitute maple syrup for the sweetener.

Dairy-free
Gluten-free

K STEAMED BROCCOLI
with Collard Greens & Red Pepper

Just a touch of crushed red pepper flakes and lemon enlivens this duet of Kapha-balancing vegetables. Serves 2

Ingredients

1 head broccoli, broken into florets
2 packed cups stemmed collard greens
¼ teaspoon crushed *or* ground red pepper
Squeeze lemon juice

1   Bring the filtered water to a boil in a steamer or in a saucepan with a steamer insert. Add the broccoli and collard greens, cover, and steam until tender, about 10 minutes.

2   Transfer the vegetables to a serving bowl, season with the red pepper and lemon juice and serve immediately.

V Use zucchini and spinach in place of the broccoli and collard greens.

P Use black pepper in place of red pepper.

Dairy- and gluten-free

FRESH FRUIT

Serve a variety of light, fresh fruits rich in astringent taste such as pomegranates, peaches, apples, cherries, pears, and strawberries.

V Choose heavier fruits with sweet and sour tastes, such as mangoes, bananas, dates, oranges, grapes, and grapefruits.

P Choose sweet, cooling, and astringent fruits such as pears, mangoes, apples, coconut, figs, cranberries, and pomegranate.

CHICORY "COFFEE"

Chicory "coffee," a popular substitute for the morning drink, is made from the roasted, ground roots of the chicory plant, available in health food and some grocery stores. Sweeten with stevia, an all-natural sweetener derived from the leaf of the stevia herb. You can find it in liquid or powder forms in health food stores. Serves 4

Ingredients

1 cup organic almond milk (p. 232)
1 cup filtered water
1 tablespoon roasted and ground chicory root
1 tablespoon cut dandelion root (optional)
Stevia

1. In a small saucepan, bring the almond milk and water to a boil over medium-high heat. Reduce the heat and stir in the chicory and, if you like, the dandelion. Simmer for 5 minutes.

2. Pour the drink into individual mugs or cups. Sweeten to taste with 4 drops liquid stevia.

V Substitute chai spice mix for the chicory powder.

P Also recommended

Dairy- and gluten-free

CELERY, APPLE & CARROT
Juice Cocktail

Freshly prepared vegetable juice makes an energy-boosting beverage for Kapha types. Serves 2

Ingredients

3 *or* 4 stalks celery
2 apples
2 carrots, scrubbed
1 small beet (optional)
2 sprigs parsley

1   Cut all the ingredients into pieces small enough to fit through the feed tube of a juicer.

2   Pass all the ingredients through the juicer. Stir briefly to blend them thoroughly.

3   Pour the cocktail into 2 glasses and drink immediately.

V Use peach or apricot in place of the apple, omit the celery, and add ½ cup water and 2 tablespoons coconut milk.

P Omit the beet and use mint in place of parsley.

Dairy- and gluten-free

MIXED SPROUT
& Shredded Jicama Salad with Basil Sauce

A simple salad of fresh sprouts makes a light, refreshing start to the day. For instructions on how to make sprouts at home, see page 105. Jicama is a light, crispy root vegetable that is widely available in health food and well-stocked grocery stores. Serves 4

Ingredients

For the sauce:
2 tablespoons organic plain yogurt (p. 227)
2 tablespoons filtered water
1 tablespoon finely chopped fresh basil leaves, *or* 1 teaspoon dried basil
½ teaspoon honey
Freshly ground black pepper

For the salad:
½ cup sunflower sprouts
½ cup mung bean sprouts
⅓ cup fenugreek sprouts (optional)
⅓ cup shredded jicama
⅓ cup shredded carrot
½ cup seedless raisins
3 tablespoons finely chopped fresh parsley

1   In a small bowl, stir together all the sauce ingredients, and season to taste with black pepper.

2   In a mixing bowl, combine all the salad ingredients. Pour the chilled dressing over them, toss well, and serve.

V Not recommended due the light, astringent qualities of the sprouts and jicama

P Also recommended

For dairy-free, use coconut milk in place of yogurt.
Gluten-free

CREAM OF ASPARAGUS
Soup

The fresh flavor and vivid color of in-season asparagus can brighten any lunchtime table. Fennel fronds add a delicate hint of licorice taste to this elegant soup. You'll usually find them still attached to the stalk when you buy fennel bulbs. Serves 4

Ingredients

1 teaspoon ghee (p. 227)
½ pound asparagus, trimmed and cut into ½-inch pieces
2 cups Vegetable Stock (p. 231) *or* Whey (p. 231)
1 cup filtered water
1 teaspoon chopped fennel fronds *or* fresh marjoram
2 tablespoons organic cream
Salt
Freshly ground black pepper
Chopped parsley *or* toasted sliced almonds, for garnish

1   Heat the ghee in a large saucepan over medium-high heat. Add the asparagus and fennel and sauté for 4 to 5 minutes.

2   Pour in the stock and water. Bring the mixture to a boil, then reduce the heat and simmer for 10 to 12 minutes.

3   Transfer the soup to a blender, add the cream, and blend until smooth. Return to the saucepan, gently rewarm, and season to taste with salt and pepper.

4   Ladle the soup into individual serving bowls, garnish with chopped parsley or toasted almonds, and serve immediately.

P Also recommended

K Use almond cream or goat cheese in place of the cream. Prepare without the whey and use minimal ghee.

Dairy-free when prepared without ghee
Gluten-free

MIXED SEAWEED SALAD

The naturally salty taste found in this salad is highly beneficial for Vata types, due to its moistening effect on bodily tissues. Hijiki and arame are varieties of dried Japanese seaweed, while dulse is dried, coarse seaweed found in parts of the British Isles. You can find these seaweeds in health food stores and Japanese grocery stores. Serves 4

Ingredients

½ cup hijiki
½ cup arame *or* dulse
2 cups coarsely chopped endive leaves
½ cup shredded daikon
½ cup shredded carrot
6 to 8 lettuce leaves, chopped
3 tablespoons shredded fennel bulb
½ cup cottage cheese
3 tablespoons sunflower seeds
2 tablespoons sesame oil
1 teaspoon lime juice *or* rice vinegar

1   Put the hijiki and arame in a bowl and add filtered water to cover them well. Soak for 1 hour. Drain, rinse well, and drain again.

2   Put the seaweed, endive leaves, daikon, carrot, lettuce, fennel, cottage cheese, and sunflower seeds in a large salad bowl. Mix together gently.

3   In a small bowl, whisk together the sesame oil and lime juice. Pour the dressing over the salad. Toss well and serve immediately.

P Not recommended due to the salt content

K Not recommended due to the salt content

For dairy-free, omit the cottage cheese.
Gluten-free

V PASTA
with Stir-Fried Vegetables & Cilantro Pesto

A classic combination of flavors and textures from Italy, the sweetness of the pasta and the unctuousness of the vegetables and pesto make this a soothing dish for Vata.
Serves 4

Ingredients

For the pasta:

8 ounces fresh *or* dried durum-wheat pasta spirals

2 tablespoons extra-virgin olive oil

1 tablespoon lemon juice

1 tablespoon organic unsalted butter

1 tablespoon finely chopped parsley

1 tablespoon finely chopped basil

1 tablespoon finely chopped fresh thyme leaves

Salt

Freshly ground black pepper

For the vegetables:

3 tablespoons extra-virgin olive oil

½ pound fresh pumpkin, peeled and cut into ½-inch cubes

2 medium zucchini, sliced

3 tablespoons finely chopped leek

3 tablespoons torn fresh basil leaves

2 teaspoons dried marjoram

6 to 8 asparagus stalks, cut into ¾-inch pieces,

or about 2 dozen fresh green beans, cut into 1-inch pieces

½ cup Vegetable Stock (p. 231)

1 tablespoon lemon juice

3 tablespoons organic heavy cream

3 tablespoons Cilantro Pesto Sauce (recipe follows)

1 Bring a large saucepan of filtered water to a rolling boil over high heat.

2 Start preparing the vegetables. In a sauté pan, heat the 3 tablespoons of olive oil over medium heat. Add the pumpkin, zucchini, and leek and sauté for 3 to 4 minutes. Stir in the torn basil leaves, marjoram, and asparagus. Add the stock and remaining lemon juice. Cover and simmer until the vegetables are tender, 8 to 10 minutes.

3 While the vegetables are cooking, add the pasta to the saucepan of boiling water. Cook until al dente, tender but still chewy, following the manufacturer's suggested cooking time. Drain in a colander. Return the saucepan to low heat. Add the 3 tablespoons of olive oil along with the 2 tablespoons lemon juice, the butter, parsley, chopped basil, and thyme. Stir until the butter has melted. Add the drained pasta, season to taste with salt and pepper, toss well to coat the pasta, and set aside, covered to keep warm.

4 As soon as the vegetables are tender, stir the cream into the vegetable mixture.

5 Transfer the pasta to a serving dish or bowl, or to individual serving plates or bowls. Spoon the vegetables over the pasta, drizzle with pesto, and serve immediately.

P Use sunflower oil instead of olive oil and omit the leek, basil and marjoram.

K Use corn pasta or amaranth pasta in place of the regular pasta, and substitute eggplant for the zucchini, bok choy or Jerusalem artichoke for the pumpkin, sunflower oil for the olive oil, and goat cheese mixed with 1 tablespoon water; omit the salt.

Dairy-free if made with sunflower oil and coconut milk
Gluten-free if made with corn pasta, amaranth pasta, or wild rice

 Cilantro Pesto Sauce

Enjoy this fresh, vibrant variation on the classic northern Italian sauce of basil, pine nuts, and Parmesan. In addition to pasta, try serving it over roasted potatoes and grilled vegetables. Makes 1½ cups

Ingredients

2 tablespoons pine nuts, walnuts, *or* cashews
1 cup packed fresh cilantro leaves
2 to 3 tablespoons extra-virgin olive oil
3 tablespoons organic plain yogurt (p. 227)
2 teaspoons lemon juice
2 tablespoons filtered water
Salt
Freshly ground black pepper

1   Preheat the oven to 350°F.

2   Spread the pine nuts in a single layer on a baking sheet. Bake, stirring occasionally, until toasted a light golden brown, 8 to 10 minutes. Alternatively, toast them in a dry skillet over medium-low heat, stirring frequently to avoid burning. Transfer to a dish or plate and let them cool for several minutes, until room temperature.

3   Put the toasted pine nuts, basil, olive oil, Parmesan cheese, and lemon juice in a blender or in a food processor fitted with the stainless-steel blade. Blend or process until the mixture forms a thick, fairly smooth paste. Season to taste with salt and pepper.

P   Use sunflower oil in place of olive oil, sunflower seeds in place of pine nuts, and cottage cheese in place of Parmesan cheese.

K   Replace the Parmesan with 1 tablespoon unsalted goat cheese and 1 to 2 tablespoons sunflower seeds.

Dairy-free if made with soy cheese.
Gluten-free

 ## Sweet Potato and Butternut Squash
with Parsley & Thyme

*Soothing and easily digestible, this simple dish is beautifully colored
with rich orange and golden yellow tones, accented by bright green.
If you pack a bag lunch for work, try preparing this quick dish in the
morning. Asafetida, a garlic-like flavoring also known as hing is available in powder or lump form in health food stores and Indian markets.*
Serves 2

Ingredients

2 tablespoons ghee (p. 227) *or* extra-virgin olive oil

1-inch piece leek, finely chopped

¼ teaspoon asafetida

1 large sweet potato, peeled and cut into ¼-inch wedges

1 cup raw peeled, seeded, and coarsely chopped butternut squash

3 tablespoons finely chopped parsley

3 tablespoons chopped fresh thyme leaves

2 tablespoons lemon juice

½ cup Vegetable Stock (p. 231), filtered water, *or* Whey (p. 231)

3 tablespoons cream

Herb Salt (p. 230)

Freshly ground black pepper

1 Heat the ghee in a saucepan over medium heat. Add the
leek and sauté for 3 minutes.

2 Stir in the asafetida, then the sweet potato and squash.
Sauté, stirring frequently, for 2 minutes.

3 Add the parsley, thyme, lemon juice, and stock. Bring the
liquid to a boil, then reduce the heat to low, cover, and
simmer until the vegetables are tender, 8 to 10 minutes.

4 Stir in the cream and season to taste with herb salt and
pepper. Cook until thoroughly heated through, 2 to 3
minutes more. Serve immediately.

P Omit the leek, asafetida, and thyme and use minimal salt and
pepper. Use ghee and season with fresh dill.

K Try cauliflower and green beans in place of the squash and sweet
potato. Use corn oil or safflower oil instead of the ghee, and omit
the salt.

Dairy-free in the Kapha version, Gluten-free

VANILLA ROSEWATER
Currant Rice Balls

Rosewater, an aromatic Middle Eastern, Indian, and Chinese flavoring distilled from rose petals, gives exotic allure to these sweet treats. Look for it in health food stores, Middle Eastern supermarkets and the ethnic sections of well-stocked grocery stores. Serves 4

Ingredients

2 cups cooked basmati rice
3½ cups filtered water with ⅓ teaspoon salt
1 tablespoon dried currants, ground in a food processor
2 whole vanilla beans *or* 1 teaspoon vanilla extract
⅓ cup raw organic sugar, such as Sucanat *or* rice syrup
4 tablespoons whole dried currants
4 teaspoons rosewater
Mint leaves and organic rose petals, for garnish

1 Thoroughly rinse the rice and place it in a pan with 3 ½ cups filtered water and ⅓ teaspoon salt. Bring to a boil, lower the heat and simmer with a lid on, slightly ajar, until all the water is absorbed, about 20 minutes.

2 Put the cooked basmati rice, ground currants, and sugar in a food processor or blender. With a small, sharp knife, split each vanilla bean lengthwise in half; use the knife tip to scrape out the tiny vanilla seeds from each split bean into the processor or blender. Pulse the machine until all the ingredients are just blended but still coarse in texture.

3 Transfer the mixture to a mixing bowl and stir in the whole currants.

4 With moistened hands, form the mixture into 1-inch balls, placing them on a serving platter. Drizzle with the rosewater. Refrigerate, covered, for at least 1 hour.

5 Line a serving platter with rose petals and mint leaves. Arrange the rice balls on top and serve.

P Also recommended

K Not recommended due to the sweet, oily qualities of the rice and sugar

Dairy-free
Gluten-free

P AVOCADO SOUP
with Cucumber

Light and refreshing, this summer soup is sublimely flavored and requires no cooking. Toasting the cumin and coriander unlocks the essential oils and true flavors of the spices. To toast spices, place them in a dry skillet over medium-low heat. Stir constantly for about 1 minute, or until their aromas blossom. Serves 4

Ingredients

1 tablespoon sunflower oil

2 ripe avocadoes, halved, pitted, peeled, and sliced

2 cups fresh carrot juice

3-inch piece cucumber, peeled and coarsely shredded

Juice of 1 orange, about 3 tablespoons

1 teaspoon ground cumin, toasted (see note)

1 teaspoon ground coriander, toasted (see note)

1 tablespoon Bragg's amino acids

2 tablespoons chopped fresh fennel leaves

2 cups filtered water

1 teaspoon maple syrup

½ cup finely shredded zucchini

Salt

1 Put all the ingredients, except the zucchini, in a blender or a food processor fitted with the stainless-steel blade. Blend or process until smooth. Pour into a large mixing bowl.

2 Stir in the zucchini, season to taste with salt, cover, and chill in a refrigerator for 20 minutes before serving.

V Serve warm; omit the cucumber; and add 1 tablespoon lemon juice and a pinch of black pepper.

K Not recommended due to the sweet, oily qualities of avocado.

Dairy- and gluten-free

SUMMER SALAD
with Herbed Croutons

You can make a vibrant salad using just some of the wide variety of leaves available in markets today. Feel free to substitute other seasonal greens from your local farmer's market, health food store, CSA (see page 108) or Co-op (see page 108). Serves 6

Ingredients

1 cup rinsed, dried, and torn romaine lettuce leaves

1 cup rinsed, dried, and torn curly endive leaves

1 cup rinsed and dried arugula leaves

1 cup rinsed, dried, and torn radicchio leaves

½ bunch watercress, stems removed, leaves rinsed, dried, and torn into sprigs

½ cup alfalfa sprouts, rinsed and dried

12 thin slices cucumber

1 avocado, halved, pitted, peeled,

2 slices organic whole wheat bread

Summer Salad Dressing (recipe follows)

1   Put the romaine, curly endive, arugula, radicchio, watercress, and alfalfa sprouts in a large mixing bowl. Add the cucumber, avocado, and croutons.

2   To make the croutons, cut a few slices of organic whole wheat bread into small cubes. Heat up a little sunflower oil or ghee in a frying pan over medium-low heat. Add the bread cubes and 1 tablespoon of mixed dried herbs. Stir until the cubes begin to turn golden brown, about 5 minutes. Add to the other salad ingredients.

3   Pour the dressing over the salad. Toss gently and serve immediately.

Serve with extra dressing at room temperature.

Recommended with the Kapha alternative dressing

Dairy-free if the croutons are made with sunflower oil
Gluten-free without the croutons

SUMMER SALAD DRESSING

Light and fresh-tasting, this creamy dressing is excellent for both Pitta and Vata.

Ingredients

3 tablespoons sunflower oil

2 tablespoons organic cream *or* plain yogurt (p. 227)

2 tablespoons filtered water

1 tablespoon lemon juice

1 tablespoon chopped fresh dill

1 teaspoon maple syrup

1   Put all the ingredients in a blender. Blend until smooth.

Use olive oil in place of the sunflower oil.

Omit the cream or yogurt.

Dairy-free in the Kapha version
Gluten-free

SUMMER SPRING ROLLS
with Almond Cream & Mint Sauce

Fresh vegetables and filo pastry can be easily transformed into these spectacular appetizers. If you like, try substituting Asian rice paper wrappers for the filo, which you merely soften briefly in cold water before filling. Makes 10 rolls

Ingredients

For the spring rolls:

1 pound organic, frozen filo pastry, thawed, cut into 8-inch squares

Sunflower oil *or* ghee (p. 227) (if using filo)

For the filling:

½ cup thin strips of tofu sprinkled with Chef Johnny's Pitta Seasoning (p. 228)

2 ounces white cabbage, shredded

1 ounce purple cabbage, shredded

½ cup finely shredded carrot

¼ cucumber, sliced very thinly

½ cup bean sprouts *or* sunflower sprouts

½ cup organic cottage cheese

For the almond cream sauce:

2 tablespoons raw almond butter *or* 12 blanched almonds

1 tablespoon Bragg's amino acids

1 teaspoon maple syrup

2 teaspoons lemon *or* lime juice

2 tablespoons filtered water

For the mint sauce:

½ cup packed fresh mint leaves

2 teaspoons maple syrup

2 tablespoons lemon juice

2 tablespoons filtered water

1 If using filo dough, preheat the oven to 350°F.

2 Sprinkle the tofu strips with the Pitta seasoning. In a mixing bowl, toss together all the filling ingredients. Set aside.

3 Place all the almond sauce ingredients in a blender. Blend until they form a smooth, light, creamy sauce. Transfer to a bowl, set aside, and thoroughly rinse out the blender.

4 Place all the mint sauce ingredients in the blender. Blend until smooth. Transfer to a bowl and set aside.

5 On a work surface, stack 3 or 4 filo pastry squares together for each wrap, making 10 separate stacks. Divide the filling equally among the filo stacks, placing it along one edge of each stack. Drizzle the almond sauce over the filling. Starting at the edge with the filling, roll up the filo to enclose it, folding in the sides over the filling as you roll, to enclose the filling in a compact cylinder.

6 Place the rolls on a baking sheet and brush with ghee or sunflower oil. Bake until their tops are light golden brown, 5 to 10 minutes. Carefully turn the wraps over and bake until uniformly golden, 5 to 10 minutes more. Serve the spring rolls hot with mint sauce for dipping.

V Recommended in moderation; substitute Chef Johnny's Vata Seasoning (p. 228) for the Pitta seasoning (p. 228).

K Substitute Chef Johnny's Kapha (p. 229) seasoning for the Pitta seasoning and omit the almond sauce.

Dairy-free
Gluten-free if using rice paper wrappers instead of filo

 ## BRAISED BOK CHOY, FENNEL & TOFU
with Lemon & Coriander

*Fennel seeds, fresh ginger, and ground coriander give crisp,
juicy bok choy leaves a delightful flavor. As an alternative
to the tofu, try using seitan, a protein-rich food made from
wheat gluten and often used as a substitute for chicken in
vegetarian cooking. Serves 2*

Ingredients

2 tablespoons organic plain yogurt (p.227)

2 tablespoons plus ¼ cup filtered water

⅓ cup raw organic sugar, such as Sucanat

2 tablespoons ghee (p. 227) *or* sunflower oil

2 teaspoons grated fresh ginger

1 teaspoon ground fennel seeds

1 teaspoon ground coriander

½ teaspoon ground turmeric

1 fennel bulb, cut into small chunks

1 cup tofu cubes (about ½-inch on a side)

¼ cup Vegetable Stock (p. 231) (optional)

1 tablespoon lemon juice

1 head bok choy, *or* 1 bunch curly *or* flat-leaf kale, *or* 6
    cups chopped collard greens

Salt

1   In a small bowl, stir together the yogurt, 2 tablespoons water, and
    sugar. Set aside.

2   Melt the ghee in a large sauté pan over medium-low heat. Add the
    ginger and sauté for 2 to 3 minutes. Add the fennel seeds, coriander,
    and turmeric and sauté for 1 to 2 minutes more. Add the chopped
    fennel and sauté an additional 2 to 3 minutes.

3   Add the tofu, remaining water or optional stock, and lemon juice.
    Bring to a boil, then reduce the heat to a simmer, cover the pan, and
    cook for 10 to 12 minutes. Add the bok choy and stir to combine
    the ingredients. Cover the pan again and continue cooking until the
    fennel and bok choy are tender-crisp, about 5 minutes more.

4   Stir in the reserved yogurt mixture. Simmer gently, stirring
    occasionally, until the sauce is thoroughly heated through, about 5
    minutes. Arrange on a serving platter or on individual plates. Season
    to taste with salt. Serve with Mint Coconut Sauce (p.203).

V.   Omit the kale and add more bok choy.

K.   Recommended without the tofu

Dairy-free if made with sunflower oil and coconut milk in place of the yogurt
Gluten-free

QUICK COUSCOUS
Milk Pudding

Reminiscent of a traditional rice pudding, this dessert features the tiny, grainlike North African pasta shapes called couscous. It can be served warm or cold. Serves 4

Ingredients

3 cups whole organic milk

1 cup filtered water

1 cup couscous

½ cup seedless raisins

5 tablespoons coarsely chopped almonds

⅓ cup raw organic sugar, such as Sucanat

¾ teaspoon ground cardamom

2 cinnamon sticks *or* ½ teaspoon ground cinnamon

3 tablespoons rosewater

1 In a medium saucepan, stir together the milk, water, couscous, raisins, almonds, sugar, and cinnamon.

2 Put the pan over low heat. When the mixture starts to simmer, cook gently, stirring occasionally, until the couscous is tender and the liquid has thickened, 5 to 10 minutes.

3 Remove the pudding from the heat. Before serving, remove the cinnamon sticks and stir in the rosewater. Spoon into individual bowls.

4 Alternatively, transfer to a bowl, cover, and refrigerate until cold, at least 1 hour. Garnish the top of each pudding with a cinnamon stick.

V Also recommended

K Not recommended due to the rich, heavy qualities of whole milk and sugar

Dairy-free if made with coconut milk, almond milk, or rice milk
Contains gluten

SPICY WHITE BEAN, BARLEY & VEGETABLE SOUP

Enjoy this warming soup during the Winter months. The astringent taste found in beans and barley makes them balancing foods for Kapha. Serves 4

Ingredients

1 tablespoon sunflower oil

2 cloves garlic, finely chopped

1 tablespoon finely chopped ginger root

2 teaspoons Chef Johnny's Kapha Seasoning (p. 229) *or* curry powder

2 tablespoons chickpea flour *or* falafel mix

8 cups filtered water

1 organic vegetable stock cube

1 cup large dried butter beans

½ cup red lentils

⅓ cup barley

⅓ cup coarsely chopped bok choy *or* asparagus

2 cups green beans, cut into ¾-inch pieces

4 Brussels sprouts, sliced in half

2 cups baby spinach leaves

4 bay leaves

2 tablespoons chopped parsley

½ teaspoon freshly ground black pepper

Pinch rock salt

Sun Dried Tomato Pesto (p. 298), for garnish

1   In a large bowl, soak the butter beans, red lentils, and barley in 6 cups cold, filtered water overnight.

2   In a large stockpot, heat the sunflower oil over medium heat. Add the garlic and ginger and sauté until fragrant, 2 to 3 minutes. Stir in the Kapha seasoning, chickpea flour, water, and stock cube.

3   Drain the soaked butter beans, red lentils, and barley. Add them to the pot along with the bok choy, green beans, Brussels sprouts, spinach, and bay leaves. Raise the heat, bring the liquid to a boil, and then reduce the heat and simmer, partially covered, for 30 minutes.

4   Remove the bay leaves. Stir in the parsley, pepper, and salt and simmer for 5 minutes more.

5   Ladle the soup into individual heated serving bowls. Drizzle pesto over each serving.

V   Omit the Brussels sprouts and substitute 1 tablespoon Chef Johnny's Vata Seasoning for the Kapha seasoning.

P   Use brown lentils in place of the red lentils. Replace the garlic and pepper with Chef Johnny's Pitta Seasoning and mint for the bay leaves.

Dairy- and gluten-free

 TOSSED SALAD
with Arugula

Enjoy the lively combination of colors, tastes, and textures in this simple salad.
Serves 2

Ingredients

For the salad:
½ cup shelled roasted pumpkin seeds
1 teaspoon Bragg's amino acids
1 large red bell pepper, stemmed, seeded, and cut into ½-inch slices
1 large leek, cut into 1-inch pieces
3 tablespoons ghee (p. 227)
1 bunch arugula
1 cup alfalfa sprouts *or* adzuki bean sprouts
1 cup finely shredded daikon
1 cup watercress

For the dressing:
2 tablespoons sunflower oil
1 tablespoon lemon juice
1 teaspoon honey
1 teaspoon organic mustard
1 teaspoon dried thyme
1 teaspoon dried basil
½ teaspoon ground turmeric
¼ teaspoon paprika
Salt
Freshly ground black pepper
Seedless raisins, for garnish

1 Preheat the oven to 350°F.
2 Spread the pumpkin seeds in a single layer in a baking dish. Bake until golden brown, about 7 minutes. Remove them from the oven, sprinkle with the Bragg's, and stir well.
3 Raise the oven temperature to 400°F. Spread the bell pepper and leek pieces on a baking sheet, drizzle them with ghee, and bake until soft, about 30 minutes.
4 In a large salad bowl, toss together the pumpkin seeds, bell pepper, leek, arugula, alfalfa sprouts, daikon, and watercress.
5 In a mixing bowl, whisk together all the dressing ingredients. Pour the dressing over the salad, toss well, and serve.

P Use finely shredded white cabbage or jicama in place of the daikon; omit the mustard, paprika, thyme, and basil and use maple syrup in place of honey.

V Use garden cress instead of arugula.

Dairy-free if made with sunflower oil in place of ghee.
Gluten-free

K | SOFT TACOS
with Spicy Black Beans & Mango Salsa

The hot peppers, cumin and garlic in this Mexican dish are perfect for kickstarting the digestive system. You can make your own organic tortillas (p. 304) or buy them in health food stores. To save time, cook the beans for 30 to 35 minutes in a pressure cooker, following the manufacturer's instructions. Serves 4

Ingredients

For the soft tacos:

1 cup black beans

8 cups filtered water

2 teaspoons chopped fresh ginger

Pinch asafetida

2 teaspoons Chef Johnny's Kapha Seasoning (p. 229) *or* curry powder

4 organic corn tortillas (p. 304)

2 tablespoons sunflower oil

2 tomatoes, peeled and seeded

1 small red bell pepper, stemmed, seeded, and thinly sliced

⅓ cup mung bean sprouts

6 mustard green leaves, stemmed and torn into bite-sized pieces

For the salsa:

1 ripe mango, peeled and chopped

½ teaspoon finely chopped green chili

½ teaspoon crushed garlic

1 teaspoon paprika

1 tablespoon lime juice

1 tablespoon whole cumin seeds

1 tablespoon chopped fresh parsley

1   Rinse the black beans and soak them overnight in 4 cups cold, filtered water to cover.

2   Drain the soaked black beans. Put them along with the 8 cups filtered water in a large stockpot.

3   Bring to a boil over high heat. Stir in the ginger and asafetida. Reduce the heat and simmer until the beans are tender, 1 to 1 ½ hours.

4   Meanwhile, prepare the salsa. Roast the cumin seeds in a small dry sauté pan over low heat until fragrant, 1 to 2 minutes. Stir together all its ingredients in a mixing bowl. Cover and refrigerate until serving time.

5   When the beans are done, stir in the Kapha seasoning or curry powder.

6   Place a tortilla on each of 4 serving plates. On top of each tortilla, neatly distribute and arrange the tomato, bell pepper, sunflower sprouts, and mustard greens. Top the vegetables on each tortilla with 1 to 2 tablespoons of the bean mixture. Add a generous spoonful of the salsa. Or encourage each person to create their own taco.

V   Use wheat flatbread and adzuki beans and leave out the tomatoes and chili pepper.

P   Substitute wheat flatbread for the tortillas and leave out the chili pepper, paprika, and tomato; use endive or Swiss chard in place of the mustard greens and omit the garlic.

Dairy- and gluten-free

RED LENTIL DHAL
with Beets & Coriander

With its strong yet subtle spices and brilliant color of fresh beets, this lentil dish makes quite an impression. Serve as a side dish or main course. Serves 6

Ingredients

2 cups red lentils, rinsed

2 medium beets, peeled and cut into 1-inch chunks

3 cups filtered water

2 teaspoons ground coriander

¼ teaspoon asafetida

½ teaspoon ground turmeric

1 teaspoon dried sage

¼ teaspoon freshly ground black pepper

1 tablespoon lemon juice

1 Rinse the lentils and soak in 4 cups cold, filtered water for 30 minutes and strain.

2 Put the lentils, beets, and water in a large saucepan. Bring to a boil over high heat, stirring occasionally.

3 Meanwhile, put the coriander in a dry skillet. Cook over medium-low heat until it darkens slightly and its fragrance blossoms, about 1 minute. Stir in the asafetida, remove the skillet from the heat, and stir the spices into the lentil mixture along with the turmeric, sage, pepper, and lemon juice.

4 When the mixture reaches a boil, reduce the heat and simmer, partially covered, stirring occasionally, until very thick, 45 to 60 minutes. Serve hot.

V Substitute split mung dhal for the red lentils.

P Substitute split mung dhal for the red lentils and omit the asafetida.

Dairy- and gluten-free

 # BAKED APPLES
with Cranberries & Cloves

 # FRESH FRUIT

Baked apples with a sweet, spicy filling makes a simple, yet classic dessert. It's also a fun dessert for children to help make. Serves 4

Serve a variety of fresh fruits such as apples, berries, cherries, peaches, or persimmons.

Ingredients

4 large apples, any variety, cores removed

¼ cup cranberries *or* dried blueberries

½ cup raisins

4 dried figs, finely chopped

2 dried apricots, finely chopped

1 teaspoon ginger powder

2 teaspoons cinnamon

1 cup apricot *or* peach juice

16 whole cloves

4 teaspoons honey (optional)

1   Preheat the oven to 350°F.

2   Remove the core from each apple, without cutting all the way through the skin.

3   Place the cranberries, raisins, figs and apricots in a mixing bowl. Sprinkle in the ginger and cinnamon and pour in the apricot juice. Mix the ingredients thoroughly and then fill the apples with the fruit mixture, allowing some to sit on top of the apples.

4   Place the apples in a baking dish and pour any remaining fruit mixture over them.

5   Pierce each apple with 4 cloves.

6   Bake for 20 minutes or until the apples appear tender. Remove from the oven and place on individual serving plates. Drizzle with honey, if desired.

V Substitute peaches for the apples.

P Substitute cardamom powder for the ginger powder.

V ROASTED LEEK
& Fennel Bisque

Fennel, with its intriguing anise flavor and smooth texture, yields a soothing soup ideal for Vata. Roasting vegetables before putting them into a soup gives them a more luxurious texture and richer flavor. To toast walnuts for the garnish, spread them on a baking sheet and bake in a 300°F oven just until they darken slightly in color, about 7 minutes. Serves 4

Ingredients

½ cup coarsely chopped leeks

2 cups sliced fennel bulb

2 cups filtered water

1 cup Vegetable Stock, made fresh (p. 231) *or* from a stock cube

2 tablespoons lemon juice *or* lime juice

1 tablespoon chopped fresh basil, *or* 1 teaspoon dried basil

½ teaspoon paprika

5 bay leaves

Salt

Freshly ground black pepper

3 tablespoons organic heavy cream

Salt and freshly ground black pepper, to taste

1 cup toasted walnuts, for garnish

1   Preheat the oven to 400°F. Spread the leeks in a baking dish and roast them until soft, about 30 minutes. Remove from the oven and set aside.

2   Put the fennel in a large saucepan along with the water, stock, lemon juice, basil, paprika, bay leaves, and salt and pepper to taste. Bring to a boil over high heat.

3   Reduce heat to a simmer. Stir in the roasted leeks and continue simmering for 20 minutes.

4   Remove and discard the bay leaves. Ladle the soup into a blender, add the cream, and blend until puréed. Adjust the seasoning to taste with salt and pepper. Ladle the soup into individual heated bowls and garnish with toasted walnuts.

P   Omit the walnuts and leek.

K   Substitute eggplant for fennel and soy milk for the cream; also add a pinch of cayenne.

Dairy-free if using soy milk
Gluten-free

V GREEN BEANS & CARROTS
with Fried Almonds

This simple vegetable dish gains added interest with crunchy almonds and a flavorful sauce. Serves 4

Ingredients

1 tablespoon plus 2 teaspoons ghee (p. 227)
½ cup slivered almonds
1 cup fresh green beans cut into ½-inch pieces
1 cup very thinly sliced carrots
1 tablespoon organic cream
2 teaspoons dried mint
1 teaspoon lemon juice
Salt
Freshly ground black pepper

1 Heat 1 tablespoon of the ghee in a small sauté pan over medium-low heat. Add the almonds and sauté until lightly browned, about 6 minutes. Remove from the pan and set aside.

2 Fill a medium saucepan with 1½ inches of filtered water. Add the green beans and carrots. Bring the water to a boil over high heat. Simmer on medium heat until the vegetables are tender, about 15 minutes. Drain, reserving the cooking liquid.

3 In a serving bowl, toss together the drained vegetables and the almonds.

4 In a separate bowl, whisk together the cream, mint, lemon juice, remaining 2 teaspoons ghee, and reserved cooking juices. Pour the mixture over the vegetables and toss well.

5 Season to taste with salt and pepper and serve while still hot.

P Substitute sunflower seeds for the almonds.

K Substitute pumpkin seeds for the almonds.

Dairy-free if made without cream and with sunflower oil in place of the ghee
Gluten-free

Mint Coconut Sauce

Rich-tasting and aromatic, this sauce makes a delicious addition to rice dishes. *Makes around 2 cups*

Ingredients

2 tablespoons ghee (p. 227)
1 tablespoon chickpea flour
2 tablespoons mild curry powder
1½ cups organic coconut milk, preferably fresh (p. 233)
3 tablespoons organic plain yogurt (p. 227)
10 to 20 fresh mint leaves, torn into small pieces
Salt
Freshly ground black pepper

1 Heat the ghee in a small saucepan over medium low heat. Add the chickpea flour and stir with a wire whisk to form a paste. Cook for 2 minutes, stirring constantly. Add the curry powder and stir for 2 minutes more.

2 Whisking continuously, slowly pour in the coconut milk. Continue whisking until the mixture begins to thicken to a creamy consistency. Remove the pan from the heat.

3 Whisk in the yogurt and mint leaves. Season to taste with salt and pepper.

Also recommended

Substitute soy milk for the yogurt, basil leaves for the mint, and add a pinch of cayenne.

For dairy-free, use sunflower oil instead of ghee.
Gluten-free

V BIRIYANI
with Mint Coconut Sauce

Biriyani is a traditional Indian pilaf of rice elaborated with other ingredients, such as nuts and dried fruit. Most are accompanied by a curry (p. 271), dhal (p. 250), or the yogurt dish known as raita (p. 301) to moisten the rice. Here, a minty coconut sauce is served alongside. Serves 4

Ingredients

1½ cups basmati rice, rinsed well with filtered water

⅓ cup split mung beans

3 cups filtered water

1 teaspoon turmeric powder

1 tablespoon ghee (p. 227)

2 tablespoons finely shredded carrot

2 tablespoons roasted pistachio nuts, shelled, coarsely chopped

2 tablespoons Chef Johnny's Vata Seasoning (p. 228) *or* curry powder

5 cardamom pods

6 whole cloves

2 tablespoons seedless raisins, chopped

1 tablespoon finely grated lemon zest

¼ cup Vegetable Stock (p. 231) *or* filtered water

Salt

Freshly ground black pepper

Mint Coconut Sauce (see previous page)

1 Soak the mung beans in 1 cup cold, filtered water for 2 hours and drain.

2 Put the rinsed rice, drained soaked mung beans, and 3 cups water in a large saucepan. Add the turmeric and bring to a boil over high heat, then reduce the heat, cover, and simmer for 45 minutes.

3 About 10 minutes before the rice and mung beans are done simmering, heat the ghee in a sauté pan over medium heat. Add the carrots and sauté for 2 minutes. Add the pistachio nuts and sauté for 2 minutes more. Stir in the Vata seasoning or curry powder, cardamom pods, cloves, raisins, lemon peel, lemon juice, and stock.

4 Bring to a boil, reduce heat and simmer for 3 minutes.

5 Stir the carrot mixture into the rice mixture when its 45 minutes of cooking time is over. Simmer until the rice is tender and moist but no excess liquid remains in the pan, 5 to 10 minutes more.

6 Season the biriyani to taste with salt and pepper. Serve with Mint Coconut Sauce on the side.

P Substitute Pitta Seasoning (p. 228) for the Vata seasoning.

K Substitute Kapha Seasoning (p. 229) for the Vata seasoning.

For dairy-free, use olive oil instead of the ghee and omit the yogurt in the sauce. Gluten-free

V FRESH CILANTRO SAUCE

Cilantro is in fact the fresh leaves of the coriander plant. In its fresh uncooked form, the widely available herb is an effective digestive aid for all three doshas. Also try this delicious sauce over pasta. Serves 4

Ingredients

1 cup chopped fresh cilantro

1 date, pitted

2 teaspoons grated fresh ginger

2 to 3 tablespoons extra-virgin olive oil

Juice of 1 lemon

2 tablespoons organic plain yogurt (p. 227)

1 teaspoon maple syrup *or* jaggery

Salt

Freshly ground black pepper

1 Put all the ingredients except the salt and pepper in a blender. Blend until smooth.

2 Adjust the seasonings to taste by pulsing in salt and pepper.

P Substitute coconut milk for the yogurt.

K Use sunflower oil in place of the olive oil; try goat cheese in place of the yogurt or just omit the yogurt.

For dairy-free, omit the yogurt or use coconut milk. Gluten- free

 ## Roasted Tuscan Vegetables
with Fresh Cilantro Sauce

This colorful baked dish immediately evokes the Italian countryside. When you take it out of the oven and pour the fresh, bright green sauce over the vegetables, you'll have a piece of edible art! Serves 4

Ingredients

1 red bell pepper, stemmed, seeded, and cut into bite-sized chunks

1 whole butternut *or* acorn squash, halved, peeled, seeded, and cut into bite-sized cubes

2 zucchini, cut diagonally into bite-sized chunks

1 fennel bulb, cut into bite-sized chunks and steamed for 10 minutes

2 parsnips, peeled and cut into bite-sized chunks

2 tablespoons chopped fresh basil

4 tablespoons extra-virgin olive oil

2 tablespoons ground fennel seeds

¼ teaspoon asafetida

Juice of 1 lime

Herb Salt (p. 230)

Freshly ground black pepper

Fresh Cilantro Sauce (p. 204))

1 Preheat the oven to 350°F.

2 In a deep baking dish, spread the bell pepper, squash, zucchini, fennel, and parsnips.

3 Sprinkle with the olive oil, fennel seeds, asafetida, basil, lime juice, herb salt and black pepper to taste. Toss well.

4 Bake until the vegetables are soft and beginning to caramelize, 45 to 55 minutes.

5 Serve the vegetables hot, along with the Fresh Cilantro Sauce for each person to spoon over them.

P Substitute sunflower oil for the olive oil, and use dried mint in place of the asafetida, basil, salt, and pepper.

K Use jicama, eggplant, cauliflower, Brussels sprouts, and leeks in place of the squash, zucchini, and parsnips; replace the olive oil with safflower oil or corn oil.

Dairy- and gluten-free

CREPES WITH SUMMER FRUITS
and Whipped Cream

Rich and Summery, this dessert has a cooling effect due to its predominance of sweet taste. Amaranth flour is made from the ground seeds of the amaranth plant. The cooked seeds can also be used as a morning cereal. Look for amaranth flour and seeds in health food stores or Caribbean and Asian markets. Serves 4

Ingredients

For the crepes:
1 cup quinoa flour
²/₃ cup amaranth flour
3 tablespoons rice flour
1½ cups filtered water
1 cup organic coconut milk (p. 233)
Sunflower oil *or* ghee (p. 227) for cooking the crepes

For the filling:
2 cups mixed strawberries, blackberries, *or* pitted cherries
3 tablespoons raw organic sugar, such as Sucanat
1 tablespoon filtered water

For the topping:
1 cup organic cream, whipped

1   Preheat the oven to its lowest setting.

2   To make the crepe batter, put the quinoa, amaranth, and rice flours into a blender with the water and coconut milk. Blend until smooth. The batter should be thin but creamy. Transfer the batter to a bowl and leave it to rest at room temperature for 10 minutes.

3   Heat a little sunflower oil or ghee in a small nonstick sauté pan over medium-low heat. Stir the batter and ladle it into the pan just enough to cover the bottom thinly. Tilt the pan back and forth to spread the batter evenly. Cook the crepe until its underside is golden brown, 1 to 2 minutes, using a spatula to lift an edge to check.

4   Flip the crepe over and cook the other side until golden, 1 to 2 minutes more.

5   Remove the crepe from the pan, transfer it to a covered baking dish, and keep it warm in the oven while you prepare more crepes.

6   When the crepes are almost done, start the fruit filling. Put the berries or cherries and the sugar and water in a saucepan. Cook over medium heat, stirring occasionally, until the fruit juices form a syrupy sauce, about 10 minutes.

7   To serve, divide the fruit filling among the crepes, rolling each one up around the filling. Carefully transfer to serving plates and top with whipped cream.

P Also recommended

K Recommended in moderation; use soy cream in place of dairy cream.

Dairy-free if made with soy cream, Gluten-free

 # GARDEN PEA & ZUCCHINI
Soup

 # COLESLAW
with Toasted Pumpkin Seeds

Despite carrying the distinction of being one of the smallest vegetables in the cook's repertoire, the garden pea offers a bold flavor, as fresh as Springtime. After taking the time to shell fresh peas, you'll be rewarded by a creamy, green soup that encapsulates the delivery of the season. Serves 4

Enjoy this Pitta-pacifying version of a picnic favorite. Serves 4

Ingredients

4 cups Vegetable Stock (p. 231)
or 4 cups filtered water and 1 organic vegetable stock cube
1 tablespoon chickpea flour
1 medium zucchini, sliced
1 cup fresh shelled peas *or* trimmed snow peas
2 teaspoons dried mint *or* 4 tablespoons chopped fresh mint
2 tablespoons organic cream
Salt

Ingredients

⅓ cup shelled pumpkin seeds
1 teaspoon Bragg's amino acids
1 cup finely shredded white cabbage
½ cup shredded carrot
⅓ cup seedless golden raisins *or* black raisins (optional)
2 tablespoons sunflower oil
1 tablespoon lemon juice
1 teaspoon maple syrup
¼ teaspoon ground turmeric
3 tablespoons organic crème fraîche *or* cream cheese
2 tablespoons organic heavy cream
1 teaspoon dried dill
1 teaspoon dried mint

1   Put ¼ cup of the stock in a small mixing bowl. Add the chickpea flour and whisk until smooth. Set aside.

2   Put the remaining stock, zucchini, peas, and mint in a saucepan. Bring the mixture to a boil over high heat. Reduce the heat and simmer for 10 minutes. Whisk in the chickpea flour–stock mixture. Simmer for 5 minutes more.

3   Ladle the mixture into a blender, add the cream, and blend until smooth.

4   Season to taste with salt. Serve immediately.

V Add a little ghee.

K Omit the cream.

Dairy-free in the Kapha version
Gluten-free

1   Preheat the oven to 350°F. Spread the pumpkin seeds in a single layer in a baking dish. Bake them until golden brown, about 7 minutes.

2   Remove the pumpkin seeds from the oven and immediately toss them in a mixing bowl with the Bragg's. Add the cabbage, carrot, pumpkin seeds, and, if you like, the raisins and toss well.

3   In a small mixing bowl, whisk together the oil, lemon juice, maple syrup, turmeric, crème fraîche, cream, dill, and mint. Pour this dressing over the cabbage mixture, toss well, and serve.

V Use shredded daikon instead of cabbage; add watercress, basil, and marjoram.

K Substitute honey for the maple syrup and use goat cheese mixed with a little goat's milk or water instead of the cream and crème fraîche; substitute basil and thyme for the mint and dill; add a pinch of black pepper.

Dairy-free if made with soy cream in place of the cream and crème fraîche.
Gluten-free

SATAY-MARINATED TOFU & SUMMER SQUASH
Wraps

Traditionally used to season the Southeast Asian kebabs known as satays, this simple marinade adds great flavor to a hearty Pitta-friendly wrap. Serve with Fresh Mango Chutney (p. 285) or Ginger-Raisin Chutney (p. 301).
Serves 4

Ingredients

For the marinade:

¾ cup organic coconut milk, preferably fresh (p. 233)

3 tablespoons Bragg's amino acids

3 tablespoons ground almonds

2 to 3 tablespoons lime juice

1 tablespoon grated fresh ginger

1 tablespoon maple syrup

1 tablespoon Chef Johnny's Pitta Seasoning (p. 228) *or* mild curry powder

For the wraps:

1 cup firm tofu cut into ½-inch strips

3 tablespoons ghee (p. 227), extra-virgin olive oil, *or* sunflower oil

2 teaspoons grated fresh ginger

2 tablespoons finely chopped fennel bulb

3 tablespoons finely shredded unsweetened coconut

1 teaspoon Chef Johnny's Pitta Seasoning (p. 228) *or* mild curry powder

1½ cups ½-inch chunks zucchini, summer squash, *or* peeled and seeded butternut squash

¼ cup filtered water *or* Vegetable Stock (p. 231)

3 tablespoons chopped fresh cilantro

4 sprouted wheat tortillas *or* flatbreads

1 cup curly *or* Belgian endive leaves, torn into bite-sized pieces

1. Preheat the oven to 350°F.

2. In a small mixing bowl, stir together all the marinade ingredients.

3. Put the tofu in a baking dish. Pour the marinade over the tofu and leave it at room temperature to marinate for 20 minutes. Then, put the baking dish in the oven and bake the tofu for 20 minutes.

4. Meanwhile, heat the ghee in a medium saucepan over medium heat. Add the ginger and sauté, stirring constantly, for 1 minute. Add the fennel and sauté, stirring frequently, until soft, 3 to 5 minutes. Add the coconut and the 1 teaspoon of korma powder. Sauté, stirring continuously, until the coconut browns slightly, about 3 minutes.

5. Add the zucchini or squash and sauté, stirring continuously, for 3 to 4 minutes.

6. Add the water or stock and continue to cook until the zucchini is just tender, about 6 minutes more or 12 minutes more if using squash.

7. Remove the pan from the heat and let the mixture cool for several minutes.

8. Then, stir in the cilantro and baked tofu.

9. Arrange the tortillas or flatbreads on a work surface and divide the filling mixture evenly among them, spooning it across the center of each one. Spoon the filling into the center of each tortilla or flatbread and add a few leaves of endive.

10. Fold the side of each wrapper over the filling, then fold the edge nearest you over the filling and continue to roll up the wrapper to enclose the filling completely. Serve immediately.

V Substitute Chef Johnny's Vata Seasoning (p. 228) for the Pitta seasoning.

K Use corn tortillas (p. 304); substitute Chef Johnny's Kapha Seasoning (p. 229) for the Pitta seasoning; reduce the quantity of tofu or use cooked chickpeas instead; substitute Jerusalem artichoke for the summer squash; omit the coconut milk, and add a pinch of black pepper to the marinade.

Dairy-free if using olive or sunflower oil
Gluten-free

BARLEY KITCHARI

One of the great balancing and easily digested complete meals in Ayurvedic cooking, the simply prepared and endlessly varied grain recipe called kitchari combines protein and carbohydrate in a single dish. Barley is considered the best grain for balancing Pitta, due to its mildly astringent taste and cooling properties. Serves 4

1   Rinse the mung beans and soak in 1 cup cold, filtered water for 2 hours.

2   Heat the coconut oil or ghee in a large saucepan over medium heat. Add the celery seeds, fennel, and coriander. Sauté, stirring frequently, until fragrant, 3 to 4 minutes.

3   Add the barley, mung beans, water or stock, and vegetable stock cube.

4   Bring to a boil, reduce the heat, and simmer, covered, for 45 minutes, stirring occasionally.

5   Season to taste with salt and pepper. Serve warm.

V   Substitute brown basmati rice for the barley.

K   Substitute sunflower oil for the coconut oil.

Dairy-free if using coconut oil
Gluten-free if using basmati rice

Ingredients

2 tablespoons coconut oil *or* ghee (p. 227)
1 tablespoon celery seeds
2 tablespoons ground fennel seeds
2 tablespoons ground coriander
1 cup pearl barley, rinsed
⅓ cup mung beans
3 cups filtered water *or* Vegetable Stock (p. 231)
½ organic vegetable stock cube
Salt
Freshly ground black pepper

POACHED PEARS
with Sweet Orange & Date Glaze

At once elegant and simple, this dessert makes a beautiful finale to any meal. Choose pears that have fairly firm flesh suitable for cooking, such as Anjou, Bartlett, Bosc, or Winter Nellis. Serves 6

Ingredients

6 ripe, but firm pears

Filtered water

4 dates, preferably Medjool, pitted and finely chopped

Juice of 1 orange

2 teaspoons maple syrup

1 teaspoon ground cinnamon

½ teaspoon grated fresh ginger

⅛ teaspoon orange oil *or* ½ teaspoon grated orange zest

2 tablespoons finely shredded unsweetened coconut

 Also recommended

K Also recommended in moderation

Dairy- and gluten-free

1   With a vegetable peeler or a small knife, peel each pear, leaving it whole and with its stem intact. Cut a thin slice off the base of each pear so that it can stand upright. Place the pears upright in a saucepan just large enough to hold them side by side. Add an inch of water to the pan.

2   Place the pan over medium heat and bring the water to a simmer. Add the dates, orange juice, maple syrup, cinnamon, ginger, and orange oil or zest. Reduce the heat and simmer gently, uncovered, until the pears are tender enough to be pierced easily with the tip of a sharp knife, about 12 minutes.

3   With a slotted spoon, carefully remove the pears from the pan, placing them upright on either a large flat serving dish or on individual serving plates.

4   Continue to simmer the liquid in the pan over low heat, stirring continuously, until it thickens enough to coat the back of a spoon. Spoon this glaze over the pears, garnish with coconut, and serve.

KASHMIRI PARSNIP
& Apple Soup

Often overlooked, the parsnip has a wonderfully subtle flavor and distinct texture. The natural sweetness harmonizes well with apples in this delicious soup. The heating spices and light consistency make it balancing for Kapha. Serves 6

Ingredients

3 medium parsnips, peeled and chopped
2 apples, peeled, cored, and sliced
4 cups Vegetable Stock (p. 231)
or 1 organic vegetable stock cube and 4 cups filtered water
2 cups filtered water
1 tablespoon ghee (p. 227) *or* sunflower oil
1 tablespoon Chef Johnny's Korma Powder (p. 229) *or* curry powder
2 teaspoons ground roasted caraway seeds
¼ teaspoon freshly ground black *or* red pepper
5 bay leaves
Salt

1   Put the parsnips, apples, stock, and water in a stockpot.

2   Bring the vegetable stock and 2 cups filtered water to a boil over high heat. If using a stock cube, boil the 6 cups filtered water together with the stock cube. While the liquid is coming to a boil, heat the ghee or sunflower oil in a small sauté pan. Stir in the korma powder, caraway seeds, and pepper. Cook, stirring occasionally, for 2 minutes.

3   Stir the sautéed spice mixture and the bay leaves into the pot. When the mixture comes to a boil, reduce the heat and simmer, partially covered, for 15 minutes.

4   Remove the pot from the heat. With a ladle, transfer a third of the mixture into a blender or a food processor fitted with the stainless-steel blade. Carefully blend or process until smoothly puréed.

5   Stir the purée back into the soup. Season to taste with salt before serving.

V   Also recommended

P   Also recommended

Dairy- and gluten-free

GRATED DAIKON SALAD

To add a little color to your table, try this lively salad full of Kapha-balancing vegetables. Serves 4

Ingredients

5 cups torn beet greens
1 cup peeled, shredded daikon
1 cup endive leaves
½ cup shredded beet
½ cup toasted shelled pumpkin seeds
⅓ cup sunflower sprouts
2 teaspoons lime juice *or* lemon juice
2 teaspoons dried basil
1 teaspoon honey
1 teaspoon dried thyme
8 red radishes, sliced
Freshly ground black pepper

1   Put all the ingredients in a large bowl. Toss well.

V   Omit the endive and use cress or watercress. Use less or no red radish and toasted blanched almonds in place of the pumpkin seeds.

P   Substitute grated cucumber in place of the daikon. Use a few endive leaves in place of the beet greens. Omit the basil and thyme and add some chopped dill.

Dairy- and gluten-free

RATATOUILLE

Evoking Mediteranean colors, fragrances and herbs, this classic dish provides a satisfying main course for Kapha. Serve with a grain dish or salad. Serves 6

Ingredients

1 tablespoon sunflower oil

3-inch piece of leek, thinly sliced

1 small green bell pepper, quartered, stemmed, seeded, and thinly sliced

1 globe eggplant, peeled and thickly sliced

2 zucchini, thickly sliced

3 ripe tomatoes, peeled, and seeded, and coarsely chopped

1 clove garlic, minced (optional)

1 cup Vegetable Stock (p. 231) *or*
⅓ organic stock cube boiled in 1 cup filtered water

2 teaspoons dried oregano

1 teaspoon dried marjoram

Salt

Freshly ground black pepper

4 ounces organic fresh, creamy goat cheese, sliced

1 Preheat the oven to 350°F.

2 In a saucepan, heat the oil over medium-low heat. Add the leek, bell pepper, eggplant, and zucchini and sauté, stirring frequently, for 5 minutes.

3 Stir in the tomatoes, garlic, stock, oregano, marjoram, and salt and black pepper to taste.

4 Transfer the mixture to a casserole, cover, and bake for 30 minutes.

5 Remove the casserole from the oven and take off the lid. Preheat the broiler.

6 Arrange the goat cheese slices on top of the ratatouille. Broil, uncovered, until the cheese begins to melt and turn golden, about 5 minutes.

V Recommended in moderation

P Not recommended due to the heating spices, eggplant and tomato

Dairy-free without the goat cheese
Gluten-free

BUCKWHEAT PILAF
with Chickpeas

Equally colorful and delicious, this festive dish is perfect for any Summer gathering. Buckwheat is one of the ultimate Kapha-balancing grains. You can give it extra flavor by toasting it for 5 minutes before adding water to the pan.
Serves 6

Ingredients

2 cups buckwheat groats *or* amaranth seeds

4 cups filtered water (*or* 5 cups if using amaranth)

3 tablespoons ghee (p. 227) *or* sunflower oil

1 tablespoon grated ginger

2 teaspoons whole cumin seeds

1 tablespoon Chef Johnny's Korma Powder (p. 229) *or* curry powder

1 cup chopped kale

1 cup chopped mustard greens

3 tablespoons Vegetable Stock (p. 231) *or* filtered water

2 tablespoons finely chopped red bell pepper

2 tablespoons finely chopped yellow bell pepper

1 cup cooked chickpeas

3 tablespoons seedless raisins

2 tablespoons finely chopped parsley

2 tablespoons finely chopped cilantro

1 tablespoon Bragg's amino acids

Freshly ground black pepper

6 whole lettuce leaves

1 Put the buckwheat or amaranth in a large saucepan. Place the pan over medium heat and cook, stirring continuously, for 5 minutes to toast the grains.

2 Add the water to the saucepan. Raise the heat and bring the water to a boil. Then reduce the heat and simmer, uncovered, without stirring until the water has been absorbed, about 12 minutes.

3 Heat the ghee in a large frying pan over medium heat. Add the ginger and cumin seeds and sauté for 3 minutes. Stir in the korma powder and cook for 2 minutes more. Add the kale, mustard greens, peppers, and vegetable stock and cook for 4 to 5 minutes more.

4 Add the chickpeas, raisins, parsley, cilantro, and Bragg's and stir well. Continue cooking briefly until all the ingredients are heated through.

5 To serve, arrange the lettuce leaves cupped sides up on a platter or individual serving plates. Spoon the pilaf into the lettuce cups.

V Use adzuki beans in place of the chickpeas and leeks in place of the mustard greens.

P Use white basmati rice in place of the buckwheat and Chef Johnny's Pitta Seasoning (p. 228) in place of the korma powder; omit the garlic and leek.

Dairy- and gluten-free

K STRAWBERRIES & PEARS
in Suspension

The secret to this dazzling dessert is agar-agar, a dried seaweed used as a jelling agent, which has about five times the gelling power of gelatin and will set at room temperature. You'll find it in health food stores or Asian markets in blocks, powder, or flakes; the flakes are easiest to use. Serves 6

Ingredients

3 tablespoons agar-agar flakes
3 cups apple juice mixed
2 cups filtered water
2 pears, peeled and cut into ½-inch pieces
12 ripe strawberries, stemmed and halved
½ teaspoon ground cinnamon *or* cardamom
4 cloves
6 to 8 fresh mint leaves, chopped finely, plus extra for decoration
Organic, pesticide-free rose petals

1 Put the agar-agar flakes in a mixing bowl. Add the apple juice and leave the agar-agar to soften at room temperature for 20 minutes.

2 Pour the agar-agar and apple juice into a saucepan. Add the water. Place the pan over medium heat and, as soon as it reaches a simmer, reduce the heat to low and simmer for 2 minutes.

3 Gently stir in the pears, strawberries, cinnamon, and cloves. Continue simmering for 6 minutes more. Remove the pan from the heat and gently stir in the chopped mint.

4 Ladle the mixture into 6 cocktail glasses or individual clear glass bowls, taking care to distribute the fruit evenly. Leave at room temperature to set.

5 Before serving, garnish with mint leaves and rose petals.

V Also recommended

P Also recommended

Dairy- and gluten-free

V DATE & AMARANTH ENERGY BARS

Fruits, nuts, and seeds combine here to make a grounding and energizing snack for Vata. It's easiest to grind sesame seeds in a small coffee grinder designated for herbs, nuts, seeds, and spices. Makes 16 bars

Ingredients

½ cup sesame seeds
½ cup amaranth
1 cup pitted dates, preferably Medjool
¼ cup whole sesame seeds
½ teaspoon ground cardamom
½ teaspoon ground ginger
½ cup lightly toasted walnuts, chopped
½ cup toasted blanched almonds, chopped
4 drops orange oil *or* 1 teaspoon grated orange zest
1 tablespoon molasses
¼ cup honey
1 to 2 tablespoons almond milk (p.232) *or* rice milk

1 In a dry skillet over low heat, toast the sesame seeds until golden, about 4 minutes. Remove and grind coarsely.

2 In the same skillet, sprinkle the amaranth seeds evenly. Cover over medium heat until all the amaranth pops, about 4 minutes. Transfer the popped amaranth to a serving bowl.

3 Put the dates in a food processor fitted with the stainless-steel blade. Pulse the machine until the dates form a thick paste.

4 Transfer the date paste to a mixing bowl and add the ground sesame seeds. Stir and mash with a wooden spoon to mix them together. Add the popped amaranth and remaining ingredients and stir well.

5 Transfer the mixture to an 8-inch square baking pan, pressing it down evenly to cover the bottom of the pan. Refrigerate for 1 hour.

6 With a table knife, cut the mixture into 16 pieces. Use the knife to pry them from the pan. Wrap each piece individually in waxed paper or parchment paper. Refrigerate in a sealable container.

P Omit the ground ginger and replace the molasses with maple syrup.

K Not recommended due to the sweet, heavy qualities of the dates and the oily quality of the nuts

Dairy- and gluten-free

ROASTED SUNFLOWER PÂTÉ

on Bruschetta or Oatcakes

To make bruschetta, the Italian-style toasted bread slices, cut a loaf of wholewheat French bread into ¼-inch slices. Brush lightly with extra-virgin olive oil and toast in a 350°F oven until lightly browned, about 7 minutes. Makes 5 cups

Ingredients

2 cups shelled sunflower seeds
3 tablespoons Bragg's amino acids
2 cups cooked chickpeas
¼ cup sunflower oil
3 tablespoons chopped parsley
3 tablespoons lemon juice
2 tablespoons organic plain yogurt (p. 227) (optional)
1 teaspoon paprika
1 teaspoon maple syrup
1 teaspoon chopped fresh mint
1 teaspoon chopped fennel leaves

1 Sprinkle the sunflower seeds on a baking tray. Place in a 300 degree oven and bake until golden brown, about 9 minutes. Add the Bragg's to the sunflower seeds and stir together on the tray. Remove and grind until medium-coarse.

2 Put all the ingredients except the sunflower seeds in a blender or a food processor, fitted with the stainless-steel blade. Blend or process to form a smooth paste.

3 Add the roasted sunflower seeds and mix well. Serve immediately.

4 Serve with Bruschetta (see intro above) or Oatcakes (recipe follows).

V Also recommended

K Replace the maple syrup with honey and omit the yogurt.

Dairy-free if made without the yogurt
The pâté is Gluten-free

OATCAKES

This Scottish and Irish favorite is simple to make and a delicious companion to appetizers, soups, or salads. Makes 8 oatcake wedges

Ingredients

1 tablespoon organic unsalted butter
5 tablespoons filtered water
1 cup medium-ground oatmeal, plus extra for rolling out dough
½ teaspoon salt
Pinch baking soda

1 Preheat the oven to 350°F. Grease a 10-inch round cake pan.

2 In a small saucepan, put the water and butter and place over low heat until the butter melts.

3 Meanwhile, in a mixing bowl, stir together the oatmeal, salt, and baking soda. Stir in the butter-water mixture to form a smooth dough.

4 Sprinkle a work surface with some more oatmeal. Turn out the dough onto the work surface and, with a rolling pin, roll out the dough to form a 9-inch circle.

5 Carefully transfer to the prepared cake pan.

6 Bake until the oatcake is crisp and browned, about 50 minutes. Turn it out onto a cutting board and, with a sharp knife, cut it into 8 wedges. Serve warm or at room temperature.

V Also recommended

K Not recommended due to the dairy and gluten

Contains dairy and gluten

 SPROUTED CHICKPEA HUMMUS
with Parsley on Rye Crackers

Sprouting your own chickpeas is easy to do. First, thoroughly rinse and drain 2 cups of dried chickpeas. Put them in a mixing bowl and add filtered water to cover them by at least 2 inches. Leave at room temperature to soak for 24 hours. Drain and rinse the chickpeas and put them in a clean jar or bowl. Cover with a clean cloth and put them in a dark place at warm room temperature. Rinse and drain the chickpeas every 6 hours. They will begin to sprout after 24 hours. Let them continue to grow for 2 days before use. Makes 3 cups

Ingredients

2 cups sprouted chickpeas
1 tablespoon sunflower oil
3 tablespoons lemon juice
½ teaspoon freshly ground black pepper
½ teaspoon ground paprika
½ cup grated carrots
½ cup finely chopped fresh parsley
Salt
Rye crackers

1   Put the chickpeas, sunflower oil, lemon juice, pepper, and paprika in a food processor fitted with the stainless-steel blade. Process until the mixture forms a fairly smooth paste.

2   Wash and finely grate the carrots.

3   Transfer the mixture to a bowl, stir in the parsley, grated carrots and season to taste with salt.

4   Serve with rye crackers for dipping or spreading.

V Recommended in moderation

P Leave out the pepper and paprika.

Dairy- and gluten-free

 SPICED DATE-NUT BALLS

Vata types will find these energy-packed morsels especially satisfying.
Makes 16 balls

Ingredients

⅓ cup blanched almonds
⅓ cup shelled walnuts
⅓ cup shelled pumpkin seeds *or* sunflower seeds
10 pitted dates, preferably Medjool
¼ teaspoon cardamom
¼ teaspoon cinnamon
Few drops orange oil

1   Put all the ingredients in a food processor fitted with the stainless-steel blade.

2   Pulse the machine until the mixture forms a thick paste. Refrigerate for 1 hour before serving.

3   With a spoon, form the mixture into bite-sized balls, shaping them gently with your hands and putting them on a plate or tray.

P Recommended in moderation

K Not recommended due to the sweet, heavy qualities of the dates and oily quality of the nuts

Dairy- and gluten-free

TROPICAL FRUIT TRAIL MIX

Keep this mixture close at hand as an easy snack for busy Pitta types.

Ingredients

Shelled fresh coconut, cut into bite-sized pieces
Dried mango, cut into bite-sized pieces
Dried pineapple, cut into bite-sized pieces
Dried figs, cut into bite-sized pieces
Seedless raisins *or* pitted dates

1 In a mixing bowl, toss together the ingredients.
2 Store in an airtight container at room temperature.

V Not recommended due to the dried fruit

K Omit the coconut.

Dairy- and gluten-free

POPPED AMARANTH

Light, toasty popped amaranth seeds provide an energizing Kapha snack. Popcorn works equally well. Serves 2

Ingredients

1 cup organic dried amaranth seeds
1 tablespoon Chef Johnny's Kapha Seasoning (p. 229) *or* curry powder
1 tablespoon Bragg's Amino Acids (optional)

1 Sprinkle enough of the amaranth seeds to cover the bottom of a cast-iron skillet. Cover over medium heat until all the amaranth pops, about 4 minutes. Turn off the heat.
2 Add the seasoning and Bragg's to the skillet and stir until thoroughly coated.
3 Transfer the popped amaranth to a serving bowl.

P Recommended in moderation

V Not recommended due to the light, drying qualities of the popped amaranth

Dairy- and gluten-free

V CHAI

Also known as Yogi tea, the hot, soothing Indian mixture of water, milk, spices, and sugar has become a popular drink in the West, with good reason. For another version made with black tea, see page 306. Serves 6

Ingredients

3 pints filtered water

8 crushed cardamom pods

4 whole cloves

2 whole star anise pods

2 cinnamon sticks

1 tablespoon grated fresh ginger

1 tablespoon whole fennel seeds

1 cup organic whole milk

Raw organic sugar, such as Sucanat

1 In a large saucepan, bring the water to a boil over high heat. Add the cardamom, cloves, star anise, cinnamon, ginger, and fennel. Reduce the heat and simmer for 10 minutes.

2 Stir in the milk. Add the sugar to taste. Continue to simmer until the sugar has dissolved, 2 to 3 more minutes.

3 Pour the chai through a strainer into heated cups or mugs.

P Not recommended due to the heating spices

K Also recommended; see page 306 for a Kapha chai made with black tea.

For dairy-free, add coconut milk, rice milk, or soy milk in place of the cow's milk.
Gluten-free

BEVERAGES

 MINT & CINNAMON LASSI

 WARM CRANBERRY JUICE
with Cloves

Whether sweet or savory, the yogurt-based Indian drink called lassi always refreshes. Enjoy thirty minutes before or after a meal or on its own as a mid-afternoon beverage. Serves 3

On a chilly day, you'll find this as satisfying as mulled cider or wine. Look for stevia powder or concentrate at your local health food store. Serves 4

Ingredients

2½ cups filtered water

½ cup organic plain yogurt (p. 227)

¾ cup raw organic sugar, such as Sucanat

20 fresh mint leaves

1 teaspoon ground cinnamon, for garnish

1 Put the water, yogurt, sugar, and mint leaves in a blender and blend until frothy.

2 Pour into tall glasses and garnish each serving with a dusting of cinnamon powder.

V Also recommended

K Recommended in moderation with less sugar

Contains dairy
Gluten-free

Ingredients

4 cups pure unsweetened cranberry juice

or 1 cup whole fresh *or* frozen cranberries

5 cups filtered water

1 apple, peeled, cored, and chopped

5 whole cloves

1 cinnamon stick

4 to 6 drops liquid stevia concentrate *or* 2 teaspoons honey

1 Put the cranberry juice, cranberries, and apple in a blender and blend until smooth.

2 Transfer the thick liquid to a saucepan, add the cloves and cinnamon stick, and cook over medium-low heat until steaming, about 15 minutes.

3 Pour through a fine-meshed strainer into heated mugs. Sweeten each serving to taste with stevia or honey.

V Not recommended due to the astringent taste of the cranberries

P Also recommended

Dairy-free
Gluten-free

 # SWEET LASSI

The popular Indian yogurt drink, enjoyed in both sweet and salty versions, is a refreshing digestive aid and excellent source of protein.
Serves 4

Ingredients

5 cups cold filtered water
1 cup organic plain yogurt (p. 227)
¼ cup raw organic sugar, such as Sucanat
¼ teaspoon ground cardamom
¼ teaspoon sandalwood powder *or* 1 drop sandalwood oil (optional)
1 tablespoon rosewater (optional)

1 Put all the ingredients in a blender and blend until smooth.
2 Pour into chilled glasses and serve immediately.

P Also recommended

K Not recommended due to the sour taste and heavy qualities of the yogurt and sweetness of the sugar

Contains dairy
Gluten-free

 # SOY MILK
with Peach & Pear

Enjoy the spicy overtones of this warming Kapha beverage. *Serves 4*

Ingredients

2 cups organic soy milk
1 cup water
½ cup peach nectar
½ cup pear nectar
1 teaspoon raw honey
½ teaspoon ground allspice
Pinch nutmeg
Pinch ground ginger

 # WARM ALMOND MILK
with Coconut & Mango

Warm and soothing, this tropical toddy is ideal for both Pitta and Vata.
Serves 4

Ingredients

2 cups organic almond milk (p. 232)
1 cup filtered water
½ cup mango purée *or* mango nectar
½ cup organic coconut milk, preferably fresh (p. 233) , *or* 1
    tablespoon grated coconut
½ teaspoon ground cardamom
1 drop sandalwood oil (optional)
1 teaspoon maple syrup (optional)

1 Put all the ingredients in a small saucepan over medium heat. Stir continuously with a whisk until the mixture is thoroughly warmed through.
2 Pour or ladle the almond milk into individual heated mugs and serve immediately.

V Also recommended

K Not recommended due to the sweet, oily qualities of the coconut milk

Dairy-free
Gluten-free

1 Put all the ingredients in a blender. Blend until smooth.
2 Pour the mixture into glasses and serve.

V Substitute maple syrup for the honey.

P Omit the ground ginger and substitute maple syrup for the honey.

Dairy-free
Gluten-free

 # GHEE

 # YOGURT

Ghee, also known as clarified butter, is butter that has had the solid fats and salts removed by slow simmering. Usually associated with Indian cooking, ghee is also widely used in French cuisine for making sauces. Classical Ayurvedic texts describe the many medicinal, nutritional and healing benefits of ghee. It is said to balance all three doshas, and lead to the production of ojas, or vital energy, in the mind and body. Kaphic types are advised to use ghee in smaller quantities due to its oily nature. Ayurvedic herbology also values ghee for its ability to carry herbs and other medicines deep into the tissues of the body.

Ghee is excellent for sautéing vegetables and panir or tofu and also for frying spices. It has a smooth, slightly nutty taste and an opaque, deep yellow color when cool. Try adding a teaspoon to rice at the beginning of cooking to achieve a delicious, subtle effect. Ayurveda considers ghee one of the most stable cooking oils, due to its ability to withstand high temperatures without burning or becoming rancid.

For the best results, I recommend always starting with organic unsalted butter when possible. If organic butter is unavailable, however, the process of clarification will remove the majority of impurities found within commercial butters today.

Ingredients

1 pound *or* more organic unsalted butter

1   Cut the butter into cubes and put in a large, heavy bottomed saucepan over medium heat. When all of the butter has melted, reduce the heat to a simmer and cook, stirring occionally, with a slotted spoon. After about 5 minutes, the butter will begin to form a white froth on its surface and will also create popping sounds as moisture evaporates from the butter. During this stage, it is important to keep stirring at regular intervals.

2   After about 10 minutes, the froth will begin to sink to the bottom of the pan where it will collect and form a golden-brown crust. Turn off the heat and skim off residual foam with a teaspoon. When the butter becomes clear, turn off the heat and let it sit for 15 minutes.

3   Finally, carefully pour the contents through a fine sieve into a bowl or jar, leaving the residue at the bottom of the cooking pan.

4   Transfer the ghee to a clean storage container. Ghee is best stored at room temperature and is said to get better with age, such as fine wine. The key, however, is always to use a clean spoon when taking ghee from the jar, in order to avoid spoilage resulting from contamination with other foods. I recommend having two containers: a large one for general storage and a smaller one that you refill every few weeks or when needed for daily use.

Contains dairy, gluten-free

Rich in protein and highly beneficial for replenishing intestinal flora, yogurt is a versatile dairy product with many culinary uses. Try using it as a thickener for sauces, soups and salad dressings or mixed with 4 parts filtered water to create the traditional Indian drink known as lassi (see recipe below).

Ingredients

1 quart organic whole milk

1 tablespoon organic yogurt *or* 1 teaspoon yogurt culture

1   In a saucepan over medium heat, bring the milk to a boil. Remove the pan from the heat and stir in the yogurt or culture.

2   Pour the milk into a wide-necked vacuum bottle, or just transfer to a clean bowl, cover, and put somewhere at warm room temperature. Leave overnight. The next morning you will have yogurt.

Try mixing 1 cup water with ¼ cup yogurt, 2 tablespoons honey or maple syrup and ½ teaspoon ground fennel and cumin each for a lassi drink, which is excellent for digestion.

P K Yogurt is best taken diluted with water for Pitta and Kapha types.

Contains dairy
Gluten-free

Note: If you do not have time to prepare your own ghee, organic varieties are also now widely available in health foods stores.

CHEF JOHNNY'S
VATA SEASONING

This useful blend of traditional spices is a must for the Ayurvedic kitchen. Use it in dhals, soups, kitchari, rice, sauces and curries. It will bring an authentic Eastern flavor to Indian, Thai and other Asian dishes, while helping balance the Vata body type. Note the inclusion of the spice asafetida and salt, which are both very grounding for Vata. You can also add the seasoning at the end of cooking, sprinkling it onto rice or legume dishes as a condiment.

Ingredients

2 tablespoons whole fennel seeds

1 tablespoon whole coriander seeds

1 tablespoon whole cumin seeds

1 tablespoon ground turmeric

1 tablespoon dried basil

2 teaspoons powdered ginger

2 teaspoons salt

1 teaspoon asafetida

1   Put all of the ingredients in an electric grinder or spice mill and grind them. Pour the ingredients into a bowl and stir further with a spoon until well combined. Transfer to an airtight container and store at cool room temperature. I recommend using the mixture within a month for the best potency. You can also cut the ingredient amounts in half to ensure freshness.

For a slightly sweet version, try adding 1 heaped teaspoon raw organic sugar, such as Sucanat, to the mixture.

CHEF JOHNNY'S
PITTA SEASONING

Similar to the Vata seasoning, there are many uses of this flavorful spice and herb mixture. The combination is designed to add an enticing flavor to dishes while helping to keep the fires of Pitta in balance.

Ingredients

2 tablespoons whole coriander seeds

2 tablespoons whole fennel seeds

2 tablespoons whole cumin seeds

2 tablespoons chopped fresh mint leaves

1 tablespoon whole cardamom seeds

1 tablespoon ground turmeric

1   Put all of the ingredients in an electric grinder or spice mill and grind them. Pour the ingredients into a bowl and stir further with a spoon until well combined. Transfer to an airtight container and store at cool room temperature. I recommend using the mixture within a month for the best potency. You can also cut the ingredient amounts in half to ensure freshness.

For a slightly sweet version, try adding 1 heaped teaspoon raw organic sugar, such as Sucanat, to the mixture.

Chef Johnny's
KAPHA SEASONING

Kapha types will find this mixture useful for those times when a dish requires bold flavor and a little kick. It's excellent in curries, dhals, and vegetable dishes. Also try sprinkling it into popcorn for a spicy snack (see page 222).

Ingredients

2 tablespoons whole coriander seeds

1 tablespoon whole cumin seeds

1 tablespoon whole fungreek seeds

1 tablespoon ground ginger

1 tablespoon ground turmeric

1 tablespoon ground cinnamon

1 tablespoon dried sage leaves

1 teaspoon ground clove

½ teaspoon cayenne *or* chili powder

1 Put all of the ingredients in an electric grinder or spice mill and grind them. Pour the ingredients into a bowl and stir further with a spoon until well combined. Transfer to an airtight container and store at cool room temperature. I recommend using the mixture within a month for the best potency. You can also cut the ingredient amounts in half to ensure freshness.

Chef Johnny's
KORMA POWDER

This versatile spice mixture was inspired by korma, a rich creamy curry made from yogurt, coconut milk, ground almonds, and spices, and one of my personal favorites. See Vegetable Korma Curry (p. 247).

Ingredients

1 tablespoon whole coriander seeds

1 tablespoon whole cumin seeds

1 tablespoon whole fennel seeds

1 tablespoon whole mustard seeds

1 tablespoon whole fenugreek seeds

1 tablespoon whole cardamom seeds

1 tablespoon poppy seeds

1 tablespoon ground cinnamon

1 tablespoon ground ginger

1 tablespoon ground turmeric

1 teaspoon ground cloves

1 Put all of the ingredients in an electric grinder or spice mill and grind them. Pour the ingredients into a bowl and stir further with a spoon until well combined. Transfer to an airtight container and store at cool room temperature. I recommend using the mixture within a month for the best potency. You can also cut the ingredient amounts in half to ensure freshness.

For a slightly sweet version, try adding 1 heaped teaspoon raw organic sugar, such as Sucanat, to the mixture.

 GARAM MASALA POWDER

 HERB SALT

Garam masala, a traditional Indian spice blend is an intriguing and highly variable mixture that can be added to a dish at the end of cooking for extra punch and flavor.

Ingredients

2 teaspoons whole cumin seeds
6 whole dried bay leaves
4 whole star anise
2 teaspoons paprika
2 teaspoons ground cloves
1 teaspoon freshly ground black pepper
1 teaspoon freshly grated nutmeg

1 In a dry cast-iron skillet over low heat, toast the cumin until it turns gold-brown and fragrant, about 7 minutes. Let cool for several minutes. Put the cumin and all other ingredients in an electric spice mill or grinder. Grind until finely ground and blended. Store in an airtight container at cool room temperature. I recommend using the mixture withn a month for the best potency. You can also cut the ingredient amounts in half to ensure freshness.

P Replace the cloves with the seeds from 8 cardamom pods and reduce the pepper by half.

Herbs salt offers a lively twist on plain salt. This mixture contains a number of easy-to-find dried herbs.

Ingredients

7 tablespoons sea salt
1 teaspoon dried basil
1 teaspoon dried thyme
1 teaspoon dried marjoram
1 teaspoon dried mint
1 teaspoon dried rosemary
1 teaspoon dried sage
3 whole dried bay leaves

1 Grind all of the ingredients to a fine powder, using an electric grinder.
2 Store in an airtight container at cool room temperature.

FRESH PANIR CHEESE
and Whey

You may well recall from childhood nursery rhymes how "Little Miss Muffet, sat on her tuffet eating her curds and whey." Curds are, in fact, fresh cheese, also known in India as panir, produced by curdling fresh milk. Whey is the yellowish liquid that separates from the curds, which float in the whey, during this process. Both foods are highly nutritious and rich in protein.

Panir is a light, slightly crumbly cheese that goes great in many dishes. Try cutting it into cubes, frying it in ghee until golden brown, and then adding your favorite spices halfway through cooking to give a delightful, savory taste. One of my favorite versions is a savory mixture of sesame seeds, cumin, ground fennel, salt and pepper. Fry until golden brown. The subtle flavor offers a unique undertone to soup stocks, sauces, and vegetable dishes. Makes 2 cups Panir and 4 cups Whey

Ingredients

½ gallon whole organic milk
Juice of 1 lemon

1 Pour the milk into a large saucepan that will leave plenty of room for the milk to foam up when boiled. Have the lemon juice ready near the stove.

2 Over medium-high heat, bring the milk to a boil, stirring occasionally, to avoid any sticking or burning on the base of the pan.

3 The moment the milk reaches a full boil, pour in all of the lemon juice and stir gently. After a few moments, the curds will separate from the whey. Pour the contents through a fine sieve or colander set over a mixing bowl. Refrigerate the whey for up to 2 days in a glass or plastic container with a lid. Use the panir fresh.

K Not recommended due to the dairy content

Contains dairy
Gluten-free

VEGETABLE STOCK

A discovery worth making, fresh vegetable stock is sweet and full-bodied in taste, and adds a significant boost of unifying flavor to many dishes, particularly soups, sauces and legume dishes. For a simple and nutritious stock, simply use the leftover water from steaming vegetables. Alternatively, dissolve 1 organic vegetable stock cube in 4 cups boiling water (or follow the manufacturer's instructions).

Ingredients

8 cups filtered water
4 inches of leek white, cut in half lengthwise
     and thoroughly rinsed
5 carrots, coarsely chopped
4 bok choy leaves with stalks, coarsely chopped
2 fennel bulbs with stalks, coarsely chopped
2 zucchini, coarsely chopped
1 sweet potato, peeled and coarsely chopped
Bouquet garni of fresh rosemary, thyme, parsley sprigs,
     tied together in a bundle with kitchen string

1 Put all the ingredients in a large saucepan. Bring to a boil over high heat and simmer for 40 minutes.

2 Place a sieve over a large heatproof mixing bowl. Pour the stock through the strainer, discarding the solids. Let cool to room temperature, then refrigerate for up to 3 days in an airtight glass or plastic container with a lid.

Dairy- and gluten-free

 ALMOND MILK

 RICH, HERBED
Flaky Pastry

Almond drinks are very nourishing and strengthening, as they increase ojas and energy levels. Try adding 2 teaspoons of rosewater or a pinch of cardamom powder. Also as a digestive aid, add ½ teaspoon ground, roasted fennel and ¼ teaspoon ground, roasted cumin seed or just a pinch of ginger powder and extra honey. Makes 2 cups

Use this easily-made dough for pies, pastries, and empanadas. Make it with cold grated butter or hardened coconut cream. The instructions work best if you take care to handle the dough very little or not at all. The lumps of butter that permeate the dough form tiny holes in the finished pastry, producing its characteristic crisp flakiness. The quantities yield enough dough for 4 single-crust pies. Follow the baking instructions in whatever recipe you are using.

Ingredients

½ cup organic almonds (about 40 almonds)

4 cups filtered water

2 teaspoons honey

Ingredients

2 cups organic whole-wheat *or* organic spelt flour

2 cups organic white bread flour

2 teaspoons paprika

1 teaspoon salt

¾ cup sesame seeds

⅓ cup mixed dried herbs such as marjoram, basil, and thyme

3 cups organic unsalted butter, chilled until cold enough to grate, *or* 3 cups organic coconut cream (p.233), chilled until hard

1½ to 2 cups cold filtered water

1   First blanch the almonds: boil 2 cups water and add the almonds. Boil for 3 to 4 minutes. Pour the almonds into a strainer in the sink, then rinse thoroughly with cold water. Remove the skins by rubbing the almonds between both hands. Discard the skins.

2   Put the almonds, 2 cups water, and honey in a blender. Blend on high speed until thoroughly and finely puréed.

3   Line a strainer with several layers of cheesecloth and place it over a clean bowl. Pour the almond milk through the cheesecloth. Refrigerate in a glass container for up to 2 days.

Dairy- and gluten-free

1   Sift the flours, paprika, and salt into a large mixing bowl. Add the sesame seeds and herbs seeds. Grate the butter or coconut cream into the bowl. Stir gently with a fork to combine the ingredients. Gradually stir in the water until the dough comes together in a ball. Take care not to overstir.

2   Divide the dough into 4 equal pieces. Lightly sprinkle each piece with flour, wrap in plastic wrap, and chill in the freezer for 30 to 40 minutes.

3   This makes more dough than you will need for any one recipe. Follow the preparation and baking instructions in the individual recipe. Wrapped tightly in plastic wrap, the dough will keep in the freezer for several months.

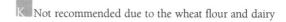 Not recommended due to the wheat flour and dairy

Dairy-free if using coconut cream
Gluten-free if using spelt flour

Coconut Milk

Coconut milk is widely used in Indian, Thai, and Malaysian cooking. Its creamy texture and distinctive flavor add a luxurious touch to a wide variety of dishes. Although coconut is often shunned in the West due to its high fat content, it contains many healthful nutrients such as protein, fiber, and lauric acid – a nutrient only found elsewhere in mother's milk. Ayurveda considers coconut a particularly beneficial food, when consumed in moderation, for Vata and Pitta types, due to its nutrient-rich and alkalizing properties. Organic, unrefined coconut oil is also used in Ayurvedic cooking for its ability to withstand high temperatures without becoming rancid.

Try preparing this fresh, easy version of coconut milk at home. If you aren't lucky enough to have coconuts in your front yard, choose ones that are heavy, with no moisture or mold on the shell. Always shake a coconut before buying it to ensure that it has liquid inside. This liquid is known as coconut water and is rich in electrolyte minerals. Either drink it on its own or use it in place of water in the recipe below. If you're unable to find fresh coconuts, or simply don't have time to prepare coconut milk, organic canned varieties are now available in most health food stores.
Makes 2 cups

Ingredients

2 fresh coconuts
3 to 4 cups warm filtered water

1 First, carefully pierce 2 of the eyes at the top of each coconut with a sharp knife and drain out the coconut water.

2 Carefully crack each coconut in two by hitting the middle of each nut with a hammer or the back of a heavy kitchen cleaver. Once a crack has appeared, carefully pry it open with a large knife.

3 Using the tip of a sharp knife, score the meat down to the hard shell with 1-inch X's. Then carefully pry the meat away from shell and peel away any thin, dark brown skin still clinging to the meat.

4 Put the coconut meat into in a blender, adding enough of the water to cover the meat. Blend on high until the coconut meat is very finely chopped.

5 Place a sieve lined with cheesecloth over a bowl and pour the liquid into the sieve, squeezing handfuls of the coconut meat to extract as much liquid as possible. Pour the liquid into a glass container and refrigerate for up to 2 days. For coconut cream, allow the milk to sit in the bowl for 45 minutes, and then skim away the top, thick layer of cream.

K Not recommended due to its heavy quality.

Dairy- and gluten-free

Note: Coconut milk will separate into 2 layers when refrigerated. The top, thick layer is coconut cream and is also used in cooking. To re-use coconut milk after refrigeration, simply place the liquid in a blender with a little filtered water to reconstitute.

AYURVEDIC BASICS

THE EXPANDED RECIPES

V TRUMPET DOSA
with Potato-Coconut Subji and Cilantro Dip

Dosas are large Indian crepes or pancakes made with a wheat-free batter of rice and lentils, which you should begin preparing the night before. Here, the unbelievably crisp and light dosas are rolled into trumpet shapes, filled with a spiced vegetable mixture, and accompanied by a cooling dip. Serves 4

Ingredients

For the dosas:

3 cups white basmati rice,

1 cup urad dhal (black lentils *or* black gram)

2 teaspoons whole fenugreek seeds

Ghee (p. 227) for frying

For the subji filling:

1 tablespoon ghee *or* extra-virgin olive oil

2 teaspoons grated fresh ginger

1 teaspoon mustard seeds

¼ teaspoon asafetida

1 tablespoon Chef Johnny's Vata Seasoning (p. 228) *or*
    Korma Powder (p. 229)

1 pound potatoes, peeled and cut into ¾-inch cubes

1 cup shelled green peas

½ cup sliced leek

2 cups Vegetable Stock (p. 231)

or 1 organic vegetable stock cube and 2 cups filtered
    water

6 tablespoons organic coconut milk (p. 233)

2 teaspoons lime juice

½ teaspoon salt

⅓ teaspoon freshly ground black pepper

2 tablespoons chopped fresh cilantro

For the dip:

½ cup finely diced or shredded cucumber

½ cup chopped fresh cilantro

3 to 4 tablespoons organic coconut milk (p. 233)

2 tablespoons organic plain yogurt (p.227) (optional)

1 teaspoon whole cumin seeds, toasted in a small, dry
    sauté pan over medium-low heat until fragrant, 1 to 2
    minutes, then transferred to a bowl to cool

1 teaspoon lime juice

½ teaspoon maple syrup

1 teaspoon grated fresh ginger

¼ teaspoon turmeric

¼ teaspoon freshly ground black pepper

1 First, prepare the batter: Wash the rice and dhal separately, until the water runs clear. Place the rice in one bowl and the dhal and fenugreek seeds in another bowl. Soak overnight in cold water to cover by 2 inches.

2 Grind both mixtures into a fine paste using a large mortar and pestle, hand grinder or blender, adding a little water as needed. Combine the two batters, cover with a damp cotton cloth and allow to sit in a warm place for 2 hours.

3 Next, prepare the subji filling: First, heat the ghee in a large sauté pan over medium-high heat. Add the ginger, mustard seeds, and asafetida. Sauté, stirring constantly, until the seeds pop, 1 to 2 minutes. Add the Vata seasoning and sauté, stirring constantly, for 2 minutes. Stir in the potatoes, peas, leeks, vegetable stock, coconut milk, lime juice, salt, and pepper. Bring the liquid to a boil, reduce the heat, and simmer until the vegetables are soft, about 20 minutes.

4 Meanwhile, prepare the dip: Put all the ingredients in a blender and blend until smooth. Transfer to a bowl, cover, and refrigerate until serving time.

5 About 10 minutes before the filling is done, make the dosas. Heat a nonstick griddle or large frying pan over medium heat. Stir the dosa batter, adding a little water to bring it to a creamy, pourable consistency. Brush the griddle with ghee and ladle in a thin layer of batter to form a pancake about 9 to 10 inches in diameter. Cook until its underside is golden brown, 1 to 2 minutes; then, with a spatula, flip the pancake over and cook about 1 minute more. Transfer the dosa to a large warmed plate or platter and cover with a clean kitchen towel. Repeat.

6 Before serving, stir the fresh cilantro into the subji filling. Roll each dosa into a cone or trumpet shape and place it on a serving plate. Generously spoon the filling into the opening of each trumpet. Serve the dip alongside.

P Substitute Chef Johnny's Pitta Seasoning (p. 228) for the Vata seasoning, and omit the mustard seed, asafetida, and yogurt.

K Substitute eggplant for the potato, grated daikon for the cucumber, honey for the maple syrup, and sunflower oil for the ghee; omit the yogurt; and reduce the amount of coconut milk.

For dairy-free, omit the yogurt.
Gluten-free

AMARANTH CREPES

with Saffron Cream Sauce

The ancient Latin American grain amaranth, actually the tiny seeds of a plant related to spinach, have a delightfully nutty, slightly sweet, and malty flavor. Here they combine with other healthful grains to make rich-tasting crepes with a chestnut-vegetable filling and golden saffron sauce. Makes 8 crepes

Ingredients

For the filling:

1 cup filtered water

8 asparagus spears, trimmed and cut into ¼-inch pieces

6 green beans, cut into ¼-inch pieces

1 carrot, cut into ¼-inch slices

1 cup fresh chestnuts, roasted and peeled, *or* dried chestnuts

For the sauce:

Pinch saffron threads

1 tablespoon ghee (p. 227)

¼ teaspoon asafetida

1 teaspoon thyme

1½ tablespoons organic amaranth flour

¼ teaspoon nutmeg, plus extra for garnish

¼ teaspoon paprika, plus extra for garnish

Herb Salt (p. 230) to taste

¼ teaspoon black pepper

2 cups reserved steaming liquid from vegetable filling, *or* Vegetable Stock (p. 231)

3 tablespoons organic heavy cream

For the crepes:

¼ cup organic wild rice flour

½ cup organic amaranth flour

¼ cup organic whole wheat flour

1 cup organic coconut milk, preferably fresh (p. 233)

1 cup filtered water

¼ teaspoon salt

Ghee

Note: If using fresh chestnuts, score an X through their flat sides and roast in a 350°F oven for 12 minutes. Peel when cooled. For dried chestnuts, soak for an hour in room temperature water and drain.

1 Put the wild rice in a blender or food processor and blend until coarsely ground. Add the amaranth flour, whole wheat flour, coconut milk, water, and salt. Blend until smooth. Pour the batter into a mixing bowl, cover and leave to rest for 30 minutes.

2 For the filling, in a steamer or a large saucepan with a steamer basket insert, bring 3 cups water to a boil. Add the green beans and carrot and steam for 5 minutes. Then add the asparagus and steam for an additional 10 minutes. Transfer to a bowl and set aside. Reserve 2 cups of the steaming liquid.

3 For the sauce, first crumble the saffron threads into a small bowl. Add 1 tablespoon of the reserved steaming liquid and set aside to soften.

4 In a medium saucepan over low heat, warm the 1 tablespoon ghee. Sprinkle in the asafetida, thyme, and amaranth flour. Stir with a wire whisk until the mixture forms a smooth paste. Cook, stirring frequently, for 4 to 5 minutes, until the paste is fairly thick. Stir in the nutmeg, paprika, herb salt, and pepper. Whisk in the remaining reserved steaming liquid. Reduce the heat to very low and whisk in the saffron mixture and the heavy cream. Cover, remove from the heat, and set aside.

5 To make each crepe, smear enough ghee to cover the bottom of a 10-inch nonstick sauté pan over medium heat. Stir the reserved crepe batter and whisk in a little water. Ladle in enough batter to cover the bottom of the pan. Cook until golden brown, about 3-4 minutes per side.

6 To assemble, spread ½ cup of the vegetable-chestnut mixture along one half of a crepe. Drizzle the filling with ¼ cup of the sauce and fold the crepe over to enclose the filling. Place 2 filled crepes on each serving plate. Drizzle the crepes with the remaining sauce and sprinkle with nutmeg and paprika.

V Substitute wheat flour for the amaranth flour.

K Substitute buckwheat flour for the wheat flour, millet flour for the rice flour and soy milk for the coconut milk. For the sauce, add ¼ teaspoon cayenne pepper, substitute sunflower oil for the ghee, and use 2 teaspoons chickpea flour or cornmeal with 3 tablespoons soy cream in place of dairy cream.

The Kapha version is dairy-and gluten-free.

GNOCCHI
with Pumpkin Sauce

The popular Italian potato dumplings, usually served as a pasta course, gain robust flavor from amaranth flour and yogurt and bright golden color from fresh pumpkin.
Serves 4

Ingredients

For the gnocci:

2 large potatoes

3 ½ oz amaranth *or* quinoa flour, plus extra for kneading

2 teaspoons organic egg substitute (potato-starch based)

2 tablespoons organic plain low-fat yogurt (p. 227)

Salt

Fresh ground black pepper

For the sauce:

3 tablespoons ghee (p. 227) *or* olive oil

½ cup chopped leeks

2 teaspoons maple syrup

2 teaspoons minced fresh basil leaves

1 teaspoon minced fresh marjoram leaves

10 fresh sage leaves, minced

2 cups peeled, seeded, and cubed fresh pumpkin

2 tablespoons plain low-fat yogurt

1 teaspoon lemon juice

Salt

Freshly ground black pepper

Freshly grated Parmesan cheese *or* rice cheese

Fresh basil *or* marjoram leaves, for garnish

1 Put the potatoes, peels still on, in a saucepan of cold salted water. Bring to a boil over high heat and cook the potatoes until tender, about 12 minutes. Drain the potatoes, peel, and set aside in a mixing bowl to cool.

2 With a hand-held electric mixer on medium speed, break up the potatoes and beat them until fluffy. Beat in the flour, egg substitute, and yogurt to form a dough. Knead the dough just until soft and smooth.

3 Divide the dough into 4 equal portions and shape each into a sausage shape about ¾-inch thick. Cut each sausage diagonally into 1-inch pieces. Flatten each piece slightly with a fork, then curve it with your fingers into a crescent shape. Transfer each shaped gnocchi to a tray. Cover and chill in the refrigerator for at least 30 minutes.

4 About 30 minutes before serving time, prepare the sauce. Heat the oil in a saucepan over medium-high heat. Add the leek and sauté just until it softens, 2 to 3 minutes. Stir in the basil, marjoram, and sage and sauté about 1 minute more. Stir in the pumpkin and maple syrup, cover the pan, reduce the heat to low, and simmer until the pumpkin is tender, about 20 minutes. Set aside.

5 Bring a large pot of water to a boil. Drop in the gnocchi, stir gently, and boil until they look plump and float on the surface, about 3 minutes.

6 To finish the sauce, transfer the hot pumpkin mixture to a blender or a food processor. Add the yogurt and lemon juice and process until smooth. Pulse in salt and pepper to taste.

7 Drain the gnocchi and transfer to a warm serving dish and pour the pumpkin sauce over them. If you like, sprinkle with grated Parmesan cheese or rice cheese and garnish with whole fresh basil or marjoram leaves.

For dairy-free, replace the yogurt with coconut milk.
Gluten-free

GRILLED EGGPLANT PARCELS

There's a novelty about this beautiful Mediterranean dish that makes it perfect for entertaining. As the instructions show, you don't even need an outdoor grill to prepare. It's a great dish for satisfying, yet not weighing down Kapha types. Serves 4

Ingredients

For the sauce:

1 large tomato, stemmed, cored, peeled and seeded

1 tablespoon lemon juice

1 teaspoon raw honey

2 teaspoons apple cider vinegar

2 tablespoons toasted pine nuts, plus extra for garnish

1 tablespoon organic plain yogurt (p. 227)

½ teaspoon dried marjoram

For the parcels:

2 large, long Asian-style eggplants

4 medium tomatoes

2 medium logs organic fresh, creamy goat cheese, about 5 ounces each

16 fresh basil leaves, plus extra for garnish

Salt

Freshly ground black pepper

2 teaspoons minced fresh thyme leaves

2 tablespoons sunflower oil *or* ghee (p. 227)

Fresh basil leaves, for garnish

Note: To quickly peel tomatoes, simply place the tomatoes in boiling water for 1 minute, submerge them immediately in cold water, and peel off the skins using your hands.

1 Put all the sauce ingredients in a food processor fitted with the stainless-steel blade or a blender. Pulse until coarsely blended. Transfer to a bowl, cover, and refrigerate until needed.

2 For the parcels, bring a saucepan of water to a boil. Meanwhile, trim the ends off the eggplants and cut each one lengthwise into 8 equal slices, about 3/16-inch thick. Blanch the eggplant slices in the boiling water for 2 minutes. Drain and transfer the slices to paper towels to dry.

3. With a sharp knife, trim and core the tomatoes and cut each one crosswise into 4 slices. Cut each log of goat cheese into 4 equal slices.

4. On a baking sheet or chopping board, place 2 slices of eggplant in a cross shape. At the center of the cross, layer 1 tomato slice, 1 basil leaf, 1 slice of goat cheese, another basil leaf, and another tomato slice. Sprinkle with salt, pepper, and thyme and fold over the ends of the eggplant slices to enclose the filling in a neat package. Repeat. Chill in the refrigerator for 15 to 20 minutes.

5. Preheat an outdoor or indoor grill, broiler, or grill pan. Brush the parcels with sunflower oil or ghee and cook them until golden brown, about 5 minutes per side.

6. Transfer the eggplant parcels to a heated platter or serving plates and spoon the dressing over them. Garnish with basil and pine nuts.

V Replace the eggplant with zucchini, substitute mozzarella for the goat cheese, and use maple syrup in place of honey in the sauce.

P Same as Vata, except substitute extra lemon juice for the vinegar.

For dairy-free, substitute 2 teaspoons tahini or cashew butter for the yogurt. Gluten-free

V STUFFED SHELL
with Asparagus and Roasted Red Pepper Sabayon

There's a hint of Greek and Mediterranean flavors in this charming dish inspired by the sea. Children can have fun helping construct the pastry shell. Serves 4

Ingredients

½ recipe Rich Herbed Flakey Pastry dough (p. 232)

For the vegetable filling:

1 teaspoon ghee (p. 227)

½ cup thinly sliced leek

¾ chopped asparagus

½ cup filtered water *or* Vegetable Stock (p. 231)

1 teaspoon lime juice

1 teaspoon dried thyme

1 teaspoon dried rosemary

⅓ teaspoon salt

¼ teaspoon freshly ground black pepper

2 teaspoons extra-virgin olive oil

2 teaspoons Chef Johnny's Vata Seasoning (p. 228) *or* Korma Powder (p. 229)

2 teaspoons chopped almonds

¾ cup small curd

For the sabayon:

1 teaspoon organic unsalted butter

½ cup plus 2 tablespoons organic cream

½ teaspoon paprika

¼ teaspoon nutmeg

1 bay leaf

¼ teaspoon salt

¼ teaspoon freshly ground black pepper

¼ teaspoon grated lemon zest

½ cup roasted red bell pepper

2 tablespoons filtered water

1 Preheat the oven to 350°F. On a lightly floured work surface, roll out the pastry to a thickness of about ⅛-inch. Using a shell shaped pastry cutter or working freehand with a knife, cut out 8 seashell shapes, each about 5 inches by 7 inches. On a baking sheet, form 8 small mounds of dried soybeans or lentils and drape each pastry piece over a mound. Bake the shells until crisp and golden, about 20 minutes. Remove from the oven and keep warm.

2 Slice the red pepper into quarters, lengthwise. Remove the stem and seeds and rub with 1 teaspoon olive oil. Place in the 350°F oven with the pastry shell until the skin begins to char, about 30 to 40 minutes.

3 For the vegetable filling, in a saucepan, heat the ghee over medium heat. Add the leek and asparagus and sauté for 3 minutes. Add the water or vegetable stock, lime juice, thyme, rosemary, salt, and pepper. Simmer for 5 minutes and remove from the heat. With a slotted spoon, remove the leek and asparagus, and set aside in a covered bowl. Keep the cooking liquid in the saucepan for the sabayon.

4 In a small sauté pan, heat the olive oil over medium heat. Add the Vata seasoning, chopped almonds, and the leek and asparagus. Cook, stirring frequently, for 5 minutes. Add the cottage cheese and stir to mix well. Remove from the heat and cover to keep warm.

5 For the sabayon, bring the reserved cooking liquid to a boil. Reduce the heat, add the butter, and simmer until the mixture thickens, about 5 minutes. Stir in the cream, paprika, nutmeg, bay leaf, salt, pepper, and lemon zest. Keep warm over low heat.

6 Put the roasted pepper, remaining cream, and water in a blender. Blend until smooth. Add to the saucepan and stir until blended.

7 Place a pastry shell in the middle of each serving plate. Distribute the vegetable filling evenly among the shells. Invert another pastry shell on top of each, positioning it to form a closed seashell. Drizzle the sauce around the shells. Garnish with chopped parsley and serve immediately.

P For the leek, substitute thinly sliced green zucchini; replace the rosemary and thyme with fennel and mint.

K Use the Kapha version of the pastry recipe and goat cheese in the filling. Also add ½ teaspoon powdered ginger and ¼ teaspoon cayenne pepper to the sabayon.

For dairy-free, use soy cheese.
For gluten-free, use the gluten-free Herbed Flakey Pastry (p. 232).

KALAN-BUTTERNUT SQUASH
& Zucchini Coconut Stew

Immensely flavorful and easy to make, this juicy curry from Kerala in Southern India looks as delicious as it tastes. Ideal for balancing Vata and Pitta. Serves 4

Ingredients

1 cup organic coconut milk, preferably fresh (p. 233)

1 cup organic flaked coconut, preferably fresh

1 cup organic plain yogurt (p. 227)

1 ⅓ cups filtered water

1 butternut squash, 3 to 4 pounds, halved, peeled, seeded, and cut into ½-inch cubes

⅓ teaspoon ground black pepper

3 tablespoons ghee (p. 227) *or* olive oil

1 teaspoon whole cumin seeds

1 tablespoon finely chopped leek (optional)

1 large zucchini, diced

1 tablespoon Chef Johnny's Pitta Seasoning (p. 228)

1 teaspoon ground fennel seeds

½ teaspoon salt

12 fresh *or* dried kari leaves (*or* ½ cup fresh cilantro leaves)

1 tablespoon maple syrup

1 In a blender, combine the coconut milk and flaked coconut. Blend until smooth. Add the yogurt and ⅓ cup of the water. Blend until smooth. Set aside.

2 In a large saucepan, put the butternut squash, 1 cup of water, and pepper. Place the pan over medium heat. When the water simmers, cover the pan and reduce the heat to low. Steam the squash just until tender enough to be pierced with a fork, about 12 minutes.

3 Meanwhile, heat the ghee in a small frying pan over medium heat. Add the cumin seeds, leek, and zucchini. Sauté, stirring frequently, until the zucchini is tender, about 4 minutes. Remove from the heat and set aside.

4 Remove the squash from the heat and gently stir in the coconut mixture, Pitta seasoning, fennel seeds, kari leaves, zucchini mixture, and maple syrup. Serve immediately.

V Substitute Chef Johnny's Vata Seasoning (p. 228) or Korma Powder (p. 229) for the Pitta seasoning.

K Substitute broccoli for the zucchini, sunflower oil for the ghee, and stock for the coconut milk; add ⅓ teaspoon cayenne pepper; omit the sweetener and, for the yogurt, substitute ⅓ cup soy milk mixed with 1 teaspoon cornmeal.

For dairy-free, follow the Kapha alternative.
Gluten-free

"En papillote" is a French cooking technique in which the food is sealed inside parchment paper and baked. As the food cooks, it lets off steam that causes the paper to puff up. The paper is usually cut open at the table so guests can enjoy the freshly cooked aroma of the food. Serves 4

Ingredients

For the marinated tofu:

3 tablespoons organic coconut milk (p. 233)

2 tablespoons Bragg's amino acids

2 tablespoons finely chopped fresh fennel leaves

2 teaspoons freshly grated ginger

1 tablespoon finely ground blanched almonds (p. 232)

1 tablespoon lime juice

1 tablespoon finely chopped fresh parsley

1 teaspoon brown rice syrup

¼ teaspoon freshly ground black pepper

1½ cups tofu, cut into 1-inch cubes

For the vegetable filling:

2 cups filtered water

½ cup florets purple sprouting *or* regular broccoli

½ pound chopped green beans, shelled fava beans, *or* chopped asparagus

1 medium zucchini, cut into ½-inch slices

1 pound pre-washed baby spinach leaves

1 medium sweet potato, peeled and chopped into 1-inch cubes

4 pieces of parchment paper, each 12 by 12 inches

2 tablespoons ghee (p. 227)

 Papillotes
of Spring Vegetables & Marinated Tofu

1   First, marinate the tofu: In a mixing bowl, stir together the coconut milk, amino acids, fennel, ginger, almonds, lime juice, parsley, brown rice syrup, and pepper. Add the tofu and toss gently to coat it evenly. Cover with plastic wrap and marinate in the refrigerator for 1 to 2 hours.

2   Preheat oven to 400°F.

3   For the filling, bring the water to a boil in a large saucepan. Add the broccoli, green beans, zucchini, and sweet potato. Cover and cook for 4 minutes. Add the spinach and cook for 1 minute more. Drain well.

4   Add the vegetables to the tofu mixture and toss gently to coat the vegetables with the marinade.

5   Place the 4 sheets of parchment paper on a work surface. Divide the tofu-vegetable mixture evenly among the 4 pieces of paper, spooning it just to one side of the center of each piece. Drizzle the filling with ghee.

6   Fold the empty side of each piece of parchment paper over the filling to enclose it. Seal the edges together by making small crimping folds all along the seam of each parchment parcel. Carefully transfer the parcels to an oiled baking sheet and bake until the paper parcels puff up, about 15 minutes.

7   Remove the baking sheet from the oven and transfer each parcel to a serving plate. Let guests use sharp table knives to cut open their parcels, instructing them to be careful of the steam inside.

For dairy-free, substitute sunflower oil for the ghee.
Gluten-free

EMPANADAS
with Black Olives, Goat Cheese, and Sun-Dried Tomato Pesto

Great flavor and crunchy texture come together in a satisfying main course that also makes a filling snack, perfect with a side salad or a sauce. Try serving with the Toasted Fennel, Leek and Tomato Sauce (p.294). Serves 6

Ingredients

½ recipe Rich Herbed Flakey Pastry dough (p. 232)

1 cup Sun-Dried Tomato Pesto (p. 298)

1 cup pitted Kalamata *or* other brined black olives, cut in halves

2 medium logs organic fresh, creamy goat cheese, about 5 ounces each

1 tablespoon minced fresh thyme leaves

2 tablespoons minced fresh marjoram leaves

⅓ teaspoon ground black pepper

Salt

1 Place the pastry on a floured work surface. With a rolling pin, roll it out into a rectangle about 10 by 18 inches and about ³⁄₁₆-inch thick. With a large, sharp knife or pastry cutter, cut the pastry lengthwise into 6 equal strips about 3 inches by 10 inches.

2 Preheat the oven to 375°F. Lightly oil a baking sheet.

3 In a mixing bowl, stir together the pesto, olives, goat cheese, thyme, marjoram, black pepper, and salt to taste. Divide this filling evenly among the pastry strips, spooning it along the length of each one. Starting at a narrow end, roll up each strip. Pinch its edges to seal it shut and bend it into a crescent moon shape. Transfer to the baking sheet.

4 Bake in the preheated oven until the empanadas are light golden brown, 30 to 35 minutes. Serve hot or warm.

V Substitute basil pesto for the sun dried tomato, Fresh Panir Cheese (p. 231) for the goat cheese, artichoke hearts or asparagus for the olives, and rice flour for the cornmeal.

P Same as Vata version, except use cilantro pesto in place of traditional basil pesto and substitute mint and fennel leaf for the marjoram and thyme.

For dairy-free and gluten-free, use the alternative pastry labeled "Dairy-Free and Gluten-Free" (on page 232).

V P K VEGETABLE KORMA CURRY

One of my personal favorites, Korma is a quick-to-make, mild curry. The rich sauce is exquisitely creamy and characterized by flavors of coconut, yogurt, almonds, and spices. Serve with basmati rice and Chapatis (p. 305) or Naan Bread (p. 305). Serves 4

Ingredients

2 cups water *or* vegetable stock

1 small potato, cut into ¾-inch pieces

1 fennel bulb, cut into ¾-inch pieces

½ cup zucchini *or* summer squash, cut into ¾-inch pieces

¾ cup broccoli florets *or* ¾-inch asparagus pieces

2 tablespoons ghee (p. 227) *or* sunflower oil

1 tablespoon Chef Johnny's Korma Powder (p. 229)

2 tablespoons ground almonds

2 tablespoons finely chopped leek

1 teaspoon chickpea flour

¼ teaspoon asafetida

1 date, chopped

¼ cup organic coconut milk, preferably fresh (p. 233)

2 tablespoons finely chopped cilantro

2 tablespoons organic plain yogurt (p. 227)

½ teaspoon salt

⅓ teaspoon freshly ground black pepper

1 In a saucepan over high heat, bring the water or stock to a boil. Add the potato, fennel, zucchini, and broccoli. Reduce the heat and simmer, uncovered, until the vegetables are tender, about 10 minutes. Place a colander or strainer over a heatproof mixing bowl and drain the vegetables, reserving the cooking liquid. Rinse out and dry the saucepan.

2 In the pan, heat the ghee or oil over low heat. Add the korma powder and cook, stirring, until fragrant, about 3 minutes. Add the almonds and leek and cook, stirring occasionally, for 3 to 4 minutes more. Stir in the chickpea flour and asafetida and cook for 2 minutes. Pour in the reserved cooking liquid, chopped date, and coconut milk.

3 Whisk until smooth and simmer for 2 to 3 minutes. Stir in the cilantro, yogurt, salt, and pepper. Add the vegetables, stir to coat them with the sauce, and serve immediately.

For dairy-free, omit the yogurt and add 1 to 2 tablespoons cashew butter. Stir thoroughly until blended.
Gluten-free

V SWEET POTATO AND PANIR TOWER
with Raisin Chutney

Some chefs say that presentation is everything, and this dish certainly has a stunning visual impact! It tastes wonderful, too, with the fresh Indian-style cheese called panir, accompanied by a spicy fruit chutney. Serves 4

Ingredients

For the spiced cream:
2 tablespoons organic crème fraîche
1 tablespoon organic cream
1 tablespoon ghee (p. 227)
1 tablespoon chopped fresh dill
1 teaspoon apple cider vinegar
⅓ teaspoon turmeric
⅓ teaspoon asafetida
½ teaspoon salt
½ teaspoon black pepper

For the chutney:
1 tablespoon extra-virgin olive oil or ghee (p. 227)
1 teaspoon ground coriander
1 teaspoon whole cumin seeds
1 cup grated apple
½ cup raisins, soaked in filtered water for 1 hour and drained
¼ cup sun dried tomatoes
2 tablespoons chopped fresh mint
1 tablespoon lemon juice or lime juice
2 dates
1 teaspoon raw organic sugar, such as Sucanat
Whey (p. 231) or filtered water, as needed

For the towers:
1 green bell pepper, quartered, stemmed, and seeded
1 red bell pepper, quartered, stemmed, and seeded
4 tablespoons extra-virgin olive oil or ghee
Leaves from 4 sprigs fresh thyme
2 purple or orange sweet potatoes, peeled and cut into ½-inch pieces
1 red potato, skin on, cut into ½-inch pieces
1 tablespoon finely shredded carrot
2 tablespoons garden cress (optional)
1½ pounds Fresh Panir Cheese (p. 231), cut into 4 triangles, each about 2½-inches on a side and about ¾-inch thick
2 teaspoons whole cumin seed
Salt
Freshly ground black pepper

For assembly:
20 dandelion leaves
Edible flowers (pesticide-free), for garnish

1 First make the spiced cream: Put all its ingredients in a blender or food processor. Blend until smooth. Transfer to a bowl, cover, and refrigerate until needed.

2 To make the chutney, heat the 1 tablespoon olive oil or ghee in a small sauté pan over medium-low heat. Add the cumin seeds and coriander and sauté until aromatic, 1 to 2 minutes. Transfer the oil and spices to a blender. Add the remaining chutney ingredients and blend thoroughly, adding a little whey or filtered water if it's too thick. Transfer to a bowl, cover, and refrigerate until serving time.

3 Preheat the oven to 375°F. To begin preparing the towers, first put the peppers in a baking dish and sprinkle with 2 tablespoons of the olive oil or ghee and the thyme leaves. Bake until their edges start to brown, about 20 minutes. Remove them from the oven and set aside.

4 While the peppers are roasting, bring the water to a boil in a steamer or a saucepan with a steam basket insert. Add the sweet potato and red-skinned potato, cover, and steam until tender, about 15 minutes. Transfer the potatoes to an ovenproof bowl and mash until smooth. Stir in the carrot, garden cress, and reserved spiced cream. Cover with foil and place in the warm oven until ready to use.

5 Sprinkle each side of the panir triangles with cumin seeds, salt, and black pepper. Heat 2 tablespoons of the olive oil or ghee in a non-stick sauté pan. Cook the panir triangles until golden brown, about 4 minutes per side, turning them over carefully with a spatula.

6 To assemble the towers, place 3 dandelion leaves with their ends touching at the center to form a 3-pointed star shape. Spoon a circular mound of the warm sweet potato mixture in the center of the plate and flatten its top with the back of the spoon. Place a roasted pepper on top, then a fried panir triangle. Spoon some chutney on top of the panir. Dot the plate with additional chutney and garnish with more dandelion leaves and edible flowers.

P Omit the asafetida and substitute 1 teaspoon roasted fennel powder and 1 teaspoon lime juice for the vinegar.

K Substitute tofu for the panir, celeriac root for the sweet potato, carrot for the potato, and goat cheese for both the cream and crème fraîche. Use honey in place of Sucanat in the spiced cream.

For dairy-free, use the dairy substitutions in the Kapha version.
Gluten-free

V YELLOW SPLIT MUNG DHAL

A time-honored Ayurvedic dish, mung dhal is easy to digest and balancing to all three doshas. Mung beans are used whole or, more commonly, split and hulled, a form called mung dhal in India. These beans don't need pre-soaking and are a snap to cook to butter-soft consistency. The versatility of this soupy dhal makes it a great protein-rich starter or side dish. Serves 4

Ingredients

1½ cups mung dhal (split hulled yellow mung beans)

4 to 5 cups filtered water

1 cinnamon stick

4 bay leaves

2 teaspoons ghee (p. 227)

2 tablespoons mustard seeds

1 tablespoon Chef Johnny's Vata Seasoning (p. 228) *or* curry powder

1 tablespoon grated fresh ginger

¼ teaspoon asafetida

2 to 3 teaspoons organic plain yogurt (p. 227)

2 tablespoons finely chopped fresh cilantro

1 tablespoon lemon juice

1 teaspoon raw organic sugar, such as Sucanat, *or* maple syrup

Salt

Freshly ground black pepper

Note Many Indian markets and health food stores carry split hulled yellow mung beans (mung dhal); however, if you can only find whole mung beans, soak them in filtered water for 1 hour, then drain, before proceeding with the recipe.

1 Put the mung dhal and its soaking water in a saucepan with the cinnamon sticks and bay leaves. Bring to a boil over high heat, then reduce the heat and simmer until tender, about 25 minutes, adding more water if the dhal gets too thick.

2 In a small sauté pan, heat the ghee over low heat. Add the mustard seeds and, when the seeds pop after a few minutes, stir in the ginger and Vata seasoning. Sauté, stirring, for 2 minutes; then, stir in the asafetida, cook 1 minute more, and remove from the heat.

3 Stir the mustard seed mixture into the dhal. Stir in the yogurt, cilantro, and lemon juice. Season to taste with salt and pepper. Remove the bay leaves and cinnamon stick before serving.

P Substitute crushed fennel seeds for the mustard seeds, Chef Johnny's Pitta Seasoning (p. 228) for the Vata seasoning and omit the asafetida and bay leaves (using curry leaves instead, if available).

K Omit yogurt and substitute sunflower oil for the ghee.

Dairy-free without the ghee
Gluten-free

SPLIT PEA DHAL

Indian dhals can be thin like soup, thick like cream, or in the case of this recipe, so thick that a spoon can stand up in it! For a traditional Ayurvedic meal, enjoy this dhal with basmati rice, Cauliflower Subji (p. 269) Chapatis (p. 305), Mango Chutney (p. 285) and Cucumber Raita (p. 301).
Serves 4

Ingredients

1½ cups yellow split peas

5 bay leaves

2 cinnamon sticks

5 cups filtered water

2 tablespoons ghee (p. 227)

2 teaspoons whole cumin seeds

½ teaspoon whole fenugreek seeds

3 teaspoons Chef Johnny's Pitta Seasoning (p. 228),
    or curry powder

¼ teaspoon asafetida

5 whole cloves

3 tablespoons chopped cilantro leaves

3 tablespoons lemon juice

1 teaspoon ground cardamom

Salt

Freshly ground black pepper

Ghee *or* melted butter, for garnish

Lemon juice, for garnish

1 Rinse the yellow split peas. Put them in a mixing bowl, add enough filtered water to cover them well, and leave at room temperature to soak for 2 to 3 hours. Drain.

2 Put the split peas, bay leaves, cinnamon sticks, and filtered water in a large saucepan. Simmer until the peas are mushy, about 40 minutes. In a small sauté pan, heat the ghee over low heat. Add the cumin seeds and sauté until light brown, 1 to 2 minutes. Stir in the fenugreek, cook for 15 seconds, and then stir in the korma powder and asafetida.

3 Pour the cumin mixture into the split peas and stir in the cloves, cilantro, lemon juice, and cardamom. Season to taste with salt and pepper.

4 Transfer to a serving bowl or individual dishes, drizzle with ghee, and sprinkle with lemon juice.

V Substitute mung dhal (whole or split hulled mung beans) for the split peas, remembering to soak whole mung for 6 to 8 hours before cooking.

K Substitute sunflower oil for the ghee.

For dairy-free, follow the Kapha version.
Gluten-free

TEMPEH AND GARDEN VEGETABLE KEBABS
in a Smoked Almond Marinade

Kebabs originated in Turkey, a land of rich tastes and exotic architecture. These hearty kebabs are especially good for satisfying hungry Pitta types. Tempeh is a traditional Indonesian food made from fermented soybeans. With its mild flavor, hearty texture, and high protein content, tempeh is a popular meat-substitute in vegetarian cooking. You can find it in the freezer section of your local health food store.
Makes 4 kebabs

Ingredients

For the kebabs:

1 pound organic tempeh, cut into 1-inch cubes

8 broccoli florets

8 cauliflower florets

1 red bell pepper, stemmed, seeded, and cut into 1-inch pieces

2 zucchini, cut into 1-inch pieces

For the marinade:

1 cup blanched almonds soaked for at least 4 hours and drained

½ cup filtered water

¼ cup organic coconut milk, preferably fresh (p. 233)

2 tablespoons sunflower oil

2 tablespoons Bragg's amino acids

1 tablespoon lime juice

2 teaspoons grated fresh ginger

2 teaspoons ground coriander seeds

2 teaspoons ground fennel seeds

½ teaspoon raw organic sugar, such as Sucanat, or 1 teaspoon date sugar or maple syrup

Pinch saffron threads, softened in 1 tablespoon filtered water

Salt

Freshly ground black pepper

Mint leaves, for garnish

Black sesame seeds, for garnish

1 Put the tempeh and vegetables in a large mixing bowl.

2 Put the almonds, water, and coconut milk in a blender or a food processor fitted with the metal blade. Process until thoroughly puréed. Add the oil, amino acids, lime juice, ginger, coriander, fennel, sugar, and saffron. Pulse several times to combine.

3 Pour the marinade over the vegetables and toss to coat evenly. Place in a casserole dish with a lid and set aside to marinate for at least 2 hours.

4 Preheat the oven to 350°F.

5 Meanwhile, thread the vegetables and tempeh onto skewers, alternating the pieces attractively. Arrange the skewers side by side in a large baking pan. Pour the marinade remaining in the bowl over the kebabs. Bake until the vegetables are hot and tender-crisp, about 30 minutes.

6 Serve the kebabs over rice or pasta and garnish with torn mint leaves and black sesame seeds.

V Substitute firm tofu for the tempeh.

K Substitute firm tofu for the tempeh and enjoy in moderation.

Dairy- and gluten-free

BLACK BEAN PATTIES
with Carrot-and-Cardamom Jus

These light patties melt in the mouth, with their crisp and savory coating. The sauce, by contrast, is delicate, aromatic and has a gem-like orange color—a magical combination! Enjoy as a distinctive starter or side dish. Serves 4

Ingredients

For the patties:

1 cup dried black beans
4 cups filtered water
1 tablespoon sunflower oil
3 tablespoons chopped leeks
1 tablespoon finely chopped fresh cilantro
1 clove garlic, finely chopped (optional)
⅓ teaspoon asafetida
2 teaspoons ground cumin seeds
2 teaspoons dried thyme
1 teaspoon dried sage
2 teaspoons grated fresh ginger
1 teaspoon ground turmeric
⅓ teaspoon freshly ground black pepper
½ teaspoon salt
1 tablespoon tomato purée
2 teaspoons lime juice
3 tablespoons cornmeal
3 tablespoons sunflower oil

For the sauce:

3½ cups fresh carrot juice
½ teaspoon ground cardamom
½ teaspoon ground coriander
½ teaspoon cornmeal

1. Soak the black beans in water for 8 hours or overnight. Drain the water, rinse, and place in a medium saucepan. Add 4 cups filtered water and bring to a boil. Simmer until tender, about 35-45 minutes.

2. Drain the black beans and put them in a mixing bowl. Mash well.

3. Heat the sunflower oil in a small sauté pan over medium heat, add the leeks and sauté until soft, 3 to 5 minutes. Stir in the herbs and spices, tomato purée, lime juice and 1 tablespoon of the cornmeal. Pour the mixture over the mashed beans and stir until thoroughly combined.

4. Sprinkle the remaining 2 tablespoons of cornmeal on a work surface. Take a heaping tablespoonful of the bean mixture and, on the cornmeal-dusted surface, pat it into a circular patty about ⅜-inch thick, using a spatula to help form it. Repeat with the remaining bean mixture.

5. Heat the sunflower oil in a large frying pan over medium heat and sauté the patties until golden, 2 to 3 minutes per side. Alternatively, brush the patties on both sides with the oil, put them on a baking sheet, and bake them in a preheated 350°F oven until golden brown, about 20 minutes.

6. Meanwhile, make the sauce: Put the carrot juice in a saucepan and simmer briskly over medium heat until reduced by half. With a whisk, stir in the cardamom, coriander, and cornmeal and continue stirring and simmering until lightly thickened, 3 to 4 minutes.

7. To serve, place the patties on individual heated serving plates. Drizzle some of the carrot jus over the patties and serve the remainder from a sauceboat.

V Substitute adzuki beans for the black beans, rice flour for the cornmeal, and basil for the cilantro.

P Omit the cayenne pepper and substitute rice flour for the cornmeal.

Dairy- and gluten-free

V P K CHICKPEAS IN MASALA SAUCE

In this rich dish from India, chickpeas provide a nourishing source of protein, while adding wonderful texture and flavor. Serve with Chapatis (p. 305) or Naan bread (p. 305). The traditional spice blend known as Garam Masala (p. 230) is also available in health food stores and Indian markets. Serves 4

Ingredients

2 tablespoons ghee (p. 227)

1 tablespoon grated fresh ginger

2 teaspoons whole cumin seeds

1 tablespoon Chef Johnny's Korma Powder (p. 229)
  or 1 tablespoon mild curry powder

1 teaspoon Chef Johnny's Garam Masala (p. 230)

½ cup fresh tomato, stemmed, peeled, and seeded

½ cup organic coconut milk, preferably fresh (p. 233)

½ cup dry chickpeas *or* 1 cup if using canned chickpeas

4 tablespoons chopped fresh cilantro leaves

1 tablespoon lemon juice

1 tablespoon maple syrup, 1 teaspoon jaggery,
  or 1 chopped date

1 teaspoon tamarind paste (optional)

3 bay leaves

5 kale leaves, stemmed and coarsely chopped

1 medium potato, coarsely chopped and steamed until
  tender

Salt

Freshly ground black pepper

1 Soak the chickpeas in 2 cups cold filtered water overnight. Drain water, rinse, and place in a medium saucepan. Add 1 ½ cups filtered water and bring to a boil. Simmer covered for 2 hours and drain.

2 Heat the ghee in a large sauté pan over low heat. Add the ginger and sauté until lightly browned, about 2 minutes. Add the cumin seed and cook 1 to 2 minutes more. Add the korma powder, garam masala, and tomato, and stir constantly until heated through.

3 Pour in the coconut milk, add the kale, and cook, stirring frequently, until the sauce becomes thick and sticky, about 8 minutes.

4 Stir in the chickpeas, cilantro, lemon juice, maple syrup, tamarind, bay leaves, and potato. Season to taste with salt and pepper.

For dairy-free, substitute sunflower oil for the ghee.
Gluten-free

K QUINOA AND VEGETABLE PILAF

A favorite grain of the Inca, quinoa is light, easy to digest and has one of the highest protein contents of any grain. Here, quinoa provides the foundation for a colorful and flavorful dish. Serves 4

Ingredients

1 cup quinoa

1½ cups filtered water

1 cup Vegetable Stock (p. 231)

or 1 organic vegetable stock and 1 cup filtered water

2 tablespoons sunflower, safflower, *or* mustard oil

1 tablespoon grated fresh ginger

2 teaspoons ground coriander

⅓ cup finely chopped white cabbage

6 spears fresh asparagus, trimmed and cut in small pieces

1 teaspoon freshly grated turmeric *or* ½ teaspoon dried turmeric

1 teaspoon minced fresh basil

1 teaspoon minced fresh marjoram leaves

½ cup coarsely chopped almonds

2 tomatoes, chopped

1 tablespoon lime juice

1 tablespoon Bragg's amino acids

Salt

Freshly ground black pepper

1 Put the quinoa in a saucepan and add the water and stock. Bring to a boil over high heat, reduce the heat to low, cover, and cook until the grains are tender and the liquid has been absorbed, about 17 minutes.

2 Put the almonds on a baking sheet and broil for 8 minutes, or until golden brown.

3 Meanwhile, heat the oil in a small saucepan over low heat. Add the ginger and coriander seeds and sauté until fragrant, about 1 minute. Stir in the cabbage and sauté, stirring occasionally, until softened, about 5 minutes more. Stir in the asparagus, turmeric, basil, and marjoram. Cook until the asparagus is tender-crisp and heated through, 3 to 4 minutes more. Stir in the almonds, tomatoes, lime juice, and Bragg's.

4 As soon as the quinoa is done, stir in the vegetable mixture just until thoroughly combined. Serve immediately.

V Substitute equal parts wild rice and brown basmati rice for the quinoa, using 3 times as much cooking liquid as grains.

P Omit the tomato.

Dairy- and gluten-free

ROLLED OAT PILAF
with Sage

For people who ordinarily think of oats as a breakfast cereal, this savory grain dish may seem somewhat unusual. Its hearty texture makes it a great dish to help Vata types keep grounded. Serves 4

Ingredients

2 tablespoons ghee (p. 227) *or* sunflower oil
2 cups rolled *or* baby oats
4 teaspoons chopped fresh sage
3 to 4 cups filtered water
1 teaspoon paprika
½ teaspoon salt
Freshly ground black pepper

1. Heat the ghee in a medium saucepan over medium heat. Gently stir in the oats and cook, stirring occasionally, for about 3 minutes. Stir in the sage and cook 2 to 3 minutes more.

2. Stir in the water, paprika, and salt. Cover, reduce the heat to low, and cook, stirring occasionally, until the water has been absorbed and the oats are fluffy and a little sticky, about 12 minutes. If necessary, stir in a little more water to keep the oats from drying out. Season to taste with salt and pepper.

P Omit the paprika and use mint in place of sage.

K Not recommended due to the sweet and heavy qualities of oats

For dairy-free, use oil instead of ghee.
Contains gluten

PENNE
with Saffron Cream Sauce

A golden yellow saffron sauce, here accented by orange and lemon zest, offers luxurious appeal to this quickly prepared pasta dish. Ideal for both Pitta and Vata. Serves 4

Ingredients

8 ounces dried penne pasta
1 teaspoon ghee (p. 227) *or* extra-virgin olive oil
Pinch saffron threads
1 tablespoon chopped fresh fennel fronds
¼ teaspoon grated lemon zest
¼ teaspoon grated orange zest
1½ teaspoons sweet paprika
6 tablespoons cream
Salt
Freshly ground black pepper

1. Bring a large pot of salted filtered water to a rapid boil. Add the penne and cook until al dente, tender but still chewy, following the manufacturer's suggested cooking time, about 8 minutes. Drain and return to the pot. Cover to keep warm.

2. In a saucepan, heat the ghee over medium heat. Pinch the saffron threads between your finger and thumb, hold them over the pan, and rub the saffron to crumble it into the oil. Stir in the fennel, lemon zest, orange zest, and paprika. Add the cream and cook gently, stirring continuously, until slightly thickened, 3 to 4 minutes. Season to taste with salt and pepper.

3. Pour the cream sauce over the penne and toss well to coat evenly. Serve immediately.

V Also recommended

K Use corn tagliatelle, omit the cream, and substitute sunflower oil for the ghee.

For dairy- and gluten-free, follow the Kapha version.

Angel Hair Pasta
with Tomato Caramelized Sauce

Plum tomatoes, also known as Roma tomatoes, offer exceptional flavor year round, making them perfect for this sweet and tangy traditional Italian sauce. Try serving with Bruschetta (p. 282). Serves 4

Ingredients

3 tablespoons extra-virgin olive oil

3 tablespoons chopped leek

1 clove garlic, crushed (optional)

1 tablespoon minced fresh thyme leaves

2 pounds plum *or* Roma tomatoes, peeled and seeded

½ cup fresh basil leaves, cut into thin julienne strips

3 teaspoons tomato purée

Salt

Freshly ground black pepper

8 ounces dry angel hair pasta

2 tablespoons extra-virgin olive oil

2 teaspoons lemon juice

½ cup chopped fresh herbs such as parsley, marjoram *or* sage

4 tablespoons freshly grated Parmesan cheese

Note: To quickly peel tomatoes, simply place the tomatoes in boiling water for 1 minute, submerge them immediately in cold water, and peel off the skins using your hands.

1   In a large sauté pan, heat the oil over medium heat. Add the leek and garlic, sauté, stirring frequently, until tender, 3 to 4 minutes, then stir in the thyme and sauté just until it is fragrant, about 30 seconds more.

2   Stir in the tomatoes, basil, and tomato purée. Reduce the heat to low and cook, stirring occasionally, until it reaches a thick sauce consistency, about 40 minutes, stirring in a little water or olive oil if it becomes too dry or sticks to the pan. Season to taste with salt and pepper.

3   Bring a large pot of salted filtered water to a rapid boil. Add the pasta and cook until al dente, tender but still chewy, following the manufacturer's suggested cooking time, about 5 minutes. Drain the pasta, transfer it still dripping to a bowl, and cover to keep warm.

4   In the pasta cooking pot over low heat, warm the olive oil and stir in the lemon juice and fresh herbs. Return the drained pasta to the pot and toss to coat evenly with the oil and herbs.

5   Mound the pasta on warmed serving plates or shallow pasta bowls. Ladle a small serving of tomato sauce on top and sprinkle with Parmesan.

P   Substitute bell peppers for the tomatoes, roasting them well in the oven and then puréeing them in a processor or blender along with the rest of the sauce ingredients; omit the leek and substitute fennel for the thyme and soy cheese for the Parmesan.

K   Substitute corn or rice noodles for the angel hair and goat cheese for the Parmesan.

For dairy-free, use soy cheese.
Gluten-free

K BARLEY RISSOLES
with Bell Pepper

The old-fashioned grain patties known as rissoles make a comforting yet lively treat when seasoned with herbs and spices and coated with crunchy sunflower seeds. Try serving with Toasted Fennel, Leek, and Tomato Sauce (p. 294) or Ginger and Raisin Chutney (p. 301). Serves 6

Ingredients

1¾ cups dried barley

1 medium red *or* green bell pepper, halved, stemmed, seeded, and finely chopped

½ cup mustard greens *or* collard greens, stems removed, leaves finely chopped

3 tablespoons finely chopped leek

3 tablespoons finely chopped fresh parsley

2 tablespoons Bragg's liquid amino acids

1 tablespoon Chef Johnny's Kapha Seasoning (p. 229) *or* curry powder

1 tablespoon crumbled dried sage

2 teaspoons whole fenugreek seeds

Freshly ground black pepper

1 cup roasted shelled sunflower seeds, coarsely ground in a food processor

Olive oil for frying

1 Put the barley in a mixing bowl, add plenty of filtered water to cover, and leave at room temperature to soak for 2 hours. Drain and rinse the barley, transfer it to a large saucepan, and add 5 cups filtered water. Bring the water to a boil over medium heat, reduce heat to low, cover, and simmer until all the water is absorbed, about 35-40 minutes.

2 In a large mixing bowl, stir together the bell pepper, greens, leek, parsley, Bragg's, korma powder, sage, fenugreek, and black pepper to taste. Stir in the barley until thoroughly combined.

3 Spread the sunflower seeds on a plate. Form the barley mixture into patties, or rissoles, about 2½-inches wide by ¾-inch thick. As you form each patty, press it into the sunflower seeds to coat it, then transfer it to a clean plate or platter.

4 In a large frying pan, heat the olive oil over medium-low heat. Carefully add the rissoles, in batches if necessary to avoid overcrowding, and fry until nicely browned, about 5 minutes per side. (Alternatively, brush the patties on both sides with ghee and broil them.) Serve hot.

V Substitute brown or white basmati rice for the barley and dandelion leaves for the mustard greens. Refer to the 'Grain Cooking Chart' on p. 327.

P Substitute chopped fresh mint, Chef Johnny's Pitta Seasoning (p. 228), and dandelion leaves for the sage, fenugreek, mustard greens, and korma powder.

Dairy-free
For gluten-free, replace the barley with 3 cups amaranth cooked in 6 cups filtered water.

 KITCHARI

One of the great balancing and easily digested complete meals in Ayurvedic cooking, the simply prepared and endlessly varied grain dish called kitchari combines protein and carbohydrate in a single dish. The English added smoked fish to the mixture and respelled the name as kedgeree. Although it is typically made with white basmati rice and mung dhal, feel free to substitute other types of rice and lentils. See p. 212 for a another simple kitchari traditionally eaten during periods of fasting or cleansing. Serves 4

Ingredients

1 cup white basmati rice, rinsed thoroughly

⅓ cup split mung dhal (split hulled mung beans), rinsed thoroughly

2½ cups filtered water

1 zucchini, chopped

1 small sweet potato, peeled and chopped

2 tablespoons ghee (p. 227)

3 tablespoons shelled pumpkin seeds

2 tablespoons chopped scallions

2 teaspoons Chef Johnny's Korma Powder (p. 229) *or* curry powder

2 tablespoons Bragg's amino acids (optional)

½ cup organic coconut milk, preferably fresh (p. 233)

2 tablespoons lemon juice

1 teaspoon maple syrup *or* jaggery

Salt

Freshly ground black pepper

Fresh cilantro, for garnish

Ghee, for garnish

1   Put the rinsed rice and mung dhal in a saucepan and add 2½ cups filtered water. Bring to a boil over high heat. Reduce the heat to low and simmer for 10 minutes.

2   Add to the pan even layers of zucchini and sweet potato on top of the rice mixture. Cover the pan again and cook until the rice mixture has absorbed all the water, about 20 minutes.

3   Meanwhile, in a sauté pan, heat the ghee over medium heat. Add the pumpkin seeds and scallions and cook, stirring, until the seeds turn light brown, about 4 minutes. Stir in the korma powder and then the Bragg's until thoroughly combined. Stir in the coconut milk, lemon juice, and maple syrup and cook for 2 minutes more.

4   When the rice mixture is done, pour in the scallion mixture and stir to blend well. Season to taste with salt and pepper. Garnish with cilantro and ghee and serve immediately.

For dairy–free, substitute olive oil for the ghee.
Gluten-free

BROILED SALMON
with Almond Dill Sauce

A subtle, elegant sauce complements rich salmon steaks perfectly. Vata types benefit from the healthy Omega 3 oils found in salmon. Always favor fresh salmon over farmed varieties. Serves 4

Ingredients

For the sauce:

1 tablespoon ghee (p. 227)

⅓ cup finely chopped almonds

½ teaspoon ground fennel seeds

2 tablespoons finely chopped leeks

¼ cup Vegetable Stock (p. 231)

2 teaspoons lemon juice

1 cup organic cream

2 tablespoons chopped fresh dill

Pinch saffron threads

Salt

Freshly ground black pepper

For the fish:

4 salmon steaks *or* fillets (fresh, non-factory farmed)

Salt

Freshly ground black pepper

1 tablespoon ghee (p. 227)

1 tablespoon organic unsalted butter

¼ cup dry white wine (optional)

1 teaspoon lemon juice

3 tablespoons chopped fresh dill

1 tablespoon finely chopped fresh parsley, for garnish

1 Preheat the oven to 400°F.

2 To make the sauce, heat the ghee in a saucepan over medium heat. Add the almonds, fennel, leek and salt and sauté, stirring continuously, until golden brown, 2 to 3 minutes. Stir in the stock and lemon juice and bring to a boil. Add the cream, dill, and saffron. Simmer gently, stirring occasionally, until the liquid has reduced by half, about 8 minutes. Season to taste with salt and pepper. Keep warm.

3 While the sauce is reducing, prepare the fish. Season the salmon on both sides with salt and pepper. Heat the ghee and butter in a large sauté pan over high heat. Cook the salmon until lightly browned, 1 to 2 minutes per side. With a spatula, transfer the salmon to a baking dish.

4 Pour the wine and lemon juice over the fish, sprinkle with dill, and bake until just cooked through but still moist in the center, about 5 minutes. Carefully pour the juices from the baking dish into the pan of sauce, stir to blend them in, and adjust the seasoning to taste if necessary.

5 With the spatula, transfer the salmon to individual heated serving plates. Spoon some of the sauce over each serving, transferring the remainder to a sauceboat.

6 For a beautiful and delicious presentation, serve the salmon on a bed of mashed celery root, roasted fennel slices, or grilled mixed vegetables such as zucchini, peppers, eggplant, and cherry tomatoes.

P Use river salmon or trout and omit the wine.

K Omit the cream and thicken the sauce with 2 tablespoons cornmeal.

Dairy-free if using coconut milk or coconut cream in place of the dairy cream in the sauce.
Gluten-free

K CHARMOULA BASS
with Root Vegetable Purée and Sage Sauce

Charmoula is a traditional Moroccan blend of seasonings that adds a wonderfully complex flavor to savory dishes. Especially good with freshwater bass, the charmoula and accompanying sauce go well with other mild white fish, too. Serves 4

Ingredients

For the root vegetable purée:

2 carrots, peeled and quartered

2 parsnips, peeled and quartered

1 celery root, peeled and quartered

Salt

Freshly ground black pepper

2 teaspoons chopped parsley

For the charmoula bass:

2 cloves garlic

2 tablespoons grated fresh ginger

1 tablespoon mixed dried herbs such as sage, rosemary, and thyme

1 tablespoon lemon juice

2 teaspoons paprika

2 teaspoons Chef Johnny's Kapha Seasoning (p. 229) *or* Korma Powder (p. 229)

½ red chili pepper, seeds removed

½ teaspoon salt

4 fresh water bass fillets

For the scallion sauce:

2 tablespoons safflower oil

4 scallions, chopped

2 tablespoons chopped fresh sage leaves

2 cups Vegetable Stock (p. 231)

or 1 organic stock cube and 2 cups filtered water

1 tablespoon prepared organic mustard such as Dijon

1 Preheat the oven to 350°F.

2 First, make the root vegetable purée: Put the carrots, parsnips, and celery root in a large saucepan with enough filtered water to cover them well. Bring to a boil, reduce the heat, and simmer until the vegetables are fork-tender, about 15 minutes.

3 Meanwhile, prepare the charmoula bass. In a food processor fitted with the stainless-steel blade or in a blender, combine the garlic, ginger, lemon juice, mixed herbs, paprika, korma powder, chili pepper, and salt. Pulse until the mixture forms a paste. Put the fish in a baking dish and spread the paste on top of each fillet. Bake in the preheated oven until the fish is cooked through, about 15 minutes, testing for doneness by inserting the tip of a small, sharp knife between the flakes in the center of a fillet to check that the flesh is opaque.

4 When the root vegetables are done, drain them and, in the saucepan or a bowl, mash them together with salt and pepper to taste. Sprinkle with chopped parsley and cover to keep them warm until serving time.

5 Make the sauce while the vegetables and fish are cooking. Heat the oil in a saucepan over medium heat. Add the scallions and sage leaves and sauté for 3 minutes. Stir in the stock and mustard and simmer until the volume is reduced by half, about 15 minutes. Season to taste with salt and pepper.

6 To serve, mound the vegetable purée in the middle of individual heated serving plates. With a spatula, arrange a fish fillet atop each mound of vegetables. Drizzle the sauce decoratively over and around the fish on each plate.

V Substitute sea bass, cod, or hake for the freshwater bass.

P Substitute Chef Johnny's Pitta Seasoning (p. 228) for the Vata Seasoning, 1 tablespoon each of crushed fennel seed and crushed coriander seed for the garlic and chili, and dill leaves and fennel leaves or kari leaves for the rosemary and thyme; omit the mustard.

Dairy- and gluten-free

P SEARED SESAME TROUT
with Coconut Curry Sauce

Fresh water trout with a cooling sauce is a balancing choice for Pitta types. Trout is easy to find nowadays cleaned, skinned, and ready to cook. Serve this quick dish atop a mixture of brown and wild rice. Serves 4

Ingredients

For the sauce:

1½ cups organic coconut milk, preferably fresh (p. 233)

1 tablespoon chopped fresh parsley

1½ teaspoons Chef Johnny's Pitta Seasoning (p. 228)

¼ teaspoon salt

¼ teaspoon freshly ground black pepper

1½ teaspoons lemon juice

For the fish:

3 whole trout, cleaned, filleted, and skinned (about 2½ pounds total), cut crosswise into strips about 1-inch wide

2 tablespoons sunflower oil *or* ghee (p. 227)

2 teaspoons grated ginger

4 tablespoons sesame seeds

Lemon juice

1 First, start the sauce: In a saucepan, heat the coconut milk over medium heat. Add the parsley, Pitta seasoning, salt, and pepper and simmer for 10 minutes. Stir in the lemon juice. Taste and adjust the seasonings if necessary.

2 While the sauce is simmering, prepare the trout. Heat the oil in a large frying pan over medium heat. Add the ginger and sesame seeds and sauté, stirring continuously, until the seeds begin to brown, about 1 minute.

3 Add the fish and cook, stirring gently, until the pieces are uniformly seared, 1 to 2 minutes. Sprinkle with lemon juice and continue to sauté until cooked through, about 6 minutes. Remove from heat and cover to keep warm until the sauce is ready.

4 To serve, arrange the fish over the rice, if using, and spoon the sauce on top.

V Substitute mahi mahi, plaice, sole, cod, or salmon for the trout, and Chef Johnny's Vata Seasoning (p. 228) for the Pitta seasoning.

K Add 1 to 2 cloves crushed garlic to the sauté pan with the fish and ¼ teaspoon cayenne pepper to the sauce.

Dairy- and gluten-free

BRAISED CHICKEN
with Cilantro Reduction Sauce

The cooling cilantro sauce and white chicken meat makes this a balancing choice for Pitta types. To make saffron rice, add 5 strands of saffron to the rice and water before cooking. Serves 4

Ingredients

4 boneless skinless chicken breast halves

2 tablespoons ghee (p. 227) *or* sunflower oil

Salt

Freshly ground black pepper

1 cup organic chicken stock *or* Vegetable Stock (p. 231)

1 bunch cilantro, about 2 cups

2 cups filtered water *or* Whey (p. 231)

1 teaspoon grated fresh ginger

1 teaspoon ground fennel seed

¼ teaspoon ground turmeric

½ teaspoon Herb Salt (p. 230)

½ teaspoon maple syrup

10 mint leaves, chopped

1 to 2 tablespoons chickpea flour

1 Preheat the oven to 350°F.

2 Grease a baking dish with half of the ghee. Put the chicken breasts in the baking dish, coat them with the ghee in the dish, and season with salt and pepper. Pour in the stock. Put the dish in the oven and bake until the chicken is cooked through, about 25 minutes.

3 As soon as the chicken goes in the oven, put the cilantro and 1 cup water in a blender or a food processor fitted with the stainless-steel blade. Blend or process until smoothly puréed.

4 Heat the remaining ghee in a large saucepan over medium heat. Add the ginger and sauté 2 minutes. Add the fennel and sauté 1 minute more. Stir in the turmeric, herb salt, syrup, mint, cilantro purée, and remaining water. Simmer until reduced by half, about 20 minutes. Whisk in the chickpea flour and continue cooking, stirring continuously, until the sauce thickens, 2 to 3 minutes. Season to taste with salt and pepper.

5 To serve, arrange the chicken breasts on a platter or individual serving plates and pour the sauce over them.

[V] Also recommended

[K] Substitute basil for the cilantro.

Dairy-free with the sunflower oil option
Gluten-free without the whey

 CHICKEN & FENNEL BROTH

 CHICKEN SOUP
with Almonds

Nourishing and rejuvenating, the healing properties of chicken broth are widely known. You'll be enticed by the fragrant aroma that rises from the pot while this hearty soup simmers away. Serves 4

The presence of almonds and mild spices in this thick purée makes it an especially soothing and satisfying version of chicken soup. Serves 4

Ingredients

6 cups organic chicken stock

1¼ pounds boneless skinless chicken, chopped (about 2 cups)

2 cups filtered water

1 fennel bulb, chopped

2 carrots, thinly sliced

½ cup finely chopped leek

3 tablespoons coarsely mashed cooked chickpeas

2 tablespoons uncooked red lentils

2 bay leaves

1 tablespoon Bragg's amino acids

1 teaspoon dried oregano

½ teaspoon freshly ground black pepper

½ teaspoon Herb Salt (p. 230)

1 tablespoon chopped fresh parsley

Ingredients

2 tablespoons ghee (p. 227)

½ cup chopped leek

1 teaspoon grated ginger

1 teaspoon ground fennel seed

¾ teaspoon salt

½ teaspoon freshly ground black pepper

½ teaspoon ground turmeric

½ teaspoon ground cardamom

1 medium carrot, sliced

½ cup shelled fresh *or* frozen peas

1 cup blanched almonds

¾ cup coarsely chopped skinless boneless chicken

3 cups organic chicken stock

1 cup organic light cream

1 tablespoon finely chopped cilantro, for garnish

1 Put all the ingredients except the parsley in a large soup pot. Bring to a boil, reduce the heat, and simmer for 40 minutes. Taste and adjust the seasonings, if necessary.

2 Ladle the soup into individual heated serving bowls. Garnish each serving with parsley.

P Substitute Puy lentils for the red lentils and cilantro for the parsley; omit the leek.

K Also recommended in moderation.

Dairy- and gluten-free

1 Soak the almonds in filtered water for 1-2 hours, drain and remove skins.

2 Heat the ghee in a large frying pan over medium heat. Add the leek and ginger and sauté, stirring frequently, until the leek softens, 3 to 4 minutes. Add the fennel and cook for 1 minute more. Stir in the salt, pepper, turmeric, and cardamom. Add the carrot, peas, almonds, and chicken and stir continuously for 2 minutes.

3 Pour in the stock, bring to a boil over high heat, then simmer the soup for 20 minutes. Remove the soup from the heat and let it cool at room temperature until warm, about 30 minutes. Purée the soup until smooth in blender or food processor.

4 Return the puréed soup to the saucepan and stir in the cream. Bring to a simmer over medium heat, then reduce the heat and continue cooking until very hot, 2 to 3 minutes. Taste and adjust the seasonings if necessary.

5 Ladle the soup into heated serving bowls and garnish with cilantro.

Dairy-free if substituting coconut milk for the cream and sunflower oil for the ghee

Gluten-free

K CHICKEN TIKKA

One of the most popular dishes in Indian restaurants, these chicken breasts get their lively flavor and extra-tender texture from a marinade of yogurt and spices. Serve with saffron rice (see introduction on page 264) and Naan bread (p. 305). Serves 4

Ingredients

4 skinless chicken breast halves

¾ cup organic plain yogurt (p. 227)

2 tablespoons sunflower oil *or* ghee (p. 227)

1 tablespoon lemon *or* lime juice

2 tablespoons tomato purée (optional)

2 teaspoons Chef Johnny's Korma Powder (p. 229)

1 teaspoon salt

½ teaspoon chili powder

2 teaspoons paprika

1 teaspoon minced garlic

1 teaspoon grated ginger

¼ teaspoon ground turmeric

6 kari leaves, chopped, *or* 1 tablespoon chopped fresh
   mint

1   With a sharp knife, make several deep slits all over the meaty side of each chicken breast. Put the chicken in a baking dish, bone down.

2   In a mixing bowl, whisk together the yogurt, sunflower oil, lemon juice, tomato purée, korma powder, salt, chili, paprika, garlic, ginger, turmeric, and kari leaves. Spread the yogurt mixture evenly over the chicken. Cover and refrigerate for at least 3 hours or overnight.

3   Preheat the oven to 475°F.

4   Place chicken on a baking pan and cook until tender, about 25 minutes.

V   Add 4 tablespoons coconut milk.

P   Substitute Chef Johnny's Pitta Seasoning for the korma powder; omit the garlic, chili, and tomato purée; add ¼ teaspoon saffron powder to sauce; and 4 tablespoons of coconut milk.

For dairy-free, use soy yogurt and sunflower oil.
Gluten-free

ROASTED PLUM TOMATOES

Roasting concentrates the flavor of tomatoes and lightly caramelizes their natural sugars, resulting in an almost candy-like intensity and sweetness. Serves 4

Ingredients

1 pound stemmed plum *or* cherry tomatoes
1 tablespoon extra-virgin olive oil
½ teaspoon Herb Salt (p. 230)
⅓ teaspoon freshly ground black pepper
1 clove garlic, minced
3 *or* 4 sprigs fresh thyme
2 tablespoons torn *or* chopped fresh basil, for garnish

1 Preheat the oven to 300°F. If using plum tomatoes, cut out their cores and cut the tomatoes lengthwise in half. Leave cherry tomatoes whole.

2 Put the tomatoes in a baking dish, cut sides up if using plum tomatoes. Drizzle them with olive oil and sprinkle with herb salt, pepper, garlic, and thyme. Bake the tomatoes for 20 minutes. Remove the thyme sprigs and garnish with basil.

P Replace the tomatoes with red bell peppers and the thyme with mint; omit the garlic.

K Follow the Pitta version, while keeping the garlic and thyme.

Dairy- and gluten-free

STEAMED KALE
with Lemon and Dill Butter

Robust-tasting, slightly bitter kale gets an added lift from a quickly prepared seasoned butter. Serves 4

Ingredients

3 to 4 cups chopped curly *or* flat kale leaves
⅓ cup organic unsalted butter, softened
1 tablespoon chopped fresh dill *or* fennel leaves
2 teaspoons lemon juice
½ teaspoon grated lemon zest
Salt
Freshly ground black pepper

1 Bring about 1 inch of water to a boil in the bottom half of a steamer or in a saucepan with a steamer insert. Put the kale in the steamer, cover, and cook until just tender, 4 to 5 minutes.

2 Put the butter, dill, lemon juice, and lemon zest in a small bowl and mash them together with a fork. Season to taste with salt and pepper.

3 To serve, spoon a dollop of butter on each serving of kale.

V Add thyme or rosemary.

K Replace the butter with safflower oil, and the dill with thyme or rosemary.

The Kapha version is dairy-free.
Gluten-free

THAI VEGETABLE
Stir Fry

Stir frying is a rapid method of cooking lively vegetables dishes. The trick comes in cutting vegetables to uniform size and adding the harder ones earlier in cooking. Five-spice powder, the distinctive seasoning in this easy stir-fry, is widely available in health food and grocery stores. Serves 4

Ingredients

3 tablespoons sesame oil *or* ghee (p. 227)

1 carrot, cut into julienne strips

1 cup broccoli florets

1 zucchini, cut into julienne strips

1 bok choy, cut crosswise into thin strips

2 teaspoons five spice powder

1 cup Fresh Panir Cheese (p. 231) *or* tofu, cut into cubes *or* slices

4 tablespoons organic coconut milk, preferably fresh (p. 233)

¾ cup bean sprouts

1 cup sliced water chestnuts

1 to 2 cups Vegetable Stock (p. 231), filtered water, *or* whey

1 tablespoon Bragg's amino acids

2 teaspoons lime juice

Salt

3 tablespoons finely chopped cilantro, for garnish

1   In a wok or large saucepan, heat the oil over high heat. Add the scallions and carrot and stir-fry for 1 minute. Add the broccoli and stir-fry for 1 additional minute. Add the zucchini and bok choy and stir-fry for 1 minute more.

2   Sprinkle the five-spice powder over all the vegetables. Add the panir and coconut milk and stir gently to combine it with the vegetables without breaking up the cheese. Then add the bean sprouts and water chestnuts along with the stock, Bragg's, lime juice, and salt to taste.

3   Cook, stirring constantly, until the vegetables are all brightly colored and tender-crisp and the panir has heated through, 2 to 3 minutes. Serve immediately, garnished with cilantro.

V   Also recommended

K   Add 2 tablespoons grated fresh ginger.

Dairy- and gluten-free

CAULIFLOWER SUBJI

Spiced mixtures of cauliflower and potato, cooked to almost melting softness, are among the most satisfying and flavorful side dishes of the Indian kitchen. Serves 4

Ingredients

2 tablespoons sunflower *or* safflower oil

1 teaspoon black mustard seeds

2 teaspoons whole cumin seeds

1 tablespoon grated fresh ginger

1 tablespoon Chef Johnny's Kapha Seasoning (p. 229) *or* curry powder

1 plum tomato, peeled, seeded, and chopped

2 cups cauliflower florets

1 cup diced potato with the peel on

¼ teaspoon asafetida

½ small red chili, dried *or* fresh, finely chopped

1 cup filtered water *or* Vegetable Stock (p. 231)

3 tablespoons organic plain yogurt (p. 227)

2 tablespoons finely chopped cilantro

Salt

Freshly ground black pepper

1   In a wok or large saucepan, heat the oil over medium heat. Add the mustard seeds. When they begin to pop, after about 1 minute, add the cumin and ginger and stir-fry for 2 minutes. Add the korma powder and cook for 1 minute more.

2   Add the tomato, stirring well to combine. Add the cauliflower, potato, asafetida, chili, and water or stock. Cover, reduce the heat, and simmer until all the vegetables are tender, 15 to 17 minutes.

3   Stir in the yogurt and cilantro. Season to taste with salt and pepper.

V   Replace the cauliflower with asparagus, bok choy, green beans, or a mixture of all three.

P   Replace the Kapha seasoning with Chef Johnny's Pitta Seasoning (p. 228), yogurt with coconut milk, and black mustard with crushed fennel seed; omit the asafetida and chili.

Dairy- and gluten-free in the Pitta version

ASPARAGUS WITH BASIL PESTO & PINE NUTS

One of the great culinary inventions of Italy, pesto is widely known for its rich taste and remarkable simplicity. It provides a green, jewel-like complement to pasta or vegetables. Serves 4

Ingredients

1 cup fresh basil leaves

¼ cup plus 1 tablespoon extra-virgin olive oil

4 tablespoons pine nuts

2 tablespoons freshly grated Parmesan cheese *or* soft cheese

1 clove garlic (optional)

1 teaspoon lemon juice

Salt

Freshly ground black pepper

2 cups coarsely chopped fresh asparagus

¼–½ cup filtered water

1 In a blender or a food processor fitted with the stainless-steel blade, combine the basil, ¼ cup olive oil, 2 tablespoons of the pine nuts, the Parmesan cheese, garlic, and lemon juice. Pulse a few times until the mixture forms a coarse paste. Pulse in salt and pepper to taste.

2 In a wok or saucepan, heat the remaining tablespoon of olive oil over medium heat. Add the asparagus and cook, stirring gently, until bright green, 3 to 4 minutes. Add the water, cover, and simmer just until the asparagus is tender-crisp, 1 to 2 minutes more.

3 Transfer the asparagus to a serving bowl or individual plates. Spoon the pesto over it, garnish with the remaining pine nuts, and serve immediately.

K Replace the basil with cilantro and the olive oil with sunflower oil; omit the cheese or substitute soy cheese.

P Substitute goat cheese for the Parmesan and sunflower oil for the olive oil.

Dairy- and gluten-free in the Pitta version

V P K 20-MINUTE CURRY

Who says delicious, nourishing curries take hours to prepare? Offer this quick, flavorful combination with basmati rice and Chapatis (p. 305) for a satisfying side dish or main course. Serves 4

Ingredients

1 tablespoon ghee (p. 227)

2 tablespoons finely chopped leeks

1 teaspoon grated fresh ginger

1 teaspoon kalonji seeds (also called nigella) (optional)

1 tablespoon Chef Johnny's Korma Powder (p. 229)

1 cup coarsely chopped green beans *or* shelled peas

2 purple *or* regular potatoes, peeled *or* cut into chunks

²/₃ cup Vegetable Stock (p. 231) *or* filtered water

2 teaspoons lime juice

2 teaspoons chickpea flour

2 teaspoons organic plain yogurt (p. 227)

1 teaspoon maple syrup *or* agave syrup

Salt

Freshly ground black pepper

1 tablespoon finely chopped cilantro, for garnish

1 In a wok or a large saucepan, heat the ghee over medium heat. Add the leek and ginger and sauté for 3 minutes. Add the kalonji and korma powder, and cook, stirring frequently, for 2 minutes.

2 Add the green beans, potato, stock, and lime juice. Cover, reduce the heat, and simmer for 12 minutes.

3 Stir in the chickpea flour, yogurt, and maple syrup. Simmer for 2 to 3 minutes more. Season to taste with salt and pepper. Serve immediately, garnished with cilantro.

Dairy-free with coconut milk or cashew butter substituted for the yogurt and olive oil for the ghee.

Gluten-free

PEYA SOUP
with Okra

This traditional Ayurvedic soup helps kindle the digestive fire without overheating Pitta. Serves 4

Ingredients

1 cup basmati rice, rinsed well

½ cup mung dhal (split hulled yellow mung beans), sorted and rinsed well

8 cups Vegetable Stock (p. 231) *or* filtered water

1 tablespoon ghee (p. 227)

2 teaspoons grated fresh ginger

6 to 8 fresh okra pods, cut into bite-sized pieces

2 teaspoons Chef Johnny's Pitta Seasoning (p. 228), *or* mild curry powder

1 tablespoon lemon juice

2 *or* 3 kari leaves *or* fenugreek leaves

Salt

Freshly ground black pepper

Finely chopped fresh parsley, for garnish

1 Put the rice and dhal in a large mixing bowl, add all the stock or water, and leave at room temperature to soak for 1 hour.

2 In a large pot, heat the ghee over low heat. Add the ginger and okra and cook, stirring frequently, 3 to 4 minutes. Add the Pitta seasoning or mild curry powder and cook, stirring, for 1 minute more.

3 Stir in the rice, dhal, soaking liquid, lemon juice, and kari leaves. Raise the heat, bring the liquid to a boil, and then reduce the heat and simmer, covered, until the dhal is tender, about 1 hour. Season to taste with salt and pepper.

4 To serve, ladle into heated serving bowls and garnish with parsley.

V Substitute Chef Johnny's Vata Seasoning for the Pitta seasoning and add 4 to 5 tablespoons coconut milk if desired.

K Substitute red lentils for the mung dhal and Chef Johnny's Garam Masala (p. 230) or regular curry powder for the Pitta seasoning; add ¼ teaspoon cayenne pepper.

For dairy-free, use the sunflower oil option.
Gluten-free

K YELLOW SPLIT PEA SOUP
with Artichoke and Jicama

Split peas and spices make a nourishing soup that balances Kapha. I also refer to this recipe as a 'Soup to Savor.' Jicama, is a widely available root vegetable whose tough brown skin conceals its crisp, white flesh and sweet, slightly nutty flavor. Serves 4

Ingredients

2 tablespoons ghee (p. 227)

2 tablespoons grated fresh ginger

2 teaspoons whole cumin seeds

1 teaspoon whole fenugreek seeds

1 teaspoon Chef Johnny's Kapha Seasoning (p. 229) *or* curry powder

5 whole star anise pods

2 cinnamon sticks

2 bay leaves

¾ cup diced jicama

¾ cup chopped fresh artichoke hearts

3 tablespoons organic coconut milk (p. 233)

1 tablespoon maple syrup

¼ teaspoon asafetida

2 cups yellow *or* green split peas

6 cups Vegetable Stock (p. 231) *or* filtered water

2 tablespoons lime juice

2 tablespoons fenugreek leaves

2 tablespoons organic plain yogurt (p. 227)

¼ teaspoon ground cardamom

Salt

Freshly ground black pepper

Lime slices and paprika, for garnish

1 Rinse the split peas and soak in filtered water for 2 hours.

2 Heat the ghee in a large saucepan over low heat. Add the ginger and sauté for 1 minute. Add the cumin and fenugreek seeds and cook, stirring frequently, until lightly browned and fragrant, 2 to 3 minutes. Stir in the korma powder, cinnamon sticks, bay leaves, and star anise. Add the jicama, artichoke, coconut milk, maple syrup, and asafetida, stirring to combine.

3 Add the split peas and enough of the stock or water to cover the peas well. Raise the heat, bring to a boil, then reduce the heat and simmer, partially covered, until the peas are tender and the soup is thick, about 50 minutes.

4 Remove and discard the star anise, cinnamon sticks, and bay leaves. Stir in the lime juice and the fenugreek leaves. Whisk in the yogurt and cardamom. If the soup's consistency seems too thick for your liking, stir in more stock or water and continue cooking until heated through. Season to taste with salt and pepper.

5 To serve, ladle the soup into heated bowls and garnish with lime slices and a sprinkling of paprika.

V Substitute split mung dhal for the split peas and sweet potato or pumpkin for the jicama; add 2 to 3 tablespoons finely chopped leek in step 1 if desired.

P Use 4 teaspoons Chef Johnny's Pitta Seasoning (p. 228) and leave out the grated ginger, bay leaves, and asafetida.

Dairy-free if using sunflower oil in place of ghee
Gluten-free

 CREAM OF SWEET
CORN SOUP

 CHILLED BERRY SOUP

Sublimely delicate and sweet, this simple soup highlights one of summer's best gifts from the garden or farm. Serves 4

Ingredients

2 ears fresh sweet corn, kernels cut off

2 cups Vegetable Stock (p. 231) *or* Whey (p. 231)

1 cup filtered water

3 tablespoons organic cream *or* 2 teaspoons organic unsalted butter

1 tablespoon chopped fresh marjoram, *or* 1 teaspoon dried marjoram

Salt

Freshly ground black pepper

Toasted shelled pumpkin seeds *or* toasted slivered almonds, for garnish

1 In a medium saucepan over low heat, cook the corn kernels in the stock or whey and water until tender, about 5 minutes.

2 Working in batches if necessary, put the corn and its cooking liquid in a blender or food processor fitted with the stainless-steel blade, add the cream and marjoram, and pulse until smooth. Season to taste with salt and pepper.

3 Serve immediately, ladling the soup into heated bowls and garnishing each serving with pumpkin seeds or almonds.

For dairy-free, substitute coconut cream for the cream or butter and use vegetable stock.
Gluten-free

Berries of any kind make a refreshing soup in hot weather. If fresh berries are unavailable, use unsweetened frozen organic berries. Serves 4

Ingredients

3 cups hulled fresh berries such as blueberries, loganberries, raspberries, blackberries, *or* pitted fresh sweet red *or* black cherries

1 peach *or* nectarine, peeled, pitted, and chopped

2 cups bottled unsweetened raspberry juice

2 cups organic plain yogurt (p. 227)

1 cup filtered water

1 teaspoon lemon juice

½ teaspoon allspice

Organic raw sugar, such as Sucanat

Organic plain yogurt (p. 227), for garnish

Fresh mint sprigs, for garnish

1 In a large saucepan, combine the berries, peach, raspberry juice, yogurt, water, lemon juice, and allspice. Bring to a boil over medium-high heat, reduce the heat, and simmer gently for 10 minutes.

2 Ladle half of the soup into a food processor fitted with the stainless-steel blade or a blender. Process until puréed, taking care to avoid splattering. Pour the purée into a mixing bowl along with the remaining cooked berry mixture and stir to combine. Stir in sugar to taste.

3 Cover the bowl with plastic wrap and chill the soup in the refrigerator for at least 1 hour.

4 To serve, ladle the chilled soup into chilled bowls. Garnish each bowl with a swirl of yogurt and a sprig of mint.

V Serve the soup warm.

K Serve the soup warm, omit the yogurt; substitute honey for the sugar.

Kapha version is dairy- and gluten-free

Mixed Vegetable Miso
with Rice Noodles

There's a clarity that comes from eating a good miso soup. It has been known to elicit an almost Zen-like contemplation of the vegetables floating in the clear, savory broth. The naturally salty taste of miso makes it a balancing choice for Vata types. Serves 4

Ingredients

2 teaspoons ghee (p. 227)

2 teaspoons grated fresh ginger

¼ teaspoon asafetida

1 bok choy, sliced crosswise into thin strips

1 medium carrot, sliced

½ red pepper, stemmed, seeded, and sliced into thin strips

½ cup thinly sliced daikon radish

12 fenugreek leaves

4 okra pods, sliced

3 tablespoons thinly sliced leek rings

2 tablespoons Bragg's amino acids

1 teaspoon dried marjoram

2 teaspoons finely chopped fresh parsley

8 cups Vegetable Stock (p. 231)

or 2 organic stock cubes and 8 cups filtered water

2 teaspoons miso paste

Small handful dried rice noodles *or* potato *or* soy noodles, broken into small pieces

1   In a saucepan, heat the ghee over low heat and sauté the ginger until fragrant, about 3 minutes. Stir in the asafetida and then the rest of the ingredients except the noodles. Raise the heat, bring the liquid to a boil, and then reduce the heat and simmer for 10 minutes.

2   Stir in the noodles. Simmer for 20 minutes more. Ladle into heated bowls and serve immediately.

P   Substitute jicama for the daikon, parsnip or green beans for the carrot, and cabbage for the leek; omit the asafetida.

K   Substitute buckwheat noodles for the rice noodles and sunflower oil for the ghee.

For dairy- and gluten-free, use sesame oil instead of ghee.

AVOCADO SALAD
with Roasted Walnuts

Crunchy walnuts and ripe, rich avocado make this a winning salad combination, enhanced by the creaminess of the dressing. Serves 4

Ingredients

For the salad:
1 large ripe avocado, halved, pitted, peeled, and cut into chunks
2 ripe tomatoes, coarsely chopped
¾ cup shelled walnut pieces, toasted in a small, dry sauté pan over low heat
½ cup diced feta cheese *or* brie (optional)

For the dressing:
3 tablespoons organic plain yogurt (p. 227)
2 tablespoons extra-virgin olive oil
1 tablespoon lemon juice
1 tablespoon filtered water
1 teaspoon tahini
1 teaspoon maple syrup
½ cup chopped watercress
2 teaspoons dried basil
1 teaspoon chopped fresh marjoram leaves
½ teaspoon ground turmeric
Salt
Freshly ground black pepper

1   In a large mixing bowl, combine the avocado, tomato, walnuts, and, if you like, the cheese.

2   In another bowl, whisk together all the dressing ingredients. Add them to the avocado mixture and toss well. Season to taste with salt and pepper.

P   Substitute cottage cheese for the feta or brie and sunflower oil for the olive oil; omit the walnuts.

K   Substitute artichoke heart for the avocado, sunflower oil for the olive oil, and honey for the maple syrup; omit the walnuts and yogurt, and try 2 tablespoons goat cheese instead of the feta or brie.

Dairy-free if you omit the yogurt and cheese

POTATO SALAD
with Watercress

An old-fashioned favorite gets a flavorful makeover with a dressing based on yogurt and herbs. Pitta types will benefit from the mildly bitter watercress leaves and cooling mint and fennel. Serves 4

Ingredients

For the salad:
3 *or* 4 potatoes, cut into bite-sized cubes
1 cup watercress leaves

For the dressing:
3 tablespoons organic plain yogurt (p. 227)
2 tablespoons filtered water
1 tablespoon sunflower oil
1 teaspoon maple syrup
1 teaspoon dried mint
1 teaspoon fennel fronds *or* dill
1 tablespoon lime
Salt

1   Put the potatoes in a saucepan, add enough filtered water to cover them well, season with some salt, and bring to a boil over high heat. Reduce the heat and simmer, uncovered, until the potatoes are tender, 15 to 20 minutes. Drain well and let cool.

2   Put the potatoes and watercress in a large mixing bowl. In a separate bowl, whisk together all the dressing ingredients. Add the dressing to the potatoes and watercress and toss well, adjusting the seasoning to taste with more salt if necessary.

V   Use sweet potato and substitute ground cumin and thyme for the mint and fennel.

K   Substitute cooked Jerusalem artichoke for the potato and parsley and thyme in place of the mint and fennel; add ⅓ teaspoon asafetida and replace the maple syrup with honey.

Dairy-free if using almond milk or coconut milk in place of the yogurt
Gluten-free

STUFFED ARTICHOKE HEARTS

This attractive starter or side salad combines the complimentary flavors of walnuts, sage, and fresh cheese in a lotus-shaped vegetable. Serves 6

Ingredients

6 globe artichokes, trimmed down to
  their cup-shaped hearts
½ tablespoon ghee (p. 227)
2 tablespoons chopped leek
1 cup Fresh Panir Cheese (p. 231)
½ cup cooked basmati rice
10 walnuts, ground
1 teaspoon crumbled dried sage
1 teaspoon Bragg's liquid amino acids
Salt
Freshly ground black pepper
Mint and Cream Dressing (p. 290), made with fresh
  marjoram, basil, *or* thyme instead of mint

1 Bring the water to a boil in the bottom of a steamer or in a saucepan with a steamer insert. Put the artichoke hearts in the steamer, cover, and cook until tender, about 25 minutes.

2 To cook the rice, place ⅓ cup white basmati rice in a pan with ⅓ cup water and ⅔ teaspoon salt. Bring to a boil, lower heat and simmer, covered, with the lid slightly ajar, until all the water is absorbed, about 15 minutes.

3 Meanwhile, in a small sauté pan, heat the ghee over low heat. Add the leek and sauté until lightly cooked, about 3 minutes. Put the leek in a mixing bowl with the panir, rice, walnuts, sage, and Bragg's. Stir in salt and pepper to taste.

To serve, transfer the artichoke hearts to individual plates and spoon the cheese mixture into their centers. Drizzle each serving with the dressing.

P Substitute sunflower seeds for the walnuts, finely chopped asparagus or peas for the leeks, and fresh dill for the sage.

K Substitute barley or buckwheat for the rice and goat cheese for the panir; add extra black pepper.

For dairy- free, use corn oil and no panir or ghee.
Gluten-free

Mixed Bean Salad
with Lemon Herb Dressing

Mixed beans and a tasty dressing make a simple salad. The astringent taste of the tender legumes and slightly bitter taste of the greens naturally balance the moist, heavy nature of Kapha. Serves 4

Ingredients

For the salad:
1 cup cooked mixed beans
  (lima, chickpeas, brown lentils *or* black eyed beans)
Handful arugula leaves, coarsely chopped
3 tablespoons grated daikon radish

For the dressing:
2 tablespoons sunflower oil
1 tablespoon lemon juice
1 tablespoon organic plain yogurt (p. 227)
1 teaspoon apple cider vinegar
1 teaspoon tahini
1 teaspoon thyme
1 teaspoon oregano
½ teaspoon raw honey
¼ teaspoon black pepper
Pinch cayenne pepper

For the garnish:
3 tablespoons shelled pumpkin seeds *or* flax seeds, lightly toasted in
  a small, dry saucepan over low heat

1 Soak the beans in 3 cups water overnight. Rinse and cook together in 6 cups boiling water, until tender, about 45 minutes. Add 1 teaspoon of fresh grated ginger and a pinch salt during cooking.

2 In a mixing bowl, stir together the beans, arugula, and daikon.

3 In a separate bowl, combine all the dressing ingredients. With a wire whisk, whisk them together until thoroughly blended.

4 Pour the dressing over the beans and toss well. Garnish with pumpkin seeds.

V Not recommended

P Leave out the cayenne pepper, oregano, thyme, vinegar, and honey, replacing them with mint, fennel leaf, and maple syrup.

For dairy-free, use coconut milk in place of yogurt.
Gluten-free

Garden Island Salad

This brightly colored salad is inspired by the lush greens of Kauai, the "Garden Island." Enjoy it in the hot Summer months. Serves 4

Ingredients

For the dressing:
½ cup almonds, soaked in water for 6-8 hours and peeled
1 teaspoon raw honey or maple syrup
2 tablespoons sunflower oil
1 tablespoon lime juice
1 teaspoon paprika
1 clove roasted chopped garlic (optional)
½ teaspoon ground turmeric dried
  or 2 teaspoons fresh grated turmeric
3 tablespoons chopped fennel fronds or dill leaves
⅓ cup water

For the salad:
½ cup sliced green pepper
1 cup watercress leaves
½ cup steamed Jerusalem artichoke, sliced
2 cups baby spinach leaves
½ cup finely shredded carrot
3 tablespoons chopped parsley
3 cups green salad leaves
5 tablespoons toasted sunflower seeds

1 Put all the dressing ingredients in a blender. Blend until smooth and creamy.

2 Put all the salad ingredients except the sunflower seeds in a bowl and pour the dressing over them. Toss to coat the leaves. Garnish with the sunflower seeds and serve.

Dairy- and gluten-free

Warm Lentil Salad
with Roasted Peppers and Honey-Lemon Dressing

Sometimes referred to as the gourmet lentil, Puy or French lentils, have an earthy flavor and delicate texture, reminiscent of caviar. When combined with bitter salad leaves, roasted red pepper, and a creamy dressing, you'll have a salad symphony! Serves 4

Ingredients

For the salad:

6 handfuls dandelion, endive, *or* arugula leaves, torn

¾ cup Puy *or* brown lentils

1 roasted red pepper, stemmed, seeded, and cut into thin strips

2 tablespoons torn fresh basil leaves

2 teaspoons chopped fresh thyme leaves

For the dressing:

2 tablespoons organic plain yogurt (p. 227)

2 tablespoons extra-virgin olive oil

1 tablespoon lemon juice

1 teaspoon honey

Salt

Freshly ground black pepper

½ cup shelled pumpkin seeds, toasted in a small dry sauté pan, for garnish

1 Soak the Puy or brown lentils in 1½ cups filtered water for 2 hours. Then place in a medium saucepan with 2¼ cups filtered water. Bring the water to a boil and simmer until the legumes become tender, 25 to 30 minutes (or 40 minutes if using brown lentils). Drain any remaining water.

2 Arrange the greens on individual plates or a large platter.

3 In a large mixing bowl, combine the lentils, red pepper strips, basil, and thyme.

4 In another bowl, whisk together the dressing ingredients. Season to taste with salt and pepper. Add the dressing to the lentil mixture and toss well.

5 Mound the lentil salad on the greens and garnish with pumpkin seeds.

V Substitute adzuki or mung beans for the lentils; winter cress for the dandelion leaves, and maple or agave syrup for the honey.

K Substitute goat cheese or cashew butter for the yogurt.

For dairy-free, omit the yogurt.

BRUSCHETTA

VEGETABLE SUSHI ROLLS

A luscious bean spread (p. 221) stands in for the rice in this colorful version of popular sushi rolls. Accompany with Tarragon Aioli (p. 297) for dipping. Serves 4

Ingredients

2 sheets nori seaweed
1 cup Sprouted Chickpea Hummus (p. 221)
1 ripe avocado, halved, pitted, peeled, and sliced
2 carrots, shredded
½ cup sunflower seed sprouts
1 small red bell pepper, halved, stemmed, seeded, and cut into thin strips
Lemon juice
1 tablespoon black sesame seeds
1 tablespoon white sesame seeds
⅓ teaspoon salt
⅓ teaspoon freshly ground black pepper

1 Place a sheet of nori flat on a work surface. Spread half of the bean spread over its surface. Sprinkle bean sprouts with lemon juice, Bragg's and a pinch of salt. Top each sheet with half each of the avocado, carrot, sunflower sprouts, and red pepper, arranging them neatly. Sprinkle with half of the lemon juice, sesame seeds, salt, and pepper.

2 Roll up the topped nori into a tight, neat roll. Cut it crosswise with a diagonal cut.

3 Repeat with the second sheet. Serve the rolls immediately.

P Also recommended.

K Substitute grilled eggplant or endive for the avocado.

Dairy- and gluten-free

The popular Italian antipasto, highlighting fresh summer tomatoes, makes a perfect Vata appetizer. Serves 4

Ingredients

8 slices French bread, sourdough bread, *or* foccacia
4 cloves garlic, sliced in half
3 tablespoons extra-virgin olive oil
3 plum tomatoes, peeled and diced
¼ cup chopped fresh basil leaves
½ teaspoon salt
½ teaspoon freshly ground black pepper

1 Preheat the oven to 350°F.

2 Arrange the bread slices on a large baking sheet and bake until lightly toasted, about 10 minutes.

3 Remove them from the oven and immediately rub each slice with the cut side of a garlic clove. Drizzle the bread with olive oil and top with tomatoes, basil, salt, and pepper. Serve immediately.

P Omit the garlic and substitute sunflower oil for the olive oil.

K Substitute Cornbread (p. 303) for the French bread and sunflower oil for the olive oil.

Dairy-free and gluten-free in the Kapha alternative

V P K CREAM OF BEET SOUP
with Puy Lentils

Puy lentils were originally grown in the volcanic soils of Puy in France, but now they're also grown in North America and Italy. A wonderful addition to this elegant soup, they remain firm after cooking and provide a rich flavor. Serves 4

Ingredients

1½ cups Puy lentils

4 cups Vegetable Stock (p. 231) *or* filtered water

1 potato, skin on, diced

1 small sweet potato, peeled, cut in half lengthwise, and thinly sliced

1 medium beet, peeled and shredded, 1 tablespoon reserved for garnish

1 cup organic coconut milk, preferably fresh (p. 233)

2 cups Whey (p. 231), Vegetable Stock (p. 231) *or* filtered water

Extra-virgin olive oil

1 tablespoon grated ginger

2 tablespoons chopped leek (optional)

1 tablespoon ground coriander

1 tablespoon ground fennel

1 teaspoon ground cumin

½ teaspoon ground turmeric

½ teaspoon asafetida

2 to 3 tablespoons organic heavy cream

1 teaspoon tomato purée

Salt

Freshly ground black pepper

Organic fresh, creamy goat cheese slices, for garnish

3 tablespoons finely chopped cilantro, for garnish

1 Put the lentils and stock or water in a large saucepan. Bring to a boil over medium heat. Reduce the heat, add the potatoes, and simmer until the lentils and potato are tender, about 15 minutes.

2 Add the beets, coconut milk, and whey. Continue simmering, stirring occasionally, until the beets are tender, about 5 minutes.

3 Meanwhile, heat the olive oil in a small sauté pan over medium heat. Add the ginger and leek and cook until softened, 3 to 5 minutes. Add the coriander, fennel, cumin, and turmeric. Cook, stirring occasionally, for 3 minutes more. Stir in the asafetida, cream, and tomato purée.

4. Stir the ginger-leek mixture into the lentil mixture. Continue to simmer gently, stirring occasionally, until the soup thickens. Season to taste with salt and pepper.

5 Ladle the soup into heated bowls. Garnish each serving with a slice of goat cheese, the reserved grated beet, and cilantro.

Dairy-free if substituting extra coconut milk and stock for the cream and whey
Gluten-free

SAMOSAS
with Mango Chutney

The vegetable-filled Indian turnovers called samosas make a satisfying starter or snack, and are easy to make using store-bought filo pastry, usually found in the freezer or refrigerated case. Makes 16 samosas

Ingredients

½ cup potatoes

1 tablespoon plus ⅓ cup ghee (p. 227)

1 teaspoon grated fresh ginger

1 teaspoon ground coriander seed

1 teaspoon ground fennel seed

1 teaspoon whole cumin seeds

¼ cup organic coconut milk, preferably fresh (p. 233)

¼ teaspoon ground turmeric

½ head cauliflower, trimmed, cut into small florets, and boiled in water for 1 minute

1 cup green peas, boiled in water for 7 minutes

1 teaspoon lemon juice

Pinch salt

6 kari leaves *or* 1 tablespoon chopped cilantro

½ teaspoon brown rice syrup

2 tablespoons organic plain yogurt (p. 227)

1 (16-ounce) package organic filo pastry

Fresh Mango Chutney (recipe follows)
   or Cilantro Chutney (p. 300)

1   Peel the potatoes and cut into ½-inch cubes. Place in a pan of 2 cups salted water and boil until tender, about 15 minutes, then drain.

2   Heat 1 tablespoon ghee in a large sauté pan over medium heat. Add the ginger, coriander, fennel, and cumin. Cook, stirring frequently, for 1 minute.

3   Meanwhile, in small bowl, stir together the coconut milk and turmeric. Set aside.

4   Add the cauliflower to the pan and sauté for 2 minutes. Add the peas, lemon juice, coconut milk mixture, salt, kari leaves, and syrup. Simmer, stirring occasionally, until the cauliflower is just tender, about 7 minutes. Stir in the potatoes, adding some water if the mixture becomes too dry. Set aside to cool.

5   Stir the yogurt into the cooled cauliflower mixture. Taste and adjust the seasonings if necessary.

6   Preheat the oven to 350°F.

7   In a small saucepan, melt the remaining ⅓ cup ghee and remove from the heat.

8   Carefully unroll the filo dough and keep the sheets covered with a clean, damp kitchen towel to prevent them from drying out.

9   Place a sheet of filo on a clean work surface and brush with melted ghee. Carefully lay another sheet of filo on top and brush with ghee. Repeat twice more to get 4 layers of filo. Cut the stack of filo into rectangles about 4 by 6 inches (most filo sheets are 8 by 12 inches, so you should be able to simply cut them in half). Place a generous tablespoon of filling in the center of each rectangle and fold one corner diagonally across to meet the opposite corner. Fold in the edges to seal in the filling. Brush both sides of each filo package with ghee and transfer to a baking sheet.

10 Bake the samosas until golden brown, about 12 minutes. Serve hot, accompanied by chutney.

V   Substitute sweet potato for the potato and green beans and leek for the cauliflower.

K   Omit the yogurt and ghee.

Dairy-free in the Kapha alternative
Contains gluten

V P K FRESH MANGO CHUTNEY

I remember my very first experience of tasting mango chutney in an Indian restaurant in Winchester, England, where I was attending school. I asked for seconds and then thirds of the tantalizing chutney, which tasted like nothing I had ever eaten before. The fresh, colorful version below is less vinegary than traditional chutneys and requires no cooking. Serves 8

Ingredients

2 large ripe mangoes, peeled and pitted

½ cup extra-virgin olive oil

4 tablespoons grated fresh ginger

3 tablespoons lemon juice

1 tablespoon rosewater

3 tablespoons raw organic sugar, such as Sucanat

1 teaspoon ground cinnamon

1 teaspoon ground cardamom

¼ teaspoon ground cloves

4 tablespoons chopped cilantro

1 In a blender or a food processor fitted with the stainless-steel blade, combine all the ingredients except the cilantro. Pulse a few times to chop the ingredients coarsely. Taste and adjust the seasonings if necessary.

2 Transfer the chutney to a serving bowl and sprinkle with cilantro.

Dairy- and gluten-free

 Green Papaya Salad

A classic Thai salad makes a fresh, tangy start to a meal. By stimulating the digestive fire or Agni, the natural enzymes in green papaya work in concert with heating spices to fulfill the true meaning of the term "appetizer". For a more exotic presentation, serve the salad atop a fresh green banana leaf, available in some Asian and Latin American markets. Serves 2

Ingredients

3 tablespoons organic coconut milk (p. 233)

2 tablespoons lime *or* lemon juice

1 tablespoon sesame oil

2 teaspoons cumin seeds, toasted in
   a small dry sauté pan until fragrant

1 teaspoon honey

½ teaspoon ground cardamom

⅓ teaspoon cayenne powder

½ teaspoon salt

⅓ teaspoon freshly ground black pepper

1 medium green papaya, peeled, pitted, and shredded

1 carrot, shredded

1 tablespoon black sesame seeds, for garnish

Cilantro, for garnish

1 In a mixing bowl, whisk together the coconut milk, lime juice, sesame oil, cumin, honey, cardamom, cayenne, salt, and pepper. Taste and adjust the seasonings if necessary. Add the papaya and carrot and gently toss with the dressing.

2 Mound the salad on a serving platter and garnish with black sesame seeds and cilantro.

V Substitute maple or agave syrup for the honey.

P Substitute cucumber or jicama for the papaya, and sunflower oil for the sesame oil.

Dairy- and gluten-free

RICE, NUT, & SOY CHEESE BALL

These savory rice balls make a great snack with their crunchy coating and hints of sage. Try serving with Fresh Mango Chutney (p. 285), Ginger Raisin Chutney (p. 301) or tomato salsa. Serves 4

Ingredients

1 cup white basmati rice
1 ¾ cups filtered water
1 cup coarsely chopped walnuts *or* mixed nuts
½ cup finely grated organic soy cheese *or* other hard cheese
1 to 2 teaspoons ground sage
Pinch Herb Salt (p. 230)
Pinch freshly ground black pepper
Ghee (p. 227)

1   Preheat the oven to 350°F.

2   To cook the rice, place the basmati rice in a pan with the filtered water. Bring to a boil, lower heat and simmer, covered, with the lid slightly ajar, until all the water is absorbed, about 15 minutes.

3   Meanwhile, in a large mixing bowl, thoroughly stir together the rice, nuts, soy cheese, herb salt, and pepper. Pour a thin coating of ghee onto a small plate. Lightly grease a baking sheet. Using one hand, squeeze together handfuls of the mixture to form 12 balls, lightly rolling each ball as it is formed on the plate to coat it with ghee and then placing the ball on the baking sheet.

4   Bake the balls until they begin turning golden brown, about 15 minutes. Serve them hot or cold, accompanied by a chutney of your choice.

P   Substitute pumpkin or sunflower seeds for the walnuts and ground cumin for the sage.

K   Substitute cooked millet for the rice and goat cheese for the soy cheese.

Dairy-free if using soy cheese and no ghee
Gluten-free

CRUNCHY CHICKPEAS
in a Spiced Coating

This popular snack from India is flavorful and filling and is said to restore sexual energy. The light, astringent qualities of baked chickpeas make them a great snack for both Kapha and Pitta types. Serves 4

Ingredients

1 pound chickpeas, boiled in filtered water until tender, then drained
1 tablespoon Chef Johnny's Kapha Seasoning (p. 229)
Salt
Ghee (p. 227)

1   Preheat the oven to 350°F.

2   In a large bowl, toss the cooked chickpeas with the Kapha seasoning and salt until thoroughly coated.

3   Spread out the chickpeas in a greased baking pan. Bake until crunchy, 45 to 55 minutes.

V   Not recommended, due to the dry quality of the chickpeas

P   Use Chef Johnny's Pitta Seasoning (p. 228) in place of the Kapha seasoning.

Dairy- and gluten-free

V TAMARI PUMPKIN SEEDS

Rich in iron, zinc, and fiber, toasted pumpkin seeds make a quick, savory snack. Together with the naturally salty flavor of tamari sauce, they also serve as a perfect garnish for soups, dhals, and rice dishes. Tamari is a wheat-free soy sauce from Japan that is loaded with enzymes. It is widely available in health food stores and Japanese markets. Serves 4

Ingredients

1 pound raw, shelled pumpkin seeds

3 tablespoons tamari sauce *or* Bragg's amino acids

1 Preheat the oven to 350°F.

2 Spread the pumpkin seeds evenly on an ungreased baking sheet. Bake them until they swell and turn bright golden-green, about 11 minutes. Immediately remove from the oven and sprinkle with tamari.

3 Serve the seeds warm or at room temperature.

Dairy- and gluten-free

P MELON MEDLEY

Try this refreshing medley during the Summer months. For an exotic variation, try adding a few drops of sandalwood oil to the sauce. Serves 4

Ingredients

For the sauce:

1 cup sweet orange juice

2 teaspoons lemon juice

1 teaspoon maple syrup

A few saffron threads

1 vanilla bean

For the melon:

1 cup watermelon balls, formed with a melon scooper

1 cup honeydew melon balls, formed with a melon scooper

1 cup cantaloupe melon balls, formed with a melon scooper

10 fresh mint leaves, snipped into strips with kitchen scissors, for garnish

1 In a small bowl, stir together the orange juice, lemon juice, maple syrup, and saffron. With a small, sharp knife, cut the vanilla bean lengthwise in half; then, scrape the tiny seeds from the inside of each half and add the seeds to the mixture.

2 Divide the melon balls among individual cocktail glasses or serving dishes and pour the sauce over them. Sprinkle with mint leaves and serve.

Dairy- and gluten-free

 # SESAME DRESSING

The nutty flavor of sesame finds perfect partners in ginger and lime. Enjoy this dressing with steamed vegetables and Roasted Tuscan Vegetables (p. 206). Tahini is a paste made from finely ground sesame seeds, traditionally used in Middle Eastern cooking. You can find tahini at any health food store or well-stocked grocery store. Serves 6

Ingredients

3 tablespoons extra-virgin olive oil *or* sesame oil

3 tablespoons raw tahini paste

1 tablespoon lime *or* lemon juice

1 teaspoon honey

1 tablespoon chopped scallion

1 tablespoon chopped fresh basil

2 teaspoons grated fresh ginger

2 teaspoons chopped fresh oregano leaves

1 teaspoon black sesame seeds

1 teaspoon paprika

⅓ teaspoon salt

⅓ teaspoon freshly ground black pepper

1 Put all the ingredients in a mixing bowl. With a wire whisk, stir them briskly until thoroughly combined.

P Substitute sunflower oil for the olive oil, maple syrup for the honey, and dill leaves for the oregano.

K Not recommended due to the rich, heavy qualities of the oil, tahini, and sesame seeds.

Dairy- and gluten-free

 # GARLIC, GINGER & PARSLEY
Dressing

This lively dressing adds sparkle to simple salads. Serves 2

Ingredients

1 tablespoon safflower oil *or* corn oil

1 tablespoon lime juice

4 cloves garlic, roasted in a baking dish, peeled, and minced

2 tablespoons minced fresh parsley

1 tablespoon grated fresh ginger

1 teaspoon honey

½ teaspoon minced fresh red chili pepper

¼ teaspoon freshly ground black pepper

1 Peel and mince garlic. Roast in a baking dish in a 300°F oven until golden brown, about 10 minutes.

2 Put all the ingredients in a mixing bowl. With a wire whisk, stir them briskly until thoroughly combined.

V Substitute sesame oil for the safflower or corn oil.

P Not recommended, due to the heating qualities of the garlic and ginger

Dairy- and gluten-free

MINT & CREAM DRESSING
Dressing

PAPAYA SEED
Dressing

Fresh mint contributes a refreshing flavor to this simple dressing, while the combination of cashew butter and cream provides a rich, silken texture. Try serving over steamed vegetables, sliced avocado, as a dip for raw vegetables, or with the Summer Salad (p. 191). Serves 4

Papaya seeds lend a spicy note reminiscent of black pepper. Use fewer seeds if you prefer a milder taste. Try this dressing with Green Papaya Salad (p. 286) and other salads. Serves 6

Ingredients

¼ cup sunflower oil

¼ cup organic cream

2 tablespoons lemon juice

¼ cup chopped fresh mint

2 tablespoons raw cashew butter

1 tablespoon chopped fresh thyme leaves

2 teaspoons maple syrup

1 teaspoon paprika

Ingredients

3 tablespoons fresh *or* dried papaya seeds

3 tablespoons organic plain yogurt (p.227) *or* crème fraîche

1 tablespoon sunflower oil

1 teaspoon lime juice

1 teaspoon apple cider vinegar (optional)

1 teaspoon maple syrup

1 teaspoon minced sage *or* fennel fronds

½ teaspoon salt

⅓ teaspoon freshly ground black pepper

1 Combine all the ingredients in a blender or a food processor fitted with the stainless-steel blade. Pulse several times to form a smooth, thick mixture.

2 Transfer to a bowl and refrigerate, covered, until ready to use.

 Also recommended.

K Substitute goat cheese for the cream and sunflower seed butter for the cashew butter; add ¼ teaspoon cayenne pepper.

For dairy-free, omit the cream or replace with coconut milk.
Gluten-free

1 Combine all the ingredients in a blender or a food processor fitted with the stainless-steel blade. Pulse several times to form a smooth, thick mixture.

2 Transfer to a bowl and refrigerate, covered, until ready to use.

For dairy-free, replace the yogurt with coconut milk.
Gluten-free

 K TOMATO & BASIL DRESSING    V BALSAMIC VINAIGRETTE

Visually enticing and delicious, this spicy dressing is ideal for Kapha. Serve it over salads, such as the Grated Daikon Salad (p. 214) and Warm Lentil Salad (p. 281, and grain dishes such as the Barley Rissoles (p. 258). Serves 4

Ingredients

2 tomatoes, peeled and seeded

2 tablespoons sesame oil

2 tablespoons chopped fresh basil

1 tablespoon lime juice

1 tablespoon grated fresh ginger

1 teaspoon honey

Pinch cayenne pepper

Salt

Freshly ground black pepper

1 Combine all ingredients in a blender or a food processor fitted with the stainless-steel blade. Pulse several times, until the tomatoes are finely chopped and the ingredients are thoroughly combined. Pulse in salt and pepper to taste.

2 Transfer to a bowl, cover, and refrigerate until ready to use.

V Also recommended.

P Not recommended due to the heating qualities of the tomatoes, ginger and cayenne.

For dairy-free, omit the yogurt.
Gluten-free

Hot yet mellow mustard, sweet honey, and creamy yogurt temper the rich, sharp flavor of aged balsamic vinegar in a dressing ideal for Vata. Try serving over steamed vegetables and salads. Serves 6

Ingredients

6 tablespoons extra-virgin olive oil

2 tablespoons balsamic vinegar

2 tablespoons organic plain yogurt (p. 227)

1 tablespoon organic yellow mustard

2 teaspoons honey

2 teaspoons minced fresh parsley

2 teaspoons minced fresh thyme

¼ teaspoon salt

¼ teaspoon freshly ground black pepper

1 Put all the ingredients in a mixing bowl. With a wire whisk, stir them briskly until thoroughly combined.

P Not recommended due to the heating qualities of the vinegar, mustard, and spices.

K Omit the yogurt.

For dairy-free, omit the yogurt.
Gluten-free

SPICED GREEN PEA SAUCE
with Saffron

When blended with yogurt, as in this easy sauce, peas make a sweet green sauce which is distinctive yet subtle, providing an attractive accompaniment to vegetable and rice dishes. Makes about 3 cups

Ingredients

1 tablespoon ghee (p. 227) *or* sunflower oil

2 teaspoons chopped leek

2 teaspoons ground fennel seed

1 teaspoon coriander seed

1 cup shelled fresh *or* frozen peas

1 cup Vegetable Stock (p. 231), Whey (p. 231), *or* filtered water

3 tablespoons chopped fresh mint leaves

Pinch saffron threads

1 teaspoon lemon juice

1 date, minced

½ teaspoon salt

⅓ teaspoon freshly ground black pepper

¾ cup organic cream *or* organic plain yogurt (p. 227)

1   Heat the ghee in a saucepan over medium heat. Add the leek and cook, stirring occasionally, until soft, 3 to 5 minutes. Stir in the fennel and coriander and cook for 2 minutes more.

2   Stir in the peas and stock. Raise the heat, bring to a boil, and then reduce the heat and simmer until the peas are tender, about 15 minutes for fresh peas or 5 minutes for frozen. Stir in the mint, saffron, lemon juice, and date. Season to taste with salt and pepper.

3   Stir the cream or yogurt into the pan, adding extra stock if needed to make a pourable sauce.

V   Substitute green beans or chopped artichoke hearts for the peas.

K   Substitute 2 tablespoons goat cheese for the cream, thyme and marjoram for the mint, and add ¼ teaspoon cayenne.

For dairy-free, substitute coconut milk for the cream.
Gluten-free

MANGO SAUCE

Exotically sweet and mildly spicy, this orange sauce goes deliciously with tofu or panir slices, and Barley Rissoles (p. 258). Serves 4

Ingredients

2 ripe mangoes, peeled, fruit cut from the pit and chopped

½ cup Vegetable Stock (p. 231) *or* filtered water

1 tablespoon Bragg's amino acids

½ teaspoon Chef Johnny's Korma Powder (p. 229) *or* mild curry powder

1 teaspoon grated fresh ginger

1 teaspoon lemon juice

1 teaspoon amaranth flour *or* cornmeal

½ teaspoon brown rice syrup

1   Put all the ingredients in a blender and blend until smoothly puréed.

2   Transfer the purée to a saucepan. Cook over medium-low heat, stirring frequently, until heated through, about 5 minutes.

V   Substitute rice flour for the amaranth flour.

P   Substitute Chef Johnny's Pitta Seasoning (p. 228) for the korma powder, maple syrup or agave syrup for the brown rice syrup, and rice flour for the amaranth flour.

Dairy- and gluten-free

V P K   ALL-PURPOSE KORMA SAUCE

The style of Indian cooking known as korma is character-ized by a sauce rich in the creamy flavors and textures of coconut and almonds, complemented by multiple mild spices. Korma sauce is especially balancing for Vata types. Try it over sweet baked potatoes, steamed vegetables such as broccoli or zucchini, rice dishes, and panir or tofu. Serves 4

Ingredients

3 tablespoons ghee (p. 227)

2 tablespoons grated fresh ginger

1 teaspoon mustard seeds

1 tablespoon finely chopped leek

3 tablespoons finely ground almonds

2 tablespoons dried coconut

1 tablespoon Chef Johnny's Korma Powder (p. 229)

1 tablespoon chickpea flour

2 cups Whey (p. 231) *or* Vegetable Stock (p. 231) *or* filtered water

1 cup Vegetable Stock (p. 231) *or* filtered water

1 cup organic coconut milk, preferably fresh (p. 233)

2 tablespoons organic cream

1 tablespoon lemon juice

1 teaspoon tomato paste

1 finely chopped date *or* 1 teaspoon jaggery

3 tablespoons organic plain yogurt (p. 227)

3 tablespoons chopped cilantro leaves

Salt

Freshly ground black pepper

1 Heat the ghee in a saucepan over medium heat. Add the ginger and mustard seeds and sauté, shaking the pan frequently, until the seeds pop, about 4 minutes. Stir in the leek and continue sautéing, stirring occasionally with a whisk, until it has softened, about 3 minutes.

2 Add the almonds, coconut, and korma powder. Sauté, stirring occasionally, until the coconut begins to brown, about 5 minutes.

3 Stirring constantly, sprinkle in the chickpea flour, and continue stirring until the mixture thickens slightly, about 2 minutes. Still stirring, pour in the whey and stock. Reduce the heat to low and continue stirring over low heat until the sauce begins to thicken to a gravylike consistency, about 5 minutes.

4 Stir in the coconut milk, cream, lemon juice, tomato paste, asafetida, and chopped date or jaggery. Continue cooking, stirring frequently, until the sauce is just heated through. Stir in the yogurt and cilantro and season to taste with salt and pepper.

For dairy-free, replace the yogurt and cream with coconut cream and the ghee with sunflower oil.
Gluten-free

 Toasted Fennel, Leek & Tomato Sauce

Fennel seeds offer an enticing lift to numerous dishes, here used as a focal point for an exquisite sauce. See p.152 for the healing properties of these versatile seeds. Try serving this fragrant sauce over grilled vegetables, tofu, or grains such as buckwheat and millet. Serves 4

Ingredients

1 tablespoon whole fennel seeds

2 teaspoons sunflower oil *or* corn oil

1 cup chopped leek

1 teaspoon minced fresh thyme leaves

1 teaspoon minced fresh sage

2 tomatoes, cored, peeled, seeded, and coarsely chopped

2 cups Vegetable Stock (p. 231) *or* filtered water

1 tablespoon organic yellow mustard

½ teaspoon salt

2 teaspoons cornmeal

2 tablespoons organic fresh, creamy goat cheese

⅓ teaspoon freshly ground black pepper

Salt

1 Put the fennel seeds in a small, dry sauté pan and toast them, stirring frequently, over low heat until fragrant, 2 to 3 minutes. Transfer to a small plate to cool, and then grind them in a clean spice grinder. Set aside.

2 Heat the oil in a saucepan over medium-high heat. Add the leek and sauté, stirring occasionally, until softened, about 3 minutes. Add the thyme and sage and cook for 2 minutes more.

3 Stir in the tomatoes and continue cooking, stirring occasionally, until they break down into a coarse purée, about 5 minutes.

4 Stir in the stock, ground fennel, and mustard. Reduce the heat and simmer, stirring occasionally, for 7 minutes.

5 While stirring continuously, sprinkle in the cornmeal. Continue cooking and stirring until the sauce thickens, about 1 minute. Crumble in the goat cheese and continue stirring until it melts into the sauce, about 1 minute more. Add the black pepper and salt to taste.

V Substitute yogurt for the goat cheese and rice flour for the cornmeal.

P Substitute cream or coconut cream for the goat cheese, rice flour for the cornmeal, and bell pepper for the leek.

Dairy-free when using the coconut cream option
Gluten-free

V Savory Lentil Gravy

There's no doubt that pouring a warm, flavorful gravy over a dish of steaming food is both comforting and appetizing. You'll be surprised by how much this vegetarian gravy recalls the rich savor of traditional pan gravies. *Serves 6*

Ingredients

2 tablespoons ghee (p. 227)

1 teaspoon mustard seeds

3 tablespoons chopped leek

2 tablespoons chopped almonds

1 teaspoon ground cumin

2 cups Whey (p. 231) *or* filtered water

1 cup Vegetable Stock (p. 231)

or 1 organic vegetable stock cube and 1 cup filtered water

1 cup filtered water

⅓ cup red lentils, soaked in filtered water to cover for 1 hour

½ small zucchini, finely diced

2 teaspoons chopped fresh basil

2 teaspoons *or* more chickpea flour

Salt

Freshly ground black pepper

1 Heat the ghee in a saucepan over medium heat. Stir in the mustard seeds and sauté just until they begin to pop, about 4 minutes. Stir in the leeks, almonds, and cumin and continue sautéing, stirring occasionally, until the leeks soften, 3 to 5 minutes.

2 Add the whey, stock, water, lentils, zucchini, and basil. Cover and simmer over low heat until the lentils are tender, about 30 minutes.

3 Raise the heat to medium and, stirring with a whisk, sprinkle in the chickpea flour. Continue cooking, stirring constantly, until the gravy thickens to a coating consistency, about 5 minutes. If you like thicker gravy, stir in a little more chickpea flour.

4 Ladle the mixture into a blender and blend until smoothly puréed. Return the gravy to the pan and rewarm it over very low heat. Season to taste with salt and pepper.

P Substitute Puy lentils for the red lentils, roasted ground fennel seeds for the mustard seeds, and bell pepper for the leek.

K Omit the yogurt and substitute sunflower oil for the ghee.

Dairy-free, if made without ghee or whey
Gluten-free

WHITE SAUCE
with Parsley

*The classic flour-thickened white sauce, often known by
the French name Béchamel in honor of Louis the XIV's
head steward, provides a versatile embellishment to
many dishes. Use the sauce to dress up vegetables such as
cauliflower and broccoli, or with nut or lentil loafs. Makes
about 2¼ cups*

Ingredients

2 cups organic milk *or* organic rice milk

1 tablespoon ghee (p. 227)

1½ tablespoons spelt flour *or* chickpea flour

Salt

Freshly ground black pepper

3 tablespoons finely chopped fresh parsley

1 teaspoon finely chopped fresh thyme

1 Heat the milk in a saucepan over low heat until hot.

2 Heat the ghee in a small sauté pan over low heat. Sprinkle in the flour, stirring constantly with a whisk until the flour begins to turn pale golden. Stir in a pinch of the salt and ¼ teaspoon of the pepper.

3 Whisking continuously, pour the milk into the flour mixture. Continue cooking, stirring continuously, until the sauce thickens to the consistency of very heavy cream and is smooth and lump free, about 6 minutes. Stir in the parsley and thyme and add more salt and pepper to taste, if necessary.

V Substitute chopped fresh dill for the parsley.

K Not recommended due to sweet, heavy qualities of the milk or rice milk

Dairy-free if made with rice milk.
Gluten-free

 # OLIVADA

 # TARRAGON AIOLI

Enjoy the rich flavor of this earthy Italian spread. Try it on Bruschetta (p. 282) or toasted pita bread. Makes about 2 cups

Classic French aioli is a garlicky variation on mayonnaise, rich with egg yolks. In this recipe, cream and crème fraîche produce the rich results. Try serving with steamed beets, carrots or Vegetables Sushi (p. 282). Makes 1¼ cups

Ingredients

2 cups pitted black olives
2 tablespoons extra-virgin olive oil
2 tablespoons pine nuts
1 clove garlic
1 teaspoon dried thyme
1 tablespoon lemon juice
Pinch freshly ground black pepper

Ingredients

3 tablespoons extra-virgin olive oil
1 tablespoon roasted garlic
½ teaspoon minced fresh garlic
2 teaspoons lemon juice
½ teaspoon apple cider vinegar
½ cup organic crème fraîche
½ cup organic cream
⅓ teaspoon freshly ground black pepper
2 tablespoons finely chopped fresh tarragon
½ teaspoon salt
½ teaspoon ground turmeric

1 In a small dry sauté pan over low heat, toast the pine nuts for about 3 minutes.

2 Put the ingredients in a food processor fitted with the stainless-steel blade. Pulse until coarsely chopped.

P Not recommended due to the heating quality of the olives and garlic

K Not recommended due to the heavy, oily qualities of the olives and pine nuts

Dairy- and gluten-free

1 To roast garlic, place whole unpeeled cloves in a baking dish and bake in a preheated 300°F oven for 12 minutes; then, let them cool and squeeze the now-soft caramel-brown pulp from the skin of each clove.

2 Put the ingredients in a blender or a mixing bowl. Blend, or beat with a wire whisk or a hand-held electric mixer, until thoroughly combined.

3 If not using immediately, transfer to an airtight container and refrigerate for up to 3 days.

P Omit the garlic and vinegar and substitute sunflower oil for the olive oil and chopped fresh dill or fennel fronds for the tarragon.

K Not recommended due to the rich, heavy qualities of the cream and crème fraîche

Contains dairy
Gluten-free

PÂTÉS AND SPREADS

 ROSE PETAL JAM

 SUN DRIED TOMATO PESTO

For those of you who have yet to experience this heavenly jam, you are in for a treat of fragrant sweet taste and exquisite texture. Use fresh petals from pesticide-free flowers, cutting above the white base of each petal. Pink roses make a more delicate jam than red roses, which have a stronger flavor. For the best flavor, harvest the roses early in the morning when the dew is still on the leaves. You can find rose water in your local health food store. Makes four 8-ounce jars

Serve over quinoa pasta with fresh herbs sprinkled on top. This recipe is suited for Kaphas in moderation, with the pungency of the basil and other herbs off-setting the oily quality of the pesto. Makes about 2 cups

Ingredients

1 quart fresh pesticide-free rose petals

1¾ pounds fructose

¾ cup apple juice *or* filtered water

½ tablespoon lemon juice *or* lime juice

1 tablespoon rose water

Ingredients

1 cup sunflower oil

⅔ cup organic sun-dried tomatoes, dry-packed

10 fresh basil leaves

1 tablespoon fresh thyme leaves

1 tablespoon chopped fresh parsley

2 tablespoons chopped fresh sage (optional)

1 tablespoon lemon juice

⅓ tablespoon freshly ground black pepper

3 tablespoons hot water

Sea salt

1   In a large saucepan, arrange several layers of rose petals and fructose. Pour the water or apple juice over them. Add the lemon juice. Bring the liquid to a boil over medium-high heat. Reduce the heat and simmer for 15 minutes, stirring occasionally. Add the rose water and continue cooking until the mixture has thickened, about 5 minutes. Test for doneness by placing a drop on a cold surface. If it forms a globule, it is ready.

2   Immerse resealable glass jam jars in boiling water for 5 minutes to sterilize. Transfer the jam to the jars and store in a cool, dark place.

1   Put the sun-dried tomatoes in a bowl and pour the oil over them. Stir in the basil, thyme, parsley, and sage and leave to marinate at room temperature for 2 hours.

2   Put the mixture of tomatoes, herbs, and oil in a small saucepan. Place the pan over medium-low heat for 5 minutes. Remove the pan from the heat and leave the tomatoes in the pan to soak in the oil for 2 hours longer.

3   Return the pan to low heat for 7 minutes more. Transfer the contents to a blender, add the hot water, black pepper, and sea salt to taste, and blend until smooth.

V Also recommended

K Not recommended due to the sugar

V Substitute extra-virgin olive oil for the sunflower oil.

P Not recommended due to the pungency of the tomatoes and heating herbs and spices

P SAFFRON & FENNEL BUTTER

Try this delicious flavored butter on vegetables, pasta, toast, or mashed potatoes. *Makes 1 cup*

Ingredients

8 ounces organic unsalted butter, at room temperature
3 tablespoons finely chopped fennel fronds
1 teaspoon paprika
½ teaspoon grated lemon zest
⅓ teaspoon freshly ground black pepper
⅓ teaspoon salt
Small pinch saffron strands, steeped in 1 teaspoon warm filtered water

1 Put all the ingredients in a mixing bowl. With a table fork or a wooden spoon, beat them together until thoroughly combined and slightly creamy.

2 Spoon the butter onto a sheet of waxed paper. Roll it up in the paper, shaping it into an even log shape about 1½-inch in diameter.

3 Refrigerate the butter until thoroughly chilled and solid, at least 2 hours. Use a sharp knife to slice the butter into rounds as needed.

V Also recommended

K Not recommended due to the rich, heavy qualities of the butter

Contains dairy
Gluten-free

V ALMOND & CASHEW
Nectar Delight

Try serving this sweet and spicy nut butter on crackers, Sprouted Wheat Bread (p. 174), or spelt tortillas. Look for sandalwood oil in the cosmetic department of any health food store. *Makes about 3 cups*

Ingredients

1 cup organic raw cashew butter
1 cup organic raw almond butter
¼ cup maple syrup *or* jaggery
¼ cup honey
1 teaspoon licorice powder (optional)
1 teaspoon ground cardamom
½ teaspoon ground cinnamon
5 drops rose oil
3 drops orange oil
3 drops sandalwood oil (optional)
2 drops pure vanilla extract

Note: Take care to follow the recipe amounts for the oils closely, since essential oils will aggravate the stomach lining when taken in excess.

1 Put the ingredients in a food processor fitted with the stainless-steel blade. Process until thoroughly blended.

2 Spoon into sealable glass jars and refrigerate for up to 30 days.

P Replace the cashew butter with another cup of almond butter; and replace ¼ cup honey syrup with another ¼ cup maple syrup.

K Not recommended due to the rich, oily qualities of the nut butters

Dairy-free
Gluten-free

 # CILANTRO CHUTNEY

 # GOMASIO WITH NORI

With a combination of savory and sweet tastes popular in Indian cuisine, this chutney goes especially well with such dishes as Biriyani (p. 204), roasted vegetables, and Naan bread (p. 305). Serves 8

A mixture of nori, the familiar dried seaweed from sushi, and toasted sesame seeds, this popular Japanese garnish makes a simple yet spectacular garnish for miso soup, rice dishes, and salads. The natural salty taste is particularly balancing for Vata. Makes 1½ cups

Ingredients

2 cups chopped cilantro leaves
3 tablespoons grated ginger
3 tablespoons organic plain yogurt (p. 227)
2 teaspoons maple syrup
⅓ cup filtered water
Salt

Ingredients

1 cup sesame seeds
1½ nori sheets
1 teaspoon salt

1   In a mixing bowl, stir together all the ingredients. Cover and refrigerate until ready to serve.

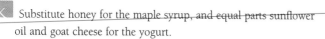 V   Add ¼ teaspoon asafetida.

K   Substitute honey for the maple syrup, and equal parts sunflower oil and goat cheese for the yogurt.

Dairy-free if substituting soy yogurt for the yogurt
Gluten-free

1   In a dry sauté pan over low heat, toast the sesame seeds, stirring continuously, until they turn fragrant and light golden, 3 to 5 minutes. Transfer to a bowl to cool. Transfer them to a clean spice grinder and pulse the machine until the seeds are coarsely ground.

2   Turn on the flame on a gas stovetop, or preheat a broiler. Carefully holding a nori sheet with tongs, hold it just above the flame and move it around continuously until it darkens slightly in color and is fragrant, about 10 seconds; alternatively, put it on a broiler pan and toast it under the broiler, about 15 seconds, keeping a close eye on it to guard against scorching. Remove the nori sheets to a bowl to cool. Then, with clean, dry hands, crumble the nori sheets to small particles about the size of breadcrumbs.

3   Put the ground sesame seeds, crumbled nori, and salt in an airtight jar big enough to hold them comfortably. Cover and shake to combine them. Store in the pantry. Shake again before using.

P   Not recommended due to the seaweed and salt

K   Not recommended due to the seaweed and salt

Dairy- and gluten-free

K GINGER & RAISIN CHUTNEY

Prepared in minutes, this sweet chutney offers a pleasing complement to many dishes. It will keep well in the refrigerator for up to 2 days.
Makes about 1 cup

Ingredients

1 cup seedless raisins
2 tablespoons grated fresh ginger
Juice of 1 orange
Juice of ½ lemon
2 tablespoons rosewater
1 tablespoon maple syrup *or* jaggery
½ teaspoon ground cinnamon
½ teaspoon ground cardamom

1 Put all the ingredients in a blender or a food processor fitted with the stainless-steel blade. Pulse the machine a few times to chop the raisins slightly and mix the ingredients thoroughly, forming a consistency resembling a juicy jam.

2 Transfer the chutney to a covered container and refrigerate until ready to serve.

V Substitute dates for the raisins.

P Also recommended

Dairy- and gluten-free

P CUCUMBER RAITA

A popular Indian mixture of plain yogurt, chopped fresh vegetables, and herbs, raita improves digestion and helps cool down spicy main dishes. Serves 4

Ingredients

1 teaspoon ground fennel seeds
1 cup organic plain yogurt (p. 227)
2 tablespoons chopped fresh dill
2 small cucumbers, peeled, seeded, and diced
¼ teaspoon freshly ground black pepper
⅓ teaspoon salt

1 In a skillet, dry roast the fennel seeds over medium heat for 5 minutes. Grind coarsely using a mortar and pestle or electric coffee grinder.

2 In a bowl, stir together the fennel seeds, yogurt, dill, and cucumber. Season to taste with salt and pepper. Cover and refrigerate for at least 30 minutes before serving.

V Add ½ teaspoon ginger powder and ¼ teaspoon asafetida.

K Recommended in moderation using the Vata substitutions

Contains dairy
Gluten-free

Hemp, Sunflower,
& Sesame Seed Sprinkle

*A nutritious, Vata-balancing condiment for salads and other dishes,
this seed sprinkle is exceptionally easy to prepare. Hemp seeds are one
of the richest plant-based sources of Omega-3 oils. Makes about 1 cup*

Ingredients

½ cup shelled raw sunflower seeds

¼ cup hemp seeds, crushed

2 tablespoons sesame seeds

2 tablespoons black sesame seeds

½ teaspoon salt

1 Put the sunflower seeds in a small dry sauté pan. Toast
   them over medium-low heat, stirring constantly, until
   light golden, 3 to 5 minutes. Transfer to a bowl to cool.
   When the seeds are cool, put them in a food processor
   fitted with the stainless-steel blade and pulse the machine
   until coarsely chopped.

2 Put the sunflower seeds and all other ingredients in an
   airtight jar large enough to hold them comfortably. Put the
   lid on and shake to mix them. Store at room temperature.
   Shake again before using.

P Recommended in moderation with minimal salt

K Recommended in moderation with minimal salt

Dairy- and gluten-free

 FLAX SEED CRACKERS

 CORNBREAD

With their crunchy texture and savory flavor, these crackers make a great snack or appetizer. Try serving with Sprouted Hummus (p. 221). Makes 16 crackers

Good old-fashioned cornbread makes a great addition to soups and also works well with spreads and pâtés. Makes 1 loaf

Ingredients

Ghee (p. 227)

3 cups organic flax seeds, soaked for 4 hours in 2 cups filtered water

1 cup sprouted buckwheat grains (see sprouting instructions on p. 105)

½ cup sesame seeds

⅓ cup Bragg's amino acids

4 tablespoons lemon juice

1 to 2 teaspoons packaged Italian seasoning blend

1 Preheat the oven to 300°F. Grease a baking sheet with the ghee.

2 Put all the remaining ingredients together in a large bowl and stir until thoroughly blended. Spread the mixture as thinly as possible on the prepared baking sheet.

3 Bake until dry, about 1 ½ hours. Remove from the oven and let cool to room temperature before cutting into desired shapes with a pizza cutter.

V Recommended in moderation with a creamy spread, such as Nectar Delight (p. 299)

P Also recommended

For dairy-free, replace ghee with corn or safflower oil.
Gluten-free

Ingredients

Ghee (p. 227)

1 cup organic yellow medium ground cornmeal

½ cup organic amaranth flour *or* organic spelt flour

4 teaspoons baking powder

¼ teaspoon salt

1 cup organic plain soy milk

½ cup applesauce

1 Preheat the oven to 350°F. Grease a 9-by-5-inch loaf pan with ghee and set aside.

2 In a large bowl, stir together the dry ingredients. Add the soy milk and applesauce and stir until combined. Pour the mixture into the prepared loaf pan.

3 Bake the cornbread until a small, sharp knife inserted into the center of the loaf comes out clean, about 30 minutes. Let the bread cool slightly before unmolding it and cutting it into slices.

V Also recommended in moderation

P Also recommended

For dairy-free, replace the ghee with sunflower oil.
Gluten-free

 SPROUTED HUMMUS
See page 221 in The Recipe Archetypes.

 SPROUTED WHEAT BREAD
See page 174 in The Recipe Archetypes.

CORN TORTILLAS

Throughout Latin America, making the perfect tortilla is a time-honored art. This quick version is made with readily available ground dried hominy, labeled masa harina. Tortillas make a great accompaniment to soups and legume dishes and are balancing for Kapha, due to the light, heating qualities of corn. Makes 12 tortillas

Ingredients

1½ cups organic dry hominy flour
½ cup plus added hot water

1 Mix the ingredients in a bowl, starting with ½ cup water and adding more, 1 tablespoon at a time, until a soft, non-sticky dough forms.

2 Knead the dough on a floured board until smooth, 5 to 10 minutes. Alternatively, knead in a food processor fitted with the stainless steel blade for 1 minute. Place the dough in a bowl, cover with a damp cloth, and leave at room temperature to rest for 30 minutes.

3 Pinch off a golf ball-sized piece of the dough, rolling it between your palms into a ball about 1½ inches in diameter. Place it between 2 sheets of waxed paper and, with a small rolling pin, roll it into a thin circle.

4 Heat an ungreased heavy skillet over medium-high heat. Gently peel off the waxed paper, place the tortilla on the skillet and cook until it looks dry and has a few dark spots, about 20 to 25 seconds. Flip over the tortilla and cook on the other side for another 15 seconds. If there are cracks around the edges, the dough is too dry. Add a little more water to the dough and divide it into 11 more pieces, shaping them in the same way. As they finish cooking, stack the tortillas, keeping them covered with a clean cloth.

V Also recommended in moderation; add ½ teaspoon salt and a little olive oil on top.

P Also recommended in moderation

Dairy-free
Gluten-free

IRISH SODA BREAD

Based on a traditional Irish recipe, this yeast-free bread gets its robust consistency from a combination of bread flours. Serve it for breakfast or enjoy it with hearty soups. Makes 4 small loaves

Ingredients

3 cups organic spelt flour
1 cup organic bread flour
2 cups organic rolled oats
2 tablespoons baking powder
1 teaspoon salt
¼ cup whole caraway seeds
¾ cup sunflower oil
2 apples, grated
2 carrots, grated
¾ to 1 cup filtered water

1 Preheat the oven to 375°F. Grease a baking sheet.

2 In a large mixing bowl, stir together the spelt flour, bread flour, oats, baking powder, salt, and caraway seeds. With your fingertips, rub in the oil until uniformly incorporated. Add the apples and carrots and stir in enough of the water to form a soft, stiff dough.

3 With your hands, divide the dough into 4 equal portions, shaping each into a flattened oval loaf and placing the loaves about 2 inches apart on the prepared baking sheet.

4 Bake the loaves until golden brown, about 40 minutes. Serve warm.

V Also recommended

K Not recommended due to the sweet, heavy qualities of the flours

Dairy-free
Contains gluten

V NAAN BREAD

Some folks say you can judge an Indian restaurant by the quality of its naan alone. The secret to this delectable favorite is the addition of yogurt to the dough, which results in its mouth-watering taste and moist, tender texture. Makes 6 pieces

Ingredients

½ cup organic sourdough starter or 1 teaspoon dried yeast

½ cup organic plain yogurt (p. 227)

4 tablespoons ghee (p. 227) or sunflower oil

½ cup organic whole-wheat flour

½ cup organic white flour

2 teaspoons raw organic sugar, such as Sucanat

1 teaspoon salt

1 teaspoon baking powder

2 teaspoons kalonji (also called nigella) seeds (optional)

1   In a small bowl, stir together the sourdough starter, yogurt, and ghee. In another large bowl, combine the dried yeast (if using), flour, sugar, salt, baking powder, and kalonji seeds.

2   Add the sourdough mixture to the large bowl and mix with your hands, adding a little water as needed, until a soft, cohesive dough forms that no longer sticks to the sides of the bowl. Knead with your hands until the dough is smooth, firm, and elastic, about 7 minutes. Cover in a bowl and leave to rise at warm room temperature for 4 hours.

3   Preheat the oven to 550°F

4   Knead the dough again and divide it into 6 equal balls. On a lightly floured work surface, using a floured rolling pin, roll each ball into an oval shape about 5 inches wide and ¼-inch thick. As they are formed, transfer the ovals to a baking sheet or a cast-iron griddle and bake until the dough puffs up, 5 to 7 minutes.

5   Preheat the broiler.

6   Transfer the naans to a wire rack and broil about 3 inches from the heat until black flecks appear on their surface, about 1 minute per side. Remove the bread from the oven and serve warm.

P Also recommended

K Not recommended due to the sweet, heavy qualities of the flour, sugar, and yogurt

Contains dairy and gluten

P CHAPATI (INDIAN FLAT BREAD)

This traditional unleavened quick bread from India makes a great accompaniment to soups, dhals, and rice dishes. A perfect chapati will puff up during the final stages of cooking; but, even if yours doesn't, it will still taste delicious. Makes 12 chapatis

Ingredients

2 cups organic fine semolina (or durum) wheat flour

¼ teaspoon sea salt

1 tablespoon ghee (p. 227) or sunflower oil

¾ cup filtered water

2 tablespoons whole cumin seeds or sesame seeds

1   In a medium mixing bowl, combine the flour, salt, and cumin or sesame seeds. In a separate bowl, whisk together the water and oil, then add to the flour and salt. Pour the water into the mixing bowl and kneed the dough with your hands until smooth and elastic, about 7 minutes. Alternatively, use an electric mixer fitted with the bread attachment.

2   Cover the bowl with a damp cloth and leave the dough to rest at warm room temperature for 2 hours. Divide the dough into 12 small balls (slightly smaller than a golf ball).

3   Lightly flour a clean work surface and roll out each piece into a thin disc, about 5 inches in diameter.

4   Preheat a large griddle over medium heat. Cook each chapati just until its surface appears dry, about 20-30 seconds on each side. Remove gently with tongs.

5   If using a gas stove, holding the chapati with the tongs, wave each chapati over an open flame for a few seconds until it puffs up. If using an electric stove, roll a clean cloth or tea towel into a firm ball and press it hard onto the chapati while still in the pan. This turns the water inside the chapati into steam, causing the chapati to puff up.

V Also recommended in moderation

K Substitute 2 cups either barley or rye flour and use only 1 teaspoon sunflower oil.

Dairy-free
For gluten-free, follow the Kapha alternative.

WARM CARDAMOM MILK
with Ground Cashew Nuts

CHAI
with Almond Milk

Vata types will find this a rejuvenating drink, especially with the sweetness of milk, ghee, and sugar. It is said to restore sexual energy and is also considered food for the brain and higher consciousness, due to its Sattvic nature. Serves 4

The spices in the traditional Indian tea blend known as chai warm the body and ignite the digestive fire. Feel free to omit the black tea for a caffeine-free version. Serves 6

Ingredients

1 pint organic whole milk

2 teaspoons ghee

2 to 3 teaspoons raw organic sugar, such as Sucanat or jaggery

¼ teaspoon ground cardamom

1 tablespoon finely ground cashews

3 or 4 strands saffron (optional)

1. Put all the ingredients in a saucepan and bring to a boil, stirring frequently, over medium heat.

2. Pour or ladle into mugs and serve immediately.

P Omit the cashews.

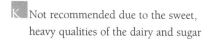K Not recommended due to the sweet, heavy qualities of the dairy and sugar

Contains dairy
Gluten-free

Ingredients

6 cups filtered water

1 tablespoon grated fresh ginger

1 tablespoon whole fennel seeds

2 teaspoons whole cardamom pods

1 teaspoon black tea leaves

2 teaspoons coriander seeds, crushed

1 teaspoon whole cloves

2 star anise pods

2 cinnamon sticks or 2 teaspoons ground cinnamon

2 cups almond milk (p. 232)

Honey or stevia

1. In a large saucepan over high heat, bring the water to a rolling boil. Add the ginger, fennel seeds, cardamom pods, black tea, coriander seeds, cloves, star anise, and cinnamon. Reduce the heat and simmer gently for 20 minutes.

2. Pour the mixture through a strainer set over a heatproof bowl. Leave the tea to cool for a few minutes before stirring in the almond milk and honey or stevia.

V Also recommended; try replacing 1 cup of the almond milk with 1 cup coconut milk for a creamier version.

P Not recommended due to the heating spices

Dairy-free
Gluten-free

GRAPE, PEAR & MINT JUICE

Fresh grapes always produce a luxurious juice drink. Here, they combine with pear and mint for an extra cooling beverage for Pitta types. To get the fresh juices, simply pass the ingredients through a quality electric juicer. Serves 4

Ingredients

2 cups fresh pear juice
2 cups fresh grape juice
Juice from ½ bunch fresh mint leaves
Juice from 2 stalks celery (optional)

1. Combine the juices in a pitcher and serve with or without ice.

V Also recommended

K Also recommended

Dairy- and gluten-free

ROSE PETAL SMOOTHIE

Rose Petal Jam (p. 298) adds a divine element to this popular beverage for Pitta types. Look for sandalwood oil in the cosmetic department of any health food store. Serves 3

Ingredients

2 cups filtered water
½ cup organic plain yogurt (p. 227)
3 tablespoons raw organic sugar, such as Sucanat
1 tablespoon Rose Petal Jam (p. 298)
¼ teaspoon ground cardamom
1-2 drops sandalwood oil

Note: Take care to follow the recipe amounts for the sandalwood oil closely, since essential oils will aggravate the stomach lining when taken in excess.

1. Combine all the ingredients in a blender and pulse a few times to mix thoroughly. Pour into tall glasses and serve immediately.

V Also recommended

K Not recommended due to the sweet taste of the sugar and jam

For dairy-free, replace the yogurt with soy yogurt.
Gluten-free

MANGO AND PASSION FRUIT CHEESECAKE

The combination of a rich, creamy filling, a nutty crust, and a tangy fruit topping equals a sublime version of the popular dessert. Serve with whipped cream, lightly flavored with freshly grated ginger, and you'll launch your guests into orbit. Serves 6

Ingredients

For the crust:
6 tablespoons organic unsalted butter, softened
½ cup raw organic sugar, such as Sucanat
¼ cup organic rice flour
⅓ cup coarsely ground almonds
⅓ cup chopped pecans
¼ cup ground shelled sunflower seeds
½ teaspoon ground cinnamon

For the topping:
1 pound cream cheese
1 cup whipping cream, chilled
⅓ cup honey
Finely grated zest of 2 lemons
2 mangoes, peeled, pitted, and pureed
2 tablespoons raw organic sugar, such as Sucanat
Pinch ground cardamom

For the garnish:
1 cup organic whipping cream, chilled
½ teaspoon grated fresh ginger, grated
Seeds from two passion fruits (optional)

1. Preheat oven to 350°F.

2. First, make the crust. In a large mixing bowl, using an electric mixer at medium-high speed, cream together the butter and sugar until light and fluffy. Beat in the flour until thoroughly combined. Add the almonds, pecans, sunflower seeds, and cinnamon and continue beating just until the mixture forms a uniform dough.

3. With your fingers, press the mixture evenly into the bottoms of 6 individual-portion 4-inch springform pans, or one 9-inch springform pan. Transfer them to the oven and bake until golden, 15 to 20 minutes. Remove the crusts from the oven and leave them at room temperature to cool completely before filling.

4. Next, make the filling. Put a clean mixing bowl in the freezer to chill. Put the cream cheese and 2 tablespoons of the cream in another clean mixing bowl. Using the electric mixer with clean beaters at medium speed, beat them together until smooth. Beat in the honey and lemon zest until the mixture is smooth and light.

5. In the chilled bowl and using clean beaters at medium speed, whip the remaining cream until thick. Fold the whipped cream into the cream cheese mixture. Spoon this filling mixture into the cooled springform pans. Cover each with plastic wrap and put in the refrigerator to chill.

6. Meanwhile, put the mango, sugar, and cardamom in a saucepan. Cook over low heat, stirring occasionally, until they form a thick sauce, about 5 minutes. Transfer to a bowl, cover, and refrigerate until thoroughly chilled. Then, uncover the cheesecakes and spread the mango sauce on top. Continue chilling for at least 4 hours or until serving.

7. Before serving, chill another mixing bowl in the freezer. Put the whipping cream for the garnish in the chilled bowl and, with clean beaters, whip the cream until it forms soft, drooping peaks when the beaters are lifted out. With a spatula, fold in the grated ginger.

8. When ready to serve, run a thin knife around the edge of each cheesecake to loosen it. Remove the side of the springform pan. With a sharp knife or thin metal spatula, carefully remove the pan bottom from each cheesecake and transfer the cheesecake to a chilled serving plate. Sprinkle the passion fruit seeds on top of the cheesecakes and decoratively spoon or pipe the whipped cream around the edge of each portion.

P Recommended in moderation

K Not recommended due to the sweet taste and heavy qualities of the butter, sugar, flour, and cream cheese

Contains dairy, Gluten-free

V CHOCOLATE COCONUT NO-BAKE COOKIES

When time is limited, no-bake cookies make it possible to create a rich, chocolaty dessert in minutes. Mahalo to our friends at the Blossoming Lotus Restaurant in Kauai for sharing this delicious treat. Serves 4

Ingredients

1 cup organic semisweet or bittersweet chocolate chips
2 tablespoons almond butter
1 tablespoon maple syrup
⅓ teaspoon vanilla extract
¼ cup seedless raisins
2 tablespoons chopped pecans
¼ teaspoon ground cinnamon
¼ teaspoon ground cardamom
2 tablespoons toasted coconut

1. Melt the chocolate in the top of a double boiler over gently simmering water. Remove the pan from the heat and stir in the chips until they have melted.

2. Stir in the almond butter, maple syrup, and vanilla extract. Sprinkle the raisins, pecans, cinnamon and cardamom over the chocolate mixture and stir well.

3. Line a tray with waxed paper. With a tablespoon, drop the chocolate mixture onto the tray to form individual bite-sized portions about ½-inch thick.

4. Immediately sprinkle the drops with toasted coconut. Refrigerate until cool and firm, about 30 minutes. Transfer to an airtight container and store at cool room temperature until serving.

P Recommended in moderation; chocolate is overly heating and acidic for Pitta when taken in excess

K Not recommended due to the sweet taste and rich, heavy qualities of the chocolate, almond butter and sugar

Dairy- free
Gluten-free

V BAKED BANANAS
with Orange & Cinnamon Sauce

The enticing combination of warm tropical fruit and spices may remind you of that old New Orleans favorite, Bananas Foster. Serves 4 to 6

Ingredients

4 to 6 ripe bananas, peeled and sliced in half lengthwise

Juice of 2 oranges

¾ cup organic coconut milk, preferably fresh (p. 233)

3 or 4 drops pure orange oil

2 to 3 tablespoons maple syrup or 1½ tablespoons raw organic sugar, such as Sucanat

½ teaspoon ground cinnamon

¼ teaspoon ground cardamom

⅓ cup seedless raisins

⅓ cup flaked almonds

1 tablespoon organic unsalted butter, cut into small pieces

1. Preheat the oven to 350°F.

2. Arrange the bananas neatly in a baking dish large enough to hold them in a single layer. In a mixing bowl, stir together the orange juice, coconut milk, and orange oil and pour over the bananas. Sprinkle them with the maple syrup, cinnamon, and cardomom. Scatter the raisins, almonds, and butter on top.

3. Bake for 25 minutes. With a spatula, carefully transfer the banana halves to individual serving plates or bowls. Spoon the sauce from the baking dish over each portion.

P. Substitute apricots for the bananas.

K Substiute peaches and dried figs for the bananas, pear juice or apple juice for the orange, and omit the butter.

Dairy-free without the butter

Gluten-free

# TAPIOCA PUDDING

Tapioca is a root vegetable which acts like a grain in puddings. Try serving this elegant pudding with cooked berries such as blackcurrants or loganberries. Serves 4

Ingredients

1¾ cups filtered water
1/3 cup dried tapioca
1 teaspoon ground cinnamon
½ teaspoon ground allspice
Pinch of nutmeg (optional)
Honey
Organic whipping cream, for decoration

1. Put the water and tapioca in a medium saucepan. Bring to a boil over high heat, then reduce the heat and simmer, stirring occasionally, until the mixture thickens, 10 to 15 minutes.

2. Stir in the cinnamon, allspice, and nutmeg. Leave the pudding at room temperature to cool. Serve either warm or at room temperature.

3. Spoon the pudding into serving dishes. Drizzle honey over the pudding to taste decorate with the whipped cream.

V Substitute amaranth for tapioca and cook in 1½ cups whole milk and 1 cup filtered water for 30 minutes.

P Use maple syrup in place of honey. Serve chilled.

Dairy-free
Gluten-free

PEAR CRISP

A homestyle English dessert perfect for Pitta types, pear crisp soothingly satisfies a sweet tooth. Serves 6

Ingredients

1 cup organic spelt flour
¼ cup coarsely chopped almonds
½ cup organic, cold unsalted butter or ghee, cut into small pieces
½ cup rolled oats
¾ cup raw organic sugar, such as Sucanat
½ teaspoon ground cinnamon
4 or 5 firm, ripe pears, peeled and sliced
8 dates, preferably Medjool, pitted and chopped in half
½ teaspoon ground cardamom
Vanilla Custard Sauce (recipe follows)

1. Preheat the oven to 350°F.

2. Put the flour, almonds, butter, oats, sugar, and cinnamon in a mixing bowl. With your fingertips, rub them together to form a crumbly mixture. Set aside in a cool place.

3. Arrange the pears and dates in a flat, deep glass or ceramic baking dish. Sprinkle evenly with the dehydrated cane sugar juice and cardamom. Sprinkle evenly with the crumble mixture.

4. Bake until the fruit is bubbling and the topping is golden brown, about 35 minutes. Spoon into individual serving bowls or plates and top with some of the Vanilla Custard Sauce, passing extra in a sauceboat.

V Also recommended

K Not recommended, due to the sweet taste and heavy quality of the butter, oats, sugar and dates

Contains dairy
Gluten-free if using amaranth flour

VANILLA CUSTARD SAUCE

The sweet, creamy quality of custard sauce makes it especially soothing for both Pitta and Vata. You can make the consistency thick or thin as you like, although a thinner custard works better as a dessert topping. Makes at least 1 cup

Ingredients

1 pint organic whole milk
¼ cup organic heavy cream
1 vanilla pod, cut in half lengthwise, or 4 or 5 drops vanilla extract
3 tablespoons finely ground oat flour
3 tablespoons filtered water
½ cup raw organic sugar, such as Sucanat
Few threads saffron
Pinch ground cardamom
1 teaspoon rosewater

1. In a large stainless-steel saucepan over medium-high heat, bring the milk and cream to a boil, stirring frequently with a wire whisk to prevent the mixture from sticking or burning. Add the vanilla. Reduce the heat to maintain a bare simmer.

2. Meanwhile, in a small bowl, whisk together the oat flour and water until smooth. Whisk this mixture into the simmering milk mixture.

3. Next, whisk in the sugar, saffron, and cardamom. Simmer, stirring continuously, until thickened to your liking, and then stir in the rosewater.

4. Keep the sauce covered and warm until serving time.

V Also recommended

K Not recommended due to the sweet taste and heavy quality of the cream, oat flour, and sugar

Contains dairy
Gluten-free if using cornmeal instead of oat flour

P MANGO MANDARIN SORBET
with Mandarin Sauce

Fresh, juicy fruit can be easily turned into a tempting sorbet. For a special party or buffet table, serve in a Floral Ice Bowl (recipe follows).
Serves 4

Ingredients

For the sorbet
2 or 3 ripe mangoes, peeled and pitted
Juice from 4 mandarins or tangerines
2 tablespoons maple syrup
1 teaspoon lemon juice
3 tablespoons filtered water
2 tablespoons organic cream
Shredded coconut or grated chocolate, for garnish

For the sauce
Juice from 4 or 5 mandarin oranges or tangerines
1 tablespoon raw organic sugar, such as Sucanat
¼ teaspoon ground cardamom

1. For the sorbet, in a food processor fitted with the metal blade or in a blender, puree the mangoes, mandarin juice, maple syrup, lemon juice, and water. Pour into a bowl and stir in the cream. Cover the bowl and freeze for 4 hours, stirring until smooth once every hour by hand with a fork or, for a finer consistency, with a handheld electric mixer.

2. Meanwhile make the sauce. In a saucepan over medium heat, simmer the mandarin juice, sugar, and cardamom until the sauce is thick enough to coat a wooden spoon, about 10 minutes. Transfer to a bowl and refrigerate until serving time.

3. To serve, scoop the sorbet into individual chilled serving bowls. Drizzle the sauce over each portion and garnish with coconut or chocolate.

V Not recommended due to the cold quality of the sorbet

K Not recommended due to the sweet taste and cold quality of the sorbet and sauce

For dairy-free, replace the cream with coconut milk
Gluten-free

P FLORAL ICE BOWL

Use your imagination and creativity to create this dazzling centerpiece container for iced desserts. To create a non-edible ice bowl, you'll need one freezerproof glass or metal bowl about 12 inches in diameter with a flat bottom, and another freezerproof glass bowl about 10 inches in diameter that can nest inside the first.

Ingredients

Filtered water
2 to 3 dozen organic, pesticide-free flowers with leaves, all about 1 to 3 inches in diameter, such as pansies, violets, nasturtiums, irises, orchids, and rose petals
1 to 2 cups neatly sliced fruit such as kiwi, star fruit, mountain pear, lime or small oranges

1. Fill the larger bowl about half full with filtered water and add most but not all of the flowers and fruit slices. Place the smaller glass bowl inside the larger one. Put a heavy object such as a can of food inside the inner bowl to weight it down to the point at which it floats on at least ½-inch of water between the bowls, pushing the flowers, fruit, and water up into the space between the sides of the bowls.

2. The inner glass bowl will allow you to see the placement of the decorative elements. Slip a few more flowers, petals, or fruit slices into the spaces between the two bowls, rearranging the flowers, if necessary, to make the bowl appear to be evenly lined with color and texture.

3. Transfer the bowls to a shelf in the freezer, double-checking to make sure that the inner bowl is centered so that the end result will have an even thickness. Leave in the freezer until solidly frozen, at least 2 to 3 hours.

4. Before presenting the ice bowl, first put a serving tray in the freezer to chill for about 30 minutes. Remove the heavy object from the center of the ice bowl. Supporting the inner bowl with your hands, gently invert the larger bowl briefly under a stream of warm tap water to loosen it from the ice bowl. Place the ice bowl upside-down on a work surface and gently slide off the outer bowl. Then, supporting the ice bowl with your hands, run a little warm water inside the inner bowl to loosen it. Place the ice bowl on the chilled serving tray and carefully lift out the inner bowl.

5. Quickly fill the ice bowl with the ice cream or sorbet you are serving. Serve immediately or return the tray to the freezer until ready to serve.

CHOCOLATE SAVEUR
with Coconut Crème

The French word for "savor" captures the way you'll enjoy this rich dessert, in small spoonfuls, so good you'll close your eyes with pleasure. Use bread flour rather than all-purpose flour to get the perfect consistency. Serves 4

Ingredients

Ghee

1 cup organic bread flour or 1 cup whole wheat flour

1 cup organic spelt flour

2 teaspoons baking powder

¾ cup raw organic sugar, such as Sucanat

¼ pound organic unsalted butter, chilled well

1 pound organic dark chocolate, grated

2 tablespoons ground blanched almonds

2 drops orange oil

1 cup organic whipping cream

¼ teaspoon ground cardamom

1½ cups organic milk

½ cup grated fresh coconut or dried coconut

Maple syrup

Raspberry syrup for garnish

1. Preheat the oven to 375°F. Grease four 4-inch crème brûlée dishes with ghee. Use the bottom of one of the dishes as a guide to draw 4 circles on a sheet of waxed paper or parchment paper. Invert the paper onto a small baking sheet and set aside.

2. Sift the flours and baking powder into a large bowl. Stir in the dehydrated cane sugar juice. Grate the butter over the flour mixture and toss, using your hands, or beat briefly with an electric mixer. Stir half of the grated chocolate into the flour mixture and set aside.

3. Melt the remaining chocolate in the top of a double boiler over gently simmering water, stirring until melted and smooth. Stir in the almonds, orange oil, half the cream, and the cardamom. Remove the mixture from the heat. Let it cool at room temperature for a few minutes, until it begins to thicken. Then, with a tablespoon, divide the chocolate mixture among the 4 circles on the sheet of paper, spreading them with the back of the spoon up to the edge of each circle. Put the baking sheet into the freezer and freeze until the mixture is solid, about 15 minutes.

4. Whisk the milk into the flour mixture. With a ladle, transfer enough of this batter to the crème brûlée dishes to fill them about one third full.

5. Place a chocolate disk in the center of each dish. Ladle the remaining batter on top. Place the dishes on a baking sheet and bake until the batter looks set, about 30 minutes.

6. While the dishes are in the oven, whip the remaining cream until it forms firm peaks. With a rubber spatula, fold in the coconut and maple syrup to taste. Cover with plastic wrap and refrigerate until serving time.

7. With a small, thin knife, loosen the chocolate saveur from each dish by running the knife around its perimeter. Invert a serving plate over the dish and, using a dry kitchen towel to hold them together, invert them and lift away the dish. (If anything sticks inside, use a knife to dislodge it and replace the piece on the serving plate. You can disguise any imperfections with whipped cream.) Garnish with the coconut whipped cream and raspberry syrup.

P   Recommended in moderation; chocolate is overly heating and acidic for Pitta when eaten in excess

K   Not recommended, due to the rich and heavy qualities of the flour, sugar, butter, and chocolate

Contains dairy and gluten

APPENDICES

DOSHA FOOD LISTS

An asterisk * indicates that these foods are OK in moderation.

The following food lists are based largely upon the research of Dr. Vasant Lad MASc., director of the Ayurvedic Institute, in Albuquerque, New Mexico. For more detailed information regarding the tastes, potencies and post-digestive effects of specific foods, please see his book: *Ayurveda: The Science of Self-Healing.*

VATA		PITTA		KAPHA	
REDUCE/AVOID	FAVOR	REDUCE/AVOID	FAVOR	REDUCE/AVOID	FAVOR

FRUITS
Note: Fruit juices are best consumed by themselves for all doshas.

Dried Fruits	*Sweet & Sour Fruits*	*Sour Fruits*	*Sweet/Astringent Fruits*	*Sweet & Sour Fruits*	*Astringent Fruits*
Apples (raw)	Apricots	Apples (sour)	Apples (sweet)	Avocado	Apples
Cranberries	Avocado	Apricots (sour)	Apricots (sweet)	Bananas	Apricots
Pears	Bananas	Berries (sour)	Avocado	Coconut	Berries
Persimmon	Berries (all)	Cherries (sour)	Bananas*	Currants*	Cherries
Pomegranate	Cherries	Cranberries	Berries (sweet)	Dates	Cranberries
Prunes	Coconut	Grapefruit	Coconut	Figs (fresh)	Figs (dry)
Watermelon	Currants	Grapes (green)	Dates	Grapefruit	Green Papaya*
	Dates	Currants*	Figs	Grapes*	Mango
	Figs (fresh)	Kiwi*	Grapes (sweet)	Kiwi	Peaches
	Grapefruit	Oranges (sour)	Green Papaya*	Lemons*	Pears
	Grapes	Peaches	Mango	Limes*	Persimmon
	Green Papaya	Pineapple (sour)	Melons	Mangos*	Pomegranate
	Kiwi	Persimmon	Oranges (sweet)	Melons	Prunes
	Lemons	Plums (sour)	Papaya*	Oranges	Raisins
	Limes	Rhubarb	Pears	Papayas	Strawberries*
	Melons (sweet)	Strawberries	Lemons*	Pineapple	
	Oranges		Limes*	Plums	
	Papaya		Plums (sweet)	Rhubarb	
	Peaches		Pomegranate	Watermelon	
	Pineapple		Prunes		
	Plums		Raisins		
	Raisins (soaked)		Watermelon		
	Rhubarb				
	Strawberries				

VEGETABLES

Frozen, Dried or Raw Vegetables	*Cooked Vegetables*	*Pungent Vegetables*	*Sweet, Bitter & Astringent Vegetables*	*Sweet & Sour*	*Bitter, Pungent, Astringent or Raw Vegetables*
Arugula*	Acorn Squash	Beets	Acorn Squash	Acorn Squash	Arugula
Beet Greens*	Artichoke	Beet Greens	Artichoke	Artichoke*	Asparagus
Bok Choy*	Asparagus	Carrots (raw)	Arugula	Butternut Squash	Beet Greens
Broccoli*	Beets	Daikon Radish*	Asparagus	Cucumber	Beets
Brussel Sprouts	Bell Pepper	Eggplant	Bell Pepper	Olives (black or green)	Bell Pepper
	Butternut Squash	Garlic		Parsnip*	

VEGETABLES (CONTINUED)

Vata REDUCE/AVOID	Vata FAVOR	Pitta REDUCE/AVOID	Pitta FAVOR	Kapha REDUCE/AVOID	Kapha FAVOR
Burdock Root	Carrots	Horseradish	Bok Choy	Potato (sweet)	Bok Choy
Cabbage	Cucumber	Green Olives	Broccoli	Pumpkin	Broccoli
Cauliflower	Daikon Radish	Leeks (cooked)*	Brussel Sprouts	Rutabagas	Brussel Sprouts
Celery	Fennel	Mustard Greens	Burdock Root	Spaghetti Squash	Burdock Root
Chili Pepper*	Green Beans (cooked)	Onions (cooked)*	Butternut Squash	Tomatoes	Cabbage
Collard Greens*	Leeks	Onions (raw)	Cabbage	Winter Squash	Carrots
Corn (fresh)*	Mustard Greens	Peppers (hot)	Cauliflower	Zucchini	Cauliflower
Eggplant	Okra (cooked)	Peppers (red)*	Celery		Celery
Jerusalem Artichoke	Olives (black & green)	Pumpkin	Collard Greens		Collard Greens
Jicama*	Onions (cooked)	Radish	Corn (fresh)		Corn (fresh)
Kale*	Parsnip	Spinach	Cucumber		Daikon Radish
Leafy Greens*	Potato (sweet)	Sun Dried Tomato	Fennel		Eggplant
Lettuce*	Pumpkin	Tomatoes	Green Beans		Fennel
Mushrooms	Radish	Turnip	Jerusalem Artichoke		Garlic
Onions (raw)	Rutabaga	Turnip Greens	Jicama		Green Beans
Parsley*	Summer Squash		Kale		Horseradish
Peas	Watercress		Leafy Greens		Jerusalem Artichoke
Peppers (red)*	Winter Squash		Collards		Jicama
Potato (white)	Zucchini		Lettuce		Kale
Spaghetti Squash*			Mushrooms		Leafy Greens
Spinach*			Okra		Leeks
Sprouts*			Olives (black)		Lettuce
Sun Dried Tomato*			Parsley		Mushrooms
Tomatoes			Parsnips		Okra
Turnips			Peas		Onions
			Peppers (green)		Parsley
			Potato (sweet)		Peas
			Potato (white)		Peppers (red)
			Rutabaga		Potato (white)
			Spaghetti Squash		Radish
			Sprouts		Sprouts
			Zucchini		Summer Squash
					Sun Dried Tomato*
					Watercress

GRAINS

Vata REDUCE/AVOID	Vata FAVOR	Pitta REDUCE/AVOID	Pitta FAVOR	Kapha REDUCE/AVOID	Kapha FAVOR
Cold, Dry, Puffed Grains	Amaranth	Amaranth*	Barley	Oats (cooked)	Amaranth*
Cereal	Couscous	Buckwheat	Couscous	Pasta	Barley
Barley*	Oats (cooked)	Corn	Oats (cooked)	Rice (brown)	Buckwheat
Buckwheat	Pasta	Millet	Pasta	Rice (white)	Corn

An asterisk * indicates that these foods are OK in moderation.

VATA		PITTA		KAPHA	
REDUCE/AVOID	FAVOR	REDUCE/AVOID	FAVOR	REDUCE/AVOID	FAVOR

GRAINS (CONTINUED)

VATA		PITTA		KAPHA	
REDUCE/AVOID	FAVOR	REDUCE/AVOID	FAVOR	REDUCE/AVOID	FAVOR
Corn	Rice (all, including brown)	Oats (dry)	Rice (basmati)	Spelt	Couscous
Granola	Spelt	Granola	Rice Cakes	Wheat	Millet
Millet	Tapioca	Oat Bran*	Rice (white)	White Flour	Oat Bran
Oat Bran	Wheat	Oat	Spelt		Oats (dry)
Oats (dry)	Wild Rice	Quinoa	Tapioca		Quinoa
Quinoa		Rice (brown)*	Wheat		Rice* (basmati, spiced)
Rice Cakes		Rye	Wheat Bran		Rice Cakes*
Rye		White Flour			Rye
Wheat Bran*					Wheat Bran*
White Flour					Tapioca
					Turnips
					Watercress

LEGUMES

VATA		PITTA		KAPHA	
REDUCE/AVOID	FAVOR	REDUCE/AVOID	FAVOR	REDUCE/AVOID	FAVOR
Black Beans	*In moderation:*	*None*	Aduki Beans	Black Lentils	Aduki Beans
Black-eyed Peas	Aduki Beans		Black Beans	Brown Lentils	Black Beans
Brown Lentils	Black Lentils		Black-eyed Peas	Kidney Beans	Black-eyed Peas
Chana Dal	Lentils		Black Lentils*	Soy Beans	Chickpeas
Chickpeas	Mung Beans		Brown Lentils	Soy Milk (cold)	Lima Beans
Kidney Beans	Red Lentils		Chana Dal	Soy Cheese	Mung Beans
Lima Beans	Soy Cheese		Chickpeas	Tempeh	Navy Beans
Navy Beans	Soy Milk (liquid)		Kidney Beans	Cold Tofu	Pinto Beans
Pinto Beans	Tofu		Lima Beans		Puy Lentils
Soy Beans	Yellow Split Mung		Mung Beans		Red Lentils
Soy Flour			Navy Beans		Soy Milk (hot)*
Soy Powder			Pinto Beans		Split Peas
Split Peas			Puy Lentils		Tofu (cooked)*
Tempeh			Red Lentils*		White Beans
White Beans			Soy Beans		Yellow Split Mung
			Soy Products		
			Split Peas		
			Tempeh		
			Tofu		
			White Beans		
			Yellow Split Mung		

DAIRY

VATA		PITTA		KAPHA	
REDUCE/AVOID	FAVOR	REDUCE/AVOID	FAVOR	REDUCE/AVOID	FAVOR
Cheese (hard)*	*All OK in Moderation*	Butter (salted)	Butter (unsalted)	Butter	Ghee*
Cow's Milk (powder)	Buttermilk	Buttermilk (commercial)	Cheese (mild, soft)	Buttermilk (commercial)	Goat's Milk
Goat's Milk (powder)	Cow's Milk	Cheese (hard)*	Cottage Cheese	Cheese of Any Kind	Yogurt (diluted)

An asterisk * indicates that these foods are OK in moderation.

DAIRY (CONTINUED)

VATA reduce/avoid	VATA favor	PITTA reduce/avoid	PITTA favor	KAPHA reduce/avoid	KAPHA favor
Yogurt (frozen)	Cheese (soft)	Feta Cheese	Cow's Milk		Cream
	Cream	Sour Cream	Cream		Cow's Milk
	Ghee	Yogurt	Ghee		Ice Cream
	Goat's Cheese		Goat's Milk		Panir*
	Goat's Milk*		Ice Cream*		Sour Cream
	Ice Cream*		Panir		Whey
	Panir		Whey		Yogurt
	Whey		Yogurt (diluted)		
	Yogurt (spiced)				

ANIMAL

VATA reduce/avoid	VATA favor	PITTA reduce/avoid	PITTA favor	KAPHA reduce/avoid	KAPHA favor
Lamb	Beef*	Beef	Buffalo	Beef	Chicken (white)
Pork	Buffalo	Duck	Chicken (white meat)	Chicken (dark)	Eggs*
Turkey (white)*	Chicken	Duck	Turkey (white meat)	Fish (saltwater)	Fish (freshwater)
Venison	Duck	Lamb	Egg Whites	Lamb	Shrimp
	Eggs	Pork	Fish (freshwater)*	Pork	Turkey (white)
	Fish	Salmon	Shrimp*	Salmon	Venison
	Seafood	Sardines	Turkey (white meat)	Sardines	
	Turkey (dark)	Seafood	Venison	Seafood	
		Tuna Fish		Tuna Fish	
		Turkey (dark)		Turkey (dark)	

NUTS

VATA reduce/avoid	VATA favor	PITTA reduce/avoid	PITTA favor	KAPHA reduce/avoid	KAPHA favor
Almonds (with skins)	Almonds (soaked, peeled)	Almonds (with skins)	Almonds (soaked, peeled)	Almonds (with skins)	Almonds (soaked, peeled)*
	Brazil Nuts*	Brazil Nuts	Coconut	Brazil Nuts	
	Cashews*	Cashews		Cashews	
	Coconut	Hazelnuts		Coconut	
	English Walnuts	Macadamia		English Walnut	
	Hazelnuts	Peanuts		Macadamia	
	Macadamia	Pecans		Peanuts	
	Peanuts*	Pine Nuts		Pecans	
	Pine Nuts	Pistachios		Pine Nuts	
	Pistachio	Walnuts		Pistachios	

SEEDS

VATA reduce/avoid	VATA favor	PITTA reduce/avoid	PITTA favor	KAPHA reduce/avoid	KAPHA favor
Psyllium*	Flax	Sesame	Flax	Sesame	Flax*
	Hemp		Hemp	Hemp	Popcorn (no salt or butter)
	Pumpkin		Popcorn (no salt or butter)		Psyllium*
	Sesame		Psyllium		Pumpkin*
	Sunflower		Pumpkin*		Sunflower
			Sunflower		

An asterisk * indicates that these foods are OK in moderation.

OILS

VATA		PITTA		KAPHA	
REDUCE/AVOID	FAVOR	REDUCE/AVOID	FAVOR	REDUCE/AVOID	FAVOR
None	All oils are fine, especially ghee, olive & sesame	Almond	Avocado	Apricot	In moderation:
		Apricot	Canola	Avocado	Almond
		Corn	Coconut	Coconut	Canola
		Safflower	Olive	Safflower	Corn
		Sesame	Sesame	Sesame	Flax
			Soy	Soy	Ghee
			Sunflower	Walnut	Sunflower
			Walnut		

SWEETENERS

VATA		PITTA		KAPHA	
REDUCE/AVOID	FAVOR	REDUCE/AVOID	FAVOR	REDUCE/AVOID	FAVOR
White Sugar	Barley Malt Syrup	Honey*	Barley Malt Syrup	Barley Malt Syrup	Fruit Juice Concentrates (especially apple & pear)
Honey*	Brown Rice Syrup	Jaggery	Brown Rice Syrup	Brown Rice Syrup	Honey (esp. raw)
	Fructose	Molasses	Fructose	Fructose	Stevia
	Fruit Juice Concentrate	White Sugar	Fruit Juice Concentrate	Jaggery	
	Jaggery		Maple Syrup	Maple Syrup*	
	Maple Syrup		Stevia	Molasses	
	Molasses		Sucanat	Sucanat	
	Stevia		Sugar Cane Juice	Sugar Cane Juice	
	Sucanat			White Sugar	

HERBS AND SPICES

VATA		PITTA		KAPHA	
REDUCE/AVOID	FAVOR	REDUCE/AVOID	FAVOR	REDUCE/AVOID	FAVOR
None	All Spices Beneficial	Ajwan	Fresh Basil Leaves*	Almond Extract	Ajwan
	Ajwan	Allspice	Black Pepper*	Tamarind	Allspice
	Allspice	Anise	Cardamom*		Anise
	Almond Extract	Asafetida	Cilantro		Asafetida
	Anise	Basil	Cinnamon*		Basil
	Asafetida	Bay Leaf	Coriander		Bay Leaf
	Basil	Caraway*	Cumin		Black Pepper
	Bay Leaf	Cayenne	Curry Powder (mild)		Caraway
	Black Pepper	Cloves	Dill		Cardamom
	Caraway	Curry Powder	Fennel		Cayenne*
	Cardamom	Garlic (esp. raw)	Mint		Cilantro
	Cayenne*	Ginger	Orange Peel*		Cinnamon
	Cilantro	Horseradish	Peppermint		Cloves
	Cinnamon	Mace	Rose Water		Coriander
	Cloves	Marjoram	Saffron		Cumin
	Coriander	Mustard Seeds	Spearmint		Curry Powder
	Cumin	Nutmeg	Turmeric		Dill
	Curry Powder	Onions (esp. raw)	Vanilla*		Fennel

An asterisk * indicates that these foods are OK in moderation.

HERBS AND SPICES (CONTINUED)

VATA REDUCE/AVOID	VATA FAVOR	PITTA REDUCE/AVOID	PITTA FAVOR	KAPHA REDUCE/AVOID	KAPHA FAVOR
	Dill	Oregano	Wintergreen		Fenugreek*
	Fennel	Paprika			Garlic
	Fenugreek*	Poppy Seeds*			Ginger
	Garlic	Rosemary			Mace
	Ginger	Sage			Marjoram
	Mace	Savory			Mint
	Marjoram	Star Anise			Mustard Seeds
	Mint	Tamarind			Nutmeg
	Mustard Seeds	Tarragon*			Orange Peel
	Nutmeg	Thyme			Oregano
	Orange Peel				Paprika
	Oregano				Parsley
	Paprika				Peppermint
	Parsley				Poppy Seeds
	Peppermint				Rosemary
	Poppy Seeds				Rose Water
	Rosemary				Saffron
	Rose Water				Sage
	Saffron				Savory
	Sage				Spearmint
	Savory				Star Anise
	Spearmint				Tarragon
	Star Anise				Thyme
	Tamarind				Turmeric
	Tarragon				Vanilla
	Thyme				Wintergreen
	Turmeric				
	Vanilla				
	Wintergreen				

CONDIMENTS

VATA REDUCE/AVOID	VATA FAVOR	PITTA REDUCE/AVOID	PITTA FAVOR	KAPHA REDUCE/AVOID	KAPHA FAVOR
Chili Pepper*	Black Pepper*	Black Sesame Seeds	Black Pepper*	Black Sesame Seeds	Black Pepper
Ginger (dry)*	Chutney (assorted)	Chili Pepper	Chutney (sweet)	Chutney (hot)*	Chili Pepper
Ketchup	Coconut	Garlic	Coconut	Coconut	Coriander Leaves
Mayonnaise*	Coriander Leaves*	Ginger	Coriander Leaves	Cottage Cheese*	Daikon Radish
Onion (raw)	Cottage Cheese	Gomasio	Cottage Cheese	Gomasio	Garlic
Radish*	Grated Cheese	Horseradish	Dulse (well-rinsed)	Grated Cheese	Ghee*
Sprouts*	Garlic	Kelp	Ghee	Kelp	Ginger (dry)
	Ghee	Ketchup	Lettuce	Ketchup	Horseradish
	Ginger (fresh)	Lemon	Mango Chutney	Lemon or Lime	Lettuce

An asterisk * indicates that these foods are OK in moderation.

VATA		PITTA		KAPHA	
REDUCE/AVOID	FAVOR	REDUCE/AVOID	FAVOR	REDUCE/AVOID	FAVOR

CONDIMENTS (CONTINUED)

VATA		PITTA		KAPHA	
	Gomasio	Lime	Mint Leaves	Mango Chutney	Mint Leaves
	Horseradish	Mayonnaise	Sprouts	Mayonnaise	Mustard
	Kelp	Mustard		Pickles	Radish
	Lemon	Onions (esp. raw)		Salt*	Sprouts
	Lettuce*	Pickles		Seaweed (well-rinsed)*	
	Lime	Radish		Sesame Seeds	
	Mint Leaves*	Salt*		Soy Sauce	
	Miso	Seaweed (well-rinsed)*		Tamari	
	Mustard	Sesame Seeds			
	Onions (cooked)	Soy Sauce			
	Pickles	Tamari*			
	Salt	Yogurt (undiluted)			
	Seaweed				

BEVERAGES

VATA		PITTA		KAPHA	
REDUCE/AVOID	FAVOR	REDUCE/AVOID	FAVOR	REDUCE/AVOID	FAVOR
Alcohol*	Almond	Alcohol	Almond	Alcohol (in excess)	Aloe Vera Juice
Apple Juice	Rejuvenative Drinks	Berry Juice (sour)	Aloe Vera Juice	Almond Milk	Apple Juice
Caffeine	Aloe Vera Juice	Caffeine	Apple Juice	Banana Shake/Smoothie	Apricot Juice
Carbonated Drinks	Banana Shake/Smoothie	Carbonated Drinks	Apricot Juice	Carbonated Drinks	Berry Juice
Coffee	Berry Juice	Coffee	Banana Shake/Smoothie*	Coconut Milk	Caffeine*
Cold Dairy Drinks	Carrot Juice	Carrot-Veg. Combinations	Berry Juice (sweet)	Chocolate	Carob
Cranberry Juice	Carrot-Veg. Combinations	Carrot Juice (in excess)	Mixed Veg. Juice	Dairy Drinks	Carrot Juice
Ice-cold Drinks	Carrot-Ginger Juice	Chocolate	Carob	Grapefruit Juice	Cherry Juice
Pear Juice	Chocolate	Cranberry Juice	Coconut Milk	Ice-cold Drinks	Cranberry Juice
Pomegranate Juice	Coconut Milk	Grapefruit	Dairy Drinks (cool)	Lemonade	Grape Juice*
	Dairy Drinks (hot)	Ice-cold Drinks	Goat Milk	Licorice Tea	Mango Juice
	Grape Juice	Lemonade	Grape Juice	Orange Juice	Mixed Veg. Juice
	Grapefruit Juice	Orange Juice*	Mango Juice	Soy Milk (cold)	Peach Nectar
	Lemonade	Sour Juices & Teas	Peach Nectar		Soy Milk
	Mango Juice	Pungent Teas	Pear Juice		(warm, spiced)
	Mixed Veg. Juice	Salted Drinks	Soy Milk		
	Milk (warm spiced)				
	Orange Juice				
	Papaya Juice				
	Peach Nectar				
	Pineapple Juice				
	Salted Drinks				
	Sour Juices & Teas				

An asterisk * indicates that these foods are OK in moderation.

VATA		PITTA		KAPHA	
REDUCE/AVOID	FAVOR	REDUCE/AVOID	FAVOR	REDUCE/AVOID	FAVOR

BEVERAGES (CONTINUED)

VATA		PITTA		KAPHA	
	Soy Milk				
	(hot & well-spiced)				
Herbal Tea:	*Herbal Tea:*	*Herbal Tea:*	*Herbal Tea:*	*Herbal Tea:*	*Herbal Tea:*
Blackberry	Chamomile	Ginger (fresh)	Chamomile	Licorice	Chamomile
Hibiscus	Elder Flowers	Ginseng	Fennel	Coffee*	Fennel*
Jasmine*	Fennel	Yerba Mate	Jasmine*		Ginseng*
Red Clover*	Ginger (fresh)		Licorice		Jasmine
	Ginseng		Lotus		Peppermint
	Licorice		Peppermint		
	Peppermint		Saffron		
	Roseflower		Spearmint		
	Saffron				
	Spearmint				

SUPPLEMENTS

VATA		PITTA		KAPHA	
Barley Green	Aloe Vera Juice	Bee Pollen*	Aloe Vera Juice	Vitamins A, D, & E	Aloe Vera Juice
Brewer's Yeast*	Amino Acids	Copper	Amino Acids*		Amino Acids
	Bee Pollen	Iron	Barley Green		Barley Green
	Royal Jelly	Royal Jelly*	Brewer's Yeast		Bee Pollen
	Spirulina & Chlorella		Spirulina & Chlorella		Brewer's Yeast*
	Vitamins A, B, B12, C, D, E		Vitamins A, B, B12, C, D, E		Royal Jelly
					Spirulina & Chlorella
					Vitamins B6, B12, C
	Minerals:		*Minerals:*		*Minerals:*
	Calcium, Copper,		Calcium, Magnesium,		Calcium, Copper,
	Iron, Magnesium,		Potassium, Zinc		Iron, Magnesium,
	Potassium, Zinc				Potassium, Zinc

An asterisk * indicates that these foods are OK in moderation.

Legume Cooking Chart

Legume	Liquid per cup of legume	Approx. cooking time (hours)	Approx. yield (cups)
Aduki/Adzuki Beans	3¼	45 min	3
Anasazi Beans	3	2	2
Black Beans (Turtle Beans)	4	1¼	2½
Blackeyed Peas	4	1¼	2
Garbanzo Beans (Chickpeas)	4	3-4	2
Great Northern Beans	4	1½	2
Kidney Beans	4	1½	2
Lentils	3	45 min	2¼
Lima Beans	3	1½	1¼
Baby Limas	3	1½	1¾
Mung Beans	3	45 min	2¼
Navy Beans (White Beans)	4	2½	2
Pinto Beans	4	2½	2
Split Peas	3	45 min	2¼
Soy Beans	4	3+	2
Soy Grits	2	15 min	2

Note: These times are for cooking dry beans. Please reduce cooking time by 25% when beans are soaked.

Grain Cooking Chart

Grain	Liquid per cup of grain	Approx. cooking time (minutes)	Approx. yield (cups)
Amaranth	2½	25	2½
Barley, pearled	3	45	3½
Buckwheat	2	15	2½
Corn Meal	3	20	3½
Couscous	1½	15	1½
Kamut	3	60	3
Millet	2½	20	3
Oats			
Steel Cut	3	30-40	3
Groats	3	60	3
Rolled	3	10	3
Quick	2	5	2
Polenta	3	10	3
Quinoa	2	20	2½
Rice			
Brown Basmati	2	35-40	2¼
White Basmati	1½	20	2
Brown Long Grain	2	45	3
Brown Short Grain	2	45	3
Wild	3	60	4
Rye			
Berries	4	60	3
Flakes	3	20	3
Spelt	3½	90	3
Teff	3	20	1½
Wheat			
Whole	3	120	2¾
Bulghur	2	15	2½
Cracked	2	25	2½

Sprouting Chart

Sprout (1 cup)	Amount	Pre-Soak hours	Days	Approximate Length
Wheat	1 cup	6-10	2-3	¼-½"
Garbanzo beans	1 cup	12	2	½"
Mung beans	½ cup	8-12	3-6	½"-1½"
Sesame seeds (hulled)	1 cup	1-1	½	¼"
Sunflower seeds*	1 cup	8-12	1-3	0"-½"
Almonds*	1 cup	12	1	0" (swells up, does not sprout)
Buckwheat	1 cup	6-10	2-3	¼"-½"
Fenugreek seeds	½ cup	8	3-5	1"-1½"
Clover	¼ cup	4-6	4-5	1"-1½"

Sprouted Greens Chart

Allowing sprouts to germinate for longer periods will create sprouted greens.

Alfalfa	2 tablespoons	2-3	7	1½-2"
Fenugreek	½ cup	8	8	1-2"
Mung Bean	½ cup	8-12	5	4"
Sunflower (unhulled)	½ cup	8-12	7-10	4-6"

*   Take off seed skins at the end of soak period to prevent spoilage

GLOSSARY

AYURVEDIC TERMS (SANSKRIT)

Abhyanga   oil massage

Agni   digestive fire

Ama   the toxic by-product of undigested food; metabolic waste

Arishta   herbal wine

Asana   a Yoga posture

Basti   herbal or oil enema

Chakras   the seven primary energy centers of the mind and body

Dhatus   the seven vital tissues of the body

Dincharya   daily routine

Doshas   the three fundamental biological energies of the mind and body

Ghee   clarified butter

Guna   quality or characteristic

Hatha Yoga   the branch of Yoga involving physical postures

Kapha   the biological energy governing structure, cohesion, and lubrication in the mind and body

Malas   waste materials of the body

Ojas   the end product of perfect digestion; vigor, strength, essence of all tissues

Panchakarma   the traditional five-step detoxification treatment of Ayurveda.

Pitta   the biological energy governing temperature, metabolism, and transformation in the mind and body

Prakruti   birth constitution

Prana   life-force energy

Pranayama   Yogic breathing practices; control of the breath

Rajas   quality of action, passion, and desire

Rasa   the sensation of taste on the tongue; also the first tissue layer

Ratricharya   nightly routine

Ritucharya   seasonal routine

Sattva   spiritual essence; quality of knowledge, purity, and truth

Srotas   channels of the body

Tamas   quality of dullness, inertia, and decay

Vata   the biological energy governing movement, communication and transportation in the mind and body

Veda   knowledge or science; the spiritual texts of ancient India

Vikruti   current state of imbalance

Vipak   the post-digestive effects of food; how food affects the building of the tissues after digestion

Virya   translates as "potency"; the heating or cooling affect of food on the physiology

Yoga   Vedic knowledge for attaining union of the Body, Mind, and Spirit

LESS COMMON FOOD INGREDIENTS

Note: All ingredients available in health food stores and well-stocked grocery stores, unless otherwise noted.

Agar-agar   a translucent seaweed used as a gelling agent in cooking; similar to gelatin

Asafetida   a traditional Ayurvedic spice with a taste similar to garlic; increases appetite and improves digestion; also known as "hing"

Aspic   a light, gelatinous dish commonly sweetened and served as a dessert in Ayurvedic cooking

Ajwan   a spice related to caraway and cumin; stimulates the digestive fire; available in Indian grocery stores

Bragg's Amino Acids   a non-fermented condiment made from soy beans; similar in taste to soy sauce

Cardamom   a mildly sweet, aromatic seed held within a greenish pod; widely used in Ayurvedic cooking; calms the nerves and improves digestion

Churna   a general Indian term for "seasoning" or "spice mixture"

Coriander seed   the seed of the cilantro leaf; widely used in Ayurevdic cooking; improves digestion and removes toxins from the body

Crème Fraîche   a lightly-cultured, slightly soured cream found throughout France

Cumin seed   a spice commonly used in Indian, Mexican and the Middle Eastern cooking; kindles the digestive fire and helps eliminate toxins from the body

Curry powder a traditional Indian spice mixture; commonly includes turmeric, fenugreek, cumin, coriander, and black pepper

Dulse a salty, dark green seaweed native to coastal countries such as Japan and England

Fennel seed a primary spice used in Ayurvedic cooking; a cousin to Dill and Anise; an excellent digestive aid; derives from the fennel plant which is also edible

Fenugreek seed a primary ingredient of Indian curry powder; promotes breast milk flow, strengthens bones, and regulates sugar metabolism

Garam Masala a traditional Indian spice mixture; commonly includes cinnamon, cardamom, cloves, cumin and black pepper

Ghee clarified butter; prepared by simmering unsalted butter over low heat and straining away the milk solids; widely used in Ayurvedic cooking

Jaggery raw, unrefined cane sugar; dark in color and available in Indian grocery stores

Jicama a crisp, mild root vegetable native to Mexico

Kanjee diluted rice water; commonly taken during periods of cleansing or strengthening in Ayurveda

Kitchari a general term for an Ayurvedic grain and legume dish; commonly prepared with basmati rice and mung beans

Quinoa a light, slightly nutty tasting grain that dates back to the Inca; contains one of the highest protein contents of any grain

Lassi a traditional drink made from yogurt, water, and spices

Medjool dates a variety of date grown in hot, dry climates; also know as "The Fruit of the Kings" in the Middle East

Miso a fermented paste made from legumes, such as soy beans and chickpeas, and grains, such as barley and buckwheat; commonly prepared as a soup in Japanese cuisine

Mung beans a small, green legume widely used in Ayurvedic cooking; split and hulled mung beans are commonly known as "mung dhal"; balances all three doshas

Nigella seeds a spice sometimes used as a substitute for black pepper; also known as celery seed or kalonji

Nori a dark green, highly nutritious sea vegetable, commonly sold in flat sheets; widely used in Japenese cooking

Panir fresh cheese made from milk; commonly used in Ayurvedic cooking

Rock salt a traditional Ayurvedic salt mined from ancient mountain ranges in India and Pakistan

Saffron a delicate, golden-orange spice traditionally used in Indian desserts; purifies the blood and improves digestion

Seitan a wheat gluten dough cooked in broth and seasoned with various spices; a popular vegetarian substitute for chicken

Subji a general Indian term for a vegetable dish

Sucanat a granular sweetener made from raw, evaporated sugar cane; abbreviation for "Sugar Cane Natural"

Tahini a paste made from finely ground sesame seeds, widely used in Middle Eastern cooking

Tamari a wheat-free condiment made from fermented soy beans; similar in taste to traditional Japanese soy sauce or shoyu

Tempeh soy beans fermented in a rice culture and then cooked; a traditional Indonesian food with a meat-like consistency

Tofu processed soy bean curd; originated in ancient China

Turmeric a small, yellow-orange root similar in appearance to ginger; widely used in Ayurvedic cooking and herbology; improves digestion and strengthens immunity

Whey the protein-rich liquid remaining after milk has been curdled and strained; a by-product of cheese-making

BIBLIOGRAPHY

Ballentine, Dr. Rudolph. *Diet & Nutrition: A Holistic Approach*. Honesdale, PA: The Himalayan Institute Press, 1978.

Ballentine, Dr. Rudolph. *Radical Healing: Integrating the World's Great Therapeutic Traditions to Create a New Transformative Medicine*. New York: Three Rivers Press, 1999.

Bell Bragg, Gina, and Dr. David Simon. *A Simple Celebration: A Vegetarian Cookbook for Body, Mind, and Spirit*. New York: Harmony Books, 1997.

Bergelson, J., Purrington, C.B., "Promiscuity in Transgenic Plants," *Nature* 3 September 1998, p. 25.

Chauhan, Dr. Partap. *Eternal Health: The Essence of Ayurveda*. Haryana, India: Jiva Institute, 2000.

Chopra, Dr. Deepak. *Perfect Digestion*. New York: Three Rivers Press, 1995.

Chopra, Dr. Deepak. *Perfect Health*. New York: Three Rivers Press, 2000.

Chopra, Dr. Deepak. *Perfect Weight*. New York: Three Rivers Press, 1994.

Cousens, Dr. Gabriel. *Conscious Eating*. Berkeley, CA: North Atlantic Books, 2000.

Filliozat, J. *The Classical Doctrine of Indian Medicine: Its Origins and its Greek Parallels*. Delhi, India: Oriental Publishers, 1964.

Frawley, Dr. David. *Ayurveda and the Mind: The Healing of Consciousness*. Twin Lakes, WI: Lotus Press, 1996.

Frawley, Dr. David and Dr. Subhash Ranade. *Ayurveda, Nature's Medicine*. Twin Lakes, WI: Lotus Press, 2001.

Gerber, Dr. Richard. *Vibrational Medicine: New Choices for Healing Ourselves*. Santa Fe, NM: Bear & Company, 1988.

Gerson, Dr. Scott. *Ayurveda: The Ancient Indian Healing Art*. Brisbane, Australia: Element Books, 1993.

Gerson, Dr. Scott. *The Ayurvedic Guide to Diet and Weight Loss*. Twin Lakes, WI: Lotus Press, 2002.

Golan, Ralph, *Optimal Healing*, New York: Wellspring/Balantine, 1995.

Haas, Dr. Elson M. *Staying Healthy With Nutrition: The Complete Guide to Diet and Nutritional Medicine*. Berkeley, CA: Celestial Arts, 1992.

Haas, Dr. Elson M. *Staying Healthy With the Seasons*. Berkeley, CA: Celestial Arts, Berkeley, CA, 1981.

Hart, Kathleen. *Eating in the Dark: America's Experiment with Genetically Engineered Food*. New York: Pantheon Books, 2002.

Hospodar, Miriam Kasin. *Heaven's Banquet: Vegetarian Cooking for Lifelong Health the Ayur-veda Way*. New York: Dutton Publishing, 1999.

Jilin, Liu. *Chinese Dietary Therapy,* London: Churchill Livingstone, 1999.

Kilham, Chris. *The Whole Food Bible: How to Select & Prepare Safe, Healthful Foods*. Rochester, VT: Healing Arts Press, 1997.

Lad, Usha and Lad, Dr. Vasant. *Ayurvedic Cooking for Self-Healing*. Albuquerque, NM: Ayurvedic Press, 1997.

Lad, Dr. Vasant D. *The Complete Book of Ayurvedic Home Remedies*. New York: Three Rivers Press, 1999.

Lad, Dr. Vasant D. *Ayurveda: The Science of Self-Healing*. Twin Lakes, WI: Lotus Press, 1984.

Lappe, Frances Moore, and Anna Lappe. *Hope's Edge: The Next Diet for a Small Planet*. New York: Jeremy P. Tarcher, 2003.

Lipson, Elaine. *The Organic Foods Sourcebook*. New York: Contemporary Books, 2001.

Lonsdorf, Dr. Nancy, Dr. Veronica Butler, and Dr. Melanie Brown. *A Woman's Best Medicine: Health, Happiness, and Long Life Through Ayur-Veda*. New York: G.P. Putnam's Sons, 1993.

Losey, J.E., Rayor, L.S., and Carter, M.E., "Transgenic Pollen Harms Monarch Larvae," *Nature,* 20 May 1999, 399: 214.

MacKenzie, D., "Can We Make Super Salmon Safe?" *New Scientist*, January 27, 1996, p. 14-15.

Morrison, Judith. *The Book of Ayurveda: A Holistic Approach to Health and Longevity*. New York: Fireside, 1995.

Nordlee, J.D., Taylor, S.L., Townsend, J.A., Thomas, L.A. and Bush,, R.K., "Identification of a Brazil nut Allergen in Transgenic Soybeans" *New England Journal of Medicine*, 1996, 334:11, p. 726.

Morningstar, Amadea. *Ayurvedic Cooking for Westerners: Familiar Western Food Prepared With Ayurvedic Principles.* Twin Lakes, WI: Lotus Press, 1995.

Morningstar, Amadea and Urmila Desai. *The Ayurvedic Cookbook: A Personalized Guide to Good Nutrition and Health.* Twin Lakes, WI: Lotus Press, 1990.

Peet, Dr. Margaret Smith, and Dr. Shoshana Zimmerman. *My Doctor Says I'm Fine…So Why Do I Feel So Bad?* Nevada City, CA: Blue Dolphin Publishing, 2001.

Pitchford, Paul. *Healing with Whole Foods: Oriental Traditions and Modern Nutrition.* Berkeley, CA: North Atlantic Books, 1993.

"Position of the American Dietetic Association and Dietitians of Canada: Vegetarian Diets" *Journal of the American Dietetic Association* 2003, 103: 6, pp.748-65.

Raichur, Pratima, and Marian Cohen. *Absolute Beauty: Radiant Skin and Inner Harmony Through the Ancient Secrets of Ayurveda.* New York: HarperCollins, 1997.

Reinfeld, Mark and Bo Rinaldi. *Vegan World Fusion Cuisine.* Kapa'a, HI: Thousand Petals Publishing, 2004.

Robbins, John. *Food Revolution: How Your Diet Can Help Save Your Life and Our World.* Berkeley, CA: Conari Press, 2001.

Rosenthal, Joshua. *The Energy Balance Diet.* Indianapolis, IN: Alpha Books, 2003.

Sachs, Melanie. *Ayurvedic Beauty Care: Ageless Techniques to Invoke Natural Beauty.* Twin Lakes, WI: Lotus Press, 1994.

Schlosser, Eric. *Fast Food Nation: The Dark Side of the All-American Meal.* New York: HarperCollins Publishers, Inc., 2002.

Schmidt, Michael A. *Smart Fats: How Dietary Fats and Oils Affect Mental, Physical and Emotional Intelligence.* Berkeley, CA: Frog, Ltd., 1997.

Sharma, Dr. Hari and Dr. Christopher Clark. *Contemporary Ayurveda: Medicine and Research in Maharishi Ayur-Veda.* Philadelphia: Churchill Livingstone, 1998.

Sharma, Priyavrat, *Caraka-Samhita* (Vols. 1-4), Varanasi, India: Chaukhambha Orientalia, 2001.

Singh, R.H. *The Holistic Principles of Ayurvedic Medicine.* Delhi, India: Chaukhamba Sanskrit Pratishthan, 1998.

Smith, Bob L. "Organic Foods vs. Supermarket Foods: Element Levels." *Journal of Applied Nutrition,* 1993, 45. pp. 35-39.

Subramuniyaswami, Satguru Sivaya. *Monks' Cookbook: Vegetarian Recipes from Kauai's Hindu Monastery.* Kapaa, HI: Himalayan Academy, 1997.

Svoboda, Robert. *Prakriti: Your Ayurvedic Constitution.* Twin Lakes, WI: Lotus Press, 1988.

Svoboda, Robert and Arnie Lade. *Tao and Dharma: Chinese Medicine and Ayurveda.* Twin Lakes, WI: Lotus Press, 1995.

Tirtha, Swami Sada Shiva. *The Ayurveda Encyclopedia: Natural Secrets to Healing, Prevention & Longevity.* Bayville, NY: Ayurveda Holistic Center Press, 1998.

Tiwari, Maya. *Ayurveda: A Life of Balance: The Complete Guide to Ayurvedic Nutrition and Body Types with Recipes.* Rochester, VT: Healing Arts Press, 1995.

Villoldo, Alberto. *Shaman, Healer, Sage.* New York: Harmony Books, 2000.

Worthington, Virginia. "Nutrition and Biodynamics: Evidence for the Nutritional Superiority of Organic Crops." *Biodynamics,* 1999, p. 224.

Worthington, Virginia. "Nutritional Quality of Organic Versus Conventional Fruits, Vegetables, and Grains." *Journal of Alternative and Complementary Medicine,* 1999, 7. pp. 161-173.

RESOURCES
AYURVEDIC HEALTH CENTERS

Ayurveda Institute of America

Dr. Jay Apte BAMS
561 Pilgrim Dr. Suite-B
Foster City, CA 94404
www.ayurvedainstitute.com

The Ayurvedic Institute and Wellness Center

Dr. Vasant Lad MASc.
11311 Menaul, NE
Albuquerque, NM 87112
Ph: (505) 291-9698
Fax: (505) 294-7572
www.ayurveda.com

Ayurvedic and Naturopathic Clinic

Dr. Virender Sodhi, M.D. (Ayurved), N.D.
2115 112th Ave. NE
Bellevue, WA 98004
Ph: (425) 453- 8022
Fax: (425) 451- 2670
www.ayurvedicscience.com

California College of Ayurveda

Dr. Marc Halpern D.C.
1117A East Main Street
Grass Valley, CA 95945
Ph: (530) 274-9100
www.ayurvedacollege.com

The Chopra Center for Well Being

Dr. David Simon M.D.
2013 Costa del Mar Rd.
Carlsbad, CA 92009
Ph: (760) 494-1608

Fax: (760) 494-1608
www.chopra.com

Kauai Center for Holsitic Medicine and Research

Dr. Thomas Yarema M.D.
Dr. Suhas Kshirsagar M.D. (Ayurved)
Kapa'a HI, 96746
Ph: (808) 823-0994
Fax: (808) 823-0995
www.hawaiiholisticmedicine.com

Ganesha Institute

Dr. Pratichi Mathur
152 Caymus Court
Sunnyvale, CA 94086
www.healingmission.com

Light Institute of Ayurveda

Dr. Bryan Miller D.C. & Light Miller N.D., D.D.
P.O. Box 35284
Sarasota, FL 34242
Ph: (941) 929-0999
Fax: (941) 346-0800
www.ayurvedichealers.com

Maharishi Ayurved at the Raj

Dr. Nancy Lonsdorf M.D.
1734 Jasmine Avenue
Fairfield, IA 52556
Ph: (800) 248-9050
Fax: (515) 472-2496
www.theraj.com

National Institute Of Ayurvedic Medicine

Dr. Scott Gerson, M.D., PhD. (Ayurved)
13 W. 9th St.
New York, NY 10011
Ph: (212) 505-8971
Fax: (212) 677-5397

www.niam.com

Natural Medicine Clinic

Dr. Vivek Shanbhag N.D., M.D. (Ayurved), BAMS
819 NE 65th St.
Seattle, WA 98115
Ph: (206) 729-9999
www.ayurvedaonline.com

Pacific Center of Ayurveda

Prashanti de Jager
P.O Box 878
Marshall, CA 94940
Ph: (415) 246-1248
www.dhanvantri.com

AYURVEDIC EDUCATION/ CLINICAL TRAINING

Aloha Ayurvedic Academy

4504 Kukui St. Ste. 13
Kapa'a, HI 96746
Ph: (808) 823-0994
Fax: (808) 823-0995
www.hawaiiholisticmedicine.com

Australian College of Ayurvedic Medicine

PO Box 322
Ingle Farm SA 5098
Australia

Ayurvedic Academy & Natural Medicine Clinic

819 NE 65th Street
Seattle, Washington USA 98115
Phone: (206) 729 - 9999
FAX: (206) 729 - 0164
www.ayurvedaonline.com

The American School of Ayurveda

460 Ridgedale Avenue
East Hanover, New Jersey 07936
Ph: (973) 887-8828
Fax: (973) 887-3088
www.lotusfair.com

California College of Ayurveda

Dr. Marc Halpern D.C.
1117A East Main Street
Grass Valley, CA 95945
Ph: (530) 274-9100
www.ayurvedacollege.com

Diamond Way Ayurveda

P.O. Box 13753
San Luis Obispo, CA 93406
Ph: (805) 543-9291
Toll Free: (877) 964-1395
www.diamondwayayurveda.com

East West College of Herbalism

Ayurvedic Program
Hartswood, Marsh Green, Hartsfield
E. Sussex TN7 4ET
United Kingdom
Ph: 01342-822312
Fax: 01342-826346

European Institute of Vedic Studies

Atreya Smith, Director
B.P. 18, 30610 Sauve, France
Tel: 33(0) 466-53-76-87
www.atreya.com

Ganesha Institute

152 Caymus Court
Sunnyvale, CA 94086
www.healingmission.com

Himalayan Institute

RR1, Box 400
Honesdale, PA 18431
Ph: (800) 822-4547
www.ayurvedichealing.com

Institute for Wholistic Education

33719 116th Street/ Box AH
Twin Lakes, WI 53181
Ph: (262) 877-9396

International Academy of Ayurved

Nand Nandan, Atreya Rugnalaya
Erandawana, Pune
411004, India
Ph:/Fax: 91-212-378532/524427
www.ayurved-int.com

LifeSpa

John Douillard
6662 Gunpark Drive East
Suite 102
Boulder, CO 80301
www.lifespa.com

Light Institute of Ayurveda

P.O. Box 35284
Sarasota, FL 34242
Ph: (941) 929-0999
www.ayurvedichealers.com

Maharishi Ayurveda Health Centre

24 Linhope St.
London, NW1 6HT
England
www.maharishi.co.uk

National Institute Of Ayurvedic
Medicine

584 Milltown Road

Brewster, NY 10509
Ph: (845) 278-8700
Fax: (845) 278-8215
www.niam.com

Vinayak Ayurveda Center

2509 Virginia NE, Suite D
Albuquerque, NM 87110
Ph: (505) 296-6522
Fax: (505) 298-2932
Website: www.ayur.com

Wise Earth School

P.O. Box 160
Candler, NC 28715
Ph: (828) 258-9999
www.wiseearth.org

CORRESPONDENCE COURSES

American Institute of Vedic Studies

P.O. Box 8357
Santa Fe, NM 87504-8357
Ph: (505) 983-9385
Fax: (505) 982-5807
www.vedanet.com

The American School of Ayurveda

460 Ridgedale Avenue
East Hanover, New Jersey 07936
Ph: (973) 887-8828
www.lotusfair.com

The Ayurvedic Institute

11311 Menaul, NE
Albuquerque, NM 87112
Ph: (505) 291-9698
Fax: (505) 294-7572
www.ayurveda.com

Light Institute of Ayurvedic Teaching

P.O. Box 35284
Sarasota, FL 34242
Ph: (941) 346-3518
Fax: (941) 346-0800
www.ayurvedichealers.com

Ayurvedic Herbs, Spices, Oils & Food Supplies

Ayush Herbs, Inc.

10025 N.E. 4th Street
Bellevue, WA 98004
Ph: (800) 925-1371
www.ayushherbs.com

Banyan Botanicals

6705 Eagle Rock Ave. NE
Albuquerque, NM 87113
Ph: (505) 821-5083; (888) 829-5722
www.banyanbotanicals.com

Bazaar of India Imports, Inc.

1810 University Avenue
Berkeley, CA 94703
Ph: (800) 261-7662; (510) 548-4110
www.bazaarofindia.com

Frontier Natural Products Co-op

P.O. Box 229
Norway, IA 52318
Ph: (800) 717-4372
www.frontiercoop.com

Internatural

33719 116th St./ Box AH
Twin Lakes, WI 53181 USA
Ph: (800) 643- 4221
Fax: (262) 889-8591
www.internatural.com

Maharishi Ayurveda Products

1068 Elkton Dr.
Colorado Springs, CO 80907
Ph: (800) 255-8332
www.mapi.com

Om Organics

3245 Prairie Avenue Suite A
Boulder, CO 80301
Ph: (888) 550-VEDA
Fax: (720) 406-9340
www.omorganics.com

Planetary Formulations

P.O. Box 533
Soquel, CA 95073
Formulas by Dr. Michael Tierra

Tri Health Ayurveda

P.O. Box 340
Anahola, HI 96703
Ph: (808) 822-4288, (800) 455-0770
Fax: (808) 822-3856
www.oilbath.com

Ayurvedic Beautycare

Auroma International

P.O. Box 1008
Dept. AH
Silver Lake, WI 53170
Ph: (262) 889-8569
Fax: (262) 889-8591
Website: www.auroma.net

Pratima Ayurvedic Spa & Skincare

110 Greene St., Suite 701
New York, NY 10012
(212) 581-8136
(212) 581-8366 Fax
www.pratimaskincare.com

Internatural

33719 116th St./ Box AH
Twin Lakes, WI 53181
Ph: (800) 643-4221
Fax: (262) 889-8591
www.internatural.com

Lotus Brands, Inc.

P.O. Box 1008/ Dept. AH
Silver Lake, WI 53170 USA
Ph: (262) 889-8561
Fax: (262) 889-8591
www.lotuspress.com

Maharishi Ayurveda Products

1068 Elkton Dr.
Colorado Springs, CO 80907
Ph: (800) 255-8332
www.mapi.com

Siddhi Ayurvedic Beauty Products

c/o Vinayak Ayurveda Center

2509 Virginia NE, Suite D

Albuquerque, NM 87110

Ph: (505) 296-6522

www.ayur.com

MEDITATION CENTERS/ ORGANIZATIONS

See websites for worldwide locations.

International Sivananda Yoga Vedanta Centers

1746 Abbot Kinney Blvd.

Venice, CA 90291

Ph: (310) 822-9642

www.sivananda.org

Self-Realization Fellowship

3880 San Rafael Ave.Dept. 8W

Los Angeles, CA 90065

Ph: (323) 255-2471

www.yogananda-srf.org

Shambala International

1084 Tower Road

Halifax, NS Canada

Ph: (902) 425-4275

www.shambhala.org

Siddha Yoga Foundation

(SYDA Foundation)

P.O. Box 600

371 Brickman Rd.

South Fallsburg, NY 12747

Ph: (845) 434-2000

www.siddhayoga.org

The Transcendental Meditation Program (TM)

639 Whispering Hills Road, Suite 704

Boone, NC 28607

Ph: (888) 532-7678

www.tm.org

Vipassana Meditation Center

P.O.Box 24

Shelburne Falls, MA 01370

Ph: (413) 625- 2160

www.dhamma.org

YOGA CENTERS/ ORGANIZATIONS

American Viniyoga Institute

P.O Box 88

Makawao, HI 96768

Ph: (808) 672-1414

www.viniyoga.com

The Ayurvedic Institute

11311 Menaul, NE

Albuquerque, NM 87112

Ph: (505) 291-9698

Fax: (505) 294-7572

www.ayurveda.com

Kripalu Center for Yoga and Health

Box 793

Lenox, MA 01240

Ph: (800) 741-7353

www.kripalu.org

Iyengar Yoga Institute

27. W. 24th St. #800

New York, NY 10010

Ph: (212) 691-9642

Omega Institute for Holistic Studies

150 lake Drive

Rhinebeck, BY 12572

Ph: (845) 266-4444

www.eomega.com

Siddha Yoga Foundation

(SYDA Foundation)

P.O. Box 600

371 Brickman Rd.

South Fallsburg, NY 12747

Ph: (845) 434-2000

www.siddhayoga.org

Sivananda Yoga Vedanta Center

234 W. 24th St.

New York, NY 10011

www.sivananda.org

Yoga Studio Directory by State

www.self-realization.com/yogadirectory.htm

VEDIC ASTROLOGY

American Council of Vedic Astrology (ACVA)

P.O. Box 2149

Sedona, AZ 86339

Ph: (800) 900-6595

Fax: (520) 282-6097

www.vedicastrology.org

American Institute of Vedic Studies

P.O. Box 8357

Santa Fe, NM 87504-8357

Ph: (505) 983-9385

Fax: (505) 982-5807

www.vedanet.com

Correspondence courses in Jyotish

FOOD-RELATED WEB SITES OF INTEREST

Organic Foods

Organic Consumers Association
www. purefood.org
Organic Farming Research Foundation
www.ofrf.org
Organic Trade Association
www.ota.org

Organic Gardening and Organic Seeds

Organic Gardening
www.organicgardening.com
Seeds of Change
www. seedsofchange.com
Victory Seeds
www.victoryseeds.com
Southern Exposure Seed Exchange
www.southernexposure.com

Educating Children

Let's Get Growing! Company Catalogue
www.letsgetgrowing.com
The Edible Schoolyard
www.edibleschoolyard.org

Community Supported Agriculture (CSA) and Gardening

American Community Gardening Association
www.communitygarden.org
Greenpeople
www.greenpeople.org
Local Harvest
www.localharvest.org
Organic Consumers
www.organicconsumers.org

Food Co-ops

Co-op Directory
www.coopdirectory.org
Greenpeople
www.greenpeople.org

Local Harvest
www.localharvest.org
Organic Consumers
www.organicconsumers.org

Composting and Herb Gardening

Avant-Gardening
www.avant-gardening.com
Organic Gardening
www.organicgardening.com

Vegetarianism

Vegetarian Resource Group
www.vrg.org
International Vegetarian Union (IVU)
www.ivu.org
North American Vegetarian Society
www.navs-online.org
Vegan Fusion
www.veganfusion.com

Modern Food Concerns

GE Food Alert Campaign
www.gefoodalert.org
GMO Free Hawaii
www.gmofreehawaii.org
Food and Water
www.foodandwater.org
Safe Tables Our Priority (STOP)
www.stop-usa.org
Humane Farming Association
www.hfa.org
People for the Ethical Treatment of Animals
www.peta-online.org
Pesticide Action Network, North America (PANNA)
www.panna.org
Citizens for Health
www.citizens.org

EarthSave
www.earthsave.org

Water Testing

Watercheck National Testing Labratories
www.ntllabs.com

Environmental Groups and Initiatives

Greenpeace
www.greenpeace.org
The Sierra Club
www.sierraclub.org
Natural Resource Defense Council
www.nrdcwildplaces.org
Friends of the Earth
www.foe.org
Rainforest Action Network
www.ran.org
Worldwatch Institute
www.worldwatch.org
Green Restaurant Association
www.dinegreen.org

World Hunger Organizations

Food First (Institute for Food and Development Policy)
www.foodfirst.org
Food Not Bombs
www.foodnotbombs.net
The Hunger Project
www.thp.org
The Hunger Site
www.thehungersite.com

*Bold numbers refer to Dosha Food Lists

Awards for *Eat·Taste·Heal*
• *Maverick Award* for Excellence in Photography
• *Writer's Digest Magazine:* Best Reference Book, International Self-Published Book Awards
• *USABookNews.com:* Award Winner: Health/Diet Category
• *USABookNews.com:* Award Winning Finalist: Health/Alternative Medicine Category
• *Nautilus Book Awards:* Award Winning Finalist: Food/Cooking/Nutrition

Photo Credits
Ed Ouellette: Winner of *Maverick Award* for *Eat•Taste•Heal*

Images on pages 51, 58, 69, 85, 88, 140 and all photos on pages 164-320 © Ed Ouellete; pages x, xiii © Kerry Oda.
Image on page xii © Bob Ellis. Images on pages 18, 64, 75, 86, 94, 106, 110, 120, 135 © Inmagine; pages 72, 90, 100, 102 © Getty Images.
Image on page 147 © iStockPhoto.

Original paintings on pages 24, 25, 124, 125, 139, 161, 163 © Johnny Brannigan; page 21 © Katy Randolph.

PLEASE VISIT US AT EatTasteHeal.com